Partners in Crime

Also by Servando Gonzalez

The Secret Fidel Castro
The Nuclear Hoax
Psychological Warfare and the New World Order
Obamania
I Dare Call It Treason
The Swastika and the Nazis
American Inventors

He is the author of the books in Spanish:

Historia herética de la revolución fidelista
Observando
La madre de todas las conspiraciones
La CIA, Fidel Castro, el Bogotazo y el Nuevo Orden Mundial.

Servando also wrote and hosted the documentaries:

Treason in America: The Council on Foreign Relations
Partners in Treason: The CFR-CIA-Castro Connection.

Servando Gonzalez

Partners in Crime

The Rockefeller, CFR, CIA
and Castro Connection
to the Kennedy Assassination

Spooks Books
Hayward, California

To Jim Garrison, *in memoriam*
To Stanley Monteith, *in memoriam*

Cataloging-in-Publication Data

Partners in Crime: The Rockefeller, CFR, CIA, and Castro Connection to the Kennedy Assassination / Servando Gonzalez.
p.   cm.

Includes notes, bibliography and index.

1. Kennedy, John F., 1917-1963   2. Castro, Fidel, 1927- 2016
3. Rockefeller, David, 1915-2017
4. United States—Politics and government—20th Century
I. Title. II. Gonzalez Servando, 1935-

q

ISBN: 9780932367358

This book was printed in the United States of America

Spooks Books
an imprint of InteliBooks
Hayward, California

CONTENTS

Appendix I

Appendix II

Notes

Bibliography

Index

Introduction

There are a thousand hacking at the branches of evil
to one striking at the root.
—Henry David Thoreau

The assassination of President John F. Kennedy on November 22, 1963, is a seminal occurrence in recent American history. Probably with the exception of the 9/11 events, nothing has affected the American mind and soul more than the JFK assassination.

Despite the concerted efforts of the U.S. Government, the media and the academia to promote the "lone nut" narrative, ever since Kennedy was assassinated many Americans have suspected foul play. Moreover, they suspect that their President was the victim of a huge conspiracy involving people at the highest levels in the U.S. Government.

In the spring of 1964, less than a year after the assassination, one third of the people interviewed by pollsters believed that Lee Harvey Oswald, the alleged "lone assassin," actually acted in complicity with others. Within two years that number had doubled. Since then, every poll taken has shown between 60% to 80% of Americans believe that President Kennedy was killed as a result of a conspiracy.

They are not wrong. In 1978 the House Select Committee on Assassinations confirmed the suspicion that JFK was assassinated as the result of a conspiracy. According to the Committee Summary of Findings, "The committee believes, on the basis of the evidence available to it, that President John F. Kennedy was probably assassinated as a result of a conspiracy."[1]

Nevertheless, for reasons I will explain in this book, most "serious" investigators who have studied the assassination of President John F. Kennedy and whose books have been published by "prestigious" publishing houses not only have denied the possibility of a conspiracy but have also avoided focusing on the three obvious suspects of the crime: the Central Intelligence Agency, Fidel Castro and David Rockefeller.

This general denial is difficult to understand, not only because the three of them had the motive, the ability, the means and the opportunity to commit such a crime, but also a proven history of resorting to assassination to protect and advance their interests.

The CIA[2] had a strong motive to kill President Kennedy. He not only openly showed his lack of appreciation for the Agency's work, but also because, after the Bay of Pigs debacle, he fired CIA Director Allen Dulles and Deputy Director for Plans[3] Richard Bissell, both of them trusted CFR members in charge of covert operations on behalf of the Rockefellers and their fellow members of the military-industrial-banking-complex. Even worse, he threatened to disband the Agency.

Castro had also enough reasons to want to get rid of Kennedy, if only because he discovered that Kennedy was trying to assassinate him. Even more important, Castro was the only one among the main suspects who had publicly threatened both John and Robert Kennedy with assassination.

Last, but not least, David Rockefeller's visceral hatred for JFK was evidenced in his strong opposition to the President, personally and through his agents in the U.S. Government and the mainstream press. It is known that he orchestrated a political campaign against the young President. Moreover, three of Kennedy's major crises during his term as President, the failed Bay of Pigs Invasion, the confrontation with the steel magnates and the Cuban missile crisis seem to have been artificially created by David's CFR agents.

Even more important, the CIA, Fidel Castro and David Rockefeller not only had the motive, the means and the opportunity, but also the expertise and the propensity to commit such a crime — the three of them were in the assassination business — and David Rockefeller controlled both Castro and the CIA. Actually, as I will show in this book, David had created both the CIA and Castro.[4] That is the reason why I have devoted so many pages in this book to study the true origins of both the CIA and Fidel Castro.

Contrary to other books about the Kennedy assassination, this book is not about the "what," but about the "who" and the "why." So, if you still believe that Oswald acted alone and there was no conspiracy, definitively this is not the right book for you to read.[5]

There are plenty of books that have devoted thousands of pages trying to prove or disprove that Oswald was the person who pulled the trigger. In contrast, I have studied Oswald only in relation to his secret ties to the CIA. Definitely, Oswald was just a tool, not too different from the Mannlicher-Carcano rifle he most likely didn't use to assassinate the President.

The Dog That Didn't Bark

In the Sherlock Holmes story "Silver Blaze," the dog that didn't bark was an important clue to solving the mystery. Similarly, most of the investigators who have studied the Kennedy assassination and have avoided pointing to Castro or the CIA as potential culprits have been directly or indirectly associated with the CFR, or the CIA, or both. This is, as I will show below, a clear indication that the omission has not been by mistake but by design. Far from wanting to solve the mystery, the true goal of these authors has been to muddy the waters even more.

Nevertheless, despite the informational blackout, at least some authors have lit the road to truth. In the case of the CIA, several authors have pointed their finger in the right direction. Probably the most damaging one was Jim Garrison's pioneering book *On the Trail of the Assassins*,[6] which won him eternal condemnation and vituperation from the CFR-controlled mainstream press and academia.

The case of Castro's possible role in the JFK assassination is a quite different story. Despite the fact that Castro was the only one among the potential suspects who publicly threatened both John and Robert Kennedy with assassination, he has been mostly invisible to most of the JFK assassination investigators.

Just recently, however, a book appeared that added to the overwhelming bibliography dealing with the assassination of President Kennedy. This book, *Target JFK: The Spy Who Killed Kennedy?*, by Robert Wilcox, added a new twist: Castro's connection to the assassination.[7] Unfortunately, Wilcox did not dig deep enough in his research and just points to the puppets while ignoring the puppeteer.

Granted, this is not the first book studying the possibility that Fidel

Castro may have played an important role in the JFK assassination. But it was not until 1988 that Gus Russo published *Live by the Sword: The Secret War Against Castro and the Death of JFK*, and in 2001 I published *The Secret Fidel Castro: Deconstructing the Symbol*, in which I devoted a whole chapter to the subject.

In 2006 the German documentary filmmaker Wilfried Huismann studied the subject again in his film *Rendevouz With Death*.[8] The film was first aired on a German television station, but the CFR-controlled U.S. mainstream media blackballed it.

In 2012, Brian Latell, a retired CIA desk analyst, published *Castro's Secrets*, in which, based on the information obtained from a former Cuban intelligence officer, asserts that Castro knew about Oswald previous to the JFK assassination and was aware that an attempt on Kennedy's life was going to be carried out.[9]

Last, but not least, Edward J. Epstein, a journalist who has extensively written about the Kennedy assassination, after writing several books and dozens of articles ignoring or denying the CIA's or/and Castro's possible participation in the assassination, finally reluctantly admitted to this connection in his 2014 book *The Annals of Unsolved Crime*.[10]

A veritable tsunami of books dealing with the JFK assassination has been published. Of those, probably twenty-five percent point to the CIA as the most likely perpetrator. In contrast, however, just a minuscule number of them have studied Castro's possible role in the assassination. In order to fill this vacuum, in this book I deal in great detail with Castro's role in the assassination.

Living in a Historical Flat Land

To explain a four-dimensional world to us, who live in a three-dimensional world, a science author described how three-dimensional entities might look to flat, two-dimensional ones.[11] So, let's visualize flat, two-dimensional beings, living in a maze somebody drew on a sheet of paper. But, what might 3-D beings look like to these 2-D creatures?

In the first place, the 2-D creatures cannot cross the lines of the maze. So, if a 3-D being staying in another part of the maze just crosses some lines and enters the part of the maze where the 2-D creatures are living, to them it would seem as if he had materialized from nowhere.

In the same fashion, CFR-controlled mainstream media, schools and universities, have created a 2-D historical universe for us to live in. In this flat historical universe people, organizations and events just pop up from nowhere like mushrooms after a summer rain and sometimes just disappear without reason or explanation.

In this flat, 2-D historical universe, Fidel Castro was a young, idealistic, Jesuit-educated lawyer who fought a guerrilla war against a corrupt, U.S.-supported Cuban president who had turned into a dictator. After many years of fighting, he gained the support of most of the Cuban farmers and workers and won the war. Once in power, he discovered that the U.S. owned most of the Island and iniquitously exploited the Cuban people and devoted himself to fight U.S. economic control over Cuba.

To get rid of Castro — the false 2-D narrative follows — the U.S. used the CIA in an effort to overthrow him, but failed miserably. They also tried to assassinate him, but without success. In a logical reaction, Castro began opposing the U.S. Then, despite a cruel economic blockade, Castro created a successful socialist society in Cuba and won the support of most of the Cuban people.

In this flat 2-D historical universe, events such as Pearl Harbor, the JFK assassination and 9/11 pop up out of nowhere. According to this view, the National Security Council and the Central Intelligence Agency were created by well-intentioned American patriots to coordinate the efforts of the several existing intelligence organizations and avoid the repetition of surprise attacks such as Pearl Harbor — which happened as the result of these organizations' failure to connect the dots.[12] People who support this view tell us that the NSC and the CIA are tools in the hands of American presidents and their job is to provide them with intelligence[13] and thus help them make better political and military decisions.[14]

In this two-dimensional view, David Rockefeller is generally depicted as a successful businessman and a devoted philanthropist. This vision willingly ignores the dark side of the man, particularly his efforts to depopulate the planet through eugenics and his push for implementing a global totalitarian society he called the New World Order.

Nonetheless, in order to escape from this flat 2-D universe,[15] in this book I have tried a radical approach, studying not only the deep roots of the Council on Foreign Relations, but also the roots of the CIA, Castro, and the man who created both of them: David Rockefeller. As Cuban patriot José Martí wrote, "To be a radical is no more than that: to go to the roots."

As I mentioned above, contrary to most books about the Kennedy assassination, my main goal in writing this book has not been finding out who pulled the trigger or if JFK was shot with a Mannlicher-Carcano or a Mauser rifle, not even if the people who pulled the trigger were working for Castro, the CIA or somebody else. My goal has been finding the sociopath[16] who ordered his psychopathic associates to carry out the assassination: the mastermind. Identifying the agents who carried out the operation is not as important as identifying the person(s) who conceived this horrendous crime.

This has not been easy. When a criminal commits a crime, the first thing he does is to disguise, erase or destroy all physical evidence linking him to the crime. These range from cleaning with a napkin all glass surfaces to erase fingerprints, to sending to a party a person disguised as him, to be later used as an alibi proving, with the support of several witnesses, that he was in a different place at the time the crime was committed.

Historical Forensics

To most people, forensics has to do with crime, autopsies, and the like. But, like Yahoo, Google, and other Internet search engines, forensic science mostly has to do with finding links. The basic principle of forensic science, as stated by Dr. Edmond Locard, one of the greatest experts in forensic science, is very simple: every contact leaves a trace.[17] Finding these traces at the scene of a crime and, through them, establishing the links to the criminal is what forensic science is all about.

The job of the forensic investigator consists in discovering these links, and revealing the links between the crime and the criminal. Unknowingly, the authors who first pointed to the CFR as the true seat of this anti-American conspiracy were practicing the science of historical forensics. And, despite the efforts of the criminal conspirators at the CFR to erase all traces linking them to their crimes against the American people, these authors discovered an amazing fact: behind every act of treason against this country and its people there were always one or more members of the Council on Foreign Relations or their parasite organizations working hard in the shadows to betray us, the American people. The JFK assassination was not an exception to this rule.

Even though I have been studying the globalist conspirators of the Council on Foreign Relations for many years and I have written four books about them,[18] in which I have briefly mentioned the assassination of President Kennedy, it was not until I read Professor Donald Gibson's book *Battling Wall Street*[19] that I fully understood how and why the CFR globalist conspirators used their assets, Castro and the CIA, to terminate Kennedy with extreme prejudice.[20]

Gibson's book is the only one I know that tells in detail how CFR members in the press fought tooth and nail against President Kennedy. Unfortunately, he doesn't mention how CFR members infiltrated into his administration betrayed him, as well as the reasons they had to do it.

Dealing with an American conspiracy, I have dedicated much of this study to the Council on Foreign Relations, the true center of a conspiracy some authors call the Invisible Government of the United States.[21] In my investigation I found out that most of the links related to the JFK assassination point to the CFR and its master, David Rockefeller.

I have devoted most of the book to analyzing the true role of the two main suspects of carrying out the JFK assassination, Castro and the CIA. Many books written about the CIA mention the Agency's inept attempts to assassinate Fidel Castro. Most of them, however, have failed to discover Castro's actions as an agent provocateur[22] working hard to help the very people he claimed to hate. The result of this effort is that Castro's true role in the Kennedy assassination has been mostly ignored or distorted.

Over the past 50 years, more than 2000 books have been published about the Kennedy assassination. Most books dealing with the role of the CIA in the assassination, however, are either anti-CIA, written by authors who consider themselves "progressive," liberal Democrats or outright leftists, or pro-CIA, written by authors who see themselves as "conservative," Republicans, or outright rightists. Also, not many books about the Kennedy assassination have noticed that most of the people participating in the cover-up were CFR members. But, paraphrasing Upton Sinclair, "It is difficult to get a man to see something, when his salary depends upon his not seeing it!"

Moreover, most of these books focus on how it happened rather than on who was the mastermind who conceived the plan, gave the orders to carry it out and why he did it. In this sense this may be a totally different kind of book, perhaps difficult to classify. I just ask the reader to read it with the same open mind I have had to write it.

Finally, I have devoted a large amount of this book to study an apparently non-related event: the assassination in 1948 of Colombian populist leader Jorge Eliécer Gaitán. The reason for this is because I have found out that the operational methodology — the *modus operandi* — used in Gaitán's assassination — in which Castro, the CIA and many important CFR members played key roles — was closely followed in the JFK assassination.

Actually, as I will show in this book, the Kennedy assassination was like a carbon copy of Gaitán's assassination. Moreover, the motive was essentially the same, because both Gaitán and Kennedy had threatened the interests of the same people.

Some Kennedy assassination scholars are salivating about a new batch of documents related to the CIA and assassination just declassified following authorization from President Trump.[23] Apparently they believe they may get lucky and find the Holy Grail of the Kennedy assassination: a smoking gun in the form of a CIA memo from somebody ordering somebody to assassinate President Kennedy, or even a memo from some very powerful individual ordering the CIA Director to assassinate Kennedy. Well, this only shows that whoever expects to find such document is using the wrong research and methodological tools to study this subject.[24]

The conspiracy surrounding the JFK assassination is like a huge puzzle of which many pieces are missing or have been intentionally put out of place in order to mislead investigators. This explains why most analysts who have studied the phenomenon using the wrong method have failed to find the true source of the problem. Nevertheless, when you look at the whole thing coldly and from a distance the pieces simply spring into place.

Consequently, rather than using the traditional research and analysis of the historian I have used in this book a methodology coming from the field the counterintelligence. It consists in tackling the problem in reverse,[25] a process called "walking back the cat."[26] It is a sort of "acid test" used to determine retrospectively the loyalty or treachery of a particular agent, or, as I will do in this book, of a whole government agency such as the CIA or a policy organization such as the Council on Foreign Relations.[27]

Historians vs Intelligence Analysts

The goal of the historian and the intelligence analyst is basically the same: search for facts and establish the truth. Their approach, however, is totally different. Give a historian a document and he will do three things: check it for accuracy; evaluate its place in the context of his own knowledge of its subject matter; and try to exploit it for producing a finished paper or book.

Now give the same document to an intelligence officer. He will do four things, but quite different ones. First, he will examine it to verify that its source is the one it purports to be; second, he will try to know if its source has disseminated it wittingly or unwittingly, and, if unwittingly, if its source knows the fact that the document has been compromised; third, he will attempt to find, guess, or intuit the source's real motives for disseminating it; and, finally, he will try to use it — by divulging it, or by not divulging it — to influence somebody, either his employers, his employees, or his enemies.

In this sense, the historian is trained to react *ad causam*, the intelligence analyst to react *ad hominem*. The historian focuses on subject matter and its relevance to understanding recorded events, the intelligence analyst focuses on people and their motives. The tools of the historian are quite different from the tools of the intelligence analysts and, therefore, the results of their research will show considerable differences.[28]

As a rule, intelligence analysts always keep in mind that some of their sources, particularly live ones, will try to intentionally deceive them. That is why, contrary to historians, intelligence analysts take vulnerability to deception into account, and do so explicitly. Therefore, one can conclude that intelligence analysts have better methodological tools than historians to successfully analyze intelligence operations such as the Kennedy assassination, where deceit and disinformation played an important role.

Moreover, the first thing intelligence analysts must keep in mind is that, despite their best efforts, in the intelligence field they will *never* find the whole picture. The best thing they can do, therefore, is to analyze the facts they have and from them do their best to infer the rest. The bottom line is that ninety percent of this final product we call intelligence[29] comes from reading critically, remembering, associating and analyzing, as well as looking for inconsistencies, implausibilities, gaps in knowledge, conflicts with known information and suspicious coincidences and, very rarely, discovering new key facts,

In the study of intelligence organizations, such as the OSS, the Mossad, the MI6, the KGB, or the CIA, we must always keep in mind that we are not dealing with innocuous aspects of history such as the origins of New Orleans Jazz, or Roman architecture during the Republic. On the contrary, this is recent history with a high content of intelligence and espionage and, therefore, deception. And, due to the fact that the basic principles of tradecraft[30] don't change much over time among its different practitioners, intelligence services are reluctant to give their past, current, or potential opponents, any feedback about the success or failure of their past operations. As a matter of fact their goal is to disinform their opponents as much as they can by keeping them in the dark.

Most of what an intelligence service claims has been its successes are most likely its failures, and vice versa. As I already mentioned above, in intelligence and espionage things are seldom what they seem. No wonder Sun Tzu's main precept is "All warfare is based on deception."[31] Under this light, events like the Bogotazo riots, the Bay of Pigs invasion, and the September 11, 2001 events, just to mention three of the CIA's alleged greatest failures, need to be reevaluated.

The bottom line is that nobody is ever going to find the smoking gun in the form of a declassified CIA document. First, for the simple reason that it doesn't exist. This is not the way these things work in this world. The orders to carry out this type of action are never written out, but given verbally, tacitly expressed in a cryptical way in highly nuanced conversations — Will no one rid me of this meddlesome priest?[32] Secondly, because, even if such document ever surfaces, taking at face value the information appearing in photocopies of documents provided by an organization that has a whole department devoted to the falsification of documents[33] is a high-level form of idiocy.

But it may not even have been this way.

When OSS Director William Donovan, following orders from his Rockefeller masters, told one of his assassins to get rid of Gen. George Patton, he most likely alleged that Patton was becoming pro-Nazi and, in order to save his image as a hero, it was necessary to terminate him.[34] When Fidel Castro told Gen. Patricio de la Guardia to assassinate Chile's President Salvador Allende, he told him that Allende was planning to surrender to the military and, in order to save for posterity his image as a hero who fought them to the end, he must to be killed.[35] In the same fashion, some of the low-level participants in the JFK assassination most likely were told that they were helping the American people to get rid of a President that had become soft on communism.

So, if it is most likely that we will never find the key document pointing to the person who gave the order to assassinate President Kennedy, what can we do? Well, as James Jesus Angleton,[36] the CIA's legendary counterintelligence chief once said, "If one could not read the enemy's files, one could at least read his mind."[37] By this Angleton meant that a patient accumulation and analysis of facts during a long period of time allows us to decipher the enemy's thinking and accurately guess his actions.

Finding the true causes of the assassination of President Kennedy is vital to understanding today's America. Nearly every form of the growing assault on freedoms that has overrun our country in the past 50 years has its roots in the assassination of President Kennedy. JFK was seemingly the last opportunity the American people had to stop the growing tyranny of the CFR conspirators' Invisible Government.

Today, a hundred years after John Fitzgerald Kennedy was born, an investigation of the true causes of his assassination is more relevant than ever because it connects directly to the communo-fascistic growth of the U.S. government and its disregard of the rule of law, the growing economic gap between the working class and the hyper rich, the erosion of the independence of the mainstream press, the growing of a pervasive surveillance society and the encroaching police state. Once the CFR conspirators were able to get away with the assassination of President Kennedy, it was a short step to the assassinations of Robert Kennedy, Martin Luther King Jr., and many others they perceived as a threat. It was also a short step to the CIA mass assassinations in Vietnam under Operation Phoenix, the Waco massacre, the 9/11 events and the official sanctioning of torture at Abu Ghraib and Guantanamo.

It seems that the conspirators' success in assassinating President Kennedy pushed them into a frenzy of assassination, abuse, theft, corruption and war. Apparently guided by the principle that the end justifies the means, they felt no constraints on their way to reach their cherished goal: a New World Order.

A long time ago Karl Marx wrote that Capital was born dripping with blood and dirt from head to toe, from every pore. I cannot think of a more accurate description of the birth of the CFR conspirators' New World Order.

Part 1

Chapter 1

David Rockefeller's New World Order

*Out of these troubled times, our objective — a New World Order —
can emerge. Today, that new world is struggling to be born,
a world quite different from the one we have known.*
—President George H.W . Bush (CFR).

I am stating below some seemingly unconnected facts. It is your job as a
reader to find the common thread connecting them.

Fact: In the past forty years, most American Presidents, Vice-
Presidents, Secretaries of State, National Security Advisors, CIA Directors, Supreme Court judges, high-ranking
Pentagon officers, Federal Reserve Bank and IRS directors have been members of the Council on Foreign Relations (CFR).[1]

Fact: Most high-circulation newspapers and magazines, TV networks and publishing houses are CFR corporate members.
Also, most influential journalists in the mainstream media
are CFR members.

Fact: The CFR is the creation of the Rockefellers and other Wall
Street bankers.

Fact: Many key CFR members believe that overpopulation and industrial civilization are the greatest threats to planet Earth.

Fact: Most key CFR members believe that nations, borders and sovereignty are obsolete and must be replaced by a global government under bankers' control.

Fact: Non-elected CFR members have infiltrated the intelligence agencies and the military, and have virtual control over the three branches of the U.S. Government. They constitute the Invisible Government of the United States.

Fact: The Council on Foreign Relations is the visible head of the Invisible Government of the United States.

Fact: Since 1945, when he appointed himself Chairman of the Board of the Council on Foreign Relations, to his death in 2017, David Rockefeller was the *de facto* president of the Invisible Government of the United States.

Currently, many Americans are aware of these easily verifiable facts and suspect that the CFR is the true Invisible Government of the United States.

The Rockefellers' Obsession With Population Reduction

Lefties and "progressives" explain the never-ending U.S. war drive as an imperialist fight for economic resources — the die-hard leftist myth of "war for oil." They seem to ignore that they are actually helping the conspirators' efforts in hiding their true eugenic goals, which they have expressed on innumerable occasions.

Early in their lives, the Rockefellers, a family of sociopaths who were obsessed with the irrational fear of losing their fortunes,[2] reached the conclusion that the world was overpopulated and that we, useless eaters,[3] were consuming too much of the Earth's natural resources that, by Natural Law, belonged to them. So, they conceived an evil plan.

The ultimate goal of the Rockefellers and their fellow globalist conspirators' plan is the elimination of at least 85 percent of the world's population. The second is the impoverishing of the survivors by the destruction of industrial civilization. This will result in the reduction of the few survivors to pre-industrial, medieval levels of consumption, with just two social classes: the super poor and the hyper rich.

This is not a figment of somebody's imagination. It has been openly mentioned by the globalist conspirators and their minions. A 2007 document published by the U.S. Space Command, "Vision for 2020," states,

"The globalization of the world's economy . . . will continue with a widening between the 'haves' and 'have-nots.'"[4]

This plan includes the total destruction of the American Republic as we knew it[5] and the creation of a global communo-fascist, feudal totalitarian society under their full control — a society they euphemistically call the New World Order.

A key component of the New World Order is population control and depopulation through eugenics. If one is to believe Jacques Cousteau, one of the conspirators' mouthpieces,

> The United Nations' goal is to reduce population selectively by encouraging abortion, forced sterilization, and control human reproduction, and regards two-thirds of the human population as excess baggage, with 350,000 people to be eliminated per day. [6]

In 1997, Ted Turner, another strong depopulation advocate, donated in $1 billion to the U.N., with the only condition that the money would be used for birth control. In 2000, Bill Gates (CFR), after being threatened by the conspirators with dismembering his dear Microsoft, saw the handwriting on the wall and, soon after, created the Bill and Melinda Gates Foundation. Its true goal, disguised under the banner of reproductive health care and family planning,[7] is depopulation in Africa, Latin America and other Third World countries.

A 1969 Memorandum from Frederick S. Jaffe, Vice-President of Planned Parenthood, to Bernard Berelson, President of the Population Council, both of them CFR members, details a carefully-conceived plan of eugenic measures to be taken to curb population. Table 1 of the Memorandum, "Examples of Proposed Measures to Reduce U.S. Fertility, by Universality or Selectivity of Impact," recommends:

> Restructure family by, a) Postpone or avoid marriage, b) Alter image of ideal family size, Compulsory education of children, Encourage increased homosexuality, Educate for family limitation, Fertility control agents in water supply, Encourage women to work, Reduce/eliminate paid maternity leave or benefits, Reduce/eliminate children's or family allowances, Compulsory sterilization of all who have two children, Confine childbearing to only a limited number of adults, Payments to encourage Sterilization and Contraception, Payments to encourage abortion, Abortion and steril-

ization on demand.[8]

As a Catholic, John F. Kennedy would have been horrified to know that some people had those ideas. If he had not been assassinated in Dallas in 1963, he would have fiercely opposed those measures proposed to drastically reduce U.S. population.

Population control was a key part of a eugenics program John D. Rockefeller III embraced with great enthusiasm since the days he funded the *Bureau of Social Hygiene*. This was in tune with the long-term interests of the Rockefellers in this issue, something evident since 1936 when the Rockefeller Foundation had provided funds to the Office of Population Research at Princeton University.[9]

John D. Rockefeller III was highly motivated by such depopulation goals, although he was always careful not to be too explicit about them, suggesting his objectives were those of an idealist. As he explained in a speech to the United Nations Food and Agriculture Organization in the *Second McDougall Lecture* in 1961, the "grand mission" of the *Rockefeller Foundation*, like the *FAO*, was the "well-being of mankind."

John D. Rockefeller III argued that there was a "relationship between population growth and social development" and that "responsible leaders" in each country needed to "decide whether population stabilization was required." ... "To my mind," he explained, "population growth is second only to control of atomic weapons as the paramount problem of the day." There is a "cold inevitability, a certainty that is mathematical, that gives the problems posed by too-rapid population growth a somber and chilling cast indeed."

The language was indeed careful, but the implications were soon apparent: "The 'grim fact' of population growth," he warned, "cuts across all the basic needs of mankind and ... frustrates man's achievement of his higher needs."[10]

In his book, *The Second American Revolution* (1973), John D. Rockefeller III persisted in likening overpopulation to nuclear war, arguing that it was the "slow way" to "render [the] planet uninhabitable"; in fact, he added, "no problem is more fundamental in long-range terms."[11]

John D. Rockefeller III noted with some pride in the findings of the *Commission on Population Growth and the American Future*, set up by Congress in 1970 with him as Chairman,[12] that the "time has come for the United States to welcome and plan for a stabilized population" and that "no substantial benefit will result from further growth of the nation's population". His warning about the population explosion was mirrored by others in the Rockefeller family and its organs. The *Rockefeller Brothers Fund* report, *"Prospect for America,"* raised the fear of "extreme nationalism" arising out of the "restlessness produced in a rapidly growing population," something magnified by "the preponderance of youth."[13]

Following his father's ideas, David Rockefeller also made his own contribution to brainwash the populace regarding the subject of population control. Using language perhaps more revealing than John D. Rockefeller III would have chosen, but still in tune with sentiments of the Rockefeller family, David observed in 1964 that the population problem was not only a matter of economic but also of political stability. "Unless we close the gap between population and food supply," he observed, we risk "unleashing upon this globe a frustration, ... an anguished fury more explosive than the growth of population itself."[14]

The Rockefellers knew that eugenic measures such as abortion, homosexuality, plagues and hunger would not be enough to curb population on this planet. Accordingly, they have always promoted the main and most effective tool of rapid population control: war. And we have to recognize that they have done an excellent job. Since the beginning of the past Century the world has been in a constant state of war, and the United States has been a main tool in this effort.[15] This has not been the result of chance but of a carefully-conceive plan.

In August, 1963, just three months before President Kennedy was assassinated in Dallas, Secretary of Defense Robert McNamara (a CFR agent) commissioned a study by a group of fifteen researchers, which included CFR members McGeorge Bundy and Dean Rusk, to evaluate the impact of world peace on the government and to suggest means other than war to keep the population under control. The Special Study Group, as it was called, first met in Iron Mountain in upstate New York. After the first meeting, they met in secrecy at various locations throughout the country over a 2 two and a half year period.

In November 1967, a strange book with an enigmatic title was published: *Report From Iron Mountain: On the Possibility or Desirability of Peace.*[16] The book purported to be a report written by a "Special Study Group" commissioned by an unknown governmental department that wanted to remain anonymous —or so they claimed. The 15 members of the study group, which also remained anonymous, addressed it to that secret department.

After their first meeting, the group, whose members had been selected because of their high level of experience, expertise and scholarship, worked for close to two and a half years, meeting in secrecy at various locations throughout the country until they produced the Report. According to Leonard Lewin, the person who published it, the Report was leaked to him by one of its members, who identified himself as "John Doe."

The name "Iron Mountain" refers to the location where the first and the last meetings of the Study Group took place. It is highly revealing that Iron Mountain in upstate New York, near the Hudson River, is not far from the Rockefeller Family's compound in the Pocantico Hills.

Deep below Iron Mountain, the Rockefellers built a huge underground bunker to be used as an emergency nuclear shelter to survive a nuclear holocaust.[17] The bunker is also the emergency headquarters for Shell, Manufacturers Hanover, Standard Oil of New Jersey, and other Wall Street firms and multinational corporations connected to the Rockefellers

Some people, however, believe that the Report is actually a think-tank study produced by the Hudson Institute, located at Croton-on-Hudson, not far from Iron Mountain and that it was commissioned by Secretary of Defense Robert Strange McNamara, a trusted CFR agent. The Hudson Institute is one of the CFR-connected think tanks. It was founded by Herman Kahn, another secret CFR agent.

In Section 6, "Substitutes for the Functions of War," the authors of the *Report* studied the possibility of artificially creating an environmental threat as a substitute for the nuclear war threat. It may be, they reasoned, that gross pollution of the environment can eventually replace the possibility of mass destruction by nuclear weapons as the principal apparent threat to the survival of the species.

According to the Report, economic surrogates for war must meet two principal criteria. They must be "wasteful," in the common sense of the word, and they must operate outside the normal supply-demand system. A corollary that should be obvious is that the magnitude of the waste must be sufficient to meet the needs of a particular society. The writers of the *Report* believed that an economy as advanced and complex as our own requires the planned average annual destruction of no less than 10 percent of the gross national product.

The Special Study Group that wrote the *Report* concluded that peace "would almost certainly not be in the best interest of stable society," because war is too much a part of the world economy, and therefore it is necessary to continue a state of war indefinitely.

In essence, the Report concluded that the return of slavery as an institution might be useful, that poverty is both desirable and necessary, and that calculating the optimum number of deaths by planned warfare is a legitimate function of government. But, after studying different ways to have population growth under control, they concluded that there is no better substitute than war to reach that goal.

Soon after the Report was published, the conspirators'-controlled mainstream press launched a coordinated damage-control campaign to disinform the public. The essence of this campaign consisted in telling the people that the Report was nothing but a joke, a well-written parody having nothing to do with reality.

Thus, CFR secret agent Walt W. Rostow, former President Kennedy's NSC adviser, declared that the Report was a hoax. The *Washington Post*, owned by CFR agent Katharine Graham, called it "a delightful satire." CFR agent Herman Kahn, director of the Hudson Institute, denied its authenticity. CFR-controlled *Time* magazine called the Report a skillful hoax. [18] According to CFR honcho Henry Kissinger, "Whoever wrote it is an idiot."[19]

There is some evidence, however, indicating that the Report was real. The same year it was initially published, Harvard professor John Kenneth Galbraith, a CFR member, blew the whistle in an article he wrote under his pen name of Herschel McLandress. It was published on November 26, 1976, in the book review section of the *Washington Post*.

According to Galbraith, he knew that the Report was authentic because he had been invited to participate in it. Also, he added, despite the fact that he was unable to officially be part of the group, he was consulted from time to time about different aspects of the discussions, and had been asked to keep the project secret.[20]

Further proof that the *Report* was not a hoax is that it suggested several substitutes for war, including creating environmental hoaxes to keep people worried about the ecology and the poisoning of the atmosphere, to introduce "a sophisticated form of slavery," encouraging "blood games" for "social purification," promoting homosexuality, and even the possibility of selling the gullible American people an extraterrestrial invasion threat by creating UFO scares. It concludes that the end of war would necessarily mean the end of the nation-state, and would bring a world government and with it the need for wasteful spending on a large scale. Obviously, JFK's plans to ease tensions with the Soviet Union and put an end to the Cold War were not well received by the Rockefellers and their allies in the military-industrial-banking-complex.

In Section 5, The Functions of War the Report deals with the possibility of finding "a viable substitute for war as a social system." But, the authors warn,

> [It] cannot be a mere symbolic charade. It must involve risk of real personal destruction, and on a scale consistent with the size and complexity of modern social systems. Credibility is the key. Whether the substitute is ritual in nature or functionally substantive, unless it provides a believable life-and-death threat it will not serve the socially organizing function of war.
>
> The existence of an accepted external menace, then, is essential to social cohesiveness as well as to the acceptance of political authority. The menace must be believable, it must be of a magnitude consistent with the complexity of the society threatened, and it must appear, at least, to affect the entire society.[21]

Consequently, as a second-best option the Report advises the use of environmental pollution as a credible global threat to keep the masses in check, even if the deliberate poisoning of the environment is required to make it credible. This way the sheeple would willingly accept without complaints the reduction of their standard of living, higher taxes and increased government control of their lives as the lesser of two evils.

Another indication that points to CFR conspirators as the true creators of the Report is that, after explaining in detail "the shortcomings of war as a mechanism for population control"[22] — despite the profusion of wars world population continues to grow — they suggest ecological measures as a possible substitute — the global warming hoax.

Three years later, in 1970, CFR agent George Kennan published an article in *Foreign Affairs* entitled "To Prevent a World Wasteland — A Proposal."[23] Essentially, Kennan proposed phasing out the military threat and phasing in the new eco-threat.

Since the end of WWII the subject of the so-called "population control" has been a key part of the Rockefellers and their CFR minion's agenda: e.g., the Population Council, founded by the Rockefeller Foundation in 1952; the Population Crisis Committee, founded by General William Draper (CFR) in 1966, which included Gen. Maxwell Taylor (CFR), McGeorge Bundy (CFR) and Robert McNamara (CFR); and the Office of Population Affairs, founded by Henry Kissinger (CFR) in 1966 as part of the State

Department. Since that, the CFR's anti-population propaganda machine continued advancing at full steam.[24]

In 1974 National Security Advisor Henry Kissinger (CFR), most likely following suggestions from David Rockefeller, wrote the National Security Study Memorandum 200 (NSSM 200), titled "Implications of World Wide Population Growth for U.S. Security & Overseas Interests." Kept hidden from public scrutiny for many years, it delineated a genocidal policy for depopulating much of the Third World, particularly the African continent. Its main goal was to allow U.S. transnational corporations, not Africans, to exploit the continent's natural resources. Among the countries targeted for depopulation were Pakistan, India, Turkey, Egypt, Indonesia, Thailand, the Philippines, Ethiopia, Nigeria, Mexico, Brazil, and Colombia. In NSSM 200, Kissinger clearly stated, "depopulation should be the highest priority of U.S. foreign policy towards the Third World." He quoted reasons of national security, and also because,

> … the U.S. economy will require large and increasing amounts of minerals from abroad, especially from less-developed countries. . . Wherever a lessening of population can increase the prospects for such stability, population policy becomes relevant to resources, supplies and to the economic interests of U.S.[25]

In 1978, under the sponsorship of the Club of Rome, an organization linked to the Rockefellers, Cyrus Vance (CFR) wrote Global 2000,[26] a secret plan to drastically reduce world population by means of war, famine, plagues diseases and getting rid of what they call the "useless eaters." As part of this plan, the HIV virus was developed from bovine leukemia virus by the Biological Warfare Center at Fort Dietrich, Maryland and injected into many Africans and others, causing the AIDS epidemic.

In October 2, 1979, after seen the optimism generated by declining birth rates in Asia and Latin America, World Bank President Robert McNamara (CFR) told a group of bankers in Belgrade, Yugoslavia, that it was a "dangerous understanding." Apparently McNamara considered it was not enough, and stressed the need for drastic actions to achieve a rapid reduction of excessive population growth. He added,

> There are only two possible ways in which a world of 10 billion people can be averted. Either the current birth rates come down more quickly or current death rates go up. There is no other way.

There are, of course, many ways in which the death rates can go up. In a thermonuclear age, war can accomplish it very quickly and decisively.[27]

In 1992, CFR agent Al Gore published *Earth in the Balance*.[28] Based mostly on false data, the book intended to scare Americans about the coming environmental crisis, particularly the fictitious global warming, which Gore sees as a strategic threat. It also claims that, as the result of human activity, particularly the burning of fossil fuels, the concentration of carbon dioxide in the atmosphere has increased by almost 25 percent since World War II, posing a worldwide threat to the earth's population [science shows that CO_2 actually is a beneficial gas necessary for both plant and animal life]. The book closely follows the scary tactics suggested in the 1963 *Report From Iron Mountain*. Nevertheless, the *New York Times* and other CFR-controlled media pushed the book with such enthusiasm that it became a best seller.

Today, after so many unnecessary wars promoted by the CFR conspirators have caused the death of millions of people, it is difficult to believe that the Report was just a hoax. But apparently its content is so damaging to the conspirators that the disinformation campaign to discredit it is still going on. In 1995 the CFR-controlled *Wall Street Journal* published a front-page story (dis)informing its readers by trying to convince them that the *Report From Iron Mountain* was a hoax perpetrated by Leonard Lewin.

In 1972 Lewin himself confessed in the *New York Times Book Review* his role in the "hoax." According to him, he wrote it "to caricature the bankruptcy of the think-tank system mentality."[29] But, was it?

Another Rockefeller Obsession: Making Us All Dirt-Poor

As I mentioned above, the Rockefellers' master plan has two main goals: depopulation through eugenics and impoverishing of the survivors through deindustrialization.

Before the industrial revolution, the world was economically divided in two classes: the very rich and the very poor. The industrial revolution, with its need for qualified workers, changed this dramatically. Eventually, beginning after the end of WWII, a middle class of well-paid workers and farmers developed in America, but, as I will show below, the globalist conspirators were not happy with this development.

Industrial civilization is based on energy sources, either mechanical, generated by internal combustion engines; electrical, generated by water (hydroelectric); by plants burning oil or coal; or nuclear fission. Due to the fact that asking people to voluntarily stop enjoying the wonders of cheap energy would have been foolish, the CFR globalist conspirators conceived a carefully-designed psychological operation to convince the people that by using energy they were destroying the planet.

To this effect they launched the ecology movement and used the mainstream media under their control to disseminate it. Through their rich nonprofit foundations, the globalist conspirators greased with lavish grants the hands of unethical scientists in universities and research institutions, as well as New Age Gaia worshippers among the fringe Left, to fiercely attack energy users in the name of saving the environment and Mother Earth.

It is highly revealing that the environmentalist movement was strongly promoted by the Rockefellers and their CFR minions in the mainstream press and the Academia. In contrast, JFK had realized that the U.S. industrial and economic base was shrinking, and he had plans to stop this. Unknowingly, his campaign motto, "Get America moving again," was a direct threat to the Rockefellers' drastic deindustrialization plans for America.

In 1970, Nelson Rockefeller published *Our Environment Can Be Saved*, a book in which he invoked international political implications as a justification for preempting environmental disaster. According to Nelson, preventing the coming "environmental crisis" should "become an area of increased cooperation between nations." He also recommended that the U.S. should "help coordinate international planning for environmental controls."

Two years later, The Club of Rome published the Rockefeller-sponsored study *The Limits to Growth* by CFR agents Dennis and Donnella Meadows.[30] According to the Study, the Earth is overpopulated and we are depleting it of its natural resources. Consequently, our only hope for survival is Zero Population Growth combined with Zero Economic Growth. The offered solution to the "problem" is to stop the profit system by direct government intervention — which can take a wide variety of forms: taxation, regulation, allocation, rationing, etc.

The book's message, considered absurd by informed demographers,[31] was promptly parroted by the CFR-controlled mainstream media. *Newsweek* magazine published a scary article entitled "Running Out of Everything," and *Time* another under the heading "Time For a New Frugality." The propaganda campaign was geared towards making Americans feel guilty for their alleged greed and profligacy.

In 1972, the Rockefellers Brothers Fund published in book form a Report under the title *The Unfinished Agenda*. The Fund's board of trustees included six members of the Rockefeller family. Chairman of the board Laurance Rockefeller (CFR) directly contributed to write one of the chapters.

The book portrayed economic growth and technology as grave problems. It advanced the idea that the U.S. and the world should move in the direction of ending population growth by promoting contraception, abortion, sterilization, and promoting female employment to discourage reproduction. It also states that giving protection to the environment has a greater importance than that of improving the standard of living.

The book also argues that the U.S. should link all foreign aid to efforts by recipient nations to achieve zero population growth. Even more important, it recommended that the U.S. be transformed into a "Conserver Society" to use fewer resources, including energy, mainly by eliminating the production of nuclear energy.[32]

In 1974, the CFR-controlled Ford Foundation's Energy Policy Project produced a study titled *A Time to Choose: America's Energy Future*. Its main recommendation was a reduction on oil consumption. Chapter Eight begins with an ominous statement: "The recognition of environmental damage as a consequence of industrial activity, and of energy use, is a relatively recent phenomenon."

The study strongly attacked nuclear energy, proposing instead the use of inefficient alternative sources or energy such as solar, wind and recycled waste. Soon after, the conspirators-controlled mainstream media began a barrage of negative propaganda against nuclear power. As a result, about 40 planned nuclear power plants to be built in the U.S. were cancelled.[33]

In a February, 1976, *Reader's Digest* article, "The Case For A Simpler Life-Style," Laurance Rockefeller (CFR) asked people to simplify their "overly complicated, overly wasteful lives . . . to protect the limited resources of which all life depends." According to him, humanity most follow a simpler path more in tune with the protection of the environment, or "authoritarian controls" may be used to force people to do it.[34]

In 1991 The Trilateral Commission published the book *Beyond Interdependence: The Meshing of the World's Economy and the Earth's Ecology*, with a Foreword by David Rockefeller (CFR) and an Introduction by Maurice Strong (CFR). The book is a desperate call for deindustrialization. According to the authors, environmental issues are "rightly moving into the central policy agenda" and we feel the need for a "new synthesis."[35] The "new synthesis" consisted in the elimination of borders and sovereignty, and the creation of a world government under bankers' control: a New World Order.

The next year, at the UN Conference on Environment and Development (UNCED) held in Rio de Janeiro in 1992, David Rockefeller's protegé Maurice Strong (CFR), Secretary General of the Earth Summit II, continued the same brainwashing discourse by telling the delegates that the only hope for planet Earth to survive is the collapse of industrial civilization. According to Strong,

> It is clear that current life styles and consumption patterns of the affluent middle class involving high meat intake, consumption of large amounts of frozen and convenience foods, use of fossil fuels, appliances, home and work place air conditioning, suburban housing are *not* sustainable. ... A shift is necessary toward life-styles less geared to environmentally damaging consumption patterns.
> It is simply not feasible for sovereignty to be exercised unilaterally by individual nation-states, however powerful. It is a principle which will yield only slowly and reluctantly to the imperatives of global environmental cooperation.[36]

The Conference produced the Biodiversity Treaty and a program called Agenda 21. Both provide the justification for the global implementation of what they call "sustainable development," necessary to reach the Conference's alleged goal of transferring the First World wealth to the Third World — actually to destroy the World's wealth. President George H.W. Bush (CFR) and 177 other world leaders who attended the UNCED agreed to pursue the implementation of Agenda 21.

According to Agenda 21, population, consumption and technology are the primary driving forces of environmental degradation. It lays out what needs to be done to reduce wasteful and inefficient consumption patterns in some parts of the world while encouraging increased but sustainable development in others.

The Agenda 21 plan openly targets private property. Its ultimate goal is the elimination of private property ownership, single-family homes, private car ownership and privately-owned small farms.[37]

As a bonus, aside from advancing their secret agenda of deindustrialization, the Rockefellers and other oil producers have profited enormously with the help of the Left. In the name of protecting the environment, the fool lefties have relentlessly worked hard to eliminate the main competitors to oil as a source of energy, such as natural gas, coal and nuclear, and pushed instead the use of inefficient sources of energy such as solar and wind which some people accepted only thanks to huge government tax incentives.

On the other hand, not all leftists support the CFR secret agenda as a result of foolishness. Some of them have done it out of material benefits. Through the myriad of non-profit corporations they control, the Rockefellers and their fellow bankers have been lavishly founding the Left in their deindustrialization efforts.[38]

As we will see in the next Chapter, President Kennedy's vision of the U.S. and the world was diametrically opposed to the vision of the Rockefellers and their CFR fellow conspirators. Kennedy's pro-development, pro-industrialization, anti-imperial policies threatened to destroy the imperial machinery of depopulation and deindustrialization David Rockefeller and his minions had in mind — and they reacted viciously against JFK.

Chapter 2

Kennedy Against David's New World Order

We shall have World Government, whether or not we like it.
The only question is whether World Government
will be achieved by conquest or consent.
— James Warburg.

In January 20, 1961, John F. Kennedy was inaugurated as the Thirty-Fifth President of the United States.[1] His inaugural address was a patriotic call for advancing America socially and economically. In it, he challenged the Soviets to use the "wonders of science" for economic progress and space exploration instead of militarism.

Soon after, Kennedy began an aggressive program to "get America moving again," and declared that the 1960s would be the decade of development for America. He stressed the importance of creating an abundant and growing supply of cheap energy. Unfortunately, however, Kennedy ignored that the CFR conspirators had already decided that the 1960s would be the decade that would mark the beginning of energy scarcity, deindustrialization and nondevelopment in America.[2]

Moreover, Kennedy wanted to end U.S. neo-imperialist policies, particularly toward Latin America, and treat smaller countries with respect and fairness.

Even a cursory analysis of Kennedy's ideas, however, show that, unfortunately, he ignored Sun Tzu's dictum: "Know your enemy and know yourself and you can fight a hundred battles without disaster." It is obvious that JFK did not know who his true enemies were.

As a senator, Kennedy once stated that he was a CFR member. Yet, his name never appeared in the CFR's official roster. It is known that the CFR has secret members, but logic indicates that they want to keep that membership secret. There is, however, evidence that JFK at least made an apparent attempt to gain the CFR's favor.

In the October, 1957, issue of *Foreign Affairs*, the CFR organ published JFK's article "A Democrat Looks at Foreign Policy," in which Kennedy mentioned "distinguished individuals" who have played important roles in U.S. foreign policy, among them John McCloy and Robert Lovett.

Also, it is known that President-elect Kennedy turned to CFR-linked Robert Lovett, a key Rockefeller agent, for counsel on his cabinet selection. As expected, all of the people Lovett suggested were CFR members. Key among those was Dean Rusk, chairman of the Rockefeller Foundation, who Kennedy chose for Secretary of State. Rusk rushed to bring his fellow CFR members to help him run State.

The CFR controlled Rusk's staff to such a point that even Kennedy was surprised. Of the 82 names on a list prepared to help President Kennedy staff his State Department, 63 were CFR members.

John Kenneth Galbraith, a close Kennedy collaborator, commented:

> Those of us who had worked for the Kennedy election were tolerated in the government for that reason and had a say, but foreign policy was still with the Council on Foreign Relations people.[3]

Kennedy began pushing his agenda to accomplish his promise to the American people clearly expressed in the motto of his presidential campaign: Get America Moving Again. He was aware that, for some reason he may not have fully understood at the time, America had stopped in its tracks to progress. Therefore, economic growth was Kennedy's main goal of his domestic agenda. He expressed this concern in a speech to the Congress on February 2, 1961, where he presented his Program to Restore Momentum to the American Economy.[4]

Moreover, Kennedy was convinced that, in order to get America moving again, the push had to come from the President. He had clearly expressed this belief on the role of the President in an interview he gave during his presidential campaign: According to Kennedy, the President,

> ... must serve as a catalyst, an energizer, the defender of the public good and the public interest against all the narrow private interests that which operate in our society. Only the President can do this, and only a President who recognizes the nature of this hard challenge can fulfill this historic function.[5]

Kennedy Wants America to Get Moving Again

President Kennedy's inaugural address was a true harbinger of big changes he planned to make in American foreign policy. In the first part of it the new president clearly expressed his intention to end with the ongoing imperial policies:

> To those old allies whose cultural and spiritual origins we share, we pledge the loyalty of faithful friends. United there is little we cannot do in a host of cooperative ventures. Divided there is little we can do — for we dare not meet a powerful challenge at odds and split asunder.
>
> To those new states whom we welcome to the ranks of the free, we pledge our word that one form of colonial control shall not have passed away merely to be replaced by a far more iron tyranny. We shall not always expect to find them supporting our view. But we shall always hope to find them strongly supporting their own freedom — and to remember that, in the past, those who foolishly sought power by riding the back of the tiger ended up inside.
>
> To those people in the huts and villages of half the globe struggling to break the bonds of mass misery, we pledge our best efforts to help them help themselves, for whatever period is required — not because the communists may be doing it, not because we seek their votes, but because it is right. If a free society cannot help the many who are poor, it cannot save the few who are rich.
>
> To our sister republics south of our border, we offer a special pledge — to convert our good words into good deeds — in a new alliance for progress — to assist free men and free governments in casting off the chains of poverty. But this peaceful revolution of hope cannot become the prey of hostile powers. Let all our neighbors know that we shall join with them to oppose aggression or

subversion anywhere in the Americas. And let every other power know that this Hemisphere intends to remain the master of its own house.[6]

The second part of his speech was a clear reference to the futility of the Cold War policy and the risks to mankind it involved,

> Finally, to those nations who would make themselves our adversary, we offer not a pledge but a request: that both sides begin anew the quest for peace, before the dark powers of destruction unleashed by science engulf all humanity in planned or accidental self-destruction.
>
> We dare not tempt them with weakness. For only when our arms are sufficient beyond doubt can we be certain beyond doubt that they will never be employed.
>
> But neither can two great and powerful groups of nations take comfort from our present course — both sides overburdened by the cost of modern weapons, both rightly alarmed by the steady spread of the deadly atom, yet both racing to alter that uncertain balance of terror that stays the hand of mankind's final war.
>
> So let us begin anew — remembering on both sides that civility is not a sign of weakness, and sincerity is always subject to proof. Let us never negotiate out of fear. But let us never fear to negotiate.
>
> Let both sides explore what problems unite us instead of belaboring those problems which divide us.
>
> Let both sides, for the first time, formulate serious and precise proposals for the inspection and control of arms — and bring the absolute power to destroy other nations under the absolute control of all nations.
>
> Let both sides seek to invoke the wonders of science instead of its terrors. Together let us explore the stars, conquer the deserts, eradicate disease, tap the ocean depths and encourage the arts and commerce.
>
> Let both sides unite to heed in all corners of the earth the command of Isaiah — to "undo the heavy burdens . . . [and] let the oppressed go free."
>
> And if a beachhead of cooperation may push back the jungle of suspicion, let both sides join in creating a new endeavor, not a new balance of power, but a new world of law, where the strong

are just and the weak secure and the peace preserved.[7]

Kennedy's inaugural address was a clear defiance of the traditional CFR-created American foreign policy. It marked the beginning of a new type of foreign policy seeking a peaceful solution to the unproductive, dangerous Cold War against the Soviet Union and changing the world's future direction. Kennedy wanted to make clear to Soviet Chairman Nikita Khrushchev that he did not want a Cold War, much less a nuclear war, but a genuine peace based on negotiations and mutual cooperation.[8] He also wanted to put and end to the U.S. imperial foreign policy, which only benefited a small group of bankers and transnational corporations, not the American people, and begin a new approach of U.S. policy towards Latin America and the Third World.

A year later, in a "Message to the Congress Presenting the President's First Economic Report," January 22, 1962, President Kennedy summarized the economic accomplishments of his first year in the presidency. Kennedy reported to the Congress that, as a result of his Administration's efforts acting under the provision of the Employment Act of 1946,

—the economy has regained its momentum;
—the economy is responding to the Federal Government's efforts, under the Act, "to promote maximum employment, production, and purchasing power;"
—the economy is again moving toward the central objective of the Act — to afford "useful employment opportunities, including self-employment, for those able, willing, and seeking to work."

In my message to the Congress on February 2, I stated that this Administration's "realistic aims for 1961 are to reverse the downtrend in our economy, to narrow the gap of unused potential, to abate the waste and misery of unemployment, and at the same time to maintain reasonable stability of the price level." In a message on the balance of payments on February 6, I added a fifth aim, to restore confidence in the dollar and to reduce the deficit in international payments.
    These five aims for 1961 have been achieved:

(1) The downtrend was reversed. Gross national product (GNP) grew from $501 billion (annual rate) in the first quarter to a record rate of $542 billion in the last quarter. In July, industrial produc-

tion regained its previous peak, and by the end of the year it showed a total rise of 13 percent.

(2) These gains brought into productive use nearly half the plant capacity which was idle at the beginning of the year. The growth of GNP narrowed the over-all gap of unused potential from an estimated 10 percent to 5 percent.

(3) Unemployment dropped from 6.8 to 6.1 percent of the labor force. The number of areas of substantial labor surplus declined from 101 in March to 60 in December.

(4) Price stability has been maintained during the recovery. Since February, wholesale prices have fallen slightly, and consumer prices have risen only one-half of 1 percent.

(5) Confidence in the dollar has been restored. Our gold losses were cut from $1.7 billion in 1960 to less than $0.9 billion in 1961. The deficit in 1961 in our basic international transactions was about one-third as large as in 1960.

The "Program To Restore Momentum to the American Economy" which I proposed to the Congress on February 2 resulted in prompt legislation to

—extend unemployment insurance benefits on a temporary basis;
—make Federal aid available, through the States, to dependent children of the unemployed;
—liberalize social security benefits;
—promote home building under the Housing Act of 1961;
—raise the minimum wage and extend it to more workers;
—provide Federal aid under the Area Redevelopment Act, to revitalize the economies of areas with large and persistent unemployment.[9]

President Kennedy continued his First Economic Report by adding that the main goals of his economic policy were, first, "full and sustained prosperity without inflation," second, "economic growth," third, "equal opportunity," and fourth, "basic balance in international payments."[10]

Then, he mentioned that his economic policies for 1962 would include taking some measures conducive to a stronger economy, among them: a program for sustained prosperity, strengthening the financial system, strengthening the U.S. manpower base, and strengthening the tax system.[11]

President Kennedy ended his Message to the Congress expressing his belief,

The momentum of our economy has been restored. This momentum must be maintained, if the full potential of our free economy is
to be released in the service of the Nation and the world. In this
Report: I have proposed a program to sustain our prosperity and
accelerate our growth — in short, to realize our economic potential. In this undertaking, I ask the support of the Congress and the
American people.[12]

In an effort to stimulate economic growth, Kennedy also envisioned a new
tax policy that channeled the flow of capital and credit from short-term
speculative and non-productive investments into long-term investment in
plants and equipment. To this effect, just three months after taking office
he submitted to the Congress a revolutionary tax program. An important
part of it was an investment tax credit, allowing companies to deduct from
their taxes a percentage of the values they had invested in plant and equipment. Even more, in order to stop the growing trend of outsourcing and
moving plants to lower wage countries,[13] this tax break would be allowed
only on capital invested in new plants and equipment located in the U.S.

Kennedy knew that existing tax laws actually were acting as an incen-
tive for U.S. corporations to avoid paying taxes by keeping income generated abroad in those countries instead of bringing it to the U.S. So, he
proposed to tax those profits generated outside the U.S. even if they were
kept abroad. In 1963 he also proposed a general tax cut for small businesses and the poor. This meant he was going to end the privileges and
special rights investors and big corporations were enjoying.

Together with economic measures, he planned to reduce poverty by
expanding job opportunities, as well as raising educational levels and standards of living. All of these measures were intended to benefit the economy
as a whole by accelerating economic progress. These new policies indicated that Kennedy was serious when he said he was to push the stalled
U.S. economy forward again.

Kennedy's Anti-Imperialist Foreign Policy

In foreign policy, Kennedy also took some policy initiatives that indicated
he was going to carry out the promises he had made as a candidate. The
measures he had in mind indicated a radical change from traditional U.S.
foreign policy. Among these were respect for the sovereignty, autonomy
and independence of other nations, as well as promoting expanded opportunities and higher standards of living in those nations.

Kennedy was opposed to neo-imperialist foreign policies based on the domination of weak, poor nations by powerful ones, conducive to perpetuating economic backwardness and exploitation of natural resources. He expressed it clearly in a message he sent to Congress just two months after he was sworn into office in which he stated: "1960s can be — and must be — the crucial 'decade of development' for Latin America, Africa, the Middle east, and Asia."[14]

This was nothing new. As a Senator, Kennedy had strongly criticized what he believed were inflexible hard loans to Third World countries by the Export-Import and other World Banks. In a 1958 speech to the Senate, he had asked for long-term multinational assistance for India's development.

During a speech he gave on December 15, 1958, in San Juan, Puerto Rico, Senator Kennedy proposed the creation of a development program which would include, among other points, the creation of an inter-American capital development bank, to which all Western Hemisphere nations would contribute and in which they all participate, with a majority of the capital being supplied by American dollars, as well as an increase in technical assistance programs of mutual cooperation between the United States and Latin America.[15]

On February 1959, in a speech to the Senate, Kennedy strongly criticized what he saw as a gap more dangerous than the missile gap.

> I am talking about the economic gap, the gap in living standards and income and hope for the future, the gap between the developed and the underdeveloped worlds; between, roughly speaking, the top half of our globe and the bottom half; between the stable, industrialized nations of the North, whether they are friends or foes, and the overpopulated, underinvested nations of the South, whether they are friends or neutrals.
>
> It is the gap which presents us with our most critical challenge today. It is this gap which is altering the face of the globe, our strategy, our security, and our alliances, more than any current military challenge. And it is this economic challenge to which we have responded most sporadically, most timidly, and most inadequately.[16]

It was precisely in that speech where Kennedy better expressed his critical view of what was wrong with U.S. foreign policy:

> As a nation, we [should] think not of war but of peace; not

of crusades of conflict but of covenants of cooperation; not of the pageantry of imperialism but of the pride of new states freshly risen to independence.[17]

Kennedy's mention of what he defined as "the pageantry of imperialism," was a direct attack on the architects of the so-called "American imperialism" — which was actually the imperialism of the oil magnates, Wall Street bankers and CEOs of transnational corporations ensconced at the Council on Foreign Relations.

This was not the first time JFK criticized the CFR conspirators' anti-American activities. As a young congressman, on January 25, 1949, he declared before the House of Representatives:

Mr. Speaker, over this weekend we have learned the extent of the disaster that has befallen China and the United States. The responsibility for the failure of our foreign policy in the Far East rests squarely with the White House and the Department of State. The continued insistence that aid would not be forthcoming, unless a coalition government with the Communists were formed, was a crippling blow to the National Government.[18]

Five days later he reaffirmed his position in a speech to the House:

This is the tragic story of China, whose freedom we once fought to preserve what our young men had saved, our diplomats and our President had frittered away.[19]

It is safe to assume that young Kennedy ignored that, since the early Thirties, the U.S. Department of State, which pushed the betrayal of nationalist China, had fully fallen under the control of CFR agents. They were the true cause of the disaster in China and the failure of the U.S. policy in the Far East.

It is also safe to assume that the CFR globalist conspirators were aware of JFK's criticism and did not ignore it.

Kennedy Creates the Alliance for Progress

Continuing the criticisms he has made in 1959 on the loan policies of the international banks, in 1960 Senator Kennedy strongly criticized the policies of private banks — most of them Rockefeller controlled — in their dealings with Third World countries, particularly in Latin America. He also asked for an increase in the flow of capital to these areas of the world. But, he added, "We must undertake this effort in a spirit of generosity, motivated by a desire to help our fellow citizens of the world — not as narrow bankers or self-seeking politicians."[20]

As we saw above, in his Inaugural Address to the American people, President Kennedy mentioned Latin America and promised:

> To our sister republics south of our border, we offer a special pledge — to convert our good words into good deeds — in a new alliance for progress — to assist free men and free governments in casting off the chains of poverty.[21]

On September 5, 1961, President Kennedy made real on his promise of a "decade of development" for Third World countries by signing a bill authorizing $4,253,500,000 in foreign aid and allowing him to commit $7,200,000,000 for development loans in the next five years.[22]

On a visit to Colombia in December 17, 1961, Kennedy not only promised a better life for the people of Latin America, but only "if past mistakes are admitted and corrected by men of influence in Latin America and Washington." He also mentioned his plan to devote $20 billion dollars for his Alliance for Progress program.[23]

Then, after stating his view of the deplorable social and economic conditions in Latin America, he admitted that forces in the U.S caused part of the problem:

> Today we face our greatest challenge to the vitality of our American Revolution. Millions of our people — scattered across a vast and rich continent — endure lives of misery. We must prove to them that free institutions can best answer their implacable demand for social justice, for food, more material welfare and above all, for a new hope — for themselves and for their children.
>
> We in the United States have made many mistakes in our relations with Latin America. We have not always understood the magnitude of your problems or accepted our responsibility for the welfare of the hemisphere.[24]

Unfortunately, Kennedy was not aware that the negative trend of the American and Latin American economies he was trying to stop and reverse had not been the result of chance or incompetence, but of a plan carefully conceived by the Rockefellers and their CFR agents to destroy the U.S. economy and change America into a Third World country. Many years before JFK was elected President, the globalist conspirators at the Council on Foreign Relations had already decided that, far from being the decade of development, the 1960s would be the decade devoted to lower the levels of education by turning it into indoctrination as well as lowering American standards of living and increasing poverty levels by systematically destroying the U.S. industrial base and encouraging the corporations to outsource their jobs abroad.

Kennedy Against the Rockefellers

If you read most of what has been published about both John and Robert Kennedy, even including the rosy stories written by court historians like Arthur Schlesinger and friends like Ben Bradlee and Ted Sorensen, you arrive at the conclusion that the Kennedy brothers were no angels. There is abundant information available showing the lack of respect for the rule of law prevailing in the Kennedy administration.

Moreover, the claim that Kennedy wanted to radically change U.S. foreign policy is not totally true. Yes, he mentioned over and over in his speeches that he sought a more peaceful world, but this was not too different from what every American president before and after had said.

Paradoxically, it was President Eisenhower who cut military spending. On the contrary, actually Kennedy increased it. So, the theory that JFK was assassinated only because he threatened the profits of the military-industrial-complex is not fully true. Most likely, the reason they hated Kennedy was because the Rockefellers and their minions in the Council on Foreign Relations and the U.S. military suspected that, in the long way, he was going to discover their secret game and become a threat to them.

In some of his speeches Kennedy criticized people lured by the pageantry of imperialism, but the evidence shows that he and his brother were lured by the pageantry of covert operations, particularly the use of assassinations to get rid of opponents. As author Henry Hurt pointed out, there was a wholesale abandonment of morality in Kennedy's Camelot, and it reached a point where murder was acceptable.[25] It is true that Kennedy used back channels to try to open a dialogue with Castro, but he also continued until his death implementing black ops against the Cuban tyrant and other foreign leaders.

He foolishly ignored that the very same CFR agents inside the CIA with whom he planned Castro's assassination were keeping Castro fully informed. JFK's naiveté most likely was a motive of amusement and contempt among the Castros, the Rockefellers, and their agents infiltrated inside the CIA.

In a speech he gave on November 16, 1961, at the University of Washington in Seattle, Kennedy elaborated upon the subject of assassination. He hypocritically declared, "We cannot, as a free nation, compete with our adversaries in tactics of terror, assassination, false promises, counterfeit mobs and crises."[26]

It seems that Kennedy fully believed the notion that the CIA was just a tool in the hands of the President. What he ignored, though, was that it was a tool in the hands of David Rockefeller, the true President of the Invisible Government of the United States, not the puppet in the White House.

Unknowingly, President Kennedy was driving painful *banderillas*[27] into the body of the CFR bull. Unfortunately, far from killing him, he was turning the bull into a furious, bloodthirsty beast. Kennedy's pro-life, pro-development, anti-war, anti-imperialist policies, jeopardized the depopulation, deindustrialization, warmongering imperialist machinery the Rockefellers and their globalist minions had so carefully assembled, and they didn't take it lightly.[28]

One of the fateful steps taken by Kennedy after he was sworn as president was to scrap the NSC mechanism. Being statutory, he could not abolish the NSC unilaterally, but he simply ignored it.[29] Then, after the Bay of Pigs debacle — which, as I will show later, actually was a very successful PsyOp carried out by the CIA on behalf of the CFR conspirators — he fired CIA Director Allen Dulles, a senior CFR conspirator closely associated to the Rockefeller gang, and told some close friends that he wanted to "splinter" the CIA "into a thousand pieces and scatter [it] to the winds."[30]

Finally, he made what were probably his three biggest anti-CFR measures.

The first one was authorizing the Secretary of the Treasury to issue currency backed by the U.S. Treasury Department, not the Federal Reserve Bank. One of the first measures taken by President Lyndon Johnson after he was sworn into office was to order the recall and destruction of the bills.[31]

The second was that, contrary to his CFR advisors' opinion, he began taking measures to end the war in Vietnam. On October 11, 1963, he ordered McGeorge Bundy to implement plans to withdraw 1,000 U.S. military personnel by the end of the year.[32] This was believed to be the first step to a complete withdrawal of American troops from Vietnam.

The third was his signing on June 28, 1961, of National Security Action Memorandum 55, Relations of the JCS to the President in Cold War Operations. The first paragraph of NSAM 55 was a slap in the face of the CFR conspirators infiltrated inside the CIA:

> I regard the Joint Chiefs of Staff as my principal military advisor responsible both for initiating advice to me and for responding to requests for advice. I expect their advice to come to me direct and unfiltered.

The second paragraph deprived the CIA of its power to conduct covert operations which, as I will show in Chapter 8, was the true and only reason why the Rockefellers had created the CIA.

> The Joint Chiefs of Staff have a responsibility for the defense of the nation in the Cold War similar to that they have in conventional hostilities. They should know the military and paramilitary forces and resources available to the Department of Defense, verify their readiness, report on their adequacy, and made appropriate recommendations for their expansion and improvement. I look to the Chiefs to contribute dynamic and imaginative leadership in contributing to the success of the military and paramilitary aspects of Cold War programs.

Kennedy further clarified his attack on CIA's covert activities on NSAM 56, Evaluation of Paramilitary Requirements, and NSAM 57, Responsibility for Paramilitary Operations, both of them dated June 28, 1961. These three NSAMs effectively stripped from the CIA all power to carry out covert paramilitary operations.

After Kennedy was assassinated, the CIA recovered its power to carry out covert operations — actually, the JFK assassination was the first step to cancel NSAM 55.

Soon after his death, his Vietnam policy of withdrawing was dismantled, and this reverse happened extremely fast. Perhaps the reason for the haste was because, just two days before Kennedy was assassinated, Dean Rusk (CFR), Robert McNamara (CFR), McGeorge Bundy (CFR) and Henry Cabot Lodge (CFR), U.S. Ambassador to South Vietnam, had secretly met in Honolulu to discuss Kennedy's new policy of troop withdrawal. Then, two days after the assassination, most of those who attended the meeting in Honolulu and CIA Director John McCone (CFR) had an emergency meeting with Lyndon Johnson, after which Kennedy's policy of withdrawal was quickly reversed.[33]

Last, but not least, Kennedy conspired with the CIA to kill his archenemy, Fidel Castro — which shows that JFK not only was a person of low moral and ethical principles, but also a fool. Trying to use the CIA to kill Castro was perhaps the most stupid thing he did in his life. So, it was a sort of poetic justice that, following the conspirators' orders, the CIA, most likely with Castro's help, terminated Kennedy with extreme prejudice.[34]

Firing Allen Dulles and mentioning that he wanted to smash the CIA into a thousand pieces was a slap in the Rockefellers' face and JFK knew it.[35] His signing of NSAM 55 was a punch in David's eye. It was his not-so-subtle way of telling David and his CFR minions that he was the one in command — or so he believed. Ignoring the NSC, and later creating his own Ex-Comm (Executive Committee of the NSC) during the missile crisis was another direct attack on the Rockefeller's power. Finally, just the fact that he signed Executive Order # 11110, authorizing the U.S. Treasury Department, not the Federal Reserve Bank, to print dollar bills and ordering the withdrawal of troops from Vietnam, were serious transgressions the CFR conspirators would never tolerate. This explains why the one who got smashed was not the CIA, but John F. Kennedy.

In synthesis:

- JFK planned to end the participation of the U.S. in the Vietnam conflict.
- He tried to overthrow or kill Castro.
- He took steps to curtail the CIA's covert operations.
- He planned the put an end to the Cold War.
- He wanted to change the U.S. neo-colonialist policy towards Latin America.
- He took a first step towards the end the Fed's monopoly on issuing currency
- He took steps to diminish the power of the National Security Council.
- He wanted to get the U.S. economy moving again.

Unknowingly, JFK had declared war on David Rockefeller and the CFR, and very soon he would pay dearly for his mistake.

Granted, JFK was no hero. Actually, there are no heroes in politics. Most politicians are extraordinarily flawed characters. Based on some newly declassified documents, some people even believed JFK was "a cunning and cagey President."[36] But, contrary to David Rockefeller and his CFR minions, John F. Kennedy did not hate his country. On the contrary, his plan to get America moving again showed that he loved his country.

Unfortunately he believed that he was the true President of the United States and tried to act as a President is supposed to do in order to protect and defend the Constitution: listening to his advisors but making his own decisions.[37] He was wrong.

Chapter 3

David Rockefeller Against President Kennedy

The question is not how to get good people to rule;
the question is how to stop the powerful from doing
as much damage as they can to us.
— Karl Popper.

As soon as he got into the White House, Kennedy began an aggressive program to "get America moving again" — quite similar to Trump's campaign motto "Make America great again" — and declared that the 1960s would be the decade of development, stressing the importance of creating an abundant and growing supply of cheap energy.

But Kennedy's enemies were decided to not allow him to accomplish his campaign promises. Soon after he was sworn into Office, his own Secretary of State Dean Dusk (CFR), as well as Chester Bowles (CFR) and other CFR agents in the State Department and in the White House, publicly expressed their displeasure with the new Kennedy policies.

David Surrounds Kennedy With CFR Agents

In 1947, CFR secret agents infiltrated into the U.S. Government pushed the creation of the National Security Act, which created the National Security Council and the Central Intelligence Agency, allegedly as tools to manage the military, intelligence, and foreign policy areas of the U.S. Government. But, soon after it was created, the CFR agents infiltrated in the National Security Council changed it into a tool to control the information reaching the eyes and ears of the Presidents, thus creating a smoke screen of disinformation around them.

Since the end of the World War II, the CFR conspirators, through their secret agents in the NSC, have been putting blinders on American Presidents, keeping them in the dark and feeding them disinformation. To make things even easier for them, the CFR conspirators created the concept of President's plausible denial — a euphemism for President's ignorance.

Soon after, they expanded the concept with the notion that "what the President doesn't know can't hurt him politically." This meant that the CFR conspirators, through their agents infiltrated in the White House, gave themselves a free hand in planning and carrying out American foreign policy with as little consultation as possible with the incumbent President.

This curtain of disinformation surrounding U.S. Presidents explains why all of them, even the ones who were not CFR members, were unknowingly advancing the goals of the Rockefellers and their CFR agents. Most of the important decisions taken by American Presidents about things they knew next to nothing had already been taken at the Harold Pratt House in Manhattan and later carefully implanted in the Presidents' brains by their CFR advisors.

Perhaps the only exception in this series of American Presidents "elected" by the CFR conspirators was John F. Kennedy, who came to be president thanks to his father's money and links to the Chicago Mafia.[1] In 1960 Richard Nixon (CFR) ran against John F. Kennedy, but Kennedy's father pulled a fast one by buying votes in Chicago and other cities, and his son was elected president by a small majority of 100,000 votes.

In his book *A Thousand Days*, Arthur Schlesinger (CFR), Kennedy's friend and biographer, wrote about the problems Kennedy faced in recruiting people to form his cabinet and close staff and how, despite his intentions to be independent from the Rockefellers and their CFR agents, he had to accept them among his close advisors and staff:

Kennedy's acquaintance had, indeed, certain limitations . . . In particular, he was little acquainted in the New York financial and legal community — that arsenal of talent which had so long furnished a steady supply of always orthodox and often able people to Democratic as well as Republican administrations. This continuity was the heart of the American Establishment. Its household deities were Henry L. Stimson and Elihu Root; its present leaders Robert A. Lovett and John J. McCloy; its front organizations, the Rockefeller, Ford and Carnegie Foundations and the Council on Foreign Relations; its organs, the *New York Times*, and *Foreign Affairs*.

The New York Establishment had looked on Kennedy with some suspicion. . . Now that he was President, however, they were prepared to rally round; and, now that he was President, he was prepared to receive them.[2]

What Schlesinger didn't mention, though, is that the way David Rockefeller — not the "Establishment" as he disingenuously calls it — rallied around Kennedy was by surrounding him by a large group of his trusted CFR agents.

Following the advice of Schlesinger (CFR) and McGeorge Bundy (CFR), Kennedy asked CFR honcho Robert Lovett,[3] one of the darkest figures in American politics, to become his Secretary of State. Lovett declined, but recommended some of his CFR buddies to fill the positions of Secretary of State, Treasury and Defense. Without exception, the three of them, Rusk, Dillon and McNamara, were selected for the cabinet.

Kennedy was somehow aware of this. He once complained to his friend Schlesinger: "I'd like to have some new faces here, but all I get is the same old names. Its discouraging."[4] He had reasons to be discouraged. The Kennedy cabinet included:

National Security Advisor, McGeorge Bundy (CFR) 1961–1963
Secretary of State, Dean Rusk (CFR) 1961–1963
Secretary of Treasury, C. Douglas Dillon (CFR) 1961–1963
Secretary of Defense, Robert McNamara (CFR) 1961–1963
Secretary of Agriculture, Orville Freeman (CFR) 1961–1963
Secretary of Labor, Arthur Goldberg (CFR) 1961–1962
Sec. Health, Ed., Welfare, Abraham A. Ribicoff (CFR) 1961–1962
Special Council to the President, Theodore Sorensen (CFR) 1961-
    1962
Special Assistant to the President, Arthur Schlesinger, Jr. (CFR) 1961-
    1963

Non-cabinet members were:

CIA Director, Allen W. Dulles (CFR) 1953–1961
CIA Director, John A. McCone (CFR) 1961–1965

Other influential CFR members in the Kennedy administration were:

W. Averell Harriman (Ambassador-at-Large)
John J. McCloy (Disarmament Administrator)
Gen. Lyman L. Lemnitzer (Chairman of the Joint Chiefs of Staff)
John Kenneth Galbraith (Ambassador to India)
Edward R. Murrow (head of the U.S. Information Agency)
Arthur H. Dean (head, U.S. Delegation to the Geneva Disarmament
    Conference)
Thomas K. Finletter (Ambassador to NATO)
George Ball (Under Secretary of State for Economic Affairs)
Paul H. Nitze (Assistant Secretary of Defense)
Charles E. Bohlen (Assistant Secretary of State)
Walt W. Rostow (Deputy National Security Advisor)
Roswell Gilpatrick (Deputy Secretary of Defense)
Henry Fowler (Under Secretary of State)
Jerome Wiesner (Special Assistant to the President)
Angier Duke (Chief of Protocol).

Altogether, fifty percent of the top foreign policy officials under Kennedy were CFR members whose true allegiance was with the CFR, not to the President.[5] Instead of new faces, Kennedy had unknowingly surrounded himself with traitors ready to stab him in the back.

David Rockefeller and the CFR globalist conspirators reluctantly accepted Kennedy simply because they thought he was too young and inexperienced, his only interest was chasing girls and, therefore, would be easy to handle. But, particularly after the Bay of Pigs debacle, Kennedy woke up to the reality surrounding him, began seeing many things he had not noticed before, and he didn't like them. Unfortunately, he underestimated the guile and evil nature of his powerful enemies.

Kennedy's speeches as Senator indicated that his ideas about America's future were quite different from what the globalist conspirators had in mind. Nevertheless, they knew that, as a boy, Kennedy attended Choate, an elite Connecticut preparatory school. After graduating from Choate and spending one semester at Princeton, he moved to London and registered as a student of the London School of Economics, mainly because he wanted to attend Prof. Harold Lasky's lectures. But, just a few days later, he fell ill — possibly with hepatitis, jaundice or the early signs of Addison's disease — and had to return to America. Once recovered, Kennedy transferred in 1936 to Harvard University

Nevertheless, despite his populist speeches, nothing indicated that he was to become an unmanageable problem for the CFR conspirators. Yet, Kennedy's actions after he was sworn into office indicated he actually believed that the President was the true source of power in this country.[6] So, they decided to give him a not-so-subtle reminder that he was wrong.

David's Globalist Mafia Shows Its Hand

The strong differences between JFK and the globalist conspirators were not only about form — where the true center of power resided in this country — but also about content. The conspirators firmly opposed Kennedy's idea of expanding America's technological and industrial base as a way to economic progress and increase the material well being of the American people through higher wages and consumption.

After WWII the United States had changed into a world hegemonic power at the same time that multinational corporations emerged as a key economic and political power in the world. These corporations, and the bankers supporting them, expected the U.S. Government to protect and advance their interests abroad, even if that included overthrowing nationalist governments and even assassinating any leaders who opposed the harmful intrusion of the multinational corporations and banks into their countries. American Presidents, most of them puppets put in power by the globalist conspirators, had accepted this *status quo* without offering resistance because they either believed it was the best way to promote U.S. interests or feared the consequences of opposing the Rockefellers and their CFR friends. But now President Kennedy was trying to destroy the *status quo*.

So, as soon as they realized that Kennedy was really going to try to accomplish his promises to the American people, the CFR conspirators unleashed their attack dogs in the mainstream press, particularly the *New York Times*, the *Wall Street Journal*, *Time*, *Life* and *Fortune*. These publications not only had strong ties to the Rockefeller and Morgan interests, but also were CFR corporate members.

Hiding behind an institutional cover of respectability, the Council on Foreign Relations is basically a criminal organization; the cover for a Mafia of Wall Street bankers, oil magnates and CEOs of transnational corporations, composed of ethically and morally challenged individuals, associated to conspire and carry out criminal activities.[7]

The criminal activities of this Wall Street Mafia have caused more death and suffering than the ones committed by all the other mafias together. As Marine General Smedly Butler expressed it clearly:

I spent most of my time being a high class muscle-man for Big Business, for Wall Street and for the Bankers. In short, I was a racketeer, a gangster for capitalism. . . . During those years, I had, as the boys in the back room would say, a swell racket. Looking back on it, I feel that I could have given Al Capone a few hints. The best he could do was to operate his racket in three districts. We Marines operated on three continents.[8]

So, why do the American people totally ignore the existence of this dangerous crime syndicate? Because, contrary to the other minor mafias, the Wall Street Mafia exerts an almost total control over the mainstream media, particularly TV, national newspapers and magazines, and the book and film industries.[9]

This control over the U.S. mainstream media began long time ago, at the beginning of the Twentieth Century, and some people saw it. As early as February 9, 1917, Representative Oscar Callaway (D-Texas) inserted a statement in the *Congressional Record* alerting his colleagues about how a group of conspirators took over the press:

In March 1915, the J.P. Morgan interests, the steel, shipbuilding, and powder interests, and their subsidiary organizations got together twelve men high up in the newspaper world and employed them to select the most influential newspapers in the United States and sufficient number of them to control generally the policy of the daily press of the United Sates.

These 12 men worked the problem out by selecting 170 newspapers, and then began, by an elimination process, to retain only those necessary for the purpose of controlling the general policy of the daily press throughout the country. They found it was only necessary to purchase the control of 25 of the greatest newspapers. The 25 papers were agreed upon; emissaries were sent to purchase the policy, national and international, of these papers; an agreement was reached; the policy of the papers was bought, to be paid for by the month; an editor was furnished for each paper to properly supervise and edit information regarding the questions of preparedness, militarism, financial policies, and other things of national and international nature considered vital to the interest of the purchasers.

This contract is in existence at the present time, and it accounts for the news columns of the daily press of the country being filled with all sorts of preparedness argument and misrepresentations as to the present condition of the United States Army and Navy and the possibility and probability of the United States being attacked by foreign foes.

This policy also included the suppression of everything in opposition to the wishes of the interests served. The effectiveness of this scheme has been conclusively demonstrated by the character of stuff carried in the daily press throughout the country since March 1915. They have resorted to anything necessary to commercialize public sentiment and sandbag the national congress into making extravagant and wasteful appropriations for the Army and Navy under the false pretense that it was necessary. Their stock argument is that it is "patriotism." They are playing on every prejudice and passion of the American people.[10]

One of the things Kennedy discovered once he became President was that some important fiscal and monetary policies were not dictated by the government, but by a small group of big corporations and bankers. Kennedy believed that most of their actions did not benefit the country as a whole. The conspirators' defense was accusing Kennedy of being anti-business. He refuted it in a speech he delivered at the Florida Chamber of Commerce four days before he was assassinated.[11]

Nevertheless, the antagonism against Kennedy did not come only from businessmen, but from the highest levels of the Invisible Government of the United States,

The Rockefeller-controlled Press Attacks President Kennedy

Less than a year after he had become the President of the United States, the CFR globalist conspirators' attack on Kennedy reached a frenzy of obfuscation, slander, vilification, disparagement and character assassination.[12] This frenzy reached a peak in mid-1962 when David Rockefeller himself showed his hostility to JFK by publicly criticizing the President's economic policies as the main cause of the U.S.'s economic problems.

On February 10, 1961, a *Life* magazine editorial began by asserting,

> The Kennedy Administration has now partly spelled out what it meant by its promise to 'set America moving.' In his State of the Union message the new President drew as dark a picture of the U.S. economy as he could find statistics for. . . . The question of whether he had correctly analyzed the 'trouble' which he says the economy is in, and whether his program is well designed to cure it.[13]

Next year, a critical *Life* editorial purposely about President Kennedy's "Appeal for a new economic thinking," ended up by telling JFK that his idea of a new economic thinking was wrong and reminding him of an old, tested principle: "The principle, in brief, is that the American economy grows best in freedom." Of course, it didn't mention that their idea of freedom was freedom just for the big banks and corporations.[14]

David Rockefeller's irritation with Kennedy grew to a point that in July 1962, *Life* magazine[15] featured an unusual exchange of letters between David and President Kennedy.

According to *Life* magazine, on the evening of May 11, 1962, President Kennedy was giving a dinner for France's Minister of Cultural Affairs André Malraux. One of the guests was art patron David Rockefeller, president of Chase Manhattan Bank and the Council on Foreign Relations. JFK and David fell into a private conversation, in which David, the virtual president of the U.S., criticized the state of the U.S. economy because Kennedy was not doing the things David would have done.

JFK politely thanked David and asked him to express his views in writing. A few days later David did that, and JFK later told *Life*'s editor to publish David's letter and his reply as an example of the kind of serious dialogue he desired to have with businessmen on these particular issues.

In his letter, in which he showed his hostility to JFK by pointing to the President's economic policies as the source of the country's problems, David expanded on his belief that "Some real progress has been achieved over the past few years in improving the basic position of our balance of payments." But he also expressed his disagreement with most of JFK's policies. In particular, David strongly disagreed with President Kennedy's intention to impose exchange controls over capital movements. He also mentioned that

the current tax burden was too heavy on investments, and suggested a reduction on corporate income tax — something JFK did not favor.

David ended his letter by telling JFK: "For all these reasons, Mr. President — because of the vital need of increased investments, the requirement
of lower taxes, and the importance of fiscal responsibility — I would urge
upon a more effective control of expenditures and a determined and rigor-
ous effort to balance the budget."

In his reply, "From the President: 'Our Basic Position is Strong,'" JFK
expressed his goal that "Our allies will be pressed to increase their share in
our joint defense costs." He also maintained that all of the domestic measures of his administration, both short-term and long-range, were designed
for ending the slowdown of the U.S. economy, preferably by rebuilding the
country's infrastructure of dams and highways.[16] Even more important,
JFK mentioned his belief that,

> Our tax laws should surely not encourage the export of dollars by
> permitting 'tax havens' and other undue preferences. The Senate
> Finance Committee is now considering what changes would be
> desirable.

Kennedy's actions were a direct threat to the Rockefellers and their
corporate friends in the area of their hidden wealth abroad parked in the
Swiss and Caribbean banks serving as tax havens.

Moreover, Kennedy's idea of U.S. Government long-term, low-inter-
est loans to Third World countries was not well received. Instead, David
was pushing — still gently at this point — for U.S. adherence to the IMF,
so rich guys could give shark loans to poor nations without the government
interfering by giving these loans under humane and reasonable terms.

Evidently, JFK's vision of America's future was quite different from
David Rockefeller's idea. This conflict sent both men on a crash course.

Continuing the trend, early in 1963 a highly critical *Life* Editorial mocked
Kennedy's "dubious arguments" of a coming recession: "His economic
program is therefore in worse shape than the U.S. Economy." The editorial
quoted New York's governor Nelson Rockefeller stating that Kennedy's
economic policies were "the heights of fiscal irresponsibility." The Kennedy
economic program, said Nelson, shows a "failure to understand the forces
underlying growth."[17]

On September 13, 1963, the Economy section of *Time* magazine mentioned that one of the most pressing problems facing President Kennedy when he took office was the growing deficit in the U.S.'s international balance of payments. Since the deficit drained U.S. gold reserves, it threatened the stability of the dollar.

By a variety of techniques, Kennedy had cut the previous year the annual deficit from the $3.9 billion he had inherited to $2.2 billion. But in the first half of 1963, the rate soared to $5.2 billion — and became one of the most painful of all subjects for the Kennedy Administration.

Time also mentioned an article by Governor Nelson Rockefeller appeared in the same issue of the magazine. In it, Nelson went a step further than his brother David in his criticism of Kennedy's economic policies. Nelson warned that the gold drain could lead to "worldwide financial collapse." It is getting worse, wrote Nelson, because Kennedy's handling of the problem "has been characterized throughout by insufficient recommendations, tardy proposals, watering down of plans already advanced, and lack of firm follow-through." He also accused Kennedy of "timid tinkering," "temporizing" and "continued drift."[18]

According to Nelson, dollars were flowing out of the U.S., "due to a failure to develop methods to support the economic development and defense of the free world without placing too great a burden on the balance of payments." Investment money was going abroad because of the "failure of the President to redeem his often-repeated 1960 campaign pledge to 'get this country moving again economically,'" and because U.S. interest rates were lower than some other countries.

Nelson offered several recommendations of his own to check the alleged gold drain. Among those he urged "an immediate federal tax cut to raise production efficiency,[19] improving our ability to compete in world markets," coupled with "a clear goal of a balanced cash budget as soon as possible." He would soften the drain caused by foreign aid by making sure that aid "does not simply pour more dollars into nations which already have balance-of-payments surpluses" and by urging "our European allies to assume a larger share of the foreign-aid program."

Kennedy Tries to End the Vietnam War

Another point of friction between Kennedy and the Rockefellers and their agents in the military-industrial-banking complex was JFK's intention of putting an end to the U.S. participation in the Vietnam War.

JFK's opposition to U.S. involvement in the war in Vietnam actually began way before he became President. In a speech to the Senate in 1954, after admitting that he supported some U.S. military help to prevent Communist domination of Indochina, he stated: "But to pour money, materiel, and men into the jungles of Indochina without at least a remote prospect of victory would be dangerously futile and self destructive."[20]

Once he was in the White House, Kennedy continued to reject his advisors' recommendations to put more American boots on the ground in Vietnam. Key among his warmonger advisors were CFR members Robert McNamara, William and McGeorge Bundy and Dean Rusk. It seems that, despite their advise, Kennedy seriously planned to retire U.S. Troops from Vietnam.

According to his nephew Robert F. Kennedy, Jr.,

> Despite the Cold War rhetoric of his campaign, JFK's greatest ambition as president was to break the militaristic ideology that has dominated our country since World War II. He told his close friend Ben Bradlee that he wanted the epitaph "He kept the peace," and said to another friend, William Walton, "I am almost a 'peace at any price' president." Hugh Sidey, a journalist and friend, wrote that the governing aspect of JFK's leadership was "a total revulsion" of war.[21]

Proof of the above is that on October 11, 1963, Kennedy signed National Security Action Memorandum 263. It no only ordered a withdrawal of 1,000 troops out of roughly 16,000 Americans stationed in Vietnam by the end of 1963, but also stated his purpose of a complete withdrawal of American troops by the end of 1965.[22]

As usual, the Rockefellers and their minions resorted to the ever-useful argument of national security to criticize Kennedy.[23] Just six days before JFK was assassinated, the *New York Times* published a speech by New York's Governor Nelson Rockefeller in which he expressed his "deep concern" that President Kennedy "was undermining the nation's security and world peace."[24]

Joining Nelson, the CFR-controlled mainstream press acidly criticized Kennedy's lack of commitment to the Vietnam conflict. On November 22, the very same day Kennedy was assassinated, a *Life* magazine Editorial stated:

> If the Delta offensive now planed is to succeed, for example, the number of Vietnamese troops, U.S. Army helicopters and U.S. Air

Force planes may have to be doubled. Now is the time to pour on more coal. It is not a time to relax or schedule U.S. Manpower withdrawals in time for our 1964 elections.[25]

On Nov 22, 1963, a few minutes after President John F. Kennedy was assassinated at Dealey Plaza in Dallas, Texas, Lyndon B. Johnson became President of the United States.

On November 26, the day after JFK was buried, Johnson signed National Security Action Memorandum 273. This was the first NSAM on Vietnam under President Lyndon Johnson. It effectively overturned Kennedy's NSAM 263 and ordered the planning of increased activity in Vietnam. The memorandum also authorized open-ended covert operations against North Vietnam.[26] A revealing detail is that the draft of NSAM 273 was dated Nov. 21, 1963, the day before the assassination, therefore Kennedy had not ordered its creation and had not seen it.

Two days after the assassination, President Johnson, following instructions from his CFR masters, reversed Kennedy's Vietnam policy and determined the course of action to follow — which paved the way for the Vietnam disaster. In addition to cancelling the troop withdrawal and providing for troop increases, the policy shift resumed the covert action program against North Vietnam.

Evidently, both David and Nelson Rockefeller wanted bankers like himself, not President Kennedy, to control the foreign and domestic policies of the United States. Many years later, David confirmed his intentions when in June 1991, during a Bilderberg meeting in Baden-Baden, Germany, he had a rare moment of candor and arrogantly told his friends in the press,

The supra-national sovereignty of an intellectual elite and world bankers is surely preferable to the national auto determination practiced in past centuries.[27]

Chapter 4

David Rockefeller Throws Obstacles Onto JFK's Path

Competition is a sin.
— John D. Rockefeller.

The one thing that mostly characterizes the Rockefellers is that they hate competition and, as soon as John F. Kennedy became the U.S. President, he began acting as the President is supposed to act. JFK's behavior not only threatened the Rockefellers' interests, but was also highly offensive to David Rockefeller, who considered himself the *de facto* president of the U.S. and that the role of the government was protecting and advancing the interests of big banks and corporations, not the American people.

So, as soon as he realized that he couldn't control Kennedy, David began throwing obstacles onto his path in order to discredit JFK and diminish his authority. The first of these obstacles was the Bay of Pigs invasion.

The Bay of Pigs Betrayal

On the morning of April 17, 1961, just three months after John F. Kennedy had been inaugurated as American president, 1400 Cuban exiles sent by the United States were wading toward disaster at a beach called Playa Girón, in a bay south of the central part of the Cuba — the Bay of Pigs. The first news about the invasion that appeared in the Soviet press reflected the general consensus that Castro's revolution was living its very last hours in the face of an American direct invasion.[1] But then, the Soviet leaders watched in disbelief how President Kennedy, with the power to command enough military force to destroy the world, did nothing as Fidel Castro's troops repelled the attack and captured prisoners off the beach.

Previous to the invasion, CIA officials had been privately assuring the Eisenhower and the Kennedy administrations that Cuba would become another Guatemala.[2] But as early as March 1960, Castro had already begun telling the world that Cuba would *not* be another Guatemala.[3] It seems that CFR agents inside CIA had been working hard to keep Castro informed about the invasion, for it was precisely in March, 1960, when President Eisenhower approved the invasion plan.[4]

The original invasion plan, on which the Joint Chiefs of Staff and the CIA had agreed, involved a one-shot confrontation of Castro's already formidable armed forces with a vest-pocket-sized force of Cuban exiles trained in regular WWII combat techniques rather than in guerrilla operations and political subversion. The plan amounted to asking the fifteen hundred patriots who landed at the Bay of Pigs to seize control of the Island from over a hundred thousand relatively well-trained, well-armed Castroite soldiers and militia.[5]

It was clear beforehand that, in the event that the invasion failed, Castro's prestige and strength were going to be greatly enhanced. Undersecretary of State Chester Bowles, who had heard of the plan, expressed precisely those concerns to Secretary of State Rusk.[6] With the benefit of hindsight, however, the evidence indicates that the whole operation had been planned to fail.

In the first place, the American government supplied the Cubans with obsolete aircraft and decrepit ships allegedly chosen with the idea that such equipment would not be identified with the ones used by American regular forces. That justification is unconvincing, because the Americans would never be able to hide their massive participation in the invasion, even if it was indirect.

Secondly, when President Kennedy approved the initial plan he had promised that the American forces would provide air cover for the invasion. Two U.S. carriers were to stand by, within easy range, their decks loaded with armed fighter planes, to secure the vital air cover for the invasion. Confident in this assurance from the highest levels of the American

Government that air support would be provided, the invaders disembarked.

Castro hurriedly sent his tanks and infantry, and the invasion force fought valiantly while waiting for the U.S. air support to arrive. But that very Sunday evening, following the advice of his CFR advisors, President Kennedy made the fateful decision to prohibit the U.S. planes from providing the vital air cover. Without that support, the invasion was doomed to fail.[7]

Several authors have popularized the notion that the failure of the invasion was not due to President Kennedy's order proscribing U.S. air cover, but because of lack of Cuban popular support to the invaders, a key assumption in the CIA's invasion plans.[8] The invasion failed, they conclude, because the people stood for Castro instead of turning to back the invaders as expected.

These authors seem to forget, however, that because of the gross error of alerting Castro two days in advance by way of an ill-planned and ineffective air attack on his planes, the Cuban dictator was put on alert. After the air raid Castro moved quickly, sending all potential enemies to jail to avoid any internal uprising.

But the most important thing they seem to ignore is that people usually support a *winning* invasion, not a failed one, and just a few hours after the invasion began it was evident that it had failed. As a matter of fact, in the first hours of the invasion some peasants of the region, including a few of Castro's militiamen, voluntarily joined the invading forces. Therefore, the invasion did not fail for lack of popular Cuban support; it failed because Kennedy's CFR advisors convinced him not to provide air support to the invasion.

A few months after the failed invasion attempt, intriguing details on why the Bay of Pigs operation had failed began appearing through the dust clouds of official excuses, explanations and disinformation evidencing a massive cover-up. The controversy raged for several months over whether or not air cover was originally planned and later withdrawn from the invasion. Then, in the last months of 1961, Ambassador Whiting Willauer provided disturbing first-hand information in testimony he gave to a U.S. Senate committee.

According to Willauer, a specialist in this type of military operations, on December 10, 1960, he was recalled from his ambassadorial post in Honduras and charged with planning an invasion of Cuba in conjunction with the Joint Chiefs of Staff and the CIA. In his initial plan, air cover, both for low-altitude and high-altitude support, was to be provided by Cuban-flown B-26 bombers and by carrier-based Navy jets.[9]

Willauer's job began before President Kennedy took office in the White House. He held the title of Special Assistant to Secretary of State Christian Herter, a CFR agent. After Kennedy's inauguration, CFR agent Dean Rusk asked Willauer to continue in this capacity. But, within two weeks, he was left out of the loop, his CIA contacts were ordered to avoid him and he was completely ignored in the State Department. For 30 days, his immediate superior, CFR secret agent Chester Bowles, refused to see him. He was never debriefed by a successor for the useful information he could have passed on. After nearly two months in "isolation," Willauer received, on April 16, 1961, the day before the Bay of Pigs invasion, a telephone call dismissing him from the State Department.[10]

Though the story was largely ignored by the CFR-controlled American mainstream press, the disturbing information provided by Willauer about the Bay of Pigs invasion was extremely important. But the invaders Castro had captured didn't need to hear Willauer's explanation. At the trial in Havana, some of the 1,179 captives of the failed operation had arrived at the same conclusion and reportedly said that false intelligence, presumably by the U.S., led them to disaster.[11] Some of them commented that the U.S. had betrayed them. They didn't know however, that it was not the U.S., but CFR agents infiltrated into the U.S. Government who had betrayed them.

Nevertheless, the Bay of Pigs invaders were not the only ones who had been betrayed. At the time of the invasion, a strong anti-Castro urban underground movement already existed in most large Cuban cities. Plans for an uprising, coordinated with the invasion, had already been laid out, but were so mismanaged in their execution as to indicate deliberate sabotage. To be successful, even with air cover, such a small force had to be supported by uprisings all over Cuba.

Moreover, one of he main reasons why the uprisings never occurred was because the leaders of the underground movement were left in the dark about the landing date and did not know whether the Bay of Pigs operation was a real or a diversionary invasion. The CIA's short wave broadcast station (Radio Swan) failed to broadcast the pre-arranged signals to trigger the waiting underground into action. Instead the station broadcasted a series of conflicting and false reports of uprisings in Cuba.[12]

In 1960 CFR agent Richard M. Bissell, Jr., a CIA Deputy Director, was made responsible for the unification of the exiled anti-Castro Cubans under a single leadership movement. The first attempt, created by CIA experts on Cuban affairs and by State Department officials, was the Cuban Democratic Revolutionary Front. Participating in the selection of anti-Castro Cubans in the U.S. who would be called to join it were former U.S. Ambassador to Brazil William D. Pawley, Head of the Caribbean Bureau of the State Department William Wieland, Assistant Secretary of State for Inter-American Affairs Roy Rubbotom and CIA's Chief of Station in Havana, James Noel.[13] All of them openly supported Castro. As expected, most of the anti-Castro Cubans they selected to direct the new organization had been former pro-Castro supporters.

Eventually, just three weeks before the April 17, 1961, invasion, the CIA dissolved the previous organization and created the Cuban Revolutionary Council.[14] Just before the invasion began, the coordinators of the Cuban Revolutionary Council, based in the U.S., and of nearly 100 underground anti-Castro organizations in Cuba, together with the invasion leaders, were rounded up by CIA agents and held incommunicado at a secluded spot in the Opa-Locka military base near Miami. They were not alerted that the invasion had started until it had already failed and were in that way prevented from alerting their contacts in Cuba.[15]

In October 1959, Huber Matos, a Rebel Army major in charge of Camagüey province who opposed Castro's alliance with the Cuban Communists, was accused of treason and condemned to 20 years hard labor. The prosecution of Huber Matos stirred strong opposition among several anti-Communist leaders in Castro's own Rebel Army. Some months after Matos was sentenced, several anti-Communist clandestine groups became active in the cities and in the countryside. By mid 1961 the Escambray Mountains in the central part of Cuba were teeming with anti-Castro guerrilla rebels. For a while the Escambray guerrillas were a virtual focus of anti-Castro resistance, and they were desperately asking for military supplies.

But the CIA apparently had decided some months before the Bay of Pigs invasion that the guerrillas were not useful to advance the secret CFR objectives. At the beginning of the operations the CIA sabotaged the guerrillas by supplying them with 30.06 caliber ammunition, but with M-3's submachine guns that fired .45-caliber ammo.

In other areas the CIA supplied .45-caliber ammunition to accompany Browning Automatic Rifles that shoot 30.06-caliber ammo. Finally, a few months before the invasion, the CIA stopped sending supplies and urged the rebel leaders to stop fighting and wait for the invasion that was about to take place. In this way the CIA paralyzed the ongoing guerrilla campaign and the spontaneous opposition against Castro's regime, bringing about the guerrilla's defeat.[16]

The Bay of Pigs invasion offered to any skeptical counterintelligence officer an incredible collection of mistakes — perhaps too many to be the product of a coincidence.

First of all, the operation was one of the worst-kept secrets in the recent military history of the United States. The CIA plans were exposed in the press more than a month before the actual invasion began. The leak started when Professor Ronald Hilton, editor of Stanford's authoritative *Hispanic American Report*, called attention to the anti-Castro bases in Guatemala. In due course the *New York Times*, *Time* magazine, *UPI* and *AP* were leading the press barrage about the coming invasion.

On April 15, 1961, rebel planes struck Havana and Santiago de Cuba. Some authors have rightly pointed out that the ineffective air strike two days before the invasion had only the effect of alerting Castro about the coming invasion.[17] But this does not seem to be the case. Early in November 1960, six months before the invasion, Castro had carefully inspected the Bay of Pigs area — the very same place where the invasion later took place. Was this a coincidence?[18]

Among the most incredible blunders, the following were paramount: In an effort to avoid identifying the invasion force with the U.S., the CIA armed the 1400 men with weapons requiring 30 different types of ammunition. The invaders made the big mistake of placing most of the ammunition and communication equipment in a single ship, the *Houston*. By another strange coincidence[19] the *Houston* was singled out as a priority target by Castro himself and sunk at the very beginning of the landing, and the vital communication and ammunition cargo in it was lost.

An aerial photograph of the Bay of Pigs taken from a U-2 plane at an altitude of more than 70,000 feet shows clearly visible a coral reef off the beaches. It is known that the photographs were used for intelligence purposes in the invasion operation. It is therefore difficult to explain how the photo analysts didn't detect the dangerous reef and alert the invaders.[20] The invaders discovered the coral reef only after the bottoms of most of their landing crafts had been ripped open by it.

Contrary to the city of Trinidad, where in case of failure the invaders could easily have gained access to the Escambray Mountains to reorganize and begin a guerilla warfare operation, the Bay of Pigs was surrounded by a swamp with no ways of escape —a veritable mousetrap. Moreover, the choice of the Bay of Pigs for the landing was strange, because, unlike Trinidad, the region was known to be a hotbed of pro-Castroism. Author Hugh Thomas manifested his surprise whith his remark, "It would have been hard indeed to have found a region in Cuba in which a rebellion could have been less easily inspired among the local people."[21]

On June 11, 1961, a New York congressman and Chairman of the Republican National Committee charged that the Bay of Pigs invasion had failed because Kennedy rescinded and revoked the Eisenhower plan to have the invaders protected by American air power. Almost two years later, in January 1963, Robert Kennedy denied the accusation in interviews with the *Miami Herald* and *U.S. News and World Report.* According to Robert Kennedy, his brother never withdrew U.S. air cover.[22]

Admiral Arleigh Burke (not a CFR agent), however, believed that the invasion very nearly succeeded and probably would have if the President had not cancelled the second air strike. The invasion might have worked even without air support of any kind, the admiral argued, if the first strike had not been scheduled two days in advance of the landing, eliminating the element of surprise.[23]

More recent information, however, shows the CFR's hands behind every single "mistake" that caused the failure of the Bay of Pigs invasion. Actually, CFR members were the ones who manipulated Kennedy to make the fateful decisions.

CIA Director Allen Dulles (CFR), for one, behind JFK's back strongly opposed the invasion. Dulles began callously calling the whole operation "our disposal problem,"[24] as if sending several thousand men to their deaths was similar to disposing of your kitchen's trash.

Publicly, however, both CIA Director Allen Dulles (CFR) and Deputy Director for Plans Richard Bissell (CFR) were so enthusiastic about the operation that Dulles told President Kennedy he was certain that "our Guatemalan operation would succeed," adding that the prospects for the invasion's plan to succeed were even better than they were for that one.[25]

Kennedy assumed that Dulles and Bissell's optimism about the success of the Cuban invasion was because the operation had "the Agency's full authority behind them." Kennedy ignored, however, that both Dulles and Bissell had never informed the analysts working in CIA's Intelligence Directorate about the upcoming invasion.[26] The reason why the CFR conspirators didn't tell the CIA's intelligence analysts about the invasion was because they knew the analysts would have opposed such a farfetched operation.

Some authors blame President Kennedy for giving the fateful order that changed the invasion's landing point. They don't tell, however, that Kennedy ordered the change following the advice of McGeorge Bundy (CFR), Adlai Stevenson (CFR), and John McCloy (CFR). A few days later, on April 4,1961, CIA's Richard Bissell (CFR), outlined an alternative plan for the invasion, with the Bay of Pigs instead of Trinidad as the landing place. The trap had been set.

It is true that Kennedy ordered the cancellation of the rest of the planned air strikes previous to the invasion. As a result, some of Castro's fighter planes were left untouched. These were the planes that shot down the invaders' planes and sank their ships, thus guaranteeing that the Bay of Pigs invasion failed. But Kennedy cancelled the air strikes only after McGeorge Bundy (CFR), Dean Rusk (CFR), and Adlai Stevenson (CFR), persuaded him to do so.

Bundy even went a step further and the day before the invasion called CIA Deputy Director General Charles P. Cabell and told him "the dawn air strikes the following morning should not be launched until planes can conduct them from a strip within the beachhead."[27] Since the strip was never operative, Bundy's order practically cancelled the air strikes.

Further proof that the CFR conspirators who control the CIA planned the invasion to fail is that they knew it beforehand. In this case, we also have the smoking gun showing that the CIA knew five months before the Bay of Pigs invasion that it was going to fail.

A declassified 300-page document with an internal CIA history shows that on November 15, 1960, five months before the Bay of Pigs invasion, a CIA task force code-named Western Hemisphere Branch Four (WH/4), in charge of plotting to overthrow Fidel Castro, met to prepare a memo for CFR agent and CIA deputy director of Plans, Richard Bissell. The memo would be used to help CFR agent and CIA Director Allen Dulles brief President-elect John F. Kennedy on foreign affairs. Present at the WH/4 meeting were not only Bissell, but also Dean Rusk, who was then Secretary of State; Robert S. McNamara, Secretary of Defense, and McGeorge Bundy, the President's special assistant for national security affairs — all of them CFR agents.[28]

The memo concluded that the invasion was unachievable as a covert paramilitary operation without the direct support of U.S. military forces.[29] The document was found in June 2005, hidden among several declassified documents in a box marked "Miscellaneous" at the National Security Archive

After accepting full responsibility for the Bay of Pigs debacle, Kennedy mentioned an old saying that victory has 100 fathers and defeat is an orphan.[30] Nevertheless, as I have shown above, the defeat and the betrayal of the Cuban and American people at the Bay of Pigs had many fathers, and all of them, without exception, were members of the Council on Foreign Relations.

With the benefit of hindsight, however, it becomes evident that, far from a failure, the Bay of Pigs operation was a total success.

As Professor Peter H. Smith rightly pointed out, it boosted Castro's political stature in Cuba, Latin America, and the developing world. And it helped him drive his revolution toward the Soviet Union; it was in December 1961, not before the Bay of Pigs invasion, that Castro declared his lifelong allegiance to Marxist-Leninism.[31]

The failed U.S. invasion gave Castro a legitimacy he could not have won any other way. No other American act could have helped him more. In addition, the invasion struck a mortal blow to the anti-Castro underground movement in Cuba and, soon after, to the anti-Castro guerrillas in the Escambray mountains. Also, CFR agent Bissell had united all anti-Castro groups in the U.S. into a single organization. The invasion's failure decapitated it with a single blow.

Moreover, since the image of the opposition to Castro had always been an American one, with Cubans in the U.S. appearing to participate in a subordinate capacity, the harsh treatment given to the anti-Castro underground seemed to be justified by the circumstances. All opposition to the regime had been identified in the Cuban people's mind as American-inspired and counter-revolutionary, thus laying right into Castro's hands.

Not surprisingly, boosting Castro's political stature and driving him toward the Soviet Union were exactly the CFR conspirator's goals. Consequently, far from being a failure, the Bay of Pigs PsyOp was a total success. Its main goals: boosting Castro's *bona fides* vis-à-vis the Soviets, and strengthening Castro's iron grip over the Island, were fully accomplished. After their success, the CFR conspirators were now dangling[32] Castro as an appetizing bait for the Soviets to bite — and they foolishly bit it with gusto.

As soon as the Soviets accepted Castro as a full fledged member of the Communist camp, the Cuban leader began an energetic campaign to heat up the Cold War and destroy Kennedy and Khrushchev's efforts to put an end to it.

Seen from this perspective it is easier to understand why CFR members in the Warren Commission made such an effort to avoid discussing any links between Castro and the Kennedy assassination.

The Steel Confrontation

The second obstacle David Rockefeller threw onto Kennedy's path was the steel crisis of 1962. At the time, the implementation of the Rockefellers' New World Order was just in its initial phase and America still had a heavy industry whose basic need was steel.

Just a year after he was sworn in office, President Kennedy, concerned about inflation, began mentioning his intention of having wage increases to match productivity increases. The United Steelworkers Union (USU) had been asking for a raise in salaries and Kennedy, knowing that the steel companies planned to raise steel prices, feared it will cause an inflation that would "quickly drive the price of everything else."[33]

Kennedy also said that it was hard to accept, for him and the American people, a situation in which "a tiny handful of steel executives whose pursuit of private power and profit exceeds their sense of public responsibility."[34] In the meantime, a steelworkers' union bargaining over a contract with the nation's steel companies was stuck because none of the parties agreed to compromise.

So, in order to avoid an inflationary trend that would paralyze the country's economy, Kennedy intervened. Using the power of the presidency, on April 6, 1962, he managed to broker a contract between the United Steelworkers Union and the steel companies. By it, the workers were to accept a modest settlement and the steel companies, in order to keep inflation down, would not raise the steel price.

Kennedy praised the agreement as obviously non-inflationary and said both the USU and the steel firms had shown industrial statesmanship of the highest order. The agreement also implicitly stated that the companies would not raise steel prices, as that would affect the whole U.S. economy and will cause inflation.[35]

Nevertheless, on April 10, Roger Blough, CEO of U.S. Steel, the largest of the steel companies with control over 25 percent of the market, unexpectedly asked to meet with Kennedy. Once at the Oval Office, Blough arrogantly told Kennedy: "Perhaps the easiest way I can explain the purpose of my visit . . .,"[36] and handed Kennedy a press release he already had passed to the CFR-controlled mainstream media. It stated that U.S. Steel was immediately raising "the price of the company's steel products by an average of about 3.5 percent . . ."[37]

Realizing that he and the steelworkers had been betrayed, Kennedy was furious. He coldly looked at Blough in the eye and said: "You've made a terrible mistake."[38]

A few hours later, Bethlehem Steel and other big steel corporations joined U.S. Steel in violating the agreement and raising their prices. Kennedy's reaction was swift. Early next day he called for a press conference in which he strongly criticized "a tiny handful of steel executives whose pursuit of power and profit exceeds their sense of public responsibility" and their "utter contempt" for the U.S.[39]

It seems that David Rockefeller and his CFR minions — Roger Blough was an influential CFR member — grossly underestimated Kennedy's courage. To their utter surprise, Kennedy's response was a swift, well-coordinated counterattack. Very soon after, Blough was going to discover the hard way that he had shot himself in the foot because, directly or indirectly, the U.S. Government was the main consumer of steel.

The first action Kennedy took in response to U.S. Steel's price increase was ordering the Defense Department to review all steel contracts and switch to lower-cost suppliers — not all steel producers had immediately joined the price increase. Within a couple of days, Defense Secretary McNamara placed a steel order for 3 submarines with Lukens Steel, one of the small steel companies that was not party to the price gouge; this contract would normally have been split among suppliers including U.S. Steel.[40]

JFK also instructed Attorney General Robert Kennedy to order the Justice Department to initiate an investigation as to whether the near-simultaneous price increases were the result of monopoly and thus subject to antitrust laws. Given the almost lockstep manner in which steel companies adjusted prices in 1962 and earlier, even a naive observer would have assumed that there was at least *de facto* price-fixing. A few hours later Attorney General Robert Kennedy explicitly included in a public statement the question of whether U.S. Steel "so dominates the industry that it controls prices and should be broken up."[41]

President Kennedy realized that the action was part of a plot, so, he went on the air and told the press and the American people why he thought the steel companies' actions were not in the public interest. He also mentioned his suspicions that the event was part of a well-coordinated conspiracy:

> The simultaneous and identical actions of United States Steel and other leading steel corporations increasing steel prices by some six dollars a ton constitute a wholly unjustified and irresponsible defiance of the public interest. ... The suddenness by which every company in the past few hours, one by one, as the morning went by came in with their almost identical, if not identical, price increases, which isn't the way we expect the competitive private enterprise system to always work. [42]

Also, Kennedy administration officials contacted board members of the other steel companies who had not yet raised prices. While they didn't specifically demand or ask for any pricing policies, they made clear the administration's preferences and the penalties arising from price increases.

As expected, these tactics alarmed some CFR-controlled business commentators. Kennedy's relationship with big business had not been warm from the start, and some saw this as JFK's "true colors" coming out — JFK had been accused of being a "socialist." From then on they would begin accusing Kennedy of something worse. Some of them began calling Kennedy a "pinko" and an outright "Communist."

In the aftermath of the crisis, *U.S. News and World Report* stated, "A planned economy, directed from Washington, is what Mr. Kennedy now has in mind." One steel company executive complained, "This is a sustained attack on the free enterprise system. It may be an all-out war."[43]

Faced with severe loss of business, on April 13, U.S. Steel and its followers began to surrender. The first corporation to yield was Bethlehem Steel, a major defense contractor.[44] Soon after, the rest followed suit.

Finally, realizing that Kennedy's actions had generated overwhelming public support, all six companies that had announced a price hike, including U.S. Steel, caved-in and announced they had rescinded the price raise.

The aftermath of the crisis brought applause for Kennedy's forceful and successful response — even many steel clients privately approved of JFK's actions. But such praise was accompanied by a fair amount of criticism in the CFR-controlled press for the tactics employed. According to a report, the president of one of the steel companies even criticized Kennedy at the subsequent annual meeting stating that Kennedy had assumed "dictatorial powers" to end the crisis.[45]

To the CFR-controlled *Wall Street Journal*, President Kennedy was
nothing but a dictator. "The Government set the price. And it did this by the
pressure of fear — by naked power, by threats, by agents of the security
police."[46] A few days later, *U.S. News and World Report* continued the
anti-Kennedy campaign in an article criticizing Kennedy's "planned
economy" and mentioning that Kennedy was acting like a Soviet Commis-
sar.[47]

But in its May, 1962, issue, *Fortune* magazine, published by CFR member Henry Luce, went a step forward and published an article whose title,
with the benefit of hindsight, may be interpreted as a threatening warning
to Kennedy, "Steel: The Ides of April." The connotation was that a soothsayer had warned Caesar of his coming assassination with the phrase: "Beware the ides of March."

The Missile Crisis That Never Was

One of the unintended consequences of the end of the Cold War was that
liars on both sides (read spies and intelligence officers) joined forces to
misinform us. This is exactly what happened regarding this bizarre event
called the Cuban missile crisis.[48]

According to the disinformers' narrative, the crisis, which began 55
years ago when an American U-2 plane allegedly discovered that the Soviet Union had installed missile bases in Cuba for medium-range strategic
nuclear missiles, is still a hot topic in the history of the Cold War. Documents declassified many years later, and countless new books on the subject, have given us a vision, indeed terrifying, of the dangerous time when,
according to these authors, the world was on the brink of nuclear war. According to them, the missing pieces of the puzzle fit together perfectly well
to give us a coherent picture of what actually happened during the crisis.

Perhaps too well.

Despite strong anti-communist rhetoric in his early speeches, evidence indicates that John F. Kennedy was a pacifist at heart and had decided to end
the Cold War. Surprisingly, he found an ally in Soviet Premier Nikita S.
Khrushchev.

In February 1956, during the 20th Congress of the Communist Party of
the Soviet Union where he denounced Stalin's crimes, Soviet Premier Nikita
Sergeyevich Khrushchev launched his doctrine of Peaceful Coexistence.
According to Khrushchev's new doctrine, the Soviet Union would con-

tinue pursuing its goal of fighting capitalism and implementing communism by competing in the fields of culture, science, commerce and the arts, but not by war, particularly nuclear war.

That same year, during a visit to the U.K. in April, Khrushchev clearly stated his position: "You do not like communism. We do not like capitalism. There is only one way out — peaceful coexistence."[49]

Pursuing this goal, on September 29, 1961, Khrushchev took the initiative of opening a back channel to the American President by secretly sending a long, friendly, confidential personal letter to Kennedy.[50] In an obvious reference to nuclear war, Khrushchev mentioned the need to find solutions to their differences in a peaceful way, even if it was,

Hard to believe that there still exist problems in the world which, due to lack of solutions, cast a sinister shadow on peaceful life, on the future of millions of people."[51]

This private correspondence between the two leaders continued for two years despite the public Cold War rhetoric. The secrecy was needed because neither Khrushchev nor Kennedy wanted to antagonize their respective military-industrial-complexes. It seems that both leaders had independently arrived at the conclusion that, far from solving a problem, a nuclear war would destroy life in most of the planet.

So, Kennedy must have felt surprised and betrayed when he received the news of the presence of strategic Soviet nuclear missiles in Cuba.

Nevertheless, Kennedy was not the only one surprised. On its 1962 September Estimate, the United States Intelligence Board (USIB), at the time not under CFR control, predicted that, though the Soviet Union could derive some military advantage from the establishment of medium and intermediate range ballistic missile bases in Cuba, this possibility was very low because it "would be incompatible with Soviet practice to date and with Soviet policy as we presently estimate it."[52]

Since then, there has been considerable debate over alleged American "intelligence failures" in the Cuban missile crisis.[53] The National Intelligence Estimate of September 19, 1962, became a *cause célèbre* because it continued to express the conviction that the Soviets would not place strategic nuclear missiles in Cuba. Several analysts have tried to prove, sometimes using the wrong arguments, that the American intelligence community, though obviously acting a little sluggish at the beginning of the crisis, nevertheless discovered the missiles just in time. Others, mainly the critics of the Kennedy administration, have tried to prove exactly the contrary, but the problem is still subject to debate.

At about 9 p.m. on October 15, 1962, CIA's Deputy Director for Intelligence Ray Cline (CFR), called McGeorge Bundy (CFR), President Kennedy's special assistant for national security affairs, to inform him that a U-2 plane flying over Cuba the previous day had photographed installations that looked like Soviet strategic missile bases on Cuban soil.

Surprisingly, Bundy didn't tell Kennedy immediately about the findings, but waited until next day to tell the President. Bundy's strange behavior was later questioned, and he explained it by saying that the President had just returned from a strenuous campaign trip, so he decided let him get the rest he would need.[54]

A few minutes before nine o'clock on the morning of October 16, McGeorge Bundy took some U-2 photographs the CIA had sent him, which allegedly depicted medium-range ballistic missiles on Cuban soil, to President Kennedy who was still in his bedroom.[55] Just a few hours after President Kennedy had been informed of the U-2 photos, the Ex Comm[56] met for the first time. Arthur Lundahl, head of the National Photographic Interpretation Center, had been invited to the meeting. Robert Kennedy's recollection of the moment is so descriptive that it is worth reproducing it in detail:

> At 11:45 that same morning, in the Cabinet Room, a formal presentation was made by the Central Intelligence Agency to a number of high officials of the government. Photographs were shown to us. Experts arrived with their charts and their pointers and told us that if we looked carefully, we could see there was a missile base being constructed in a field near San Cristóbal, Cuba. I, for one, had to take their word for it. I examined the pictures carefully, and what I saw appeared to be no more than a clearing of a field for a farm or the basement of a house. I was relieved to hear later that this was the same reaction of virtually everyone at the meeting, including President Kennedy. Even a few days later, when more work had taken place on the site, he remarked that it looked like a football field.[57]

So confused was the President with the "evidence" presented by Lundahl, that he asked him point blank: "Are you sure these are Soviet MRBMs?" [Medium Range Ballistic Missiles] Lundahl's cryptic answer was "as sure of this as a photointerpreter can be sure of anything." Unfortunately, none of those present had the knowledge, or the guts, to translate Lundahl's answer to the President. In plain English it meant, "I haven't the slightest idea!"

It seems, however, that, like lemmings, some crisis scholars stopped thinking and have just followed the disinformation provided by their CFR leaders. See, i.e., Ernest R. May and Philip D. Zelikow, *The Kennedy Tapes: Inside the White House During The Cuban Missile Crisis.*[58] In the very first line of the Introduction, the authors, both of them CFR members, affirm, "On the morning when he first saw photographs of Soviet missiles in Cuba . . ." Well, either the authors have privileged information they have not shared with the readers, or they simply still don't get it. Not only did President Kennedy not see any missiles in the photos, but also nobody saw any missiles in them for the simple reason that no photograph taken by the U.S. at the time showed even the image of a single strategic missile in Cuba. This is an undisputable fact that anybody can easily verify just by taking a look at the U-2 photos and the photos taken by low-flying reconnaissance planes, most of then now available in high resolution on the Internet.[59]

Such photos only show long objects covered with tarps, which the CIA believed were Soviet strategic missiles, and a few concrete bunkers that, according to the CIA, contained the nuclear warheads. But the vaunted nuclear missiles do not appear anywhere. Why, then, do most books and articles about the crisis continue to maintain the theory that the U-2 pictures provided incontrovertible proof that there were nuclear missiles on Cuban soil in 1962?

These authors' claims are such a gross distortion of the facts that it raises doubts about their professional competence.

In the same fashion, in his Prologue to Central Intelligence Agency, *The Secret Missile Crisis Documents,*[60] in a section entitled "The Facts," CFR member Graham T. Allison, Jr., asserts that on 14 October, 1962,

> A U.S. high altitude U-2 overflight of Cuba took photographs that provided clear evidence of an ambitious Soviet deployment of 48 medium-range ballistic missiles (MRBMs, range 1,100 nautical miles) and 24 intermediate-range ballistic missiles (IRBMs, range 2,2000 nautical miles) at four separate sites in Cuba."[61]

Allison's statement is remarkable, because a careful reading of the documents offered in the very same book he wrote the prologue for provide no evidence whatsoever to substantiate his affirmation. The references found in some of the documents offered to the reader are to "eight canvas-covered, missile-type trailers;"[62] "six canvas covered trailers of 80 feet in overall length which are of the general size and configuration of those used to transport the Soviet SS-3 (700 n.m. ballistic missile) and SS-4 (1,100 n.m. ballistic missile);" [63] "14 canvas-covered missile trailers" and "8 canvas covered missile trailers."[64]

Only on page 255 do the authors make a direct reference to actual missiles in an area near San Cristóbal, in western Cuba, "We have identified six of the launchers and seven of the sixteen missiles," but, just a few lines below it is explained that the identification is not based on direct visual confirmation but that "The keys to these identifications are the size of the missile body."[65]

Further proof of this disinformation effort is that, a few pages after, a description of the San Cristóbal site reports "seven canvas covered missiles,"[66] as well as "six canvas-covered missiles" in the San Cristóbal area. On page 176, one of the document states that "Detailed photointerpretation shows that the missiles are canvas-covered, have a blunt nose, and are 66 feet, plus or minus two feet in length" According to my view, however, the only thing this statement shows is that the CIA photointerpreters at the NPIC were either very gullible or a bunch of liars.

In the same fashion, under the title "The Real Thirteen Days: Reconnaissance Photo," The National Security Archive[67] has posted some of the U-2 photos taken during the crisis.[68] I challenge my readers to visit the site and try to find in any of the photos, particularly in the ones taken between October 14, 1962 and January 27, 1963, any object even slightly resembling a Soviet strategic missile or a nuclear warhead.

Following the same trend, in his book *Eyeball to Eyeball*, retired CIA photointerpreter Dino Brugioni wrote, "Statements by responsible U.S. officials, and articles written subsequent to the crisis, maintaining that nuclear weapons were never seen in Cuba simply weren't true."[69] After reading Brugioni's chapter twice, however, I could only find the following type of references:

> There was no evidence of a nuclear warhead storage facility, but it was *assumed* that there were nuclear warheads in Cuba, *probably* near the missile sites;"[70] "A number of nuclear warhead storage bunkers were found under construction near other missile sites in Cuba;"[71] "It was therefore *believed* that there *would be* a commu-

nication center near any nuclear weapons storage area;"[72] "It was generally *agreed* that nuclear warheads for the SS-4 missiles *would be* guarded... ;"[73] "The warheads *would be* mated to the missiles only when ... ;"[74] "Since it was *assumed* that the warheads were under control of the KGB, it also was *assumed* that the warheads *would be* stored in a ... ;"[75] "There was no doubt, however, that if the Soviet missile units in Cuba moved into an operational posture, the warhead and support elements *would be* observed at the launch pads on aerial photography;"[76] "The Soviets attempted to conceal the *nose cone containers...* ;"[77] "One of the vans had its rails extended and *appeared* to be transferring a warhead to a truck... ;"[78] "It has to be *presumed* that the warheads were also mated to the missile."[79] [Emphasis added].

It seems that the CIA phointerpreters ignored the military's wise saying: "Assumption is the mother of all fuck-ups." Most likely we are missing something here. But, even disregarding the fact that a photo of a nuclear warhead is *not* a nuclear warhead,[80] after reading Brugioni's arguments supporting his unsubstantiated, far-fetched assertion that responsible U.S. officials and people who wrote that nuclear weapons were never seen in Cuba were wrong, as well as his claims that there were nuclear warheads in Cuba in 1962, I can only say that I am an unbeliever who maintains that nuclear weapons were never seen in Cuba for the simple reason that there weren't any. Actually, the NPIC folks were never able to provide us with a single candid snapshot of a nuclear warhead on Cuban soil.

Even more farfetched is the claim, advanced by "experts" in several meetings that took place several years after the crisis, that not only were dozens of nuclear warheads in Cuba, but also that Soviet officers in the field had been allowed discretionary power to fire the missiles. This defies any logic because it goes contrary to known Soviet military doctrine and practices before *and* after the Cuban missile crisis. (See Appendix II, The Evaluation of Information.)

Perhaps the CIA has the photos, but is till keeping them secret all these years to avoid the Soviets from discovering that they had nuclear warheads in Cuba. Or probably CIA psychics trained at the Stanford Research Institute found the nuclear warheads using remote viewing, which, if confirmed, would be by far the greatest unpublished story of the Cuban missile crisis.

Sorry for being facetious, but I can't take seriously the CFR disinformers' claims that the presence in 1962 of Soviet intermediate range missiles and their nuclear warheads on Cuban soil was proved beyond a doubt.

Nevertheless, after the CFR agents inside the CIA convinced Kennedy that Soviet Premier Khrushchev had taken the fateful step of deploying inter- mediate ballistic missiles with nuclear capability on Cuban soil, he was forced to act to not look "soft on communism." To this effect, he assembled a group of experts to discuss the measures he must take. He called this group the Executive Committee of the National Security Council, later know as ExComm. Unfortunately, however, most members of the ExComm — Dean Rusk, Robert McNamara, Douglas Dillon, John McCone and Gen. Maxwell Taylor — were trusted CFR agents. Since that moment, most of Kennedy's efforts to solve the crisis were devoted to contain the trigger- happy members of his own military.[81]

The situation became so dangerous that Kennedy used his brother to convey a message to Khrushchev using unofficial channels. In it, Robert mentioned that the President was appealing directly to Khrushchev to end the conflict as soon as possible, adding: "If the situation continues much longer, the President is not sure that the military will not overthrow him and seize power."[82]

Finally, on Friday night, October 26, Kennedy received through his back channel a letter from a terrorized Khrushchev in which the Soviet Premier agreed to withdraw the missiles just in exchange for Kennedy's pledge not to do what he never intended: invade Cuba. What Kennedy ignored, and died without knowing, was that what had terrorized Khrushchev was a letter he had received from his "friend" Fidel Castro.

Late in the night of October 26, Castro visited the Soviet Embassy in Ha- vana and stayed through the early hours of the next day writing a letter to Khrushchev. The most important part of the letter is Castro's efforts to convince Khrushchev that an American invasion of Cuba was imminent, and his request that, to avoid this, the Soviet Union should launch a pre- emptive nuclear attack against the United States. Castro's words were,

> I tell you this because I believe that the imperialists' aggressive- ness is extremely dangerous and if they actually carry out the bru- tal act of invading Cuba in violation of international law and mo- rality, that would be the moment to eliminate such danger through an act of clear legitimate defense, however harsh and terrible the solution would be, for there is no other.[83]

In a letter on October 30, in which he answered Castro's plea, a terror- ized Khrushchev refers to Castro's request in very precise terms:

In your cable of October 27 you proposed that we be the first to launch a nuclear strike against the territory of the enemy. You, of course, realize where that should have led. Rather than a simple strike, it would have been the start of a thermonuclear war.

Dear Comrade Fidel Castro, I consider this proposal of yours incorrect, although I understand your motivation.[84]

Actually, however, Nikita Khrushchev never fully understood Castro's motivation. Contrary to what Khrushchev thought, had he understood it, he would had shivered in terror.

But asking Khrushchev to launch a nuclear salvo upon the U.S. was not the only way Dr. Strangelove Castro tried to push the world into a nuclear holocaust. Following Castro's orders, and disregarding Soviet advice, on the morning of October 27, antiaircraft batteries manned by the Cuban Army began firing at American low-flying reconnaissance planes, damaging at least one. As Castro himself later told his biographer Tad Szulc,

I am absolutely certain that if the low-level flights had been resumed we would have shot down one, two, or three of these planes . . . With so many batteries firing, we would have shot down some planes. I don't know whether this would have started nuclear war.[85]

Still, although Cuban crews were operating anti-aircraft guns, the powerful surface-to-air missiles (SAMs) were under the Soviets' tight control and the Cubans had no access to the bases and did not know how to operate them. Therefore, though the short-range antiaircraft guns were firing at everything flying over them, the U-2s, flying at an altitude far beyond their fire range, were safe from Castro's antiaircraft batteries.

But then, in the morning of October 27, at the peak of the crisis, a bizarre incident occurred. An American U-2, piloted by Major Rudolph Anderson, Jr., was detected over the eastern part of Cuba and a SAM site at Los Angeles, near Banes, in the Oriente province, fired one or several anti-aircraft missiles and shot it down.

According to Seymour Hersh, there is strong evidence that, on October 26, 1962, a Cuban army unit attacked and overran a Soviet-manned SAM base at Los Angeles, in the Oriente province, killing many Soviets and seizing control of the site. Hersh based his article on information partly drawn from an interview with former Department of Defense analyst Daniel

Ellsberg, who was citing classified material from a post-crisis study of the event. The speculation was based on an intercepted transmission from the Soviet base at Los Angeles indicating heavy fighting and casualties. Adrián Montoro, former director of Radio Havana Cuba, and Juan Antonio Rodríguez Menier, a senior Cuban intelligence officer who defected in 1987 and was living in the U.S., seem to confirm Ellsberg's information.[86]

Though both Castro and the Soviets categorically denied that the attack took place, Raymond L. Garthoff, Special Assistant for Soviet bloc Political/Military Affairs in the State Department during the Kennedy administration, claims that, in fact, beginning on October 28, the Cuban army *did* surround the Soviet missile bases for three days.[87]

Actually, the possibility that the Soviet SAM base had been overrun and occupied by Cuban Army units was widely circulated. An article appeared in the *Los Angeles Times* mentioned that, "It now appears from U.S. intelligence decryption that Soviet troops there transmitted a report from Cuba that a 'fire-fight' had occurred in the vicinity of a Soviet SAM site and that some Soviet soldiers had been killed."[88]

The bizarre fact seems to agree with Castro's behavior. According to Che Guevara, when Castro heard the news that Khrushchev had reached an agreement with President Kennedy to remove the missiles from Cuba, Fidel was so furious that "he swore, kicked the wall and broke a mirror in his fury."[89]

In Havana, pro-Soviet posters were torn off in rage from walls. Both militiamen and "spontaneous" conga[90] dancers marched through Havana's streets intoning: *"Nikita mariquita; lo que se da no se quita"* ("Nikita, you little sissy; what one gives, doesn't take back"), berating Khrushchev and the Soviets for leaving Castro in the lurch.

The CIA subsequently admitted that it had no agents in the field that might have physically verified the existence of the Soviet strategic nuclear missiles on Cuban soil in 1962. When the Soviets were shipping back to the Soviet Union what they claimed were strategic nuclear missiles, Kennedy had an excellent opportunity to order the Navy to board the ships and physically verify the withdrawal of the missiles, but he did not. Why did Kennedy decide not to verify the existence of the missiles and their actual withdrawal from Cuba? Nobody has provided a satisfactory answer to this question.

I am aware of later claims that nuclear warheads were actually in the island, and that more were bound for Cuba in Soviet ships. But CIA reports at the time consistently denied the presence of nuclear warheads in Cuba. A

CIA report on October 23, 1962, offering an estimate of the operational readiness of the missile in Cuba stated in very clear terms: "We are unable to confirm the presence of nuclear warheads."[91] Indeed, American planes, flying low over the missile sites and the Soviets ships, apparently never detected any of the radiation that could be expected from nuclear warheads. Nor any of the American warships sailing close to Soviet ships and submarines reported any radiation. As a matter of fact, almost no mention to gamma radiation emanating from the nuclear warheads supposedly in Cuba has been made in the hundreds of thousands of pages that have been written about the crisis.

This is remarkable, because the technology to detect radiation already existed at the time. In the 1960s the NEDS 900 series of radiation detectors had been developed and deployed in the Dardanelles as a way to monitor the presence of nuclear weapons aboard Soviet warships and submarines transiting the strait from the Black Sea.

Far from being so close to the brink, as a group of professional liars and disinformers linked to the CFR have been trying to make us believe, the Cuban missile crisis was a totally manufactured pseudo-event; a monumental hoax whose main goal was to terrorize the American public and justify the Cold War. It is not by chance that the people who made billions with the Cold War — which was mostly a propaganda product — are the same ones who control the non-profit foundations that have bankrolled most of the research whose main goal is to prove "how close to the brink" we were during the Cuban missile crisis.

The reason for this is very simple: to the CFR conspirators at the military-industrial-banking-complex our current fears translate into their profit. Their credibility would be questioned if one day the American people discover that the previous fears were totally groundless.

Kennedy's Efforts to End the Cold War

After having experienced the possibility of a devastating nuclear war that would have destroyed most of the life in the planet and having found a peaceful solution to an apparently unsurmountable problem, both President Kennedy and Premier Khrushchev continued their fight against all odds to put an end to the Cold War. But this was something the Rockefellers and their CFR co-conspirators were not going to allow them to do.

In his commencement address at American University in Washington, D.C., in June 10, 1963, President Kennedy told the students that he was there,

> To discuss a topic on which ignorance too often abounds and the
> truth is too rarely perceived — yet it is the most important topic on
> earth: world peace.
>
> What kind of peace do I mean? What kind of peace do we
> seek? Not a *Pax Americana* enforced on the world by American
> weapons of war. Not the peace of the grave or the security of the
> slave. I am talking about genuine peace, the kind of peace that
> makes life on Earth worth living, the kind that enables men and
> nations to grow and to hope and to build a better life for their chil-
> dren — not merely peace for Americans but peace for all men and
> women — not merely peace in our time but peace for all time.
>
> I speak of peace because of the new face of war. Total war
> makes no sense in an age when great powers can maintain large
> and relatively invulnerable nuclear forces and refuse to surrender
> without resort to those forces. It makes no sense in an age when a
> single nuclear weapon contains almost ten times the explosive force
> delivered by all of the Allied air forces in the Second World War. It
> makes no sense in an age when the deadly poisons produced by a
> nuclear exchange would be carried by wind and water and soil and
> seed to the far corners of the globe and to generations yet unborn.[92]

Kennedy ended his speech with a direct attack on the U.S. military-industrial-banking complex:

> Today the expenditure of billions of dollars every year on weapons
> acquired for the purpose of making sure we never need to use them
> is essential to keeping the peace. But surely the acquisition of such
> idle stockpiles — which can only destroy and never create — is
> not the only, much less the most efficient, means of assuring peace.
>
> I speak of peace, therefore, as the necessary rational end of
> rational men. I realize that the pursuit of peace is not as dramatic as
> the pursuit of war — and frequently the words of the pursuer fall
> on deaf ears. But we have no more urgent task.[93]

Maintaining his efforts for a peaceful solution of the Cold War, in September 20, 1963, in a speech at the United Nations, President Kennedy proposed:

A new approach to the Cold War — a desire not to "bury" one's adversary, but to compete in a host of peaceful arenas, in ideas, in production, and ultimately in service to all mankind.

The contest will continue — the contest between those who see a monolithic world and those who believe in diversity—but it should be a contest in leadership and responsibility instead of destruction, a contest in achievement instead of intimidation. Speaking for the United States of America, I welcome such a contest. For we believe that truth is stronger than error — and that freedom is more enduring than coercion. And in the contest for a better life, all the world can be a winner.[94]

Kennedy also informed the American people that the Soviets had expressed a desire to negotiate a nuclear test ban treaty and that the U.S had postponed some planned atmospheric nuclear tests.[95] An interesting detail is that President Kennedy's efforts to end the Cold War closely resembled Soviet Premier Nikita Khrushchev's Doctrine of Peaceful Coexistence.[96]

On October 11, 1963, President Kennedy, contrary to the opinion of his advisors, which include the CFR-controlled Joint Chiefs of Staff and some high-level people in his own administration — among them Dean Rusk, Robert McNamara, and McGeorge and William Bundy, all of them CFR members — ordered to immediately implement plans to withdraw 1,000 U.S. military personnel by the end of the year.[97] This was believed to be the first step to a complete withdrawal of American troops from Vietnam. Many years later, in a 2003 documentary entitled *The Fog of War*, McNamara confirmed that "Kennedy announced we were going to pull out all of our military advisors by the end of '65 and we were going to take 1000 out by the end of '63."[98]

Ultimate proof of Kennedy's intentions is a memo concerning a conference attended by the Secretary of Defense held at the CINCPAC headquarters in Camp Smith, Hawaii. In Part IV, Withdrawal of US Forces, the memo states, "As a matter of urgency, a plan for the withdrawal of about 1,000 US troops before the end of the year should be developed …" Part V of the memo deals with the "Phase-out of US forces."[99]

Unfortunately, JFK underestimated the guile and evil nature of his powerful enemies and paid with his live for his ignorance.

On November 22, 1963, President Kennedy was assassinated. On July 31, 1964, David Rockefeller visited the Soviet Union and had a long meeting with Soviet Premier Nikita Khrushchev. Just two months and a half later, on October 14, Khrushchev was unceremoniously deposed.

Kennedy and Khrushchev, the two main obstacles to the Cold War, had been eliminated. Peaceful coexistence was over. David Rockefeller's Cold War, with full support of his secret agent Fidel Castro, was again going full steam ahead.

Following his assigned role as an agent provocateur, Castro increased his aggressive destabilizing policies, training and providing support to guerrillas in Africa and Latin America, and, during the 1970s, outright invasion of countries such as Angola, Ethiopia and Mozambique. Also, Cuba became a haven and training ground for terrorist groups such as the Basque ETA, Argentine Montoneros, American Black Panthers, Italian Red Brigades, German Baader-Meinhof and others. All of these under the happy, approving eyes of the Rockefellers and their friends in the American military-industrial-banking complex.

Chapter 5

David's Agents Control the JFK Assassination Cover-up

> *Who controls the past controls the future.*
> *Who controls the present controls the past.*
> — O'Brien in George Orwell's *1984*.

American conservatives have consistently accused CFR members of being Communists.[1] Actually, the CFR globalist conspirators who control the Invisible Government of the United States are not guided by or attached to any particular political ideology. They are mostly pragmatists guided more by practical considerations than by ideas. Nevertheless, given their aim for total control, they unavoidably became aligned with totalitarian ideologies such as fascism and communism. This explains why, more than a democracy,[2] the Invisible Government of the United States resembles a Communist or Fascist dictatorship in power and functions as such.

Not everybody in Nazi Germany was a member of the Nazi Party, nor everybody in the Soviet Union was a member of the Communist Party. The parties, however, had full control over the government and party members had been strategically situated in economic areas where they needed specialists who were nonparty members.

Not all industrial or businesses leaders in Nazi Germany or Soviet Russia were Party members, but they were reluctantly accepted because the Party needed their expertise. But Party members inside their businesses and industries oversaw them, carefully monitored their jobs, and shadowed the non-Party member leaders. In the case of the armed forces, where not all officers were Party members, they created a similar parallel structure: the overseers in the military were called political commissars.

The CFR: a Communo-Fascist Government in Power

Communist countries maintained the fiction that there was a government elected by the people apart from the Communist Party. In order to maintain this fiction, every few years there were elections where people voted for the candidates of the only approved Party. They knew, however, that the candidates they elected had no power at all and things would continue exactly as before.

This is not too different from what has been going on in the U.S since the beginning of the past century. The only difference is that, to make things a little more credible, here in America the CFR, the visible head of the communo-fascist Invisible Government of the U.S. has allowed for the existence of two political parties apparently different, though in practice they are the two sides of the same coin. I call it the Repucratic Party.

Like in a Communist or Fascist party, CFR meetings are secret, and members are supposed to keep them secret. Divulging what has been discussed in a CFR meeting is cause for losing membership.

Like in a Communist party, in their secret meetings at the Harold Pratt House in Manhattan, CFR members are free to some extent to discuss and express their viewpoints, even viewpoints that are contrary to the CFR's policy. This is a process Vladimir Lenin called "democratic centralism." But once the policies are established — which are always the ones already decided at the CFR's nucleus meetings and brought to the outer rings meetings by senior members[3] — other members are supposed to accept and support them fully, without mental reservations. Dissidence is not permitted, and members who dare to deviate from the party line are ignored, discredited, harassed or physically eliminated.

Like in a Communist country, the CFR party nuclei inside the U. S. Government see that the foreign and domestic policies follow the lines already traced at the CFR. The CFR party nuclei inside the mainstream press guarantee that the information the American people get is the disinformation conceived at the CFR. To reinforce the charade, CFR members, infiltrated into both the Republican and the Democratic parties, oppose each other at election time and, once elected, in minor, non-important things. This guarantees that the same leaders always remain in control and keep the sheeple controlled, regardless of which political party is in "power."

The ultimate goal of those who control the Invisible Government of the U.S. is socialism, either in its Communist or Fascist varieties, or a mixture of both. This means total socialistic control of all resources, communications, commerce, wealth, and people, by a small, powerful group of bankers, oil magnates and CEOs of transnational corporations. That is what the so-called New World Order is about: a socialist, one-world government controlled by all-powerful masters, with full control over a semi-slave population of serfs living in the most abject economic and moral misery with no constitutional guarantees or personal freedoms.

The Council on Foreign Relations has been operating in a similar way since its creation. The Harold Pratt House is actually the center of the U.S. Communo-Fascist Party in power. That's where all the important political decisions are planned. Once the decisions are taken, secret CFR agents in the mainstream press and every branch of the U.S. government pass down the "orientations" (a euphemism for orders and directives from above) already taken at the CFR secret meetings.

This process was evidenced itself in stark clarity in the coordinated cover-up that followed President Kennedy's assassination.

With the benefit of hindsight, it becomes obvious that the operation did not go as planned. Oswald — a patsy and most likely a Manchurian Candidate[4] — was supposed to be killed just a few minutes after the assassination. It seems, however, that the brainwashing, conditioning process failed to some extent, Oswald realized that something wrong was going on, tried to escape and was captured alive.

After his capture, and during 48 hours of hostile interrogation during which he was denied the rights of legal counsel — photos show him with a black eye and a cut on his forehead — Oswald categorically denied he was the assassin.[5] He even said that he was just a patsy.

Moreover, the conspirators never thought about the possibility that Mr. Zapruder would have been there filming the whole show. The now famous Zapruder film clearly shows Kennedy's head moving forward as the result of the first shot from the back and, a few seconds later, moving violently backward when a bullet shot coming from the front hit him in the head.[6] Moreover, the trajectory of the bullets was almost horizontal, an impossibility if the shooter had fired from a 6th floor window. The Zapruder film forced the Warren Commission's disinformers to concoct the farfetched single-bullet theory.

So, faced with the unexpected, the first thing the CFR conspirators had to do was to silence Oswald. The makeshift job was carried out by Jack

Ruby, who eventually was silenced — dead men don't tell tales.

The CFR Launches a Cover-up Campaign

Just a few hours after Kennedy was assassinated, the very same CFR-controlled mainstream press that had been fiercely attacking President Kennedy launched a well-coordinated disinformation campaign. The main goal of the campaign was to prove that Oswald acted alone and that there was no conspiracy. To this effect, the mainstream media began disseminating their disinformation. It consisted in planting subtle hints indicating that a single assassin had carried out the assassination — what later became known as the "lone gunman" theory sanctioned by the CFR-controlled Warren Commission.

The day after the assassination, big headlines in the November 23, 1963, edition of *The New York Times* (CFR corporate member) mentioned "a rifle shot," "the killer," "killed by sniper," "an assassin," in a subtle effort to brainwash readers into believing that a single person had assassinated the President. Also, in a second-page story entitled "Why America Weeps," CFR agent James Reston, after supporting the theory of the lone gunman, advanced a convenient explanation about the assassin's motive. According to Reston, "the assassin" was the product of "some strain of madness and violence" growing in the U.S. In other words, Oswald was a crazy white supremacist and he acted alone.[7]

That same day the *New York Herald Tribune* published a story following the same lines entitled "Shame of a Nation: History of Assassinations," stating:

> Historically, assassinations has been a weapon in the struggle for political power in countries around the world, but attempts on American Presidents have not followed this pattern.
>
> In a book about Presidential assassinations, *The Assassins*, Robert J. Donovan, former bureau chief of the *New York Herald Tribune* and now of *Los Angeles Times*, points out: "They involved neither organized attempts to shift political power from one group to another, nor to perpetuate a particular man or party in office, not to alter the policy of the government, not to resolve ideological conflicts. With one exception, no terroristic or secret society planned these assaults on our Presidents or was in any way involved."[8]

To guarantee that everybody got brainwashed, the *Tribune* hit the nail again with an Editorial entitled "A Day of Grief and Shame." Commenting on the Kennedy assassination, the editorialist wrote:

> Americans take consolation from the fact that the assassins of their Presidents have, in nearly every case, been crazed individuals, representing nothing but their own wild imaginings.
>
> The heat of normal politics has its reflex on the lunatic fringe. And the "hate sheets," the rumor mongering, the unbalanced charges of the lunatic fringe affects the real lunatics, the killers.

That very same day, Dallas' Mayor Erle Cabell reached the same conclusion, declaring that the assassination was "the irrational act of a single man" and that it "could only be the act of a deranged mind."[9]

Two days later, on November 25, 1963, Deputy Attorney General Nicholas Katzenbach (CFR) wrote a memo to Bill Moyers (CFR) telling him the importance that,

> The public must be satisfied that Oswald was the assassin; that he did not have confederates who are still at large; and that the evidence was such that he would have been convicted at trial.[10]

That same day, the *Wall Street Journal*, (CFR corporate member) one of the most acerbic critics of Kennedy's' policies, supported the lone assassin theory and added its own conclusion that not only the assassin, but the assassin's assassin as well, were deranged individuals, not the tools of a conspiracy. According to the editorialist, Kennedy's sense of history,

> Would have told him that all such murders were the work of individual hysteria, just as the murder of the assassin, not the working of the historical process. We have had assassinations before, but they are not, as in many countries, the normal means of politics.[11]

That very same day also the *NYT* continued the carefully-planned brainwashing operation by publishing a story written by reporter Foster Hailey that parroted exactly the same theory: "Lone Assassin the Rule in U.S.; Plotting More Prevalent Abroad." According to Hailey, though assassination of leaders is a common event in the rest of the world, there is big difference:

> In the United States, in all except two cases, the attempts were made by a single person, often with little advanced planning, and

often without any real grievance against the personage attacked. That seems to have been the case with Lee H. Oswald, the killer of President Kennedy, who was himself slain yesterday.

A week later, *Time* magazine,[12] *U.S. News and World Report*[13] and *Newsweek*,[14] all of them CFR corporate members, joined the crazy guy, lone assassin cacophony. According to the CFR-controlled mainstream press, Oswald was a deranged individual and he acted alone. No conspiracy existed because conspiracies have never existed in America.

Really? Is this a proof of America's exceptionalism?

Actually, the United States is probably the country where more assassinations attempts on top leaders have been carried out. Before the Kennedy assassination, presidents Jackson, Lincoln, Garfield, McKinley, T. Roosevelt and F. D. Roosevelt were victims of assassination attempts. After the Kennedy assassination, there were assassination attempts on Presidents Nixon, Ford (twice), Carter and Reagan. Nevertheless, according to this author, and conveniently parroted by the author of the *Herald Tribune* editorial, none of these were the result of conspiracies.[15]

The lone, deranged gunman explanation was so convenient that it was used later to explain the assassinations of Robert Kennedy and Martin Luther King. After that, together with suicide and airplane accidents, it has been used over and over to explain the assassination of any person the CFR conspirators perceived as a threat and they decided to get rid off.

There is, however, more than meets the eye in the Kennedy assassination. Some little-known facts indicate that the cover-up had already been launched before the assassination.

Col. L. Fletcher Prouty, at the time a liaison officer between the Pentagon and the CIA, has mentioned that the day of the assassination he was in Christchurch, New Zealand, and read the news about the assassination in *The Christchurch Star*. The newspaper, apparently following an *AP* cable, reported that Kennedy had been assassinated and reported Oswald as prime suspect in the assassination.

The problem is that Kennedy was assassinated at 12:30 p.m. on November 22, 1963, and *The Christchurch Star* appeared in the street in the afternoon of November 23, New Zealand time, but still the 22nd in Dallas. According to Prouty, the information appeared to be already available before the assassination.[16]

Professor Gibson managed to read the newspaper and corroborated that the information appeared on page one of the *Christchurch Star* and it included an extraordinary amount of information about Oswald. Even more important, the newspaper reported that Oswald was the "prime suspect in the assassination of the President." The newspaper mentioned the *Associated Press*, *Reuters* and the British *United Press* as its sources.[17]

A curious detail is that the Kennedy assassination operation apparently followed the same *modus operandi* carried out by the CIA in 1948 in Bogotá, Colombia, to assassinate Colombian nationalist leader Jorge Eliécer Gaitán.[18] Not only was Gaitán allegedly assassinated by Juan Roa Sierra, a deranged, solitary drifter — most likely a Manchurian Candidate and a patsy — who was captured and conveniently killed by the mob, but also the information about the assassination appeared in some newspapers even before it had occurred.[19]

A few hours before the assassination of Gaitán took place, the newspaper *El Popular*, of Barquisimeto, Venezuela, printed on its edition of April 9, 1948 (logically prepared the night before it was printed) the news of the assassination and released it to the public.

The amazing fact was noticed and mentioned by other publications. A few days later, in April 14, another Venezuelan publication, *El Gráfico de Caracas*, reproduced a photocopy of the *El Popular*'s issue with the information. On April 29, a Colombian newspaper, *El Siglo* of Bogotá, also reproduced *El Popular*'s information.[20]

Now, if one discards the possibility of extra-sensory perception, the only thing that may explain the publication of the news about the assassination of Gaitán and Kennedy *before* they happened, is that in both cases the CIA's Mighty Wurlitzer[21] had made a mistake.

CFR Agents Control the Post-Cover-Up

On September 27, 1964, close to a year after JFK was assassinated, the United States Government Printing Office released to the public the report of *The President's Commission on the Assassination of John F. Kennedy*, better knows as *The Warren Report* because Chief Justice Earl Warren chaired it.

In an Introductory Note to a book edition of *The Warren Report* published by the Associated Press, Saul Pett, after admitting that "There was now in the minds of many, the suspicion that there must be more to the Dallas story," puts forward a series of questions:

> The questions tumbled forward. Was John Kennedy actually murdered by Lee Harvey Oswald and, if so, had Oswald acted alone?

Had Jack Ruby known Oswald? Were they somehow knowing or unknowing parts of the same conspiracy, one to kill the President and the other to kill and silence the killer? Were we to believe in an amazing coincidence of derangement: that a sullen little man, for his own twisted reasons, could kill a President and then, while in police custody, himself be killed by another little man with his twisted reasons? Did one unbalanced mind rob us of a President and another, of his murderer? And if we say that and we see that, are we then close to sensing that *the sick of the world*, though unknown to each other, may form as dangerous a conspiracy as any political plot from the left of from the right? . . . But this last question goes beyond the Commission's immediate purpose. It was the other questions which the Warren Commission was called upon to answer." [22] [emphasis added]

Of course, Pett, an employee of CFR's corporate member *Associated Press*, is maliciously disingenuous. Actually, the true and only purpose of the Warren Commission was not to discover the truth but to hide the obvious fact that the JFK assassination was the result of a conspiracy. This was somehow admitted by the Commission's members who, in the Foreword to the Report, clearly stated:

> After Oswald's arrest and his denial of all guilt, public attention focused both on the extent of the evidence against him and the possibility of a conspiracy, domestic or foreign, His subsequent death heightened public interest and stimulated suspicions and rumors. [23]

Though Justice Warren was the Commission's Chair, apparently he realized that everything was a hoax and allowed CFR members Allen Dulles and John McCloy to fully control it. This is evidenced in the Foreword to the Report,

> Because of the diligence, cooperation and facilities of Federal investigative agencies, it was unnecessary for the Commission to employ investigators other than the members of the Commission's legal staff. [24]

Translated into plain English, that meant that the perpetrators were the only ones allowed to investigate themselves. Proof of this is that some of the officials of government agencies who testified under oath were, Secretary of State Dean Rusk, Secretary of the Treasure C. Douglas Dillon and CIA Director John McCone[25] — all of them CFR members.

Finally, at the end of the Foreword, the Committee members reveal the true purpose of the Report:

> The Commission's most difficult assignments have been to *uncover* all the facts concerning the assassination of President Kennedy and to determine if it was in any way directed by unknown persons at home or abroad. . . . The task has demanded unceasing appraisal of the evidence by individual members of the Commission in their effort to *discover* the whole truth[26] [emphasis added]

The truth, however, is that the Commission's assignments were so difficult because, rather than trying to *uncover* or *discover* all the facts, their true purpose was to *cover* the facts that did not fit their lie.

Actually, this is not new. Professor Harry Elmer Barnes devoted several books and dozens of articles to fight what he called the "historical blackout."[27] In a 1947 article, Columbia University Professor Austin Beard summarized the implications of this historical blackout:

> The Rockefeller Foundation and the Council on Foreign Relations . . . intend to prevent, if they can, a repetition of what they call in the vernacular "the debunking journalistic campaign following World War I." Translated into precise English, this means that the Foundation and the Council do not want journalists or any other persons to examine too closely and criticize too freely the official propaganda and official statements relative to "our basic aims and activities" during World War II. In short, they hope that, among other things, the policies and measures of Franklin D. Roosevelt will escape in the coming years the critical analysis, evaluation and exposition that befell the policies and measures of Woodrow Wilson and the Entente Allies after World War I.[28]

The Rockefeller Foundation even openly admitted the subsidizing of a group of historians to prevent and frustrate the development of post-WWII historical revisionism as it had happened after WWI.[29] In the CFR lingo, a "revisionist" is someone who tries to uncover and re-establish the historical truth.[30]

In another paragraph, the Warren Report is even more revealing:

> The procedures followed by the Commission in developing and assessing evidence necessarily differed from those of a court conducting a criminal trial of a defendant present before it, since under our system there is no provision for a posthumous trial. If Oswald had lived he could have had a trial by American standards of justice where he would have been able to exercise his full rights under the law. A judge and jury would have presumed him innocent until proven guilty beyond a reasonable doubt. He might have furnished information that could have affected the course of his trial. He could have participated in and guided his defense. There could have been an examination to determine whether he was sane under prevailing legal standards. All witnesses, including possibly the defendant, could have been subjected to searching examination under the adversary system of American trials.[31]

Well, this is absolutely true. Actually, this is the reason why Oswald was assassinated. A trial by jury would have revealed that everything was a hoax, something that would have put the CFR conspirators in a very difficult situation.

In November 2003, CFR member Peter Jennings produced a special documentary entitled *Beyond Conspiracy*. As expected, it promoted the ridiculous magic bullet theory and pushed the lone nut assassin theory.[32]

In his 2007 book *Brothers*, David Talbot mentions how *NYT*'s columnist Anthony Lewis (CFR) "took the lead in good job in knocking down conspiracy theories." According to Talbot, "over the years, Lewis would continue to disparage critics of the Warren Report."[33]

In November 22 1993, CFR member Michael Beschloss blamed Oswald, who he describes as a "surly little egoist," as the sole culprit for the JFK assassination.[34]

Unfortunately, Pett, Jennings, Talbot, Lewis, Beschloss and the members of the Warren Commission were not alone in their disinformation efforts. Probably the author who has done more to muddying the waters in relation to the Kennedy assassination is Edward Jay Epstein.

In his book *Inquest*, after accepting that the Commission investigation "was by no means exhaustive or even thorough,"[35] Epstein explains how the Zapruder film showed that "the assassination could have been committed by one man alone only under one condition: that Kennedy and Connally were hit by the same bullet."[36] Then, he ends his book with a revealing paragraph:

> Why did the Commission fail to take cognizance in its conclusions of this evidence of a second assassin? Quite clearly, a serious discussion of this problem would in itself have undermined the dominant purpose of the Commission, namely, the settling of doubts and suspicions. Indeed, if the Commission had made it clear that very substantial evidence indicated the presence of a second assassin, it would have opened a Pandora's box of doubts and suspicions. In establishing its version of the truth, the Warren Commission acted to reassure the nation and protect the national interest.[37]

Still, Epstein is highly disingenuous. The CFR agents in the Commission[38] did not act to reassure the nation, much less to protect the national interests, but to protect the narrow interests of the sociopaths who ordered the assassination. Actually, their treachery immensely damaged the national interests of this nation. The assassination of President Kennedy and its cover-up were a dagger stuck in the very heart and soul of America.

Instead of reassuring the nation, the conclusions of the Warren Commission marked the beginning of the American people's profound distrust for their own government. This distrust increased after the events of September 11, 2001, and culminated in 2016 with the defeat of the CFR's puppet Hillary Clinton and the unexpected election of Donald Trump — a loose cannon the CFR conspirators feared immensely.

In the same fashion, Epstein's book *Counterplot* is nothing but a hatchet job on New Orleans District Attorney of Orleans Parish, Louisiana, Jim Garrison, for the sole reason that Garrison suspected the CIA had played a key role in the JFK assassination and he was trying to prove it.

In the many books he has written about the assassination of President Kennedy, Edward Jay Epstein systematically and insistently denied or simply ignored the possible participation of Castro or/and the CIA in the events. In his book *Inquest*,[39] he mildly criticizes the Warren Commission but, as CFR member Richard Rovere points out in the Introduction to *Inquest*,

"Mr. Epstein does not challenge or even question the fundamental integrity of the Commission or its staff. [40]

Rovere continues by asserting, "In late 1963 and 1964 I was one with what I am sure was a majority of Americans in that the theory of the assassination that best suited me was the one the Warren Commission in time said best suited the facts."[41] This is simply not true. As the Warren Commission Report admits in the Foreword, since the very beginning there was a widespread suspicion that the JFK assassination was the result of a conspiracy.

In 2017, however, after dozens of obvious political assassinations and mostly thanks to the role of the Internet as a new mass communication medium the CFR conspirators cannot fully control, things have changed dramatically. The American people as a whole have awakened from their media-induced dream, particularly after if became well-known than more than a hundred people related to the JFK assassination died suspicious deaths,[42] and have stopped trusting their government and believing in the disinformation provided by the mainstream media. Currently only CFR members and the most gullible Americans still believe that lone nut Oswald killed JFK and there was no conspiracy.

In the Preface to *Inquest*, Epstein clarifies that his book was not centered in the assassination itself, but only attempted to answer the question: "How did the Commission go about searching for such an elusive and many-faced quarry as the truth?[43]

This, however, does not seem to agree with the Commission's members goal. Though the purpose of the Commission was never fully stated in its report, according to Allen Dulles (CFR), a key Commission member, its main goal apparently was not to discover the truth, but to dispel rumors about a conspiracy.[44] Another key Commission member, John McCloy (CFR), agreed with Dulles when said that it was of cardinal importance to "Show the world that America is not a banana republic, where a government can be changed by conspiracy."[45] Nevertheless, after reading the draft of the Commission's Conclusion, Representative Gerald Ford (CFR), also a Commission member, carefully advised that, instead of categorically stating that there was no conspiracy, the wording should be changed to "The Commission has found no evidence of a conspiracy."[46]

But Dulles, McCloy and Ford were not isolated cases. Actually, the whole CFR disinformation machinery went into full swing to prove that there was no conspiracy. A *New York Times'* Editorial of September 28, 1964, insisted: "The facts, exhaustively gathered, independently checked and cogently set forth . . . destroy the basis for the conspiracy theories that have grown weedlike in this country and abroad."

Epstein notes that, despite the fact that some prominent witnesses, such as Secretary of State Dean Rusk (CFR), Secretary of the Treasury Douglas Dillon (CFR), FBI Director J. Edgar Hoover, and CIA Director John McCone (CFR), testified on the procedure, actually none of them revealed any new facts about the assassination itself.[47]

In the Introduction to Epstein's *Inquest*, CFR member Richard Rovere stated: "The seven Commissioners were chosen more from their known probity than for their mastery of probative techniques."[48] Really?

Apparently, neither Rovere nor Epstein questioned the fact that four of the Commission members, Sherman Cooper, Gerald Ford, John McCloy, and Allen Dulles, were members of the Council on Foreign Relations, an organization whose members fiercely opposed Kennedy's national and international policies. Seemingly, they considered perfectly normal that Allen Dulles, a key member of the Commission created to investigate the JFK assasssination, had been recently fired by Kennedy because he had intentionally mislead about the Bay of Pigs invasion.

Also, did Epstein never found it strange that it was precisely Dulles the member of the Commission chosen to advise (actually to coach) CIA officers about the possible questions his fellow commissioners most likely would ask?[49]

In a new Preface to *Inquest* Epstein wrote in 1992,[50] he explains how, when he was still a student at Cornell University preparing to write a master's thesis "On the problem of how the government goes about searching for such elusive quarry as the truth,"[51] he contacted some members of the Warren Commission about interviewing them. To his surprise, they told him they were delighted to be interviewed.

Epstein confessed that he was surprised because the members of the Warren Commission had always kept an aura of secrecy on their deliberations and refused to discuss their work with outsiders. Surprisingly, the two members who proved to be more open and collaborative were CFR honchos John McCloy and Allen Dulles. According to Epstein,

> Dulles even invited me to stay for a leisure tea while reminisced how the commission's inquiry differed from those he had conducted at the CIA, and McCloy suspended his incoming phone calls so as not to interrupt the interview.[52]

How nice! Unknowingly, however, Epstein is describing in detail a process intelligence officers call agent recruiting. As an OSS officer in Bern during WWII, one of Dulles' key activities was recruiting agents.[53] Most intelligence officers agree that the best agent is the one who doesn't know, or doesn't want to know, that he has been recruited.[54]

According to Epstein, his book *Inquest* opened up the possibility "that the members of the Warren Commission, *though honest*, had not dug deeply enough to find the evidence of a conspiracy."[55] [Emphasis added.]

Epstein's second book of his trilogy on the Kennedy assassination, *Counterplot*[56] is essentially a nasty hatchet job; a character assassination of Jim Garrison. Obviously Epstein hated Garrison for the sole reason that Garrison suspected the CIA had played a key role in the assassination and decided to investigate it.[57] According to Epstein, Garrison was a tinhat only read by UFO believers,[58] a conspiracy theorist,[59] a McCarthyist,[60] a paranoid,[61] a demagogue,[62] and a corrupt district attorney who took payoffs and graft by local gamblers.[63]

Nevertheless, in 1989, while living in New Orleans, I had the opportunity of talking to Garrison a couple of times over the phone about the possibility of creating a HyperCard multimedia presentation in the Macintosh computer[64] explaining his theories about the assassination. Contrary to what Epstein wants people to believe, Garrison sounded a very nice, rational, educated Southern gentleman, very well informed about the JFK assassination. I recall that he was interested in the idea. Unfortunately, we were never able to carry out the project.

Epstein's third book of his trilogy on the Kennedy assassination, *Legend*,[65] is basically an attempt to distract the attention from the CIA as possible participant in the assassination of President Kennedy. Most of it is focused in trying to implicate the Soviet intelligence services. Reading into it, I discovered that a key source in this endeavor was none other than James Jesus Angleton, the CIA chief of counterintelligence.

Now, writing about the assassination of President Kennedy and having as main sources of information the stories told by guys like John McCloy, Allen Dulles and James Angleton is like writing a book about the history of the National Society of Liars based on interviews with its president, vice-president and general secretary.

In 1992, the indefatigable Epstein seized the opportunity of Garrison's death to drop the final bucketload of mud to defame his memory. In a very long article for *The New Yorker* magazine, Epstein repeats over and over the same arguments he had been using for close to thirty years against Garrison.[66]

According to Epstein, Garrison had a "rarefied view of reality," lived in an "enchanted maze," and only broke it to "penetrate deep into other dimension." To prove his point, Epstein quotes from Garrison's book *Heritage of Stone* and adds his own comments,

> The main reason for the inability of the American people and the press to recognize the conspiracy to kill President Kennedy was the fact that its operations all occurred in another dimension, a dimension which is generally not known to exist in our nation.
>
> This second dimension is evil as well as manipulative. In it an "invisible government tat begins and ends with deception" appropriates power to itself through assassinations and conceals from the populace "government force that is as criminal as the Germany of Hitler or the Russia of Stalin." This elite, supported by the "military-industrial complex" was the hidden sponsor of the Viet Nam War and nuclear arms race. To assure its invisibility, this "power elite" employs technicians capable of inflicting on its enemies "heart attacks, falls, shootings by 'deranged men' and dozens of other kinds of misadventures." . . . It engages in "thought control" over the media and, in the case of those who escape this "concentration camp of the mind," it stage-manages in the media "massive discreditation."[67]

We need to keep in mind that Epstein is writing for *The New Yorker*'s brainwashed, moronic readers. Nevertheless, it is obvious that the true cause of Epstein's hatred is because Garrison was too close to the truth for the CFR conspirators' comfort.

I have been very critical of many books written about the CIA. One of them is Joseph Trento's *Prelude to Terror*.[68] Nevertheless, if I accused Trento of something it was of being too naïve by accepting at face value information offered by CIA officers trained to lie, such as James Angleton, William Corson and Robert Crowley. The case of Epstein, however, is very different. He is anything but naïve. His work evidences a systematic, conscious effort to distract the attention from the obvious suspects: Castro, the CIA, and their CFR masters, particularly the Rockefellers.

Some people have mentioned their suspicions that Epstein is a CIA asset. After reading his three books on the Kennedy assassination: *Inquest,*

Counterplot and *Legend*, I have reached the conclusion that these suspicions may be true: Edward Jay Epstein is most likely a CIA asset. Why? Simply, because it he looks *like a duck*, swims *like a duck*, and quacks *like a duck*, then he most probably *is* a duck

Still, there are questions that need to be answered: Why did the Commission members, otherwise so secretive about their job, open up to Epstein inquest? Why did such a mysterious, secretive character like James Jesus Angleton became so cozy with Epstein to the point of confiding to him his deep secrets?

As expected, the CFR conspirators mobilized their beloved CIA to help them on the disinformation campaign. A CIA memo entitled "Propaganda Notes," dated 22 September 1964, states:

> Reports from around the world indicate that there is a strong belief in many countries that the assassination of the President was the result of a "political plot;" the unwarranted interpretation that Ruby's murder of Oswald was committed to prevent Oswald from revealing the purported conspiracy adds to this belief.[69]

In order to fight these conspiracy theories, most likely advanced by "communists," the CIA ordered its officers to use its agents of influence to,

> Covert assets should explain the tragedy wherever it is genuinely misunderstood and counter all efforts to misconstrue it intentionally – provided the depth of impact warrants such action. Communists and other extremists always attempt to prove a political conspiracy behind violence.[70]

So, is it any surprise that Noam Chomsky endorsed the lone assassin and magic bullet theory in the assassination of JFK? From his emergence as a guru of the Left in the late 1960's, Chomsky made fun of anyone researching the anomalies stemming from the official story and the Warren Commission cover-up. According to him, any examination of it is a complete waste of time:

> There's just a huge amount of frittering away of energy on real absurdities. There are parts of the country, like California, where *incredible* amounts of energy go into things like trying to figure out exactly which Mafia figure might have been involved in kill-

ing John F. Kennedy or something — as if anybody should care. The energy and passion that goes into things like that is really extraordinary, and it's very self–destructive. ... [emphasis in the original][71]

Nevertheless, among the many moronic books that have been written backing the Warren Commission's conclusion that Oswald was a nutcase and he acted alone, therefore no conspiracy existed, perhaps the most asinine is Gerald Posner's 1993 book *Case Closed*.[72]

In his book, reissued with a new afterword for the 40th anniversary of the assassination, Posner examined all of the available evidence and reached the only possible conclusion to gain the favor of the CFR conspirators: Lee Harvey Oswald acted alone. He was a highly disturbed individual. There was no second gunman on the grassy knoll. The CIA was not involved. Case closed!

Closely following Posner's book is Vincent Bugliosi's pitiful *Reclaiming History*.[73] In his book, Bugliosi confirms beyond all doubt — or so he thinks — the oft-challenged findings of the Warren Commission: Lee Harvey Oswald, acting alone, shot and killed President John F. Kennedy.

More Post-Cover-Up Disinformers

Oliver Stone's 1992 film *JFK*, basically based on Jim Garrison's theories, unleashed a barrage of criticism from the usual suspects in the CFR-controlled mainstream press. Granted, I am not a Stone fan. The reason for this is that in 2003 he produced and directed *Comandante,* a documentary on Fidel Castro. The documentary, which consisted in long interviews with Castro, so overemphasized and dramatized Castro's goodness vis-à-vis U.S. evil that it bombed miserably. Even bleeding-heart liberals hated it.

Apparently, Stone, like many others, fell under Castro's Charles-Manson-like powers of fascination.[74] Another possible explanation for this strange behavior might be that most people think that, by logic, the enemy of their enemy has to be their friend. They seem to ignore, however, that the pseudo-enemy of their enemy most likely is not their friend.

Nevertheless, even before it reached the theaters, Stone's film acted like the smell of blood to the CFR sharks. Just from December 15, 1991, to January 16, 1992, the *New York Times* published 10 stories about *JFK* — an average of one every three days — strongly attacking Stone, Garrison and the film. *Newsweek's* December 23 cover trumpeted "The Twisted Truth of *JFK:* Why Oliver Stone's New Movie Can't Be Trusted."

The attacks were so nasty and uncalled for that Garry "Doonesbury" Trudeau drew a comic strip picturing Stone running through a maze while snipers from the CFR controlled mainstream media were shooting at him from every angle.

The main source for Stone's film was Garrison's book *On the Trail of the Assassins*. So, the critics concentrated their attack on Garrison. One of them, Jon Margolis, wrote an article in the *Chicago Tribune* in which he called Garrison,

> The bizarre New Orleans District Attorney who, in 1969, claimed that the assassination of President Kennedy was a conspiracy by some officials of the Central Intelligence Agency.[75]

Bizarre? Actually, of all the potential suspects the CIA is the only organization that has a department especially dedicated to carry out "executive action" – that is, assassination. Margolis continued,

> … all conspiracies that have been alleged are unsupported by credible data and require far more suspension of disbelief than does acceptance of the prosaic likelihood that poor Oswald did it himself because he was mad.[76]

Well, actually the main conspiracy theory that is unsupported by credible data and requires more suspension of disbelief to be accepted is the bizarre conspiracy theory advanced by the Warren Commission.

Another critic, George Lardner Jr., joined the attack. The title of his article tells all: "On the Set: Dallas in Wonderland. How Oliver Stone's Version of the Kennedy Assassination Exploits the Edge of Paranoia."[77] Lardner is a national security writer for the CFR's corporate member *Washington Post*.
  Margolis' and Lardner's articles unleashed a veritable tsunami of *ad hominem* abuse, insults, vituperation and vilification of both Stone and Garrison that reached new levels. Apparently, the CFR conspirators feared Stone's film so much that they fully mobilized their goons in the mainstream media to discredit it even before it hit the movie theaters.
  On June 10, 1991, *Time* magazine published an article by Richard Zoglin, "More Shots in Dealey Plaza: Oliver Stone returns to the '60s once again with a strange widely disputed take on the Kennedy assassination." The article was a vicious attack on Stone and Garrison, whom Zoglin calls

"a wide-eyed conspiracy buff," and a person "considered somewhere near the far-out fringe of conspiracy theorists."

On November 1991, *Esquire* magazine published "The Shooting of JFK," a long article by Robert Sam Anson. Hiding behind a façade on feigned objectivity, the article was basically a character assassination of Jim Garrison.

Anson's article not only kept criticizing Garrison but also viciously attacked Stone, whom — according to Anson — his opponents have accused of distorting history, recklessness, irresponsibility, mendacity, McCarthyism, paranoia and dementia as well as characterizing him "as a liar, a hypocrite, a megalomaniac, and a charlatan." He also accused Stone of being "highly susceptible to sources serious scholars[78] had dismissed years before."

On December 8 of that same year, the *Los Angeles Times*, published an opinion article by Jefferson Morley entitled "The Political Rorschach Test." According to Morley, the JFK assassination has become a sort of inkblot in which everybody sees what his political concerns indicate. Thus, people who for any reason distrust the government are the ones who see a conspiracy.

Obviously, Morley is looking at the problem through the wrong side of the binoculars. Actually, it is not that our distrust of the government has affected our perception of the JFK assassination, but that our perception of the JFK assassination — as well as the 9/11 events — has affected our trust of the government.

A few days later, on December 15, 1991, *The New York Times* struck again with an article by Tom Wicker. The title tells all: "Does *JFK* Conspire Against Reason? Oliver Stone transforms a discredited theory into the sole explanation for the assassination."

On December 17, 1991, *The Washington Post* published an article by Gerald R. Ford and David W. Belin, "Kennedy Assassination: What About the Truth?" that basically continues the retinue of criticism against Stone's *JFK* but also included in his criticism the *A&E TV* series "The Men Who Killed Kennedy."

According to Ford and Belin, "The common denominator of these commercial productions is the big lie — the assertion that the top echelons of our government were conspiratorially involved in the assassination and that Lee Harvey Oswald was not the lone gunman who killed President Kennedy and Dallas Police Officer J.D. Tippit."

Now, having CFR member Gerald Ford calling Stone a liar is tantamount to hearing the pot calling the kettle black.

Another CFR member who joined the anti-Stone Chorus was Daniel Patrick Moynihan. On December 29, the *Washington Post* published Moynihan's article "The Paranoid Style." According to him, he was at the White House sitting at Ralph Dungan's (CFR) office the hour JFK was killed. When they heard the news, McGeorge Bundy (CFR) got up and went over to a telephone and called Robert McNamara (CFR).

What a coincidence. All of them CFR members.

Following similar lines, on January 9, 1992, the *New York Times* published "Kennedy and Vietnam," by CFR honcho Leslie Gelb. Next day the *Wall Street Journal* published "JFK: Truth and Fiction," by CFR member Arthur Schlesinger, Jr.

A few days later, on January 28, 1992, the *Wall Street Journal* published "A Concoction of Lies and Distortions" by another CFR member, Joseph Califano. According to him,

> The Oliver Stone movie *JFK* is a disgraceful concoction of lies and distortions designed, among other things, to leave the impression that there was a massive conspiracy among all elements of American society — business, the media, to kill President Kennedy and that one of the conspirators was President Johnson.

The mainstream media consensus in criticizing Stone's *JFK* film was so evident that the *San Francisco Examiner* devoted a large part of its *IMAGE* magazine to the subject with two articles under the generic title "See No Evil." The Media and the JFK Assassination. Two Media Critics Examine the Response to the Shooting of *JFK* ... and JFK." [79] The first one, David Armstrong's "Killing the Messenger: Why Did the Press React So Furiously to Oliver Stone's Movie?" ends with a key question:

> It took a Hollywood moviemaker to focus the country's attention once again on its deepest and most disturbing mystery: the murder of John Fitzgerald *Kennedy*. But instead of praising Oliver Stone for renewing the national debate about the assassination, the media were much more interested in burying him. So overheated has been the elite mainstream media's response to *JFK* that their defensiveness has become part of the story. Months after the fusillade against the film began, the public may well be asking, why is Oliver Stone's refusal to accept the official story such an affront to the press?

The other article, Todd Gitlin's "Why the Journalistic Barrage at Oliver Stone? Whom Did He Shoot?"[80] also tries to understand, without much success, the true causes for such vicious attacks on Stone. Actually, Oliver Stone, perhaps unknowingly, shot the Rockefellers and their minions with the weapon their fear the most: truth. This explains why they reacted so viciously against him.

Other media stars eventually joined the anti-Stone chorus, among them, CFR members George Will, Arthur Schlesinger, Jr., Leslie Gelb, Anthony Lewis and Dan Rather.[81]

An interesting detail is that Stone devoted an inordinate amount of time writing letters to the Editor refuting his detractors to most of the newspapers and magazines that published the articles attacking him. His attitude, however, trying to offer evidence substantiating the information offered in the film, indicates that he never fully understood the true reasons for such vicious attacks.

Actually, the concerted attacks of the CFR-controlled media against Stone closely resemble the attacks by the very same people against Donald Trump after he was elected President of the United States. The only purpose of such attacks, which defy any logic or reason, is to discredit the person attacked.

Of course, it is impossible to understand the attacks unless you know that the CFR-controlled media hates any mention of a conspiracy in the JFK assassination because they were part of the conspiracy. It is not a coincidence that most of the media stars, politicians and scholars who attacked Stone were proud members of the Council on Foreign Relations.

The evidence that the critics of Stone and Garrison were not searching for truth, but following a plan most likely conceived at the CFR, is confirmed by the following facts:

1. Both the Church Committee and the Rockefeller Commission revealed that at the time of the JFK assassination the CIA already had a department dedicated to the assassination of foreign leaders.

2. According to transcripts of the deliberations of the Warren Commission, later declassified, some members of the Commission found suspicious not only that Oswald had traveled to the Soviet Union, but also his financing, his fluency in Rus-

sian, and many other unexplainable facts about his activities and well as the inaction of both the CIA and the FBI to investigate him.

3. The Church Committee[82] concluded that there was a 95 percent of probability that the JFK assassination was the result of a conspiracy.

4. Declassified CIA documents later confirmed that, as Garrison maintained, Clay Shaw not only had known David Ferrie and possible Oswald, but also was a CIA asset.

5. In 1979, the House Special Committee on Assassinations reached the conclusion that unknown conspirators had been responsible for the JFK assassination.

6. Last, but not least, we have the unexplainable fact that Allen Dulles, the key person in the investigation of the assassination of President Kennedy, had been fired two years before from his job as CIA Director by President Kennedy.

After seeing the concerted effort of these mainstream press members to destroy the reputation of both Stone and Garrison, one has to conclude that the only reason for this was because their explanation of the events was too close to the truth for CFR's comfort.

In the article I mentioned above, Jefferson Morley advances the theory that the main reason why Stone and other conspiracy theorists are criticized so fiercely today is because,

Those who believe Oswald acted alone are not only defending the anti-conspiratorial theory advanced by the Warren Commission. They are also defending the credibility of senior U.S. government officials, the integrity of U.S. law enforcement and intelligence agencies and the capabilities of the national media. [83]

What Morley fails to see, however, is that what they are really defending is the credibility of senior members of the Council on Foreign Relations infiltrated in the U.S. government, the integrity of a CFR-created Central Intelligence Agency, and the credibility of the CFR-controlled national media. Nevertheless, the truth is that none of them have any credibility, much less integrity.

Another disinformer who has recently joined the group is former editor in chief of *Salon.com* David Talbot. In a 1213 article, Talbot strongly criticizes author Philip Shenon because in his book *A Cruel and Shocking Act*,[84] "following the conspiracy trail Shenon quickly takes a wrong turn down the "Castro-as-mastermind" path.[85] One must keep in mind that to most American "progressives" Castro still is untouchable.

Nevertheless, in 2015 Talbot published a book that is a notable addition to the post-cover-up disinformation campaign.[86] In it, Talbot not only didn't mention that Castro was the only one of the suspects who publicly threatened the Kennedy brothers with assassination but puts all the blame for the JFK assassination on Allen Dulles. But, as one of the book's reviewers in Amazon.com pointed out, "Talbot has rightly castigated the Dulles brothers but is remiss in examining their puppet masters, the real wire-pullers."

I don't think that Talbot's omissions and errors are the product of sloppy research or faulty analysis of the facts. I think that Talbot is a dishonest writer who wants to push his own political agenda disregarding of the facts. Proof of this is that, far from mentioning Castro's possible links to the JFK assassination, he devotes thirteen pages of his book to paint a rose-colored, disingenuous image of Fidel Castro as a Latin American hero.[87]

Nevertheless, as the saying goes, every dark cloud has a silver lining. Perhaps taken by his admiration for the two assassins, Castro and Guevara,[88] Talbot expresses his approval because they were "backed with guns," and "put the hard-core thugs of the old regime against a wall," and shot them.[89]

So, if you believe that the progressives' reasons for wanting to ban *your* guns is just because they want to make America safe, you are wrong. Actually, they don't want you to be armed when they knock at your door to take you to the wall to be shot, and you should heartfully thank David Talbot for reminding you about that.

A question that may come to mind is why CFR members in the Warren Commission created the farfetched theory that Oswald was a lone nut and that he killed JFK with a single bullet? Also, why in a nation of 250 million people, so many of the people involved in the JFK assassination cover-up belonged to the Council on Foreign Relations, an organization with less than 3,000 members? Why so many of the people who fiercely attacked Oliver Stone and Jim Garrison were CFR members? Was the CFR involved in the assassination?

As I will show below in this book, since its creation in 1921, members of the Rockefeller-controlled Council on Foreign Relations have been behind *every* act of treason against this country and its people, including the assassination of President John F. Kennedy.

Part 2

Chapter 6

The Rockefellers: A Criminal Gang

Everything you know is wrong.
— The Firesign Theater.

Histories of the Standard Oil written by most authors, pro and con, show that John D. Rockefeller, the originator of the family empire, was a person of a deeply conspiratorial, scheming nature. U.S. Senator Robert Lafollette went a step further and called him "The greatest criminal of the age."[1] John D. himself would later in his life discover that his father's primary occupation had been pitchman and con artist.[2] "Cut from the same mold as the legendary P. T. Barnum, he was far from chagrined by his secret life. In fact, he seemed to revel in his petty larcenies." [3]

Since its very creation, John D. Rockefeller's Standard Oil Company —which other oil producers used to call "a gang of thieves"[4] — worked like an intelligence and espionage organization. It had created a cult of silence and deception and enforced a policy of total secrecy.[5] It is known that some of the people who did business with John D. were forced to sign an oath of secrecy, promising to keep any deals strictly private.[6]

John D. pioneered the use of industrial espionage to advance his business interests.[7] According to author Gary Allen, at its time the "Rockefeller's industrial espionage system was by far the most elaborate, most sophisticated and most successful that had been established."[8]

According to some witnesses, Rockefeller recruited agents everywhere, among competitors, politicians and in the media. In its continuous effort to monopolize the oil industry by eliminating all competition, Standard employed spies who gathered information about foreign and American markets,[9] as well as analysts who evaluated the raw information and produced useful intelligence.[10]

In 1897, Rockefeller sent two of his secret agents on a mission to Asia, where they gathered information to assess a probable threat by the Royal Dutch oil company.[11] As one of Rockefeller's colleagues acknowledged at the time, "We have before us daily the best information obtainable from all the world's markets."[12]

The Rockefellers' Criminal Activities

In order to disguise the criminal activities of his Standard Oil in his effort to eliminate all competition, John D. Rockefeller and some of his coconspirators created a fictitious organization under the innocuous name of South Improvement Company.[13] This was an early example of what the CIA later called a "proprietary," an ostensibly private business firm created and operated by the CIA for the sole purpose of providing cover for large-scale secret operations.

Ida Tarbell, who wrote an authoritative study of the Standard Oil, called John D. Rockefeller, "a brooding, cautious, secretive man ..."[14] Tarbell's research assistant wrote her: "I tell you this John D. Rockefeller is the strangest, most silent, most mysterious, and most interesting figure in America."[15] According to Tarbell, Mr. Rockefeller employed force, fraud and blackmailing to reach his ends.[16]

Matthew Josephson, another author who has studied the life of John D. Rockefeller, confirms Tarbell's vision. According to Josephson, "He was given to secrecy; he loathed all display. ... His wife, Laura Spellman, proved an excellent mate." She encouraged his furtiveness, Josephson relates, advising him always to be silent, to say as little as possible.[17] He also mentions how John D. Rockefeller never hesitated to resort to violence to destroy his competitors,

> But where the Standard Oil could not carry on its expansion by peaceful means, it was ready with violence; its faithful servants knew even how to apply the modern weapon of dynamite.[18]

Widespread opposition to what most people were convinced was a

Rockefeller "conspiracy" grew to the point that, on April 29, 1879, a Grand Jury indicted John D. Rockefeller, William Rockefeller and other chieftains of Standard Oil for criminal conspiracy to "secure a monopoly of the oil industry, to oppress other refiners, to injure carrying trade, to extort unreasonable railroad rates, to fraudulent control prices," to use secret rates and deceiving their competitors as to what their rates were, etc.[19]

Even in a friendly article about the Rockefellers, author Lewis Galantière had to recognize the unscrupulous monopolistic principles on which they did business,

> The classic Standard Oil schemes were: (1) to get a lower shipping rate than rivals paid, and to get in addition, in cash from the roads, the difference between the two rates paid by the competitors; (2) to choke all crude supplies from competitors; (3) to force the transport companies to deny the competing refiners access to markets; (4) to work the fifth-column game by bribing servants of other companies, putting their own people into those companies, or secretly buying up a competitor and obtaining the trade secrets of rival groups through the officials of the company secretly acquired.[20]

In his book *The Rockefeller Syndrome*, Ferdinand Lundberg expands on John D. Rockefeller's practices of intelligence and espionage. According to Lundberg,

> How, in a nutshell, cutting through volumes of apologetics, did the original Standard Oil operate? It operated in such a way as to be a model for any secret service operation such as the CIA or the GPU and KGB. Standard Oil had nothing to learn from them.
>
> In the first place, a large portion of Standard Oil's operations was illegal, as ascertained by the courts. The rule of secrecy was one constantly enjoined upon his associates by Rockefeller himself. As many of these were men of expansive temperament, they would have been, unless carefully coached, apt to tell anyone with pride what they were doing, thus showing what clever fellows they were.
>
> . . .
>
> In addition to using the aliases and disguises of satellite companies, the Standard Oil operated with a secret code and ciphers, lest anyone know what it was doing. It also had an efficient inter-

nal and external espionage system. It not only knew what every-
one in its employ was doing (and internal pilferers and loafers were
dropped at once), but it knew about the internal operations of those
trying to compete. It not only had its paid informants planted in
other companies, but through the handling of the shipments of others through apparently independent Standard-owed shipping agencies, it learned who the rival's customers were, the quantities being shipped, and the prices paid. It used this information to the
detriment of the competitor.[21]

In other part of his book Lundberg added information about how John D.
bought corrupt politicians, venal journalists and unscrupulous scientists, a
practice the Rockefeller family has successfully continued to the present
day. The only difference is that, since the beginning of the 20th century,
they have done it indirectly, through the "philanthropic" foundations under
their control. According to Lundberg,

Standard Oil not only ladled out money to politicians, in an out of
office, and to newspapers, and quickly hired for itself any spe-
cially bright lawyers it found acting for its competitors or hostile
government agencies, but it had vast success in enlisting the aid of
certified academicians. And here, in my opinion, was the worst
subversion of all — the trammeling of the very citadel of truth.[22]

Author William Manchester agrees with Lundberg. According to Manchester,

The trouble with fighting John D. was that you never knew where
he was. He ran his company as though it were a branch of the
C.I.A. All important messages were in code —Baltimore was
"Droplet," Philadelphia "Druggewt," refiners were "Douters," the
Standard itself "Doxy." Shadowy men came and went by his front
door, shadowy companies used his back door as a mailing address.
For a long time the public didn't realize how powerful he was because he kept insisting he was battling firms that he secretly owned
outright. His real rivals were forever discovering that their most
trusted officers were in his pocket. The tentacles of the octopus
were everywhere.[23]

Eventually, the opposition to Rockefeller's unethical and criminal practices rose to a point that he was accused of conspiring against his business competitors. Writs were served against him and, on April 29, 1879, John D. Rockefeller and other senior executives of Standard Oil were indicted by a Grand Jury for criminal conspiracy, to "secure a monopoly of the oil industry, to oppress other refiners, to extort unreasonable railroad rates, to fraudulent control prices," and other crimes,[24] but he managed to avoid being convicted by skillfully spreading his money.

In 1906 the accusations against John D. surfaced again when Theodore Roosevelt, an old Rockefeller critic, made public a report made by the Bureau of Corporations, revealing how Rockefeller had benefited enormously through the use of unethical business practices. At the same time, a lawsuit was initiated in the Federal Circuit Court in Eastern Missouri, with the goal of dissolving the Standard Oil as a conspiracy in restraint of trade. But, again, John D. managed to escape the laws.

On April, 1914, miners of the Colorado Fuel and Iron Company at Ludlow, Colorado, owned by John D. Rockefeller, Jr., went on strike in protest for low pay and poor working conditions and set up a tent city with their families facing the mine's entrance. Instead of trying to negotiate with the miners, Rockefeller promptly called the National Guard, who took positions on an elevation overlooking the strikers' tents. On April 20, allegedly in response to a shot fired from the miners' side, the National Guard troops opened fire on their tents, killing forty protesters and wounding countless, including women and children.[25]

After the massacre, Junior declared that he stood by the officers who committed the killings. When asked if this meant killing all his employees, he answered that it was "a great principle."[26]

Ironically, in 1913, a year before the bloodbath in Colorado, the Rockefellers had invested $50 million worth of Standard Oil assets to launch their Rockefeller Foundation with. Its charter described the Foundation's goal as the advancement of "the civilization of the peoples of the United States and its territories and possessions and of foreign lands..." But the foundation's "philanthropic" activities more often than not conveniently served the Rockefeller corporate interests, a pattern that continues to the present day.

On December 6, 1928, workers of the Rockefeller-controlled United Fruit Company in the town of Ciénaga near Santa Marta, Colombia, went on strike. Some sources put the figure of strikers throughout the banana zone at between 11,000 and 30,000 people.

The workers demanded written contracts, eight-hour workdays, six-day workweeks and the elimination of food coupons. The United Fruit Company paid contractors who then paid the workers.[27] The Company maintained that the piecework contract system was the only way to make efficient use of a mobile labor force. Its critics argued that the Company had adopted this system to circumvent Colombian labor laws.[28]

A regiment of the Colombian army was dispatched from Bogotá by the government to deal with the strikers. The troops set up their machine guns on the roofs of the low buildings at the corners of the main square and closed off the access streets. A dense Sunday crowd of workers and their wives and children had gathered in the town's square after Sunday Mass. After a five-minute warning to disperse, the soldiers opened fire on the crowd. The exact number of casualties was never established because the soldiers threw them into the sea, but it was calculated between a few hundred and as high as two thousand.

On September 14, 1971, while Nelson Rockefeller was the Governor of New York, a rebellion started at the state prison in Attica. Thirteen hundred prisoners, mostly black, had taken 38 prison employees as hostages. After a five-day standoff, during which Nelson didn't visit the prison and refused to hear the prisoners' complaints, a helicopter suddenly dropped pepper gas into the yard and the police force surrounded it and unleashed a volley that killed 10 hostages and 29 inmates. Also, 80 prisoners were wounded.

Nelson justified his actions by alleging that the prisoners' demands were political. According to Nelson, the prisoners' demands transcended prison reform and had "political implications."

Nelson and David Inherit Grandpa's Passion for Spying

It seems that the passion for intelligence, espionage and assassination runs deep in the Rockefeller clan, and Nelson and David proudly continued the tradition that began with their grandfather John D. Rockefeller.

In the late 1930s Nelson Rockefeller was appointed to oversee a secret U.S. government ideological and economic warfare offensive south of the border. In *American Propaganda Abroad*, former U.S. Information Agency official Fitzhugh Green states,

> In 1938 the United States government began its own modest cultural thrust among the Latin American republics, called the Office

of Inter-American Affairs, under Nelson Rockefeller in the State Department."[29]

The creation of the Office of Inter-American Affairs got strong support among politicians of both Rockefeller-controlled parties, who had been asking for an agency to coordinate the U.S. defense activities in Latin America and to foster Latin American attitudes favorable to the CFR conspirators' objectives, especially if its propaganda aspects were properly concealed, and good Nelson gave them what they have been craving.

The innocuous name actually disguised the true job of the OIAA: waging psychological warfare against the Latin American peoples. Soon after it was created, a secret psychological warfare team was created at the OIAA.

As an undated and formerly classified White House memorandum relates, such "psychological" activities were then still too controversial with the American public to be discussed openly. "Propaganda was still a horrid word," says the document which reads like an early history of American propaganda efforts overseas, and the national administration in 1940 could not hope to establish an admitted propaganda agency. Therefore, "American psychological operations or opinion-influencing activities had to be cloaked in the subterfuge of agency titles."[30]

Two years later, in August 1940, Nelson Rockefeller was appointed Coordinator of Commercial and Cultural Relations Among the Latin American Republics. At the time Nelson already had strong economic, financial and commercial ties in Latin America, and the primary covert function of his Office of Inter-American Affairs was to implement an extensive psychological warfare operation. This PsyWar had been carefully planned to mold Latin American public opinion into accepting the CFR conspirators' plans of economic and ideological subjugation — which included the overthrow and assassination of leaders they could not buy — for the implementation of the coming New World Order.

Nelson served in different positions in the Roosevelt administration. But Truman (not a CFR member) didn't see any need for Nelson's help in his administration and asked Nelson for his resignation.

Just after sending his resignation, Nelson sent a two-page memorandum to the President in which he expressed his conviction that the normal approach of the Secretary of State in control of foreign policy was not adequate at a time when the U.S. had become a global power. His recommendations to fix what he saw as a problem are quite revealing: Nelson suggested replacing the different cabinet agencies of the government with a sort of super government secretly acting behind the backs of the American people, responsible to a single man, the President.[31] Obviously, Nelson's idea was to become America's first dictator.

Nelson never achieved his dream, but, with the creation of the National Security Council, American presidents got dictatorial powers. The only difference with traditional dictators all around the world is that the American ones are puppets under CFR control.

Under Dwight Eisenhower, however, Nelson's star briefly rose again. He served as the President's Special Assistant on Foreign Policy (1954-55) and as head of the secret "Forty Committee" charged with overseeing the CIA's covert operations — the fox in charge of protecting the chickens.

Nelson favored the use of private organizations and foundations as government surrogates in the nation's psychological warfare effort. His idea was detailed in a secret June 4, 1952 memorandum titled "Cold War Resources of Private and Other Government Agencies," written by White House strategist William A. Korns and archived in the records of the old Psychological Strategy Board.[32]

A condition for the deployment of "private resources," the memo advised, would be a determination on "the overt-covert issue." The document further explained that non-governmental actors should be used only when necessary to conceal the involvement of the U.S. government. "If there is reason to believe that the Made in America label may in some instances thwart the achievement of our long-range objectives, it would follow that private capabilities should be used on a highly selective basis," Korns wrote.

The same memo also hinted that such American business ventures could be of use in intelligence gathering because of their experience in dealing with local officials. It specifically referred to the Standard Oil Company's negotiations in India, at which time "the State Department [was] in close touch with the corporation," and mentioned Nelson Rockefeller's International Basic Economy Corporation as one organization regarded as "sensitive to political direction," a euphemism for spying and psychological warfare.

The Family Tradition Continues

In 1953, after Iran's democratically elected Prime Minister Dr. Mohammad Mossadegh nationalized Iran's oil business, a UK/US-backed coup overthrew him in favor of strengthening the monarchical rule of Shah Mohammad Reza Pahlavi. CIA Director Allen Dulles and his brother, Secretary of State John Foster Dulles, were instrumental in the coup. Previously, Iran's oil had been controlled by the Anglo-Persian Oil Co. (i.e., British Petroleum, BP) but, after the U.S. role in this coup, U.S. companies got a 40% share and the top beneficiary was Rockefeller-owned Standard Oil of New Jersey.

In 1979, syndicated columnist Jack Anderson disclosed that the Rockefellers, who controlled Standard Oil and Chase Manhattan Bank, had "helped to arrange the CIA coup that brought down Mossadegh." According to Anderson, a grateful Shah handsomely rewarded the Rockefellers by depositing huge sums of cash in Chase Manhattan. He also gave the contract to building a new housing development to a Rockefeller firm.[33]

The next year, the Rockefeller boys were at it again orchestrating a coup in Guatemala. This one ushered in decades of fascist military governments that killed hundreds of thousands of innocent civilians. But it brought great profits for Rockefeller's United Fruit Co., in which their secret agents, the Dulles brothers, had heavily invested. CIA Director Allen Dulles had also been on United Fruit Board of Trustees.

In 1964, one of Rockefeller-controlled law firm's most important clients was M. A. Hanna Mining Company, the largest producer of iron ore in Brazil. Soon after Joao Goulart was democratically elected president in 1961, he began to talk about nationalizing the Brazilian iron ore industry, and Hanna's executives were extremely concerned about the company's investments in the country.

Following Rockefellers' orders, the CIA began to make plans for overthrowing Goulart. A psychological warfare program approved by CFR agent Henry Kissinger during his chair of the 40 Committee sent U.S. PsyOps disinformation teams to spread fabricated rumors concerning Goulart's Communist affiliations.[34] Actually, Goulart was a wealthy landowner who was opposed to communism, but he was a nationalist who believed that Brazil's resources belonged to the Brazilian people, not to foreign interests.

In early 1964 CFR agent John J. McCloy opened a channel of communication between the CIA and Jack W. Burford, one of the senior executives of the Hanna Mining Company. On February 1964, McCloy traveled to Brazil and tried to convince President Goulart not to go ahead with nationalizing the iron ore industry, but Goulart rejected McCloy's arguments. On the night of March 31, 1964, a CIA-backed military-led coup overthrew Goulart.

Similar accusations have been made about a possible Rockefeller role in the 1973 coup that toppled Chile's Salvador Allende — actually a Castro-CIA joint operation. The CIA had run a powerful propaganda campaign against Allende, directed at convincing the conservative middle classes that Allende was a radical leftist, a would-be despot and a tool of Moscow and Castro.[35]

On his part, Rockefeller agent Castro carried out a propaganda campaign directed at convincing the Left that Allende was not radical enough. If recently surfaced information is true, Allende did not commit suicide: his Cuban security chief, General Patricio de la Guardia, killed him, following Castro's direct orders.[36] Moreover, the fact that Henry Kissinger, a well-known Rockefeller agent, played a key role in the overthrowing and killing of Allende, points to a Rockefeller participation in the event.

In his book *Trading with the Enemy*, Charles Higham offered ample proof of the Rockefellers' treasonous activities during the Second World War.[37] Germany lacked the oil needed to wage the war, but Nazi bombers were dropping tons of bombs on London and other European cities thanks to the gasoline provided by the Rockefeller's Standard Oil. [38]

Nelson Rockefeller's criminal actions around the world became so outrageous that by 1947 there was widespread concern about his treasonous activities in South America. At the same time he was in charge of Latin American intelligence, but he turned a blind eye to Standard Oil's shipments of South American oil to the Nazis before and after the U.S. declared war against Nazi Germany.

After the U.S. got involved in World War II, Nelson Rockefeller moved to Washington, where President Roosevelt named him Coordinator of Inter-American Affairs. It seems, however, his main true task was to coordinate the refueling of German ships in South America from Standard Oil tanks. He also used that office to obtain important South American concessions for his private firm, International Basic Economy Corporation, including a corner on the Colombian coffee market. He immediately raised the price, a move that enabled him to buy several billion dollars worth of real estate in South America and also gave rise to the stereotype of "Yankee Imperialism." It also allowed him to buy several billion dollars worth of drug-growing real estate.

Granted, Nelson Rockefeller was not the only major figure suspected of having engaged in treasonous acts during World War II. Others were Prescott Bush and his attorney Allen Dulles, then OSS Station Chief in Bern, Switzerland, and later Director of CIA. But it is not a coincidence that both were CFR members and partners in Standard Oil Co.[39]

The Rockefellers have always used espionage as their main tool to advance their interests. For example, Stephen Schlesinger, a scholar with expertise in the field of cryptology, wrote an article in which he revealed some of the unethical espionage activities carried out by the CFR conspirators.

According to Schlesinger, before and during the San Francisco Conference of 1945, which created the United Nations Organizations, OSS officers, working on behalf of their CFR masters, spied on the delegates, and intercepted their secret communications with their respective countries to know beforehand each country's negotiating positions. The knowledge of this private information allowed the CFR conspirators to have full control the Conference, to the point that the UN Charter adopted by the delegates was the one the conspirators had already written at the Harold Pratt House in New York.[40]

The CFR: An Organization of Traitors, Thieves, Assassins and Mass Murderers

Currently, thanks mostly to the Internet, it is easy to find the list of people associate with the Clintons who have died under suspicious circumstances.[41] In contrast, there is no "Rockefeller death list" available on the Web. Nevertheless, the list of people the Rockefellers have seen as actual of potential obstacles to their globalist plans and have died under suspicious circumstances is much longer than the Clinton's.

Following orders from their Rockefeller sociopathic masters, CFR agents infiltrated inside the CIA ordered the assassination of many foreign leaders, among them Italy's oil executive Enrico Mattei and Prime Minister Aldo Moro, Dominican Republic's President Rafael L. Trujillo, Panama's Omar Torrijos, Chile's President Salvador Allende, Congo's Patrice Lumumba, South Vietnam's Ngo Dinh Diem, Sweden's Olof Palme, Pakistan's Ali Bhutto, Poland's Lech Kaczynski and Venezuela's Hugo Chavez. They also planned and carried out the assassination of American leaders, such as General George S. Patton, Admiral James Forrestal, U.S. Senator Joseph McCarthy, President John F. Kennedy, his brother Robert Kennedy, and civil rights leader Martin Luther King.

They have also ordered the assassinations of people who, for one or another reason, they have considered a threat to their plans. Among them are, singer John Lennon, Chief of Naval Operations Admiral Jeremy Boorda, ex-CIA director William Colby, Clinton's secretary of commerce Ron Brown, San Jose *Mercury News*' journalist Gary Webb, George W. Bush's biographer J.H Hatfield, editor of *George* magazine and presidential hopeful John F. Kennedy, Jr., U.S. Army corporal and football star Pat Tillman, computer hacker and activist Aaron Swartz, journalist Michael Hastings, and probably even novelists Tom Clancy and Michael Crichton as well as publisher Andrew Breitbar and comedian Joan Rivers, just to mention a few. CFR agents in the U.S. Government and the mainstream press have also played an active part in the cover-up when somebody has tried to investigate those crimes.

CFR sociopaths have also had an active participation in approving mass murder abroad, such as the infamous Phoenix program in Vietnam and the creation of death squads in Latin America. They have also planned and ordered similar crimes in America, such as the massacre of Branch Davidians in Waco, Texas, the killing of several thousand Vietnam vets as the result of Agent Orange, and hundreds of American soldiers as the result of using depleted uranium ammo in Iraq — the so-called "Gulf War Syndrome — the killing of close to 3,000 Americans on September 11th, 2001, and the killing of innocent citizens attending the Boston Marathon on April 15, 2013, just to mention a few.

None of these crimes, however, would have been committed without the tacit approval or express orders of the CFR Godfather and master sociopath, the U.S. President-for-life David Rockefeller.

Acting on behalf of the CFR sociopaths, psychopaths under CFR control have committed massive genocide and assassination,[42] waged unprovoked wars, performed psychological warfare operations against the American and other peoples around the world, and overthrown legitimate government leaders through coups d'état and assassinations, including American Presidents. They have systematically committed fraud and stolen money, property and natural resources from the American people and the peoples of the world. Their ultimate genocidal goal is the elimination of no less than 85 percent of the population of this planet — the "useless eaters"[43] — and the reduction of the survivors to pre-industrial, feudal levels of consumption, after the implementation of a global totalitarian communo-fascist dictatorship they euphemistically call the New World Order, which, of course, they plan to control.

The Rockefeller-controlled Council on Foreign Relations is the logical refuge for sociopaths with a criminal mind, where they can find both their sociopathic soul mates as well as the criminal psychopaths who can carry out their orders to commit all types of crimes.

Chapter 7

The Rockefellers Create the Inquiry, the CFR and the OSS

> *We are all born ignorant, but to stay ignorant is a choice.*
> — Chinese proverb.

U.S. Intelligence Before WWI

Prior to the 1880s, U.S. intelligence activities were mostly centered in supporting military operations in time of war. This intelligence work was mostly tactical, like providing support to deployed forces. Though some strategic intelligence was produced, it mostly consisted in intelligence on the strategic and geopolitical positions of other countries or their participation in a particular conflict.

On March 1882, however, the Office of Naval Intelligence was created within the Department of the Navy to collect intelligence on foreign navies both in peacetime and in war. This was the first permanent U.S. military intelligence organization. A similar organization was created within the Army three years later, the Military Intelligence Division. Its role was to collect foreign and domestic military data for the War Department and the Army.

It was not until the Administration of Theodore Roosevelt, however, that an American President systematically made active use of intelligence for foreign policy purposes. Roosevelt was also a pioneer in the used of illegal covert action. He sent intelligence operatives to Panama to incite a revolution he would use as a pretext to justify before the American people and the world the annexing of the territory needed to dig the Panama Canal. In 1907, Teddy Roosevelt also relied on intelligence which indicated the growing military build-up in Japan as a justification to launch the worldwide cruise of the "Great White Fleet" whose main purpose was displaying the U.S. naval muscle to the world.

Despite these early attempts, most of the early part of the Twentieth Century didn't show an expanded use of intelligence for foreign policy purposes. It did show, however, an expansion of domestic intelligence capabilities. In 1908, the Justice Department established the Bureau of Investigation (the forerunner of the FBI) out of concern that Secret Service agents were spying on members of Congress. By 1916, the Bureau had grown from 34 agents focusing primarily on banking issues to 300 agents with an expanded charter that included internal security, Mexican border smuggling activities, neutrality violations in the Mexican revolution, and Central American unrest. After war broke out in Europe, but before the United States joined the Allied cause, the Bureau turned its attention to activities of German and British nationals within our borders.

Traditionally, the U.S. never has had a civilian intelligence agency. Usually, intelligence needs had been carried out by Military Intelligence, Naval Intelligence, the Secret Service, the Customs House the Bureau of Investigation of the U.S. Department of Justice and the State Department. The first attempt to create a civilian, independent intelligence agency was made by a private group of Wall Street bankers and oil magnates, particularly the Rockefellers.

Most books about the Central Intelligence Agency claim that the CIA was an offshoot of the Office of Strategic Services (OSS). What they don't tell, however, is that the OSS itself was an offshoot of a select group of scholars handpicked by powerful Wall Street bankers to act as spies and intelligence analysts allegedly to brief president Woodrow Wilson about the U.S. options for a postwar world,[1] which eventually turned into a veritable intelligence agency.

Through the winter of 1917-18, this group of intelligence analysts and would-be spies gathered secretly in a hideaway in Manhattan, interpreting and evaluating information and producing intelligence reports they thought were vital to make the world safe. Actually, however, they were working to keep safe the assets abroad of the Wall Street bankers and oil magnates who had recruited them. This secretive group was called the Inquiry.

The Rockefellers Create the First U.S. Civilian Intelligence Agency

In the fall of 1917, Colonel Edward Mandell House, President Woodrow Wilson's confidential adviser, gathered about one hundred prominent men to discuss the postwar world. Dubbing themselves "the Inquiry," they made plans for a peace settlement, which eventually evolved into Wilson's famous "Fourteen Points" he presented to Congress on January 8, 1918.

Their plans advanced for the first time the idea of globalization, calling for the removal of "all economic barriers" between nations (now called "free trade"), equality of trade conditions, and the formation of "a general association of nations" —which later materialized in the short-lived League of Nations and later in the CFR-controlled United Nations Organization.

The idea of creating a private civilian intelligence agency — a concoction of a small group of Wall Street bankers and oil magnates conspiring to advance their interests, particularly the Rockefellers— was a meme,[2] implanted in Wilson's suggestive mind by an obscure, shady character and secret agent of the conspirators, "Colonel" Edward Mandell House, a sort of proto-National Security adviser. House had managed to recruit Wilson and, like most controllers,[3] psychologically manipulated the President until he became his most trusted aide. House developed the *modus operandi* later used by the conspirators through the National Security advisers to manage Americans Presidents — which I call the "mushroom treatment" : keeping them in the dark and feeding them manure.

Edward Mandell House was the son of an English immigrant. He grew up in Houston Texas. Like all agent controllers, House had a flair for making friends who appreciated his discretion, respected his views, and valued his counsel. This talent for winning friends and influencing people remained the basis of his remarkable achievements in politics throughout his life.

After living in Austin since 1886, House moved to New York City in 1902. His biographer, Godfrey Hodgson describes how, soon after, his social connections, acquaintances and friendships among the rich and the powerful were extraordinary.[4] Most likely it was at that time when he associated himself with some Wall Street conspirators and became a secret agent for the Rothschild-Warburg-Rockefeller banking cartel.

House assigned the job of recruiting the scholars-cum-spies for the Inquiry to Walter Lippman, another trusted secret agent of the conspirators. Lippman recruited the initial group of spies and intelligence analysts and managed it. His job was not different from any intelligence officer on the look to recruit spies and intelligence analysts: "What we are on the lookout for is genius — sheer, startling genius, and nothing else will do,"[5] Lippman told some friends.

The initial group — which eventually grew up to 126 scholars — was composed mostly of American socialist-oriented intellectuals that formed the inner circle of the Intercollegiate Society. Under the direction of House's brother-in-law Sydney Mezes,[6] they worked in secret out of the American Geographical Society, doing historical research and writing position papers with plans for the upcoming peace settlement in Paris. The Inquiry was the *de facto* first formally sanctioned civilian U.S. Central Intelligence Agency.

Since its very creation, the Inquiry was organized and acted like an intelligence agency. In the first place, it was divided into several study groups. Some of these groups studied different geographic areas and countries: Africa, Austria-Hungary, the Balkans, Far East, Italy, Latin America, Pacific islands, Russia, Western Asia and Western Europe. Other groups were devoted to study Diplomatic History, Economics, International Law and Cartography.[7] This division was quite similar to the CIA's "desks."

Secondly, the Inquiry's activities were surrounded in secrecy.[8] Even its bland, disingenuous name, "the Inquiry," was adopted to hide the true purpose of the organization.[9]

The Inquiry was an autonomous organization responsible only to the President and secretly paid with funds he controlled. Congress mostly ignored its existence.[10] It bypassed the State Department.[11] The Inquiry's work was kept secret from the American people. It was never mentioned in the mainstream press. Special armed guards patrolled its headquarters day and night.[12]

Thirdly, the Inquiry's activities were divided among four general categories: planning, collecting, digesting, and editing the raw data.[13] This roughly corresponds to what later the CIA described as the intelligence cycle: planning and direction, collection, processing, production and analysis, and dissemination.[14]

Finally, though the Inquiry's alleged sole purpose was to research and report to Wilson to prepare the U.S. case for the coming peace settlement, the fact that it had a Latin American group indicates that its scope was much wider. Actually, the Inquiry was, among other things, the first step to systematically study Latin America's natural resources for its future exploitation by Wall Street bankers and oil corporations — a job later entrusted to the Council on Foreign Relations and the CIA.

In his study of the Inquiry, CFR agent Peter Grose affirms:

> The vision that stirred the Inquiry became the work of the Council on Foreign Relations over the better part of a century: a program of systematic study by groups of knowledgeable specialists of different ideological inclinations would stimulate a variety of papers and reports to guide the statecraft of policymakers. What began as an intellectual response to a juncture of history grew into an institution that would thrive through all the diplomacy of America's twentieth century."[15]

Among the initial members of the Inquiry were Col. House himself (CFR), as well as George Louis Beer, Isaiah Bowman (CFR), Clive Day (CFR), Allen Dulles (CFR), John Foster Dulles (CFR), H. Haskins (CFR), Christian Herter (CFR), Mark Jefferson, Maj. Douglas W. Johnson (CFR), Walter Lippman (CFR), H. Lord (CFR), W. E. Lunt, Sidney E. Mezes (CFR), Charles Seymour (CFR), Whitney H. Shepardson (CFR), James Thomson Shotwell (CFR), Allyn A. Young (CFR), Frank Aydelotte (CFR), Thomas W. Lamont (CFR), Jerome D. Greene (CFR), Archibald C. Coolidge (CFR), Gen. Tasker H. Bliss (CFR), Erwin D. Canham (CFR), W. Averell Harriman (CFR) and Herbert Hoover (CFR)[16] With a few exceptions, most of the Inquiry members later joined the CFR.

There are good reasons for believing that most of them also belonged to the American chapter of the Cecil Rhodes' Round Table groups, a secret society devoted to advance the British rule in the world.

In his 1877 book *Confessions of Faith*, millionaire Cecil Rhodes exposed his idea of creating an organization to bring the whole world under British domination,

> Why should we not form a secret society with but one object, the furtherance of the British Empire, for the bringing of the whole uncivilized world under the British rule, for the recovery of the United States, for the making [of] the Anglo-Saxon race but one empire.[17]

To pursue his dream Rhodes established in 1891 a secret society formed of small cells called the Round Table groups. At his death, he left his immense fortune to the Rhodes Trust, which funded his secret society as well as a Rhodes Scholarship Fund to propagate his ideas in pursuit of a British-controlled world government [18]

On November 1918, shortly before the armistice that would put an end to WWI, Colonel House sailed to Paris with a group of twenty Inquiry members and twenty military intelligence officers, now designated as the "Territorial, Economic and Military Intelligence Division."[19] To coordinate the conspirators' presence at the forthcoming Paris Peace Conference of 1919, bankers Paul Warburg and Bernard Baruch accompanied House in the trip.[20]

A month later, Wilson himself followed suit aboard his presidential cruiser to attend the Conference. He was accompanied in his trip by 20 of the Inquiry scholars now turned into spies.[21] As soon as the Inquiry spies accommodated themselves at the Hotel Crillon, they engaged in their espionage activities. Peter Grose describes these activities in some detail:

> The historical record of the Paris Peace Conference focuses on the meetings of the major powers: Britain, France, Italy, and the United States. To those of the Inquiry, however, and the colleagues they gathered among diplomatic and military officers in Europe, these plenary sessions mattered little. For them the daily teas at the Quai d'Orsay, the bridge games, the breakfast and dinner meetings of experts from a dozen countries gave enduring personal meaning to the peace conference.
>
> In congenial and civilized encounters, they floated ideas in the noncommittal style of the Oxford Common Room; they noted each other's expertise and forged lifelong friendships without regard to age or nationality. In these unrecorded discussions the frontiers of central Europe were redrawn (subject, of course, to their principals' satisfaction), vast territories were assigned to one or another jurisdiction, and economic arrangements were devised on seemingly rational principles.[22]

House and his Wall Street masters feared the European monarchies might become an obstacle to their long-term plans of global domination. Consequently, they wanted the people to believe that "the war [WWI] had been imposed on the peoples of Europe by the monarchies and their aristocracies,"[23] an idea House himself had already implanted in Wilson's mind. Therefore, Wilson became convinced that a postwar settlement should include the elimination of the Austro-Hungarian and German empires and the creation of a number of new democratic states in central Europe.

It was to fulfill the details of this vision — which Wilson was now convinced was his own idea — the argument House used to persuade Wilson to assemble a group of experts to study the problem and suggest solutions. The plan they created was the basis for Wilson's proposals at the Versailles peace conference — later known as Wilson's Fourteen Points.

Profiting from his almost total psychological control over Wilson, House engaged actively in promoting the bankers' interests. This ultimately led to the passage in 1913 of the illegal Federal Reserve Act who created the Federal Reserve Bank and the dreaded Internal Revenue Service, an old dream of Wall Street bankers.[24] Both projects, wrongly attributed to Wilson, had actually been developed by one of the Wall Street conspirators, Nelson Aldrich.

The CFR: The Rockefellers' Secret Intelligence Agency

The newly-created intelligence agency the conspirators disingenuously called the Inquiry served the international bankers so well that they decided to make it permanent. A few days after the end of the Conference, a group of conspirators from the U.S. and Britain Round Table Groups met at the Hotel Majestic, where the British delegation was staying, to talk about how to continue their intelligence and espionage experiment. To this effect, they planned the creation of a permanent espionage agency, with branches in London and New York, to continue serving their interests. As usual, they used an innocuous, disinforming name, Anglo-American Institute of International Affairs, as a cover to hide its real espionage and intelligence activities.

Just a few months later, however, the American branch of the conspirators decided to go independent, and created their own espionage agency. It was named the Council on Foreign Relations, and Colonel House was one of the founding fathers, together with Elihu Root. The initial group of secret agents was augmented with the inclusion of promising new members anxious to get into the espionage business. Prominent among them were Herbert H. Lehman, W. Averell Harriman, and John Foster Dulles. The British conspirators changed the name of their own intelligence agency to Royal Institute of International Affairs, also called Chatham House.

Founded in 1921, the Council on Foreign Relations headquarters is located in the Pratt House, at 58 E. 68th Street, New York. Though in recent years it has opened its doors to a larger number of members (about 4,000), the few scholars who have studied the organization agree that the CFR is actually a Rockefeller front. Since its very creation, the CFR epitomizes all that is despicable, dirty, rotten and treasonous in U.S. foreign policy and most of its domestic policy as well.

The CFR describes itself as a non-partisan organization — in the conspirators' lingo, "non-partisan" actually means "CFR-controlled" — whose only goal is to promote international exchanges to reach a better understanding among countries. This, however, is just what in intelligence and espionage is called a "cover story."[25] This cover story is repeated over and over through the CFR's publications, particularly on its main organ, a quarterly magazine called *Foreign Affairs*. In addition, they frequently publish position papers advancing the Rockefellers' policies.

Nevertheless, on November 25, 1959, they made the mistake of publishing a position paper titled Study No. 7, *Basic Aims of U.S. Foreign Policy*,[26] in which the CFR's true purpose is explained in some detail. According to this study, which was accepted *in toto* by the U.S. Government for its implementation, the long-term main goal of U.S. foreign policy must be the "building (of) a new international order (which) may be responsible to world aspirations for peace (and) for social and economic change. ... An international order ... including states labeling themselves as Socialist."[27]

It was not until January 29, 1991, that President George H. W. Bush, a CFR member, let the cat out of the bag in his "Toward a New World Order," speech to a joint session of Congress.[28]

In his laudatory study about the Inquiry, CFR agent Peter Grose inadvertently exposed the true character and purpose of both the Inquiry and the CFR as veritable intelligence agencies at the service of the Rockefellers, Wall Street bankers, oil magnates and CEO's of transnational corporations.[29] He was right. The CFR is actually an intelligence and espionage agency, and operates like one.

Like all intelligence agencies, the Council on Foreign Relations is a semi-secret society: although it is not secret where its headquarters is located, and who its senior executives are, nobody really knows what are its secret activities, mush less its secret goals. Like all intelligence agencies, the CFR has listed members and secret ones.[30] Like all intelligence agencies, the CFR has a department specialized in information collection and analysis. But, contrary to conventional intelligence agencies, the intelligence analysts of this department do not work in-house, but live a parasitical life disseminated among government jobs in the CIA, the NSC, the State and Defense departments and the Pentagon, as well as in private institutions such as the mainstream press, universities, think tanks and non-profit foundations.

As needed, the CFR intelligence analysts periodically produce their own National Intelligence Estimates — they don't call them NIEs, but that is exactly what they are— but, because of the fact that they have been written from the point of view of the conspirators' interests, they greatly differ from the officially produced CIA NIEs written from the point of view of the U.S. interests. This explains why the NIEs produced by the CIA are largely ignored or forced to change according to the conspirators' political and propaganda needs.

Typical of these CFR NIEs is George Kennan's (CFR) 1947 article "The Sources of Soviet Conduct," published in *Foreign Affairs*, written under the pseudonym "X,"[31] explaining his — actually the conspirators' — theory of "containment." According to Kennan, the U.S. role in the coming Cold War should be limited to containing the expansion of Soviet Communism, not fighting to win it. Soon after, President Truman made Containment the core of "his" Truman Doctrine.

Another example of CFR NIE is the infamous National Security Study Memorandum 200, allegedly written by CFR senior secret agent Henry Kissinger but actually a CFR collective product. NSC 200, Implications of Worldwide Population Growth for U.S. Security and Overseas Interests, dated December 10, 1974, but kept secret for many years, delineated a genocidal policy of depopulating of much of the African continent, to allow U.S. transnational corporations, not Africans, exploit the continent's natural resources.[32]

A more recent example of CFR NIE is the September 2000 Report entitled "Rebuilding America's Defenses: Strategy, Forces and Resources For a New Century," published by the CFR-controlled neocon group Project for a New American [Imperialist] Century (PNAC)[33] The Report mentions that, in order to transform the U.S. military for the new challenges it will face, the process of transformation, "… even if it brings revolutionary change, is likely to be a long one, *absent some catastrophic and catalyzing event — like a new Pearl Harbor.*" [Emphasis added] As if on cue, exactly a year later the 9/11 events provided on a silver platter the new

Pearl Harbor the CFR conspirators were craving.

Like all intelligence agencies, the CFR has a department specializing in psychological warfare, subversion, insurgency, and paramilitary operations — functions that, until recently, had been mostly carried out by one of its branches: the CIA. Currently, however, after the conspirators gained more control over most key U.S. government areas, including a large segment of senior U.S. military officers, they don't need the CIA as much, and have transferred some of these functions directly to the U.S. military.

Like all intelligence agencies, the main job of some CFR members is to recruit spies and agents of influence,[34] as a way to infiltrate other organizations they want to control, in the U.S. and abroad. In the case of ambitious and intelligent, but morally and ethically challenged young people, once the CFR recruiters find them and decide to proceed with their recruitment, the first step is usually granting them a Rhodes Scholarship. If they successfully pass this first step, they are offered a grant to study at the London School of Economics.

Eventually, the ones who proved their worth are spring boarded to key positions in the government and the media where they act as secret agents of influence advancing the CFR conspirators' views and policies.

This was, for example, the case of Bill Clinton. Once Georgetown professor Carroll Quigley, a CFR recruiter, detected young Bill, and it was verified that he had the right stuff, he was offered a Rhodes Scholarship. Life proved that the selection was the right one for the CFR conspirators.

Another successful CFR recruiter is Zbigniew Brzezinski. He was the hidden hand behind the recruitment of an unknown Georgia peanut farmer who had become interested in politics. He invited him to join the recently-created Trilateral Commission and later his CFR masters pushed him into the White House.[35]

More recently, Brzezinski hit the jackpot again by bringing to the White House another potential CFR operative he had spotted. There are clues indicating that, while he was a professor at Columbia University in the early 1980s, Brzezinski recruited a young, ethically challenged, ambitious, opportunistic student: Barack Hussein Obama. One of these clues is that when Obama was studying politics, he wrote a paper whose main topic was Soviet nuclear disarmament. The paper was heavily influenced by Brzezinski's crazy ideas.[36]

As author Webster Griffin Tarpley pointed out, this may explain why

Obama is so secretive about his years at Columbia University, where all his records have been locked and placed out of the scrutiny of researchers and the press. Evidently, there are things in Obama's past the conspirators don't want the American people to know about.[37]

The CFR has been very successful in placing its agents of influence in the mainstream media. These are the cases of Dan Rather, Barbara Walters, Jim Lehrer, Diane Sawyer, Bill Moyers, Charlie Rose and George Stephanopoulos. Of lately, they have successfully recruited Hollywood stars such as George Clooney, Evangelina Jolie, Warren Beatty and Richard Dreyfuss, just to mention a few of them.

The Council on Foreign Relations has become in practice the closest the U.S. has to a Communo-Fascist Party in power. Like the Communist Party of the Soviet Union or the Nazi Party in Germany used to, CFR members have secret meetings where policies are discussed, and then they exert pressure on the government to guarantee that these policies are carried out. Like members of a Communist or Fascist party, they follow a strict party discipline: once a policy is approved in their secret councils, it becomes the Party line and they push it with all their force and resources. Like members of a Communist or Fascist party, they act in block, and no inner dissidence on key issues is allowed.[38]

This block acting was experienced first-hand by President Lyndon Johnson. In November 1967, the group of presidential advisors called the Senior Advisory Group on Vietnam, Dean Acheson, Robert Lovett, John McCloy, McGeorge Bundy, Walt W. Rostow, Robert McNamara and Paul Nitze, met with President Johnson, and all of them supported the continuation of the war.

But in early 1968, the very same advisors who had been hawkishly pushing Johnson to continue and escalate the war, had a long meeting with the President, at which Johnson asked each of them to express his personal view about the conflict. All of them, without exception, suddenly manifested themselves against the war. The hawks had turned overnight into doves. It goes without saying that all them, without a single exception, were CFR members just following the Party Line already decided at the Harold Pratt House.

According to a witness, Johnson was visibly shocked by the magnitude of the defection. A few days later he went on television to announce the de-escalation of the war and his decision not to run for a new presidential term. The *New York Times* reported that the decision was a stunning surprise even to Johnson's close associates.[39]

The ultimate goal of the CFR is the complete takeover of America to change it into a socialist communo-fascist dictatorship. The final steps of the implementation of this plan took place under the evil eye[40] of the latest CFR puppet, Mr. Barry Soetoro (a.k.a. Barack Hussein Obama).

The OSS: Covert Operations for the Rockefellers

Most authors who attribute to President Roosevelt the creation of the Office of Strategic Services miss a very important point: like most American presidents before and after him, Franklin D. Roosevelt was a puppet put in the White House and closely manipulated by the CFR puppeteers.[41] Prominent in this group of close advisors, who FDR euphemistically called his "brain trust," were Harry Dexter White, Harry Hopkins, George Marshall and Henry Morgenthau, Jr., all of them CFR secret agents. They were an early version of today's National Security Council advisors surrounding Americans presidents.

Therefore, it makes sense to conclude that, like all important decisions made by American presidents since Wilson, the creation of the OSS was an idea developed by the Rockefellers at the CFR and implanted in Roosevelt's brain by his CFR controllers. Moreover, given the fact that the Rockefellers already had their own intelligence agency, the CFR, they had no need for another one. Consequently, despite claims to the contrary the OSS was never a true intelligence agency, but just an undercover military arm of the CFR created for the sole purpose of conducting covert operations on behalf of its CFR masters.

Contrary to the widely accepted myth, the true purpose of the OSS was not to care for the interests of the American people, but the interests of the Wall Street bankers, oil magnates, and owners of big corporations who had been doing good business arming the Nazi war machine. Contrary to what is written in most history books, the true goal of the CFR conspirators was not to defeat their Nazi partners, but to save them after Germany's catastrophic collapse — a job they accomplished to a great extent thanks to the OSS.

General William Donovan, the man selected by the Wall Street bankers and oil magnates to direct the OSS, was a millionaire Wall Street corporate lawyer. In 1929 he created his own law firm, Donovan, Leisure, Newton and Lumbard.[42]

His right hand, Allen Dulles, was a Wall Street lawyer and senior member of the Rockefellers' Council on Foreign Relations. Through his OSS office in Bern, Switzerland, Dulles kept an eye in the protection of the interests of CFR members. Sullivan & Cromwell, the law firm Dulles had worked for since 1926,[43] had strong business ties with the I.G. Farben, the chemical firm producer of the Zyklon B, the lethal gas used to kill the camp's prisoners. It also represented the United Fruit Company and other Rockefellers' interests. John Foster Dulles, Allen's brother and partner in Sullivan & Cromwell, had close ties to Carmel Offie, William Bullitt, George Kennan, Paul Nitze and James Forrestal, all of them CFR agents or assets.

Most senior OSS members were secret CFR agents, and many of them had been part of the Inquiry. As such, they had played a key role in the behind-the-curtains machinations of the U.S. delegation to the Versailles negotiations. Most of them later played important roles in the development of U.S. intelligence and national security policy for many decades.

In his book *OSS: The Secret History of America's First Intelligence Service*, by far the best study written on the subject,[44] author R. Harris Smith paints a picture of systemic chaos in the OSS organization. According to Smith, a Captain who had led an OSS team behind Japanese lines in China told him that, "All officers were quite junior, and as long as everybody did his work few of us bothered with military regulations, high brass was unlikely to inspect."[45]

In 1942 Hoover's FBI began documenting what they saw as a communist group inside the OSS. But in his book *OSS*, Smith mentions the fact that "In later life he [Donovan] developed an emotional hatred of Communism."[46] Smith seems to ignore, however, that like most CFR members, Donovan's "emotional hatred of Communism" only appeared after his CFR masters had decided that Soviet Communism, a monster they had created, would be the appropriate replacement for Nazi Germany, another monster they also had created.

Actually, Donovan was not interested in ideologies. Like his CFR masters, he changed ideologies like snakes shed their skins, according to the needs of the moment. Contrary to the prevalent myth, the OSS was not an intelligence agency working for the benefit of the American public. Actually it was the conspirators' Fifth Column infiltrated into the U.S. armed forces to sabotage the efforts of true patriots such as General George S. Patton to destroy the Nazi German war machine and win the war as soon as possible to save the lives of American soldiers.

But the Rockefellers and their CFR minions had other plans. Forced to fight the Nazi war machine because the monster they had contributed to create had turned into a Frankenstein's monster, their secret plan was to substitute it with another monster they also had created: Soviet Russia.

It seems that the OSS's main mission was to prevent the American military from winning the war too quickly and capture Nazi war criminals before the OSS provide ways for them to escape.[47] Their secondary mission was to make favorable conditions for the Soviets to get control over most of Eastern Europe. This perhaps explains why leftists and outright communist militants so extensively composed the OSS.

Nevertheless, there were some obstacles in the path of their plan. Despite of the fact that the CFR conspirators controlled a few senior Army officers such as Dwight Eisenhower, George Marshall and Matthew Ridgway, most of them were true American patriots who firmly believed that their mission was defeating the Nazis. Unfortunately, they were wrong. They ignored that the true goal of the war was protecting the conspirators' investments in Germany and allowing the top Nazi criminals to escape justice.

Nevertheless, the fact that some OSS members were also true American patriots who firmly believed their main role was fighting the Nazis is irrelevant. They had been recruited under a false flag and, wittingly or unwittingly, were helping the Rockefellers and other American pro-Nazis to help the Nazi thugs avoid paying for their war crimes.

Since the beginning of the war, the Rockefeller's Standard Oil had been supplying through North Africa the gasoline the Nazi war machine needed so badly. But, after the Allied invasion of North Africa, Standard Oil was no longer able to supply their Nazi friends with oil through that route. Standard Oil then began shipping oil to the Nazis through the neutral countries of Spain and Switzerland. Therefore, it is not a coincidence that most OSS officers in Spain and Switzerland had close links to Standard Oil.

Despite Donovan's apparent openness to fill the lower ranks of the OSS with lefties and communists, corporations like J. Walter Thompson, Paramount Pictures, and Goldman, Sachs had actually loaned many of their senior executive officers to the OSS. And Standard Oil Company generously provided some of its trusted men, now changed into OSS officers, to watch operations in Spain and Switzerland to ensure that gasoline shipments to Nazi Germany went unmolested. [48] On his part, Allen Dulles kept himself busy hiding the close connections, up to shared ownership, between U.S. and Nazi corporations.[49]

On one occasion, FBI Director J. Edgar Hoover's presented Donovan with dossiers containing factual evidence showing that three OSS members had fought with the Abraham Lincoln Brigade during the Spanish Civil war and were affiliated with the Communist Party. When Hoover demanded their separation from the organization, Donovan dismissed the issue by answering, "I know they are Communists; that's why I hired them."[50]

It would be a mistake, however, to conclude that Donovan himself had any sympathy for leftists or communists. Following a policy carefully planned at the Harold Pratt House, the General was using leftists and communists as unwitting tools in preparation for the coming Cold War. Though in theory the OSS was simply an intelligence agency, it played an important role in helping the CFR conspirators implement their foreign policy decisions. But, as author R. Harris Smith noticed, the OSS was fully under the control of the CFR conspirators,

> While Donovan diligently sought left-wing intellectuals and activists for the operational and research branches of the OSS, he saw no incongruity in appointing corporate attorneys and business executives as OSS administrators. [51]

Even so, despite the widespread criticism, one has to recognize that the OSS did a wonderful job. The only problem is that it was a job on behalf of its Wall Street masters. It had nothing to do with their purported one, and the true OSS goals had nothing to do with benefiting the interests of the United States or its citizens. Unfortunately, this was a vice inherited by the CIA.

The Chase Bank: David's Private Intelligence Agency

As I mentioned above, the CFR is both an intelligence agency and a think tank. Nevertheless, for the daily gathering of information from all around the world, David created his own private intelligence agency: the Chase Bank.[52]

From the bank's 60-story Wall Street skyscraper, David controlled Chase's domestic and international banking operations. Under his command the bank expanded first in the United States and the British-dominated Caribbean area primarily through the use of simple branch banking. But it has penetrated the more difficult continental regions by acquiring "affiliates."

Chase has branches in most important cities of Central and South America as well as the Caribbean area. Its branches in Europe are in located London, Paris, Hamburg, Munich, Milan, Rome and Athens. Main branches in Asia are in Tokyo, Osaka, Seoul, Singapore and Taipei. Even in the most confrontational days of the Cold War, Chase had branches in the Soviet Union.

Like all banks, the main purpose of the Chase bank has always been using other people's money to make money. Nevertheless, since he became Chairman of the Board, David began expanding its purpose until it became veritable intelligence agency.

Chase employs more than sixteen thousand persons all around the world. Surprisingly, many of them are not banking technical experts but specialize in fields far removed from banking such as linguists, biologists, engineers, journalists, mathematicians, geologists, political scientists, anthropologists, agronomists and urbanists. These are highly talented and highly paid people.

These people are in close contact with the local politicians, businessmen and journalists, so that they are usually well informed. Given their privileged location in the main capitals and cities of most countries in the world, they perform a similar job as the officers of CIA, Mossad, MI6 and other intelligence agencies. Their main job is gathering information, analyze it and pass the resulting intelligence to the main bank in New York.

As the man on the top of this intelligence gathering apparatus David was in a privileged position to get first access to news not only about what was happening but also about what was likely to happen — sometimes as a direct result of his machinations behind the curtains like a modern Wizard of Oz.

Whenever David made one of these frequent trips abroad, his staff, using the information gathered by his spies in the local Chase branches, prepared a book-size detailed script informing him about whom he was going to meet, what to tell and what to ask. He carefully followed his script when he traveled.

Chapter 8

The Rockefellers Create the CIA

And ye shall know the truth
And the truth shall make you free.
— John VIII-XXXII.[1]

On July 26, 1947, President Harry S. Truman signed into law the National Security Act, establishing the National Security Council (NSC). It also created the Central Intelligence Agency (CIA) as well as the Secretary of Defense, the Joints Chiefs of Staff and a separate Air Force branch of the military. This marked the official beginning of the Cold War, an artificial creation of the CFR conspirators.[2]

If one is to believe the accepted myth created by the Rockefellers and their CFR agents, the CIA was to be just an obedient tool in the hands of the President. According to this view, "The agency has one main client, the President of the United States, who is also the agency's boss. Agency people are the President's men."[3]

Nevertheless, as the cases of John F. Kennedy and Donald Trump have evidenced, the U.S. President is the CIA's boss only if the Rockefellers and their CFR agents are the President's bosses.

The National Security Act and the Creation of the CIA

The NSC was allegedly created to manage the bloated foreign policy, military and intelligence apparatus of the U.S. Government to prevent events such as the Pearl Harbor surprise attack from happening again.[4] But the National Security Act, like all important documents in the history of the U.S. since the beginning of the past century, such as Wilson's Fourteen Points, the League of Nations, the Federal Reserve Bank, the Federal Income Tax, the Lend Lease, the Containment Doctrine,[5] the Marshall Plan,[6] the Alliance for Progress,[7] FEMA, as well as the nefarious Patriot Act and the Office of Homeland Security, up to Obamacare, have been written by the CFR conspirators at the Harold Pratt House in Manhattan and placed on the President's desk for him to sign.

Given the fact that at the time the NSC was created some American presidents were not fully under the conspirators' control, the NSC's true purpose was to create a shadow organization whose members, acting as blinders, controlled the Presidents by controlling the information reaching them. It is not a coincidence that, since its creation, most National Security Council members have been secret CFR agents.

According to the official history, it was mainly dissatisfaction with Roosevelt's decision-making processes what led to the creation of the National Security Council. Its creation, the official story goes, was a key initiative of President Harry S. Truman, who had assumed office in April 1945. Truman had long sought to unify the armed forces into one Cabinet department.

But information now available shows a different picture. Following the conspirators' *modus operandi*, the National Security Act was the creation of CFR agents working in the shadows behind the backs of the American people to advance the Rockefellers' interests.

In this case, two of them, Navy Secretary James V. Forrestal and his former business colleague and fellow CFR member who had served as vice chairman of the War Production Board, Ferdinand Eberstadt, were commissioned to study the effects of the unification of national security activities and to recommend a government organization that would be most effective in protecting the country.[8] The subsequent Eberstadt Report (actually the CFR Report) envisioned a National Security Council chaired by the President (or, in his absence, the Vice President), which would include the four service secretaries, the secretary of state, and the chairman of a board to coordinate allocation of resources.[9] This approach, however, drew criticism from non CFR-controlled people as being incompatible with the concept of the President as chief executive under the Constitution. According to one scholar, Eberstadt was trying to modify the Presidency as an institution[10] — which was exactly what the CFR conspirators were trying to do.

As a result of the Eberstadt Report, on December 1945 President Truman sent a special message to Congress requesting a statute to establish a single department of national defense and a single chief of staff, but without mentioning the creation of a national security council. Truman, not fully under the conspirators' control, feared that any way that the President would be bound by the council consensus it would infringe on his constitutional powers.

Finally, after several months of negotiations, the new national security legislation was enacted on July 26, 1947, as the National Security Act of 1947.[11] In addition to establishing the CIA, it created the National Security Council, which included the President, the secretary of state, the new secretary of defense, the secretaries of the military departments, and the chairman of the new National Security Resources Board.[12] Other officials who had been confirmed by the Senate could be added as NSC members by the President as needed. According to the act, the responsibility of the NSC was:

> To advise the President with respect to the integration of domestic, foreign, and military policies relating to the national security so as to enable the military services and the other departments and agencies of the Government to cooperate more effectively in matters involving the national security.[13]

The NSC Authorizes the CIA to Conduct Covert Operations

The National Security Act gave the National Security Council just advisory, not executive powers, much less gave the newly-created CIA authority to carry on covert operations abroad. Nevertheless, CFR agent Allen Dulles knew its real significance when he said that the National Security Act "had given Intelligence a more influential position in our government than Intelligence enjoys in any other government in the world."[14] Nevertheless, just a few months later, on December 1947, NSC directive 4/A made the Director of Central Intelligence responsible for psychological warfare.

Moreover, less than a year after it was created, the NSC pushed the envelope even further and illegally assumed executive powers. On June 18, 1948, the National Security Council produced NSC 10/2, a directive that superseded NSC 4/A and was kept secret from the American government and people for many long years. NSC 10/2 authorized the CIA to not only conduct psychological but also all types of covert operations.[15]

In paragraph 5 the document specified that "covert operations" were,

> Understood to be all activities conducted or sponsored by the U.S. Government against hostile foreign states or groups or in support of friendly foreign states or groups but which are so planned and executed that any U.S. Government responsibility for them is not evident to unauthorized persons and that if uncovered the U.S. Government can plausible deny any responsibility for them. Specifically, such operations shall include any covert activities related to: propaganda, economic warfare, preventive direct action, including sabotage, anti-sabotage, demolition and evacuation measures, subversion against hostile states, including assistance to underground resistance movements, guerrillas and refugee liberation groups, and support of indigenous anticommunist elements in threatened countries of the free world.[16]

NSC 10/2 created *de facto* a new semi-independent, highly secret organization within the CIA under the intentionally vague name of Office of Special Projects (OSP). Soon after, the OSP was renamed with the even more innocuous name Office of Policy Coordination (OPC).[17] Author John Loftus found out that the Office of Policy Coordination was actually a secret CFR-controlled covert action department hidden from the American public and depending directly from Secretary of Defense James V. Forrestal, a CFR agent, and what Loftus called "the Dulles [John Foster Dulles, a senior CFR agent] faction in the State Department."[18]

It seems, however, that the idea for NSC 10/2 was not the result of an afterthought but of a secret part of the initial plan. It was not a coincidence that the persons who launched the idea and backed it were CFR members James Forrestal, George Marshall and George Kennan.[19]

It was obvious that these covert operations may include the destabilization of foreign governments, as well as the overthrowing and even assassination of foreign leaders. CIA assassins even created a euphemism for it: "executive action." According to the Church Committee's congressional report,

> In addition to investigating actual assassination plots, the Committee has examined a project known as Executive Action that included, as one element, the development of a general, standby assassination capability.[20]

A few years later, in 1954, a Secret Report of a Special Study Group (Doolittle Committee) on the Covert Activities of the Central Intelligence Agency found out that the CFR conspirators had gone a step further when in a secret document they advised:

> It is now clear that we are facing an implacable enemy whose avowed objective is world domination by whatever means and at whatever cost. There are no rules in such a game. Hitherto acceptable norms of human conduct do not apply. If the United States is to survive, long-standing American concepts of "fair play" must be reconsidered. We must develop effective espionage and counterespionage services and must learn to subvert, sabotage and destroy our enemies by more clever, more sophisticated and more effective methods than those used against us.[21]

Finally, the CFR conspirators had created the perfect tool to carry out their dirty work. Translated into plain language, "communist" meant any person who threatened the interests of the globalist conspirators who control the Secret Government of the United States and their military-industrial-banking complex. Unfortunately, once they successfully carried out abroad the covert activities mentioned in these documents, the CFR conspirators realized that those covert activities could be effectively used against their main domestic enemy: the people of the United States. And they did it with extreme dedication, enthusiasm and *gusto*.

As I mentioned above, the NSC 10/2 was the document that gave the CIA *carte blanche* to carry out all types of covert operations. An interesting detail is that it was written in June 1948, just a few months after the success of the Bogotazo Operation. So, it was just authorizing *a posteriori* something that already existed. According to the NSC 10/2,

> The National Security Council, taking cognizance of the vicious
> covert activities of the USSR, its satellite countries and Commu-
> nist groups to discredit and defeat the aims and activities of the
> United States and other Western powers, has determined that, in
> the interests of world peace and U.S. national security, the overt
> foreign activities of the U.S. Government must be supplemented
> by covert operations.
>
> The Central Intelligence Agency is charged by the National
> Security Council with conducting espionage and counterespionage
> operations abroad. It therefore seems desirable, for operational rea-
> sons, not to create a new agency for covert operations, but in time
> of peace to place the responsibility for them within the structure of
> the Central Intelligence Agency and correlate them with espionage
> and counterespionage operations under the overall control of the
> Director of Central Intelligence.
>
> Therefore, under the authority of Section 102(d)(5) of the na-
> tional Security Act of 1947, the National Security Council hereby
> directs that in time of peace:
>
> a. A new office of Special Projects shall be created within the
> Central Intelligence Agency to plan and conduct covert operations;
> and in coordinations.
>
> b. A higly qualified person, nominated by the Secretary of State,
> acceptable to the director of Central Intelligence and approved by
> the National Security Council, shall be appointed as Chief of the
> Office of Special Projects.
>
> c. The Chief of the Office of Special Projects shall report di-
> rectly to the Director of Central Intelligence. For purposes of secu-
> rity and of flexibility of operations, and to the maximum degree
> consistent with efficiency, the Office of Special Projects shall op-
> erate independently of other components of Central Intelligence
> Agency.[22]

NSC. 10/2 made no mention about assassination of foreign leaders and
other people who opposed the conspirators' plans, but a letter written by a
"consultant" included among the documents gives an idea of what they had
in mind:

> You will recall that I mentioned that the local circumstances under

which a given means might be used might suggest the technique to be used in that case. I think that gross divisions in presenting this subject might be (1) bodies left with no hope of the cause of death being determined by the most complete autopsy and chemical examination, (2) bodies left in such circumstances as to simulate accidental death, (3) bodies left in such circumstances as to simulate suicidal death, (4) bodies left with residua that simulate those caused by natural diseases.[23]

By creating NSC 10/2, which authorized the CIA to break the laws of this nation, the CFR agents infiltrated into the National Security Council who wrote and approved it under the pretext of protecting this country committed themselves a major crime against America. They licensed a U.S. Government agency, whose job was to defend and protect the laws of the land as expressed in the Constitution, to break the law as they wished. NSC. 10/2, actually authorized CIA officers to do whatever they wanted, except telling the truth or getting caught.

The OPC became the espionage and counterintelligence branch of the Central Intelligence Agency. CFR agent Frank Wisner, the person the conspirators selected to run their Mafia-like organization, was given a free hand in creating a criminal organization. This initial capital sin molded the CIA's amoral ethos and marked the behavior of the Agency through all these years. But even a perfunctory look at the CIA's true origins show that its treasonous activities have never been by mistake, but by design.

Frank Wisner was a troubled, mentally unstable man,[24] with the mentality of a gangster. To fill the new positions at the OPC he needed the very best ruthless lawyers money could buy. He searched for them in Wall Street, among the lawyers and bankers who, like him, had joined the OSS gang. According to his own confession, to do this dirty work Wisner wanted amateurs, not former cops, ex-military, or ex-FBI agents.[25]

Wisner knew that professionals might easily cut through the disinformational fog and discover the true purpose of the new organization — which was not the protection of the interests of the American people. So, he recruited "patriotic, decent, well-meaning, and brave" men who, as he later admitted, "were also uniquely unsuited to the grubby, necessarily devious world of intelligence"[26] and, therefore, easy to manipulate and kept in the dark about the true purposes of the organization.

Time proved that Wisner was absolutely right. Some years later the

CIA made the mistake of hiring former FBI agent Bill Harvey, a seasoned professional. Soon after, Harvey discovered that Angleton's disciple, Kim Philby, of the British MI6, was actually a Soviet mole.[27]

Every once in a while some conspiracy theorist *aficionado* airs his suspicions that the CIA has fallen under the control of an evil, internal rogue cabal, that is using it to advance their own stingy monetary interests. This idea, however, is not new. It was mentioned long time ago, and further reinforced by Senator Frank Church, when, during the Congressional investigation he chaired to investigate the Agency's misbehavior, he called the CIA a "rogue elephant."[28]

The notion that JFK was assassinated by a rogue group of "disgruntled CIA agents, anti-Castro Cubans and members of the Mafia" is advanced by Jesse Ventura in a book he wrote about the JFK assassination.[29] The truth, however, is quite different. No rogue faction is controlling the CIA. Actually, since its very creation, the whole CIA has been a rogue organization that has nothing to do with the government of this country and has never worked for the people who foot the bill: the American taxpayers.

If there is a rogue group working inside the CIA, it is a disorganized one consisting of a small group of true American patriots (or, naive fools if you wish), who, after being recruited under a false flag,[30] have suddenly realized that they had been working for the CIA year after year under the false impression that they were doing so for the benefit of their country and the American people.[31] Actually, the true and only "rogue elephant" that has planned and ordered all the evil things the CIA has carried out and is blamed for, is the Council on Foreign Relations.

Furthermore, there is evidence that the National Security Council, like most of the aberrations created by the CFR conspirators, is a Rockefeller baby. In December 1955 Nelson Rockefeller decided to become the next President of the U.S. and resigned from his position as President Eisenhower's Assistant of Foreign Policy and as head of the secret "Forty Committee" in charge of overseeing the CIA's covert operations.

Just after sending his resignation, he also sent a two-page memorandum to the President in which he expressed his conviction that the normal approach of the secretary of state in control of foreign policy was not adequate at a time when the U.S. had become a global power. His recommendations to fix what he saw as problem are quite revealing: Nelson suggested replacing the different cabinet agencies of the government with a sort of super government secretly acting behind the backs of the American people, responsible to a single man, the President.[32] Obviously, Nelson's idea was to become America's first dictator once he became the U.S. President.

Nelson never achieved his presidential dream, but with the creation of the National Security Council, American Presidents got dictatorial powers. The only difference with traditional dictators all around the world is that the American ones are puppets under CFR control.

Just recently, in a September 15, 2017, talk at a Geoengineeringwatch.org conference, Kevin Shipp, a whistleblower who held several high-ranking positions in the CIA, told the attendants that the CIA was created through the Council on Foreign Relations with no congressional approval.[33] Well, this is new only for people whose only source of information is the CFR controlled mainstream media, because it only confirms what I wrote about in detail in my 2010 book *Psychological Warfare and the New World Order*.[34]

Why Did the Rockefellers Create the CIA?

There is a question that may come to mind: Why did the Rockefellers need a new intelligence agency, the CIA, when they already had two good intelligence agencies: the CFR and Chase?

The answer is relatively simple: they didn't need another *intelligence* agency, and did not create a new one, because, as I explained above, the CIA has never been an intelligence agency in the true sense of the word — at least, not for the Rockefellers and the CFR conspirators who created it. So, again, why did they create the CIA if not to profit from its information gathering and intelligence analysis capabilities?

According to an anecdote, when Soviet leader Joseph Stalin was informed that the Vatican had declared war against Nazi Germany after getting the news that the Red Army had already surrounded Berlin with an iron choke hold, he laughed heartily and asked: "How many divisions does the Pope have?"

Like the Vatican, the Rockefellers and other Wall Street bankers and oil magnates had enormous economic power to buy supporters and critics, but they also needed physical power to threaten the cowards and punish the rebels. So, since late in the 19th century they began using the U.S. armed forces as their military arm to enforce their policies. The long list of American military interventions all around the world, beginning with the Spanish-Cuban-American war,[35] marked the beginning of "American imperialism," — or, more properly, "Rockefeller Wall Street imperialism." These military interventions on behalf of the Wall Street Mafia, which have gained the U.S. so many enemies around the world, are the direct result of this raw deal for the American people.

CFR agent Donald Rumsfeld was known to often quote a line from Al Capone: "You will get more with a kind word and a gun than with a kind word alone." It seems that the tough talk of the Chicago mobster closely resembles the guiding philosophy of the Rockefellers and the Wall Street Mafia: "You will get more with a lie and an army than with a lie alone."

A perfunctory analysis of American military interventions all around the world since the mid-1800s shows how the Wall Street and oil magnates have used the U.S. Army and Navy, to carry out their Mafia-like criminal actions against other peoples and governments.[36]

Paradoxically, one the strongest critics of the Wall Street conspirators who used the U.S. armed forces, particularly the Marines, to advance their private interests was a military hero and a proud Marine himself: Brigadier General Smedley D. Butler.[37]

As Gen. Butler put it bluntly,

> War is a racket. It has always been. It is possibly the oldest, easily the most profitable, surely the most vicious. It is the only one international in scope. It is the only one in which the profits are reckoned in dollars and the losses in lives.
>
> A racket is best described, I believe, as something that is not what it seems to the majority of the people. Only a small "inside" group knows what it is about. It is conducted for the benefit of the very few, at the expense of the very many. Out of war a few people make huge fortunes,
>
> In the World War [he is referring to WWI] a mere handful garnered the profits of the conflict. At least 21,000 new millionaires and billionaires were made in the United States during the World War. That many admitted their huge blood gains in their income tax returns. How many other war millionaires falsified their tax returns no one knows.
>
> How many of these war millionaires shouldered a rifle? How many of them dug a trench? How many of them knew what it meant

to go hungry in a rat-infested dugout? How many of them spent sleepless, frightened nights, ducking shells and shrapnel and machine gun bullets? How many of them parried a bayonet thrust of an enemy? How many of them were wounded or killed in battle?[38]

General Butler was right. Even a perfunctory list of U.S. military interventions since 1890 shows that just few parts of this planet have not experienced first hand the presence of American troops protecting the interests of Wall Street bankers and oil magnates.

Eventually, however, the world changed, and it became more and more risky and problematic for the CFR conspirators to keep openly using the U.S. armed forces, particularly in Latin America, as the main tool to impose their will upon other peoples.

The fact was acknowledged by CFR agent Franklin D. Roosevelt himself in one of his meetings with Winston Churchill during World War II, when he pointed out that open colonialism, as it had been practiced in the past, was no longer an appropriate option in the Caribbean.[39] This was not only because the Marines had become a worldwide symbol of American aggression and oppression, but also because a growing discontent among senior officers of the U.S. armed forces, not fully under the control of the conspirators, was making more difficult to continue openly using the American military for their nefarious purposes.

Still, the Rockefellers and their CFR conspirators needed an option short of the use of direct U.S. military action when coercion and intimidation alone could not do the job. Consequently, perhaps following Sun Tzu's dictum that all warfare is based on deception,[40] they decided to create their own illegal private army. And the best way to create this army without alarming the American people and the world was by making it invisible. Therefore, they created it surreptitiously, keeping it hidden from public scrutiny under the cover of a legitimate U.S. government organization.

To such effect, using their secret agents infiltrated in the U.S. government, in 1947 the Rockefellers and their CFR conspirators forced down the throats of naive, or corrupt American politicians, the National Security Act, which created an organization they planned to use to fully exert their puppeteers' control over American Presidents: the National Security Council. And an important component of the National Security Act was the creation of a Central Intelligence Agency, which they never planned to use as an intelligence agency, but as a cover to hide their military arm, now in the form of covert operations.

When President Truman disbanded the OSS at the end of WWII and refused to create a Central Intelligence Agency, CFR member Allen Dulles went freelance and created a private, secret one. It operated from a secret room at the Harold Pratt House in Manhattan.[41] Finally Truman relented to the conspirators' pressure and created the CIA. A few years later, who was appointed CIA director? None other than Allen Dulles.

The first two CIA Directors were Admiral Roscoe Hillekoetter (not a CFR member), who was soon after substituted by General Walter B. Smith (CFR). In 1950, Bedell Smith recruited Dulles to oversee the CIA's covert operations as Deputy Director for Plans. That same year Dulles was promoted to Deputy Director of Central Intelligence, second in the intelligence hierarchy. After the election of Dwight Eisenhower in 1952, Bedell Smith moved to the Department of State and on February 26, 1953, and Eisenhower (CFR) appointed Dulles as CIA Director. After Dulles, most CIA directors have been CFR members

The CIA: the Rockefellers' Secret Military Arm

Very soon after it was created, the CIA proved to be exactly the right type of organization the conspirators needed to help them accomplish their illicit purpose of conducting their pillage and plundering all around the world. In the first place, it was for free, because the American taxpayers were paying for it. Secondly, because thanks to the CIA's operational principles of secrecy, compartmentation and need-to-know inherent to all intelligence services, it was relatively easy to hide its real activities from both the American public and non-CFR-controlled CIA employees who were ignorant of the Agency's true goals.

CIA Director Allen Dulles himself recognized the fact when he wrote,

> An intelligence service is the ideal vehicle for a conspiracy. Its members can travel about at home and abroad under secret orders, and no questions are asked. Every scrap of paper in the files, its membership, its expenditure of funds, its contacts, even enemy contacts, are secret.[42]

Though Dulles was specifically talking about the German intelligence services, everything he said could be applied to the CIA or to any intelligence service.

Political analyst Michael Parenti also noticed the fact that the CIA is nothing but a conspiracy. According to him,

> In most of its operations, the CIA is by definition a conspiracy, using covert operations and secret plans, many of which are of the most unsavory kind. What are covert operations if not conspiracies? At the same time, the CIA is an institution, a structural part of the national security state. In sum, the agency is an institutionalized conspiracy.[43]

Nevertheless, despite their cleverness, the conspirators didn't fool everybody. Former CIA Director Admiral Stanfield Turner (not a CFR member), for one, suspected that perhaps compartmentation had some secret, nonproper uses. In a book he wrote about his experiences as CIA Director, he said:

> I found the system of compartmentation eminently sensible. I couldn't help wondering, though, if it has been used deliberately to keep people from knowing what they properly needed to know.[44]

Nevertheless, the conspirators' ruse worked to perfection. A list of U.S. military interventions abroad from 1947 to 1990 shows that after the creation of the CIA in 1947 there is an appreciable shift from the use of open force by the U.S. military to covert operations carried out by the CIA.

As I mentioned above, when the CIA was created, covert operations were not included among its functions and they were added surreptitiously just a few months later. Nevertheless, just five years after its creation, the Agency had carried out major covert operations in forty-eight countries to influence the outcome of political and military events on behalf of its CFR masters.[45]

As former CIA Director Admiral Stanfield Turner observed,

> The CIA's covert activities had so increased in the 1950s and 1960s that some of them inevitably became public. Much of what leaked out seriously alarmed the public and Congress. They did not condone all the activities in which the CIA had been involved.[46]

Moreover, Turner also found out that,

> The majority of the espionage professionals, from what I could see, believed that covert action had brought more harm and criti-

cism to the CIA than useful return, and that it had seriously de-
tracted from the Agency's primary role of collecting and evaluating intelligence.[47]

Admiral Turner also discovered that during the tenure of directors Allen
Dulles, Richard Helms and William Colby, the CIA's espionage branch
which included covert operations, had become dominant to the point that
other branches feared being absorbed.[48] Obviously, most CIA officers working in the covert operations area firmly believed that this was the Agency's
most important mission, even if the overt one — preventing another Pearl
Harbor through better collection and analysis of information as well as
coordination with other intelligence agencies — was the reason why the
CIA allegedly had been created.[49]

Turner didn't mention, though, a very important fact: Allen Dulles,
Richard Bissell, Richard Helms, James Angleton, Tracy Barnes, Frank
Wisner, Desmond Fitzgerald and William Colby, were senior CFR secret
agents infiltrated into the CIA's covert operations branch to advance the
conspirators' secret goals.[50] Moreover, not being a trusted CFR secret agent,
Admiral Turner seemingly was ignorant of the fact that the CIA's true primary role was not collecting and evaluating information in order to produce intelligence but to carry out covert operations, including assassinations, on behalf of the Rockefellers and their ilk.

Covert Operations: The CIA's True and Only Purpose

Like most important documents in the recent history of the United States,
NSC 10/2 was written at the Harold Pratt House in Manhattan. It was the
work of CFR agent George Kennan.[51] It mentions as a proven fact "the
vicious covert activities of the USSR, its satellite countries and Communist groups to discredit and defeat the aims and activities of the United
States and other Western powers." These alleged "vicious covert activities" of the Soviet Union were the justification the CFR conspirators gave
to the American people, whose country was supposed to be the antithesis
of the USSR, to allow the CIA to engage in Soviet-like vicious covert activities all around the world.

Some years later, ex-OSS officer and CFR agent Arthur Schlesinger,
Jr., advanced the same idea in a 1967 article in *Foreign Affairs*, the CFR's
disinformation organ. According to Schlesinger, the West was forced to act
against the Soviet Union, mostly because Stalin was paranoid.

Some years later, CFR honcho Henry Kissinger expressed a similar twisted reasoning,

> We need an intelligence community that, in certain complicated situations, can defend the American national interest in gray areas where military operations are not suitable and diplomacy cannot operate.[52]

Just changing "American national interest" into "the Rockefellers' international interests" will reveal the true meaning of Kissinger's words.

Nevertheless, without falling into the Left's error of believing that the Soviet leaders were saints guided by high moral principles, there is ample evidence pointing to the fact that the Cold War, like the Soviet Union itself, was the globalist conspirator's baby, conceived and nurtured[53] as a credible threat to maintain the American people in a constant state of fear. This artificially-created threat justified the arms race produced by the confrontation with the artificially-created enemy. It is also a known fact that Eastern Europe was served to Stalin on a silver platter, as a sure way to increase the Communist threat all around the world.

Stanford's revisionist historian Barton J. Bernstein found evidence that, "By overextending policy and power and refusing to accept Soviet interests, American policy-makers contributed to the Cold War."[54] A similar view is expressed by H. W. Brands. According to him, "The cold war had resulted largely from the efforts of the U.S. to export capitalism across the globe."[55]

Not too different is the thesis advanced by Frank Kofsky in one of the best-documented books about the causes of the Cold War, which he attributes to a conspiracy carried out by the CFR power elite. According to him,

> Regardless of how outlandish or nonsensical most 'conspiracy theories' may be, the fact of the matter is that members of the ruling class and the power elite in the late 1940s showed themselves ready to resort to conspiratorial machinations whenever they deemed it necessary.[56]

The process by which the conspirators instilled fear into the American people by brandishing the specter of Communism was repeated in the 1990s after the unexpected implosion of the Soviet Union left the conspirators without a reason for the existence of U.S. national security state. I have always suspected that the true reason for the first war in Iraq — a trap into which Saddam Hussein foolishly fell — was to provoke the Soviets to get into the conflict. But at the time the Soviet bear was already dead, and not even that direct provocation brought him back to life. Unfortunately for the American people, this failure to resurrect Soviet Communism brought us the 9/11 events that justified the War on Terror as the makeshift replacement for the Cold War.

The Rockefeller Family's Tradition Continues

In 1953, Iran's Prime Minister Mohammed Mossadegh nationalized Iran's oil business. Soon after, a UK/US-backed coup returned the Shah to power. CIA Director Allen Dulles and his brother, Secretary of State John Foster Dulles, were instrumental in this coup. Previously, Iran's oil had been controlled by the Anglo-Persian Oil Co. (i.e., British Petroleum, BP) but after the U.S. role in this coup, U.S. companies got a 40% share and the top beneficiary was the Rockefellers' Standard Oil of New Jersey.

On December 1979, syndicated columnist Jack Anderson disclosed that the Rockefellers had helped to plan the August 1953 CIA coup in Iran. According to Anderson, a grateful Shah handsomely rewarded the Rockefellers by depositing huge sums of cash in Chase Manhattan and assigned some construction projects to a Rockefeller firm.[57]

The next year, the Rockefeller boys were at it again, orchestrating a coup in Guatemala to overthrow the country's democratically-elected President Jacobo Arbenz. This one ushered in decades of fascist military governments that killed hundreds of thousands of innocents. But, it brought great profits for Rockefeller's United Fruit Co., in which their secret agents, the Dulles brothers, had invested. CIA Director Allen Dulles had also been on the United Fruit Board of Trustees.

Similar accusations have been made about a possible Rockefeller role in the 1973 coup that toppled Chile's Salvador Allende —actually a Castro-CIA joint operation.[58] The fact that Henry Kissinger and Fidel Castro, two key Rockefeller agents, played an important role in the overthrowing and killing of Allende, indicates that it was an operation carried out on behalf of the Rockefellers.

Nelson Rockefeller's criminal activities around the world became so outrageous that by 1947 there was widespread suspicion about his treasonous activities in South America. At the same time he was in charge of Latin American intelligence, he turned a blind eye to Standard Oil's shipments of South American oil to the Nazis before and after the U.S. declared war against Nazi Germany.

Granted, Rockefeller was not the only major figure suspected of having engaged in treasonous acts during World War II. Others were Prescott Bush and his attorney Allen Dulles, then-OSS Station Chief in Bern, Switzerland, and later Director of CIA. But it is not a coincidence that both were partners in Standard Oil Co. [59]

There is overwhelming evidence proving that the Rockefellers' collaborated with the Nazis before and during the Second World War.[60] While Germany lacked the oil needed to wage the war, Nazi bombers were dropping tons of bombs on London and other European cities thanks to the gasoline provided by the Rockefeller's Standard Oil. [61]

Nelson Rockefeller moved to Washington after the U.S. involvement in World War II, where Roosevelt named him Coordinator of Inter-American Affairs. Apparently, however, his real main task was to coordinate the secret refueling of German submarines in the Caribbean and South America from Standard Oil's underwater fuel tanks.[62] He also used that office to obtain important South American concessions for his private firm, International Basic Economy Corporation, including a corner on the Colombian coffee market. In true Rockefeller fashion, he raised the price, a move that enabled him to buy several billion dollars worth of real estate in South America and also gave rise to the stereotype of the "Yankee Imperialism." It also gave rise to several billion dollars worth of drug-growing real estate.

The Rockefellers have always used espionage as their main tool to advance their interests. As I mentioned above, before and during the San Francisco Conference of 1945, which created the United Nations Organizations, OSS officers, working on behalf of their CFR masters, spied on the delegates, and intercepted their secret communications with their respective countries to know in advance each country's negotiating positions.[63] The knowledge of this private information allowed the CFR conspirators to have full control the Conference.

The CIA, the NSA, the Department of Homeland Security and large sections of the U.S. military constitute what should be properly called the Military-Industrial-Banking-Assassination Complex (MIBAC). They are fully under the control of the Invisible Government of the United states of which David Rockefeller was the virtual President since 1945 to his death in 2017. Though ostensibly the only purpose of these organizations is to advance and protect the interests of the American people, in practice they just advance and protect the interests of their creators, the oil magnates, Wall Street bankers and CEOs of transnational corporations ensconced at the Rockefellers' Council on Foreign Relations.

Chapter 9

The Rockefellers Recruit Fidel Castro

> *When you have eliminated the impossible, whatever remains,*
> *however improbable, must be the truth.*
> – Sherlock Holmes.

In early 1948, the destinies of Fidel Castro, the CIA, the Council on Foreign Relations and the Rockefellers became closely intertwined. Just a perfunctory analysis of the Castro-US relations since 1948 shows that almost every American who supported Castro was linked, directly or indirectly, to the CFR or the CIA and, despite the conspirators' efforts to hide this relationship, some people suspected it.

U.S. Ambassador Earl E. T. Smith, for one, was convinced that Castro was allowed to grab power in Cuba in 1959 thanks to the efforts of several people in the State Department, among them William Wieland and Roy Rubbotom.[1] These two shady characters, particularly Wieland,[2] were consistently accused of being pro-Castro because, their accusers believed, they were Communists. Moreover, in his book *The Fourth Floor*, Smith told in some detail how CIA officers in the U.S. Embassy in Havana, particularly Chief of Station Jim Noel, were openly pro-Castro.

The truth, however, is that, far from being Communists, these and other Castro supporters were just following orders from above. Keeping in mind that, beginning in late 1949, the U.S. State Department fell fully under CFR control,[3] and that the U.S. Secretary of State at the time was John Foster Dulles, a senior CFR secret agent, it is safe to surmise that the true protectors of Castro were not in the Kremlin but in the Harold Pratt House in Manhattan.

The CIA Recruits Castro as Agent Provocateur

On April 9, 1948, Bogotá, the capital of Colombia, was the scene of violent riots, later known as the Bogotazo.[4] The event that apparently unleashed the riots was the assassination of Colombia's populist leader Jorge Eliécer Gaitán. The rioters destroyed most of the city and several thousand people were killed. The events coincided with the celebration in Bogotá of the Ninth International Conference of American States, which had opened its sessions on March 30, 1948, chaired by U.S. Secretary of State and CFR agent General George C. Marshall.

Though apparently unconnected, a clear understanding of the true causes of the Bogotazo and the assassination of Gaitán are extremely important to understand the true causes for the assassination of President Kennedy. The reason for this is because, with the benefit of hindsight, it becomes clear that the assassination of Gaitán was a sort of dry run for the Kennedy assassination.

Both operations were carried out by the CIA with the support of dozens of CFR members in the CIA, the State Department and the military. In both operations Fidel Castro, Allen Dulles and James Jesus Angleton played important roles.

In both operations, the alleged assassins were psychologically controlled Manchurian Candidates and also patsies who ostensibly committed the crime while the true assassins really did it. In both operations the weapons allegedly used to commit the crime proved not to be the ones used by the true assassins. In both operations the alleged assassins were supposed to be captured and killed — as it happened in the Gaitán assassination but failed in the JKF assassination. Both operations were followed by a massive cover-up carried out by CFR members in the U.S. Government and the mainstream press. Both operations were carried out against men who had dared to threaten the Rockefellers' interests.

The assassination of Gaitán is a key event to understanding many similar false flag operations carried out by the CIA following the CFR conspirators' orders — including the 9/11/2001 operation. Therefore, I am going to study it in some detail because it is an event mostly unknown by the American people because the American media and scholars have mostly ignored it. As authors Loftus and Aarons rightly pointed out, "Omission from history is the hallmark of success in covert operations."[5]

On the morning of April 9, 1948, Jorge Eliécer Gaitán, a Colombian political leader and presidential candidate with a populist, nationalist agenda, was gunned down as he was leaving his office. Fidel Castro and his friend Rafael del Pino,[6] were in Bogotá when Gaitán was assassinated. Their overt purpose was to attend a student's congress that had been planned to coincide with the Conference.

Castro and del Pino had contacted Gaitán, allegedly to invite him to speak at the inaugural session of the student's congress, and Gaitán had agreed to meet them early in the afternoon. That same afternoon, less than two hours before the meeting, Gaitán was shot as he was leaving his office to have lunch with a few friends. Castro and del Pino were close by when the assassination took place.

The murder of Gaitán unleashed a frenzied, senseless orgy of killing, burning, and looting that destroyed most of the center of Bogotá and virtually cut the city off from the rest of the world for two days. The riots took the lives of more than a thousand people. Before the riot ended 150 buildings had been burned down or severely damaged. The riots marked the onset of a dark period in Colombia's history called "la Violencia," (the Violence), which claimed more than 200,000 lives in the decade following the Bogotazo and has continued almost uninterrupted to the present day.

What none of the books about the CIA mention, however, is that the assassination of Gaitán actually was the CIA's first successful large-scale psychological warfare operation (PsyOp) carried out on behalf of the CFR conspirators. In it they tested new covert warfare, propaganda and mind control techniques later employed in operations ranging from the assassination of President Kennedy to the September 11, 2001, events.

The assassination of Gaitán and the Bogotazo operations were the events in which the conspirators used for the first time their newly recruited secret agent: Fidel Castro.

For reasons one can only guess, in 1947 the CIA's talent spotters at the U.S. Embassy in Havana had already focused their attention on Fidel Castro and decided to recruit him and send him to Bogotá, Colombia, as an agent provocateur on a sensitive mission. Apparently Castro's already impressive record as a gangster, assassin and violent psychopath totally lacking in moral principles convinced them that he was the right person they were looking for to carry out a delicate and important job.

Castro's criminal activities had been reported in the Cuban press, and noticed by intelligence officers at the U.S. Embassy in Havana. A confidential Dispatch to the State Department signed by Embassy Counselor Lester D. Mallory, dated April 26, 1948, states,

> He [Castro] is the student leader of the Law School of the University of Habana [lit.] and last came to the Embassy's attention in connection with the shooting of the former FEU [University Students' Association] President Manolo Castro (no relation). Fidel Castro is believed to be a member of the Union Insurreccional Revolucionaria (UIR), the band of thugs and "student" strong-arm boys which is generally considered to have been responsible for the killing of Manolo Castro in the culmination of a long-standing police and student feud.[7]

For many years I had suspected that the only explanation for Castro's long life of unmolested anti-American hatred just 90 miles from American shores was that he actually was working for the very same people he claimed to hate, and I had found abundant circumstantial evidence proving it. It was not until 1995, however, that somebody provided the first direct evidence that Castro had been recruited by the U.S. intelligence services.

In a book self-published in 1995,[8] Ramón B. Conte, an eyewitness who used to do some minor contract work for the CIA as a heavy,[9] mentions how the recruitment of Fidel Castro took place in early 1948 during a meeting at the residence of Mario Lazo in Havana. Lazo was an American-educated Cuban lawyer who represented many American interests in Cuba. Conte and another CIA operative were on a stakeout in a car parked across the street in front of Lazo's house. They were armed and ready to intervene if Castro, known for his flaring temper and love for firearms, refused the offer he was going to get and turned violent.

Castro attended the meeting accompanied by his friend Rafael del Pino Siero, a CIA asset who had been in the U.S. Army Intelligence during WWII. Among the people who attended the secret meeting were Lazo himself, CIA officers Richard Salvatierra and Isabel Siero Pérez,[10] former U.S. ambassador to Cuba Willard Beaulac,[11] and two other Americans. Conte only identified them as Col. Roberts and a CIA officer known as Mr. Davies.[12] The true purpose of the meeting was recruiting Fidel Castro as a

CIA agent.

Some years after Conte published his book, I interviewed him over the phone. In it he added to the list of people who attended the meeting at Lazo's home an important name he failed to mention in his book: William D. Pawley.[13]

Pawley, a multi-millionaire businessman who owned the Havana Bus Company and had large investments in Cuba's mineral and sugar industries, was a close friend of President Eisenhower and Allen Dulles. At the time of the meeting he was U.S. ambassador to Peru and Brazil. He had been closely linked to the U.S. intelligence services since the time of the OSS. Author Tim Weiner calls him "a CIA consultant,"[14] but he was much more than that. Pawley was one of the main organizers of the Ninth International Conference that was going to take place in April in Bogotá.[15]

According to Conte, a week after the initial meeting, Castro and del Pino met again with CIA's Salvatierra, who had been assigned the job of Castro's controller. In this second meeting Castro took himself the pseudonym "Alex," and was told about his first mission. It consisted in traveling to Bogotá, Colombia and, acting as an agent provocateur, participate in the assassination of Gaitán, which would be used as a pretext to provoke the riots known as the Bogotazo. The secondary goal of the operation was to plant false clues that would be used later to blame the Communists for the riots. The riots would help Secretary Marshall to use the fear of communism as a threat to convince the delegates attending the Conference that the Communist threat was real and imminent.[16]

The Bogotazo Operation and the Cold War PsyOp

Most Colombians who have studied the Bogotazo still believe that the event was just a violent outburst in Colombia's national politics. But, as I will show below, they are wrong. Actually, the Bogotazo was a false flag operation,[17] a part of a psychological warfare operation (PsyOp) that had nothing to do with Colombia's internal affairs. It was the event that triggered in Latin America the beginning of a PsyOp of enormous proportions: the Cold War.

An important clue to the disinformation techniques used in the Bogotazo operation is the fact that, though the CIA allegedly failed to inform Marshall about the possibility of riots, CFR secret agents in the field kept the Colombian press well informed in advance about that possibility. As Francisco Fandiño Silva, a known Colombian journalist, later recalled, "The American Embassy informed me that it had received reports that a bomb attack was to be made against the General [Marshall]."[18]

Following the same pattern of disinformation, on March 24, Gaitán received a false warning from U.S. Ambassador to Colombia, Willard Beaulac, telling him that the Communists were planning to break up the Conference and that, if they succeeded, Gaitán's Liberal Party most likely would be blamed for the events.[19] Beulac was one of the persons who attended the secret meeting in Lazo's home where Castro was recruited.

After studying the Bogotazo case, the Senate Internal Security Subcommittee made these comments about the reasons why the CIA reports were not delivered in timely fashion:

> O.J. Libert, State Department aide in Bogotá, and Ambassador Willard L. Beaulac were charged by Admiral Hillenkoetter[20] with failure to forward these messages to the State Department in Washington. Mr. Libert vetoed sending these messages to Secretary Marshall's security officers because he thought Bogotá police protection was "adequate," and he did not wish to "alarm the delegates unduly."[21]

Beaulac's activities in blocking the intelligence report, and his insistence in blaming the Communists for the riots, as well as his participation in the earlier meeting at Lazo's residence, are consistent with him being an active part of the Bogotazo operation. Moreover, it is safe to assume that, as a high-level CFR member, Secretary of State Marshall was also an important part of the operation, and he had been informed about it.

In his testimony of April 15, 1948, before a special Congressional subcommittee investigating the CIA's "failure" to forecast the Bogotazo riots, CIA Director Adm. Hillenkoetter rebuked his critics by stating that the CIA had reported in a timely fashion about the "possibility of violence and outbreak" during the Conference, and that this information had been transmitted to officials in the State Department.[22] Hillenkoetter also charged that Embassy officials in Bogotá had blocked the transmission of a CIA key report dated March 23 to the Sate Department, alerting about the possibility of disturbances during the Conference.[23]

Moreover, according to an October 14, 1948, Report of the Office of Intelligence Research of the State Department, the assumption that the Communists were involved in the assassination of Gaitán was based on the fact that they had made, far in advance, plans to sabotage and discredit the activities of the Conference and to disrupt the activities of several of the delegations, principally that of the U.S.[24]

Just a few hours after Gaitán was assassinated and the Bogotazo riots erupted, General Marshall, a trusted CFR agent, blamed the Communists for the event. CIA Director Adm. Hillenkoetter, U.S. Ambassador Beaulac, Colombia's President Dr. Mariano Ospina, Secretary of the Presidency Rafael Azula, and other important witnesses concluded that the assassination and the Bogotazo riots were a Communist operation instigated by the Soviet Union.

Puzzled by the Agency's first intelligence "failure," CIA officer Russell Jack Smith, who knew through his contacts in the country that the Colombian Communists had nothing to do with starting the riots, telephoned a contact in Secretary Marshall's office in the State Department and asked,

> "Where did the Secretary get the information that the rioting in Bogotá was a communist plot?" "Oh," his contact said casually, "he just looked out of the window in his villa six or seven miles away and said, 'The Communists did it.'"[25]

A few days later, on April 13, 1948, the *Philadelphia Inquirer* published an article under the title "Marshall Blames World Communism for Bogotá Revolt," providing more false elements in an effort to convince the American public that the assassination of Gaitán and the Bogotazo riots had been the work of Colombian Communists with the support of the Soviet Union.

Despite the lack of evidence to prove that claim, later efforts were made by the CFR-controlled U.S. mainstream press to convince the American public that the assassination of Gaitán and the Bogotazo riots had been a KGB operation carried out with the support of Colombian communists.

CIA's Agent Provocateurs Plant False Clues

On their way to Colombia, Castro and del Pino stopped first in Panama, where they were introduced to President Enrique Jiménez, and del Pino gave a violent anti-American speech.[26] Argentina's President Juan Domingo Perón, who acted as a CIA cutout to hide the true source of the money, had provided the funds for Castro and del Pino's trip. Perón's pro-Nazi activities have been extensively documented, and he was a personal friend of CFR senior agent Allen Dulles.

A few days later, the Cubans repeated their performance in Venezuela, where they meet with a group of university students and became acquainted with former president Rómulo Betancourt, who was to head Venezuela's delegation to the Conference in Bogotá.[27] Because of his nationalist, anti-imperialist stance,[28] and the fact that as a young man he had been a leader of the Communist Party, Betancourt was seen as a troublemaker and the CFR conspirators accused him of being a Communist. Their meeting with Jiménez and Betancourt was another element used to boost Castro's cover as a Communist.

As soon as Fidel Castro and Rafael del Pino arrived at the Medellín, Colombia airport, the Colombian National Security Office immediately placed them under surveillance. Alberto Niño, former Colombian Security Chief, later wrote that he had been informed that the Cubans had come as a replacement for two Soviet agents stationed in Cuba.[29] Fulfilling their role as agent provocateurs, once in Bogotá, Castro and del Pino openly distributed pro-Communist literature just a few days before the Bogotazo and kept Communist literature in their hotel room.

In a effort to add credibility to the allegation that Castro was a Communist and a Soviet agent, William D. Pawley, U.S. Ambassador to Brazil and a Conference delegate, later declared to a U.S. Senate investigation that, while he was riding an official Embassy car the day the riots begun, he heard somebody on the radio saying,

> This is Fidel Castro from Cuba. This is a Communist revolution. The President has been killed. All the military establishments are now in our hands. The Navy has capitulated to us and this revolution has been a success.[30]

Some authors have taken Pawley's words as the ultimate proof that at this early time Fidel Castro already was a Communist. But, as I mentioned before, this goes against the evidence. In the first place, because, according to Conte, Pawley had attended the meeting at Lazo's home where the CFR conspirators recruited Castro. Secondly, because Pawley played a key role in late 1958 as a personal envoy of President Eisenhower in trying to convince Cuba's President Batista to leave the country and thus opening the way for Castro grabbing power in Cuba in January, 1959.

Since their arrival at Bogotá, Castro and del Pino devoted an inordinate amount of time to plant false clues in an effort to implicate the Colombian Communists and the Soviet Union in the coming assassination of Gaitán and the riots.

On September 22, 1949, *El Gráfico* of Caracas, Venezuela, published a confidential report filed by a Colombian police detective. The Report was originally published in the influential Bogotá daily *El Siglo*. It dealt with the results of the surveillance on Castro and del Pino prior and during the Bogotazo riots.

According to the detective, on April 3, Colombia's President, Dr. Mariano Ospina Pérez was attending an evening performance a the Colón Theatre. Then, at about 10:00 p.m., shortly after the third act of the play had begun, there was a shower of leaflets from the gallery. They were definitely Communist in style and revolutionary in phraseology.

Some police detectives proceeded to the gallery where they caught two Cubans in the act of showering "the boxes and orchestra of the Colón Theatre with their revolutionary propaganda." One of the detectives took Fidel Castro and del Pino into custody and proceeded to their lodgings — room 33 of the Hotel Claridge. There the two Cubans *voluntarily* showed the detectives various papers, some of importance. There was a letter from Rómulo Betancourt "recommending both of them," *and various Communist or leftwing books* [emphasis added], including one of Betancourt "with whom they claimed to have close relationship or friendship and political affinity.[31]

As stated in the Report, the detectives asked for written authorization from their superiors to pick up Castro and del Pino's passports and summon them to the Bureau of Detectives of the National Police for further interrogation on their Communist activities. Strangely, the permission was denied.[32] It seems that some important people needed Castro and del Pino free to continue doing their jobs as agent provocateurs uninterrupted.

The very same day Gaitán was assassinated at 1:30 p.m., Castro and del Pino were waiting in a café facing the building where Gaitán office was located, waiting for an interview they were going to have with Gaitán at 3:00 p.m. Castro had already met Gaitán briefly a few days earlier.[33] The date and time of the interview was recorded in Gaitán daily schedule book. According to journalist Jules Dubois, the interview was to be held in the offices of the newspaper *El Tiempo*.[34]

The Assassination of Gaitán and the Bogotazo Riots

Most authors who have studied the Bogotazo riots agree that, far from being a spontaneous uprising, there were signs indicating previous preparation. Fidel Castro himself has given some credibility to these suspicions.

In an interview with Indian journalist Kurt Singer in late 1960, Castro mentioned how, when he was barely 20 years old, he "participated in the realization of *a plan* [emphasis added] whose goal was the liberation of Colombia."[35] The fact that he was following a plan is confirmed by a letter his girlfriend Mirtha[36] wrote him. In it, she told Fidel that she was worried because, before the trip, he had told her that he was "going to start a revolution in Bogotá."[37]

Now, given the fact that at the time the 20 year old Castro lacked the experience, the resources and political stature to lead such a plan, one can conclude that it was somebody else's plan. Moreover, it is safe to surmise that the plan he mentioned had been conceived by the Rockefellers and their agents at the Harold Pratt House and carried out by CFR members infiltrated into the recently-created CIA.

It was not a coincidence that the Bogotazo riots flared up while the Ninth International Conference of American States was taking place. After the end of WWII in 1945, the American military-industrial-complex[38] and its Wall Street associates were desperately looking for a way to continue producing armaments and saw Latin America as the best potential market for their products. To that effect, they kept active the military bases the U.S. had acquired south of the border with the pretext of the war against the Axis, continued training officers from Latin American countries, and moved to standardize South and Central American military equipment along U.S. lines in an effort to add the military field to Latin America's economic dependency to the United States.

Moreover, the CFR conspirators infiltrated in the U.S. Government emphasized Latin America's importance as a safe source of basic materials from a geographic area where foreign powers could not interfere. The plan was to use the Latin American military as their praetorian guard to protect the natural resources that, according to their reasoning, rightly belonged to the Wall Street conspirators. The first step in that direction was the Rio Pact of 1947, a military alliance between the United States and the Latin American countries.

Nonetheless, most Latin Americans governments had signed the Pact with the hope that the U.S. would give them the economic help they badly needed — of which the corrupt politicians hoped to steal a great part — in return for their political and military cooperation. But, a year later, the economic aid had not materialized, and the politicians were not happy. Now the U.S. had asked them to meet again in Bogotá to sign new treaties.

Cardinal among these was the creation of a new tool for political and economic domination, the Organization of American States (OAS), as well as a commitment to fight the new artificially created enemy: Soviet communism. A secret memorandum dated March 22, 1948, signed by George Kennan (CFR), Director of Political Planning at the State Department, mentions that the problem of communism would be considered at the Ninth Conference, as well as anticommunist measures that would be prepared and implemented in the inter-American system.[39]

But, given their previous frustrating experience, most leaders of Latin American countries were not eager to help the U.S. to reach its goal. This was evidenced during the first days of the Conference by the delegates' reluctance to cave in to Marshall's pressures. But the sight of the angry mobs in the streets, the burning of the buildings, and the indiscriminate killing, proved to be more persuasive than Marshall's arguments. The last day of the Conference the delegates not only unanimously approved the Charter creating the OAS, but also unanimously approved and signed a document condemning international communism.[40]

The OAS Charter provided the legal mechanism for upholding the Monroe Doctrine. Due to the fact that the U.S. controlled the majority in the OAS, including several Latin American votes, this would guarantee their right to legally militarily intervene in the affairs of the OAS member countries. If the votes did not give the CFR conspirators the legal right to intervene, they reserved the right to do it unilaterally just the same.

The Bogotazo was a key part of a larger psychological warfare operation (PsyOp),[41] whose primary goal was to scare the American and Latin American people with the fear of the communism — an enemy artificially-created to substitute the CFR's artificially created previous enemy that had just disappeared: Nazi Germany.[42] Therefore, it was not by chance that the first mission assigned to the CIA's Office of Special Projects against what soon after became the CIA's new "main enemy," the Soviet Union,[43] was the Bogotazo false flag operation.

Propaganda and sabotage techniques used during the Bogotazo — broadcasting fake reports inciting the rioters, distribution of leaflets implicating the Communists, etc. — seem to have been carried out following the OSS guidelines for psychological warfare operations as specified by the OSS Morale Operations Branch.[44] The main goal of the OSS Morale Operations Branch was to create unfounded panic, intimidate, demoralize, and spread confusion and distrust among enemy civilians and military forces. A secondary goal was to stimulate feelings of resentment and rebellion among occupied populations.[45] Morale Operations mostly used "black"[46] propaganda, in which the source of the information is disguised.[47]

The Bogotazo operation was the pretext used by the CFR conspirators to initiate what is known as "the War Scare of 1948,"[48] a PsyOp that marked the true beginning of the Cold War in the Western Hemisphere. The Cold War proved to be extremely profitable to CFR's Wall Street bankers and transnational corporations who, as they had done with Nazi Germany, now were making good money selling their goods to both sides of the Cold War conflict.

Following the trend, on May 19, 1950, President Truman signed National Security Council Memorandum NSC 56/2, "United States Policy Toward Inter-American Military Collaboration."[49] It asserted, "the cold war is in fact a real war in which the survival of the free world is at stake." In 1951 the U.S. Congress voted to give $38.2 million for military assistance to Latin America and the following year it jumped to $51.7 million.[50] As expected, most of the money went directly to the big pockets of U.S. weapons manufacturers.

In synthesis, everything indicates that the riots, which apparently were spontaneously provoked by the assassination of Gaitán, actually had been planned and prepared way in advance, and the assassination was only a cover to hide its true causes.

Was Gaitán's Assassin a Patsy?

Though his motive is still a matter of discussion, most of the people who have studied the Bogotazo events agree that Gaitan's assassin was Juan Roa Sierra, an uneducated 25-year-old drifter and loiterer who came from a poor family of workers. The scant information available about Roa tells that he was introverted, lazy, and had delusions of grandeur. Though he sometimes got odd jobs, he was kept alive by sleeping with a much older woman who provided for him. His opinions were violently right wing, but he was a person with no known political affiliation.[51]

On April 9, around 1:30 in the afternoon, on his way to have lunch with a few friends, Gaitán was about to exit the building where his office was located when somebody opened fire on him. Several witnesses have described the event, but some versions are contradictory. According to the press, the assassin was Roa Sierra and he acted alone, but some evidence points to the contrary.

After the assassination, a Bogotá police detective added very important information about Roa Sierra. Some time before the assassination,

... I saw del Pino standing in the door of the Colombia café, talking with a shabbily dressed individual whose photograph would later appear in the newspapers as the murderer of Gaitán.[52]

So, according to this police detective, Castro's friend and co-conspirator Rafael del Pino had contacted Roa Sierra previous to the assassination. Other sources seem to confirm the detective's assertion, and indicate that Castro and del Pino had met Roa Sierra on several occasions before the assassination. According to a *United Press* report published in *El Tiempo* of Bogotá, "Roa was seen in the company of several people who appeared to be foreigners, a few days prior to the crime."[53]

Probably one of the persons who more carefully have investigated the details of the crime is author Rafael Azula Barrera. He mentions how the efforts to save the alleged assassin from the mob were useless. The angry crowd in front of the drugstore where he took refuge grew in size and the drugstore owners forced Roa out and closed the iron grate. As soon as Roa was out, the people present began hitting him with fury.[54]

The mob killed the alleged assassin mercilessly. With terrifying speed and cruelty, they beat him to death and stomped his face into an unrecognizable, bloody mass, stripping him of his clothes as they dragged the body up the street.

But, cautioned Azula Barrera, since the first moment there were doubts as to whether the man taken by the crowd was really the assassin. Just a couple of weeks after the assassination, Milton Bracker of the *New York Times* asked himself whether Roa had accomplices who stood by ostensibly to protect him, but actually to silence and kill him.[55]

But now things get a little more complicated. According to some witnesses, there were *two* individuals implicated in the assassination of Gaitán.

A lift operator at the Nieto building, where Gaitán's office was located, mentions the presence in the scene of the assassination of a tall, dark-haired, white individual with brown, popping eyes, of about 28 years of age, carrying a trench coat draped on his left arm. According to the lift operator, since mid-March the same individual had visited the building several times stopping on the fourth floor, where Gaitán's office was located. The operator added that on the day of the assassination, around 12:30, the man went up using the stairs and down from the fourth floor using the elevator. Downstairs he joined another individual, who had been waiting for him in the alley.[56]

Another witness, who at the time had just entered the Gato Negro café, not far from Gaitán's office, noticed two individuals. One of them called his attention because he seemed unable to control his nervousness. Five minutes later, the nervous guy exited the café to stand casually on the sidewalk. This witness believed that this was actually the individual who fired at Gaitán.[57]

According to what he had told some friends and relatives in the days previous to the assassination, Roa had been trying to get a driver's license in order to work as a driver and bodyguard for some foreigners, who had told him they were explorers looking for a gold mine in the Plains. These were the ones who gave him the money to buy the gun, allegedly to protect them from possible attacks from the Indians and wild animals.[58]

The available record strongly suggests that Roa was a patsy, the fall guy whose only role was taking the blame while some professional hit men carried out the assassination. Like in the case of Lee Harvey Oswald, the killing of Roa was part of the plan to avoid him being interrogated by the authorities. Roa Sierra had never been in the military, nor had any training in the use of small arms, to the point that when he bought the revolver from an acquaintance, he was the one who tested the gun, firing a single shot.[59] If Roa fired any of the shots during the assassination, most likely it was only the last one, but even this is doubtful, because his gun was in very bad shape.

In the intelligence and espionage business there is no such thing as coincidences. There is a saying in the military stating, "Once is happenstance, twice is coincidence, but three times is enemy action." But intelligence officers, and particularly counterintelligence officers, leave no room for happenstance or coincidence. For them, just once must be seen as enemy action, and all coincidences are potentially deceptive.

For example, the fact that Castro and del Pino had an appointment to meet Gaitán just a few hours after the time he was assassinated may have been the product of a coincidence. But, after knowing, first, that Castro was suspected of having been recruited by the CIA; second, that in the days previous to the riots he had called attention upon himself like an obvious agent provocateur;[60] third, that a few days before the assassination of Gaitán he and his friend del Pino had been seen in the company of the alleged killer; and, fourth, that he was close by the very moment Gaitán was killed, even the most skeptical Army officer would have suspected enemy action.

One can only guess what was the purpose of Castro's presence so close to the place where the assassination took place, but knowing Castro's psychopathic nature[61] and his propensity to assassinate political leaders, I am inclined to think that Fidel Castro and his friend Rafael del Pino were the CIA assassination team who killed Gaitán.

Many known key participants in the Bogotazo were linked to the CFR, the OSS or the CIA. The known ones are:

> Gen. George C. Marshall (CFR), U.S. Secretary of State, Chief U.S. delegation to 9th Conference.
> Gen. Matthew B. Ridgway (CFR), military advisor to U.S. delegation to 9th Conference
> Averell Harriman (CFR), U.S. Secretary of Commerce.
> William Wieland, protégé of Sumner Welles (CFR), probably an intelligence liaison between CIA and State Dept., later became a strong Castro supporter inside the State Department.
> William Pawley, friend of Allen Dulles, links to CIA, attended Lazo meeting.
> Willard Beaulac, U.S. ambassador to Colombia, former U.S. Ambassador to Cuba, suspected of attending Lazo meeting.
> Norman Armour (CFR, OSS), Assistant Secretary of State, U.S. delegate to 9th Conference.
> Richard Salvatierra, CIA officer, attended Lazo meeting, became Castro's controller.
> John Mepples Spiritto, CIA officer, had participated in mind control project ARTICHOKE.
> John C. Wiley (CFR, OSS), former U.S. Ambassador to Colombia.
> Robert Lovett (Skull & Bones), U.S. Acting Secretary of State, with close links to CFR.
> Rafael del Pino Siero, U.S. intelligence asset, attended Lazo meeting.[62]
> Fidel Castro Ruz, attended Lazo meeting, recruited by CIA.

Apart from the information I have provided above, the activities during the Bogotazo riots of so many people linked to the U.S. intelligence services and the CFR is a strong indication that the Bogotazo was not a random outburst of violence, but a false flag operation, the key element of a carefully-planned and executed major PsyOp called the Cold War — the first of many to be carried out by the CIA and the CFR conspirators in their long battle against the American people and the peoples of the world in the pursuit of their goal of world domination.

The methodology used in this PsyOp followed the Hegelian principle of thesis-antithesis-synthesis,[63] in which the Bogotazo operation was the scaring antithesis used as a threat to force the American and Latin American people into accepting the frightening new synthesis called the Cold War.[64] The Bogotá PsyOp was so successful that the CFR conspirators felt encouraged to keep using its methodology. As I will show in this book, the assassination of Gaitán in 1948 closely followed the *modus operandi* later used in the 1963 assassination of President Kennedy.

Most authors who have written books about the CIA have simply ignored the Bogotazo riots or written just a few lines about it.[65] Nevertheless, the Bogotazo is very important not only for the reasons I have explained above, but also because the fear of communist subversion, allegedly exemplified by the Bogotazo riots, was the pretext used by the CFR conspirators George Kennan, James Forrestal and Allen Dulles to secretly approve NSC directive 10/2 authorizing the CIA to conduct covert operations, including assassinations, all around the world.[66]

The twisted logic invoked was that the Communists were so vile, foul, terrible, horrendous and atrocious that the only way to win was becoming even worse than them. This explains why many of the actions carried out by the CIA's covert operations branch were so vile, foul, terrible, horrendous and atrocious, not to mention treasonous.

Many years later, in 1976, in an epilogue to the Church Committee report, Senator Frank Church recognized how erroneous this way of thinking was:

> The United States must not adopt the tactics of the enemy. ... each time we do so, each time the means we use are wrong, our inner strength, the strength that makes us free, is lessened.[67]

The Bogotazo PsyOp marked the onset of the Cold War in the Western Hemisphere. Just a few years later, CFR conspirator Nelson Rockefeller was frantically selling the idea of building nuclear shelters in every American building, and American schoolchildren were hiding under their desks rehearsing for a coming nuclear attack. The time for Americans to live under a permanent threat of war and fear had arrived.

Chapter 10

David Rockefeller Puts Castro in Power in Cuba

A characteristic common to all intelligence officers,
East and West, is that they have an open-mindedness.
For them nothing is impossible because it is improbable.
– Thomas Powers, *The Man Who Kept the Secrets.*

During the last years President Batista was in power, Cuba experienced an economic boom unseen in all its history. Around 1956 the Cuban economy under Batista[1] began an upward swing, and 1957 — the year that Castro began fighting his guerrilla war against him in the mountains — was one of the best years for the Cuban economy since the creation of the Cuban Republic at the beginning of the 20th century.

During 1957 Cuba's economic activity reached the highest level registered since World War II, and the average income per capita soared to $400.00,[2] one of the highest in Latin America.[3] In 1958 Cuba occupied the first place in Latin America on the number of TV sets per capita, with 1 set per 18 inhabitants, followed by Venezuela with 1 set per 32, Argentina with 1 per 60 and Mexico with 1 per 70. Moreover, Cuba was the second country in America to broadcast black and white TV programs, and the first in Latin America to broadcast color TV (1957).

The year before Castro took power in Cuba, the country had 160 commercial radio stations. The country was the second in number of radio receivers in Latin America, only second to the U.S. In consumption of fresh fish Cuba was number one in America, with 5.6 pounds per capita, followed by the United States with 5.4 pounds.

Louis A. Pérez, Jr., a scholar who studied in detail the growing similarities between the American and the Cuban culture and society, pointed out, "In almost every important way Cuba was integrated directly into North American marketing strategies."[4] And added,

> In habits, in tastes, in attitudes, in other ways too numerous to fully appreciate, with consequences impossible to measure, Cubans participated daily in North American cultural transactions. They became like North Americans . . ."[5]

The standard of living and mind-set of average Cubans was so close to their American neighbors, that the Island was used by Madison Avenue marketing and advertising firms as a testing ground for the products they were promoting. In order to test their marketability, some of these products, such as some new beer brands, the kitchen cleanser Ajax, and other household products, were launched in the Cuban market several months before launching them in the American markets.

In the mid-fifties, Sears opened a big store in Havana and, soon after, began selling its products through its catalogs to the whole island. By that time the leading American telecommunication companies used Cuba to test their new microwave technology and, upon leaving, left a network that in some aspects was better than any in the United States and the world.[6] The nickel processing plant under construction in Nipe Bay, left unfinished when Castro nationalized it, was the most technologically advanced in the world at the time.

This was contrary to David Rockefeller's plans for a depopulated and deindustrialized New World Order. Obviously, Cuba was setting a bad example other nations might want to follow. So, David decided that it was time to substitute his inefficient puppet Batista with a new puppet: Fidel Castro. His secret goal was to turn Cuba into a testing ground of the New World Order.

Following David's orders, since November, 1956, Castro and a small guerrilla band had been in the Sierra Maestra Mountains in the Eastern part of Cuba fighting Batista's troops, but without much success. By late 1958 Castro's victory over Batista's troops seemed uncertain. So, David decided to give his agent Castro a helping hand.

David Helps Castro Overthrow President Batista

In late 1958, following the advice of Secretary of State John Foster Dulles (CFR), and his brother, CIA director Allen Dulles (CFR), President Eisenhower (CFR) sent William Pawley (a close friend of Allen Dulles) to Havana. Pawley's orders were to inform Batista that the U.S. no longer supported him, and to convince the Cuban President to surrender power and leave the country.[7]

Millionaire William Pawley,[8] former Ambassador to Peru and Brazil, was a personal friend of President Eisenhower and CIA Director Allen Dulles. He had owned several successful businesses in Cuba and was a personal friend of President Batista. Moreover, he is suspected of having attended the secret meeting at Mario Lazo's home where Castro was recruited by the CIA for his Bogotazo job. Also, it was not a coincidence that Pawley was in Bogotá during the Bogotazo riots, where he played an important role on behalf of the CFR conspirators.

Once in Havana, Pawley had a three-hour long interview with the Cuban President. But, despite all his persuasive arguments, he failed to convince Batista to quit and leave the country. The Cuban President told him that he had lost all faith in officials of the U.S. State Department. Pawley returned to Washington and informed President Eisenhower that his mission had failed.[9]

So, on December 14, 1958, CFR agents at the State Department formally intervened to oust Batista and bring in their secret agent Fidel Castro. To this effect they instructed U.S. Ambassador in Cuba Earl T. Smith to inform President Batista that the U.S. no longer supported him and he should leave Cuba as soon as possible.[10]

Two hours after midnight on the New Year's Eve of 1959, Batista fled the Island, leaving the door open for Castro's grabbing power in Cuba. David and the CFR's conspirators had achieved their secret goal.

An anomaly that attracted the attention of some American diplomats was the U.S. haste to recognize Castro's government after President Batista's escape on January 1, 1959. According to Ambassador Earl Smith, the U.S. was very hasty in its recognition of the Castro government. Usually the U.S. withholds recognition from a new government until it is formally established and operating. Normally, the U.S. does not want to be among the first nor among the last to recognize a new government.

The U.S. usually waits until assurances are given that the new government will honor its international obligations. In Latin America it was the custom for the U.S. to wait until several Latin American countries had recognized the new government. However, on January 7, 1959, just six days after former President Batista fled from Cuba and one day before Fidel Castro arrived in Havana, the U.S. officially recognized the Castro government.[11]

Moreover, on May 23, 1961, Drew Pearson revealed in his well-read *Washington Post* column "Washington Merry-Go-Round," that persistent rumors in the diplomatic corps indicated that the CIA had been helping to put Castro in power for years. The rumors had further stated that the CIA agents, in their efforts to get rid of President Batista, had supplied arms and ammunition to Castro during his guerrilla war in the mountains.

Nevertheless, there are more reasons to believe that the CIA in fact delivered weapons to Castro. When he was in the Sierra Maestra fighting Batista's troops, Castro received some weapons delivered by the International Armaments Corporation, the company that sent weapons to Guatemala, under the CIA's orders, to overthrow Jacobo Arbenz's government. The IAC had been founded by Samuel Cummings, a former CIA operative.[12]

Also, rumors ran that CIA officer Robert D. Chapman spent a long time in the mountains with Raúl Castro[13] and that CIA officer Robert Weicha also visited him.[14] Moreover, there is evidence that between October 1957 and the middle of 1958 the CIA gave no less than fifty thousand dollars to Castro's men in Santiago de Cuba.[15]

Castro the Fascist

When Fidel reached school age his parents sent him to Santiago de Cuba, the capital of Oriente province, to study at the LaSalle School, operated by the Christian Brothers. After a short period of time he was transferred to the Dolores School, operated by the Jesuits. In 1942, after finishing grade school, he was sent to Belén High School in Havana, also operated by the Jesuits.

At Belén, young Fidel stood out as an athlete, an indefatigable speaker and a good student — perhaps not too brilliant, but with a photographic memory. Some of his ex-classmates claim that at Belén Fidel fell under the influence of fathers Armando Llorente and Alberto de Castro (no relation to Fidel). Both priests, like most of the Spanish *padres* in Cuba, were staunch supporters of Francisco Franco's Falange,[16] a Spanish brand of fascism, and harbored strong anti-American feelings. They passed on to their young disciples at Belén their enthusiasm for their anti-American cause.

Father Alberto de Castro, who taught Latin American history, expounded on some of his ideas. According to him, the independence of Latin America had been frustrated because the adoption of materialistic Anglo-Saxon values and traditions had supplanted Spanish cultural domination. He emphasized how Franco had liberated Spain from both Anglo-Saxon materialism and Communist Marxist-Leninism.

Young Fidel seemed to have been captivated by the teachings of his Jesuit tutors, and particularly by Father de Castro's ideas.[17] It is known that Fidel read most of the works of José Antonio Primo de Rivera, founder of the Spanish Falange. José Pardo Llada, a radio commentator and politician who at some time was close to Castro, said that Fidel had Primo de Rivera's complete works at his guerrilla camp in the Sierra Maestra mountains.[18] It is also known that Fidel was fascinated by Primo de Rivera's speeches — some claim that Castro knew many of the speeches by heart — and by de Rivera's image of a wealthy man who left everything and went to fight for what he believed in.

Fidel's classmates at Belén have testified that he was an admirer of other fascist leaders, including Hitler, Mussolini, and Perón. Among Castro's preferred reading was an eight-volume collection of Mussolini's speeches.[19] Also, Castro told a friend that he had learned many things about propaganda by studying Hitler's *Mein Kampf*, which he also knew by heart. Some friends recall that young Fidel had pinned on one of his room's walls a large map of Europe, where he happily marked the victorious advances of the Wehrmacht's Panzers.

When Castro was in Mexico preparing for his invasion of Cuba, somebody informed the Mexican secret police about his illegal activities, and the police detained some of the revolutionaries and searched their house. Among the things the police came across was a copy of Hitler's *Mein Kampf*, which allegedly Castro always kept at hand.[20]

An American journalist and author found out that Castro "reportedly read Marx, and Hitler's *Mein Kampf*, during his University days and was greatly influenced by both."[21] Also, Mario Llerena, a prominent member of Castro's M-26-7 revolutionary movement, claims that many people have seen in Fidel the characteristics of a Fascist dictator, and that he often heard it said that one of Fidel's favorite books was *Mein Kampf*.[22] Evidence shows that Castro was in fact very familiar with Hitler's ideas.

For example, Hitler was called "the Führer" (the chief) by his close followers. Among his intimate circle Fidel was called *"el jefe"* (the chief).[23] Hitler used to defile his enemies calling them vermin. Castro called his opponents *"gusanos,"* literally "worms."[24] Castro used the term *"bandidos"* (bandits) for the patriots fighting guerrilla warfare against him in the Escambray Mountains as Hitler called "bandits" the partisani fighting him.

Over and over the Cuban people were recorded chanting rhythmically *"Fi-del!, Fi-del! Fi-del!,"* at rallies and mass meetings.[25] The chanting closely resembled the Nazi *"Zieg-Heil!, Zieg-Heil!, Zieg-Heil!"* and the *"Du-ce!, Du-ce!, Du-ce!"* cheers of Mussolini's Fascist thugs. A common slogan in Hitler's Germany was: "The Führer orders, let us obey!," very similar to the Italian Fascist motto *"Credere, Obedire, Combattere!"* ("Believe, Obey, Fight!"). Its Castroist counterpart was: *"Comandante en Jefe: ¡Ordene!* ("Commander-in-Chief, give us your orders!

Castro's closing words of his own defense speech at the trial for his failed 1953 attack on the Moncada garrison, "Condemn me, never mind, History will absolve me," were very similar to Hitler's final words in his own defense at the trial for the frustrated 1923 beer-hall putsch: "Condemn me, never mind, the Goddess of History will absolve me." Evidently, there were too many similarities to be just the product of coincidences.

Castro the Communist

During a televised speech on December 2, 1961, Castro delivered a long speech in which, after admitting his bourgeois prejudices, he declared that he had always been a Marxist-Leninist at heart and would remain so until the last day of his life.[26] He began his speech at about midnight on December 1 and finished his speech at 5:00 a.m. on December 2. Author Loree Wilkerson, who wrote probably the best analysis of Castro's speech, observed that Fidel's self-analysis in this speech presents the picture of a man desperately trying to modify his past so that it would conform to the present.[27]

Castro's confession of Marxist faith was received with surprise by the Soviet leadership and with extreme suspicion by the Soviet intelligence analysts in charge of Cuba. Their suspicion was understandable, because an evaluation of Castro's claims may have produced something close to an E-5 (that is, source unreliable, accuracy of information improbable. See Appendix II, The Evaluation of Information). Evidently, Fidel Castro was trying to create for himself, *a posteriori*, what in intelligence parlance is known as a "legend," a false biography or cover story, supplied mostly to illegals and sleepers,[28] enabling them to live undetected within a foreign country under a false identity. The Soviets were not alone in their misgivings about Castro's claims. Fidel's non-Communist affiliation had been so widely accepted in international circles that his speech caused a sensation abroad.[29]

In January, 1962, Fidel confessed to a French journalist that, even though he had never read beyond the first pages of the first volume of Marx's *Capital*, he had always been a Marxist. Hugh Thomas, a scholar who wrote one of the best studies of Castro and his revolution, said that Castro must be therefore the first Marxist-Leninist leader who had scarcely read any of the works of the Master and who scarcely allowed more than a few words and few expressions taken from Marxism to enter his vocabulary.[30] Thomas' remark is highly accurate. An analysis of Castro's speeches shows that, while giving lip service to Marxism, true Marxist terminology and concepts were totally absent from them.

Both Castro supporters in Cuba, and anti-Castro exiles in the U.S., uncritically accepted Fidel's claims at face value. But Herbert Matthews, the *New York Times'* journalist who first interviewed him at the Sierra Maestra Mountains, knew better. Asked a few days later about Castro's confession of Marxist faith, Matthews told a gathering of his colleagues at the Overseas Press Club in New York that he didn't believe Castro; that the Communist label didn't fit him. "Today Castro may believe he is a Communist," he said, "but tomorrow he may believe something else."[31]

Matthews, who closely followed Castro's actions and political career since his guerrilla days, was right. As a matter of fact, there is nothing in Castro's political life or speeches that allow us to conclude that Marx's or Lenin's works influenced his ideas or political behavior in any way. And Matthew's views on Castro were not an isolated case. Many people seemed to share his views.

Free lance photographer Andrew St. George, a CIA asset who acted under a journalist's cover, visited Castro at the Sierra Maestra Mountains and remained with the guerrilla for two or three weeks. Upon returning to Washington he expressed his opinion that Castro was an egomaniac and emotionally unstable individual, but not a Communist.[32] Similarly, a senior CIA officer, General C. P. Cabell, Deputy Director of Central Intelligence, testifying before the Internal Security Sub-Committee of the U.S. Senate, expressed CIA's opinion that, "We believe Castro is not a member of the Communist Party, and does not consider himself a Communist."[33] Apparently Matthews, St. George, and Cabell were not alone. Neither the Soviets, nor the Cuban Communists, true experts in communism, ever believed Castro was one of them.

On February 24, 1957, the CFR-controlled *New York Times*[34] published the first of a series of three articles written by its correspondent Herbert L. Matthews, a trusted CFR member, who had interviewed Fidel Castro in the Sierra Maestra Mountains in eastern Cuba. He depicted Castro as a liberal and a folk hero — a Latin American Robin Hood crusading against evil. Matthews' articles gave Castro instant international publicity. One of Castro's closest followers, Armando Hart, commenting about the coverage and the high impact of Matthews articles, told Mario Llerena, the M-26-7[35] public relations man in the U.S., that both Matthews and the *New York Times* could be considered practically in their pockets.[36]

Nevertheless, knowing the close links among the CFR, the CIA and the *New York Times*, one may safely surmise that the Rockefellers were behind the efforts to change Castro into a sort of Hollywood hero more palatable to the American public.[37]

Matthews' articles in the *Times* were just the beginning of a barrage of publicity about Castro. On February 4, 1958, *Look* published an extensive interview with Castro. On February 25, 1958, the *Times* continued giving coverage to Castro and published an interview with the Cuban leader.

Herbert Matthews put Llerena in contact with *CBS*,[38] which was also interested in an interview with Castro. Some weeks later *CBS* broadcasted a special program by CFR member George Taber entitled "The Story of Cuba's Jungle Fighters." On May 27, *Life* published a long, illustrated article about Castro and his struggle against Batista, and a much longer Spanish version, directed to Latin America, appeared two days later in *Life en Español*.

As 1958 advanced and the situation in Cuba tilted toward Fidel Castro and his guerrilla fighters, outside Cuba things also seemed to be going Castro's way. In the United States both the government and the press were becoming more and more favorably disposed towards Fidel Castro and his men. Thanks mainly to the selling of Fidel Castro by the CFR-controlled U.S. media, Americans were being conditioned to see Castro's guerrillas in the Sierra Maestra Mountains as legendary liberators of an oppressed people.

So, it is evident that the Invisible Government of the United States and the mainstream media under its control conveniently paved Castro's road to power.

When Ambassador Earl T. Smith was preparing to assume his new post as Chief of Mission in Havana, no one in the State Department ever mentioned to him Castro's involvement in the *Bogotazo*. Some CFR assets at the State Department arranged to have Smith briefed on Castro's virtues, not by the exiting ambassador, as it was the common practice, but by Herbert Matthews, who was portrayed as an expert in Cuban affairs.

As it is customary in the U.S. diplomatic service, when a man-on-the-spot returns from his post abroad, he is questioned by the State Department about his latest views and his estimate of the situation in the country where he has been living for some years. This process is called debriefing. After Ambassador Smith resigned in January 10, 1959, he was never debriefed. His predecessor, Ambassador Gardner, testified that he was also not debriefed at the end of his mission in Cuba.[39]

U. S. Ambassador Smith commented that, during his mission in Havana, the pro-Castro leanings of the CIA station chief at the embassy were so evident that from time to time he asked him in jest if he was not a *Fidelista*.[40] Testifying before the Senate Internal Security Committee on August 30, 1960, Smith affirmed that the chief of the CIA section in the American Embassy in Havana was pro-Castro, and that the Number 2 CIA man in the embassy encouraged a revolt of Cuban Navy officers against Batista in September 1957.[41]

Ambassador Smith went a step further and accused the United States government, i.e. certain members of the Congress, the CIA, the State Department, as well as some segments of the press, of being directly responsible for Castro coming to power. "Castro never won a military victory," declared Smith, adding,

> The fact that the U.S. was no longer supporting [President] Batista had a devastating psychological effect upon the Cuban armed forces and upon the leaders of the labor movement. These U.S. actions were mostly responsible for the rise of Castro to power."[42]

In October, 1957, one of three young American Navy men who had joined Castro that summer, was designated to go back to the U.S. in a propaganda mission on Castro's behalf. The American entered the U.S. through the U.S. Naval base at Guantánamo, with the full approval of American authorities, and received considerable publicity in the U.S. media. [43]

During his visit to the United States in April 1959, Castro received a lot of coverage in the American media. What the media barely mentioned, however, was that Castro visited the headquarters of the Council on Foreign Relations in New York, where he gave a speech on "Cuba and the United States," and had a long private meeting with David Rockefeller.[44] Nor did the media cover Castro's meeting of over an hour with a friendly, persua-sive, and fluently Spanish-speaking CIA officer. According to some wit-nesses, the CIA man emerged in a state of ecstasy over Castro's receptivity, responsiveness and understanding. The subject of the conversation still re-mains a secret.[45]

With the benefit of hindsight, the sudden efforts of the CFR-controlled press to prove that Castro was a communist seems very suspicious. The same people, who before Castro took power had denied that he was a Com-munist, now had suddenly changed their minds, and were accusing him of being a Communist. To top all, Castro *himself* was telling everybody that he was a Communist. But this made no sense, because Fidel Castro never joined the Cuban Communist Party or any of the many Cuban Communist front organizations. Moreover, Castro was not a crypto-Communist, not even a Communist sympathizer. So, why were these people so eager now to prove that he was a Communist?

It is clear that neither "Yankee imperialism" nor economic conditions were responsible for Castro's alleged turn to "communism." Adding still further to the mystery and complexity of the enigma was the fact that the Cuban Communist party never really opposed Batista. On the contrary, they op-posed all of the anti-Batista movements, including that of Fidel Castro. How could Cuba become a Communist state when the Communists op-posed the revolution that produced that state? If Castro was a Communist, why had the Communist Party initially made such a contemptuous esti-mate of his military operations? If he was a Communist, why did a CIA officer, testifying before a congressional subcommittee, declare that the available evidence did not warrant such a conclusion?

Nobody has satisfactorily explained how a small Caribbean country abruptly became an important player in world politics? How could a vul-gar, filthy gangster, with a photographic memory[46] but a second-rate intel-lect, achieve such unparalleled power and influence in the world? What was his ultimate goal when he sent his troops to Africa in 1975? What were his true intentions when he promoted guerrilla subversion in Latin America, the U.S., Africa and Europe?

Seemingly Castro was delivering to the Russians what they had never dreamed of having. A parade of Communist leaders all over the Americas had been preaching communism for thirty years, and not one of them had been ever able to attain power. Now Castro, not a Communist himself, was gratuitously presenting the Russians with a power base ninety miles from the Unites States. The Russians had ample reasons for being suspicious. Why was Castro delivering Cuba over to Communism? How could Castro become a Communist when the Communists themselves initially opposed the revolution that brought him to power?

Well, now we know: Fidel Castro was David Rockefeller's creation and Castro was advancing the Rockefellers' globalist agenda. An important part of this agenda was the creation of a credible threat South of the border in the form of Soviet Communism, but Premier Khrushchev's doctrine of Peaceful Coexistence intended to end the Cold War. So, good Fidel put all his love and enthusiasm into carrying out David's orders: warming up the Cold War and turn the fear of Communism into a credible threat.

In his *Memoirs*, David Rockefeller deceptively refers to his October 23, 1995, chance encounter with Castro at a reception commemorating the fiftieth anniversary of the U.N. as his first one.

Actually, David had met Castro several times. He had a long private meeting with Castro in April 1959, when Castro visited the CFR headquarters in New York.[47] He also had a long meeting with Castro in February 2001, when he led a high-level CFR delegation visiting Cuba.[48]

Moreover, I found a source claiming that David's first secret meeting with Castro was in 1955, while preparing his expedition to overthrow Cuban President Batista.[49] Unfortunately, I have not found independent confirmation of this Castro-David meeting, but it makes sense that it took place.

David Rockefeller, a secret Nazi supporter, must have been very happy with his selection of Fidel Castro as a secret agent provocateur to destabilize Latin America, Africa and the world as a way to warm up the Cold War Kennedy and Khrushchev had tried to end. Castro's successes proved that his selection had been the right one, and David was proud of it.[50] On the other hand, most likely David's idea of using Cuba as a testing ground for his New World Order may have come as an afterthought.[51]

Part 3

Chapter 11

Killing Presidents: Castro's Life-long Obsession

> *In politics, nothing happens by accident. If it*
> *happens, you can bet it was planned that way.*
> — Franklin D. Roosevelt.

It seems likely, as his subsequent behavior indicate, that his Jesuit precep-tors may have introduced Fidel Castro to the Theology of Father L'Amy, the guiding principle by which the Order gives its members the right to eliminate its adversaries.[1] But we know for sure that, as a student of the Jesuits at the College de Belén High School in Havana, young Fidel Castro heard about the *Compañía*'s principle of the legitimacy of assassinating tyrants and "to commit, without sin, acts which are considered criminal by the ignorant masses."[2]

Proof of it is that in his impassioned self-defense speech during the trial for his 1953 attack on the Moncada Barracks, Castro mentioned how,

> No less a man than Juan Mariana, a Spanish Jesuit during the reign
> of Phillip II, asserts in his book, *De Rege et Regis Institutione*, that
> when a governor usurps power, or even if he were elected, when
> he governs in a tyrannical manner, it is licit for a private citizen to

exercise tyrannicide, either directly or through subterfuge with the least possible disturbance.[3]

We must not blame the Jesuits for Castro's behavior, but for some unknown reason killing presidents became one of his many obsessions, and he began aggressively pursuing it very early in his life. In his massive scholarly study of Castro's revolution, Hugh Thomas mentioned Castro's "desire to carry out a student tradition of tyrannicide."[4]

Unfortunately, as we will see below, Castro's deep hatred for democratically elected presidents overcame whatever tyrannicidal desires he may have felt.

Castro's Attempts to Kill Cuban and Foreign Presidents

In 1947, when he was 21 years old, Castro and a group of University students were visiting President Ramón Grau San Martín, a populist politician democratically elected by popular vote, at the Presidential Palace. At some time during the visit, the President and the students moved close to one of the large, second floor windows facing the park. They were astonished when Castro suggested to some of them to kill the old President. "I have the formula," he whispered, "to take power at once and get rid of this old son-of-a-bitch once for all. Let's pick him up and throw him off the balcony. Once the President is dead, we'll proclaim the triumph of the student revolution and talk to the people on the radio."[5]

Most of Castro's classmates believed that he was *loco*,[6] so they didn't take his suggestion seriously. Nevertheless, it seems that killing presidents was an idea that never left his deranged mind.

In the summer of that same year, Castro joined a group of adventurers who were planning an invasion of the Dominican Republic. The main element of their plan, which eventually failed, was the assassination of President Rafael L. Trujillo and a putsch to take control of the country.[7]

In 1949, while Castro was making arrangements for a trip to the U.S., he used to visit his friend Max Lesnick at his apartment on Morro Street, close to the Presidential palace. Lesnick told Castro's biographer Tad Szulc that one day, while looking at the Presidential palace, Castro grabbed a broomstick and, pointing it like a rifle to the north terrace of the place, said to Lesnick's grandmother: "You know, if [democratically elected President] Prío steps out on that terrace to make a speech, I could get him from here with a single bullet from a telescopic sight rifle . . ."[8]

On March of 1953 Fidel Castro and a group a conspirators concocted a plan to kill President Batista. The opportunity came when Batista decided to attend a meeting of Veterans of the Cuban Independence Wars to be held in Santiago de Cuba, capital of the Oriente province in the Eastern part of the island. Castro and some of the conspirators obtained false documentation, army uniforms and official car plates and traveled to Santiago to wait for Batista's arrival. But Batista got word of the action, changed plans at the last moment, and the assassination attempt didn't take place.

Though most of Castro's early presidential assassination attempts failed to succeed, it would be a mistake to believe that they were just the daydreams of a young, feverish mind. On the contrary, Fidel Castro had a lot of practical experience in the business of political assassination, and the evidence seems to indicate that sometimes he was successful — both in the attempt and in getting away with it.

Fidel Castro's obsession with killing presidents didn't stop after he grabbed power in Cuba in January 1959. In April 26, Castro sent a hit team of eighty-four Cubans and Panamanians to Panama, to kill President Ernesto de la Guardia and spark a revolution. Within a few hours of landing, the invasion was crushed.[9]

The unsuccessful Panama expedition is a good clue to Castro's true political thinking. The Panamanian government was not a dictatorship, and its president had been elected by popular vote, therefore the attack had no ideological justification — that is, if Castro was really the leftist he claimed to be. Moreover, at the time of the attack Castro was visiting Washington in an attempt to allay American fears of his totalitarian leanings.

Just a month after the Panama affair, another group secretly departed from Cuba and headed for Costa Rica in an operation to kill Nicaraguan President/Dictator Luis Somoza, Castro's sworn enemy. On the first of June 1959, two planes full of invaders left Costa Rica and headed for Nicaragua. The invasion was suppressed in a few hours, and Castro denied any involvement in the attack.

Less than two weeks later, on June 14, 1959, Castro sent a similar group to the Dominican Republic to kill President Trujillo. Fidel Castro's personal involvement in this expedition is undeniable. The group, consisting of some 200 Dominican exiles that had been undergoing military training in Cuba, and ten Cubans, all commanded by one of Castro's Rebel Army officers, left Cuba in a plane and two small ships and headed for the northern coast of the Dominican Republic. Nonetheless, the invasion soon ended in total failure, and Trujillo's army soldiers left no survivors to tell the story.

Both the Nicaraguan and Dominican operations ended in failure, and Castro denied that he personally had authorized the ventures. However, given Castro's propensity to assassinate his opponents and his total control over Cuban events, one has to conclude that he was fully behind the attempts.[10]

A couple of months later, in mid-August, 1959, Castro struck again. This time an expeditionary force moved against Haiti. Its main goal was to assassinate François "Papa Doc" Duvalier, the dictatorial president of Haiti, another of Castro's preferred targets. Che Guevara, following Castro's direct orders, had organized the expedition. Like the expeditions on Panama and Dominican Republic, the Haitian adventure ended in total disaster, and most of the attackers were killed. Castro never responded to or denied the Duvalier's government charges of his complicity in the affair.[11]

On July 26, 1960, in a speech commemorating the failed attack on the Moncada garrison in Santiago de Cuba, Fidel Castro declared his commitment to "liberate" the rest of Latin America.[12] What he didn't make clear, however, is that his technique to achieve that goal essentially consisted in the indiscriminate application of Fascist-like putschist *coup d'ètats*, including the assassination of democratically elected presidents of the target countries.

There is evidence that Castro also tried to kill the democratically elected president of Panama, Roberto Chiari. According to an FBI report dated October 25, 1962, one of Castro's hit men, Humberto Rodríguez Díaz, in complicity with a former Cuban ambassador to Panama, planned an attempt on the life of the Panamanian president.[13]

In the spring of 1963, Castro shipped several tons of weapons and ammunition to a Venezuelan revolutionary underground.[14] Castro's obsession with killing President Rómulo Betancourt, who initially was his supporter, has been extensively documented.

That same year Bogotá's newspapers published reports that planes that had landed at Colombia's Guajira peninsula carrying a group of assassins from Cuba had been sent by Fidel Castro. Their mission was to kill President León Valencia and overthrow his government. The information was officially corroborated on October 17, 1963, by President León Valencia himself, who notified all diplomatic missions in Bogotá that he held Castro responsible for the action.

A few months later, on February 26, 1964, coinciding with a planned visit of President Valencia to Cali, another plot to kill him was uncovered. Next year President Valencia pointed to Castro as the instigator behind both assassination attempts.[15]

On July 19, 1979, Nicaraguan dictator Luis Somoza was overthrown by the Castro-backed *Frente Sandinista de Liberación Nacional* (FSLN, Sandinista Front for National Liberation), and fled the country to become a political exile in Paraguay. Just a few months later, Somoza and his body-guards were assassinated on a street of Asunción by a Sandinista hit team using machine guns and bazookas. Some members of Castro's intelligence services boasted at the time that the assassination team, mostly composed of ETA Basque separatists, had been trained in Cuba.[16]

Castro Profoundly Hated President Kennedy

Shortly after taking office in 1963, President Lyndon Johnson discovered that, as he graphically put it, "We had been operating a damned Murder Inc. in the Caribbean." According to what he told some close friends, LBJ suspected that a vengeance-seeking Fidel Castro might have triggered President Kennedy's assassination.[17]

Johnson had suspicions that John F. Kennedy's assassin had been "influenced or directed" by Fidel Castro, and his suspicions grew stronger with time. A few years after the Kennedy assassination, LBJ confided to Howard K. Smith, "I will tell you something that will rock you. Kennedy was trying to get Castro, but Castro got to him first."[18]

A book about LBJ's White House tapes shows that Johnson suspected Castro had been an important player in President Kennedy's death. But, as he expresses in some secret tapes, if the U.S. had blamed Castro or the Russians, Americans would have demanded a retaliatory attack upon Cuba or the Soviet Union, initiating a war that would have killed 40 million Americans in the first hour.[19]

In the same fashion, John Karamessines, assistant to CIA Director Richard Helms (CFR), was quoted as saying that some people at the, "CIA feared that the Cubans were responsible for the assassination," which, if proved true, might lead to an international crisis that could literally mean the end of the world.[20]

The theory, however, that implicating Castro in the JFK assassination may trigger a war with the Soviet Union was a makeshift pretext concocted by CFR agents at the CIA to justify their covering up of Castro's role in the assassination.

Nonetheless, Robert Kennedy suspected that Castro ordered his brother's assassination. When, in January 1971, Jack Anderson broke the story of the anti-Castro plotting by the Kennedy brothers, he reported that Robert Kennedy was emotionally devastated after the President's assassination by the possibility that his efforts in trying to assassinate Castro may well have led to Castro assassinating his brother.[21] What seemingly never crossed Robert's mind was that Castro and the CIA had worked together in carrying out his brother's assassination.

Among the many people who shared similar suspicions, was Chief Justice Earl Warren. He told some friends privately that he believed Castro was "one of the principal suspects" in the assassination.[22] Moreover, there is evidence that some senior intelligence officers in Cuba suspected that Castro had a direct participation in the assassination of President Kennedy.[23]

Another who had strong suspicions about Castro's role in the Kennedy assassination was Thomas Mann, former American Ambassador to Mexico. As he later expressed,

> Castro is the kind of person who would avenge himself in this way. He is the Latin type of extremist who reacts viscerally rather than intellectually and apparently without much regard for risks. His whole life story shows this.[24]

Senator Robert Morgan, a member of the Senate Intelligence Committee (the "Church Committee"), went a step further. He was not merely suspicious, but totally convinced that Castro was the assassin. According to Morgan, "There is no doubt in my mind that John Fitzgerald Kennedy was assassinated by Fidel Castro, or someone under his influence, in retaliation for our efforts to assassinate him."[25]

President Johnson and the rest of the people who had suspicions about Castro's role in the assassination were probably not too far off the mark, because Castro had strong reasons for revenge. The very same day that Kennedy was killed in Dallas, Desmond Fitzgerald, a senior CIA officer and a personal friend of Robert Kennedy, following orders from the U.S. Attorney General, was having a secret meeting with Rolando Cubela, a senior Cuban official, to discuss the assassination of Fidel Castro.[26]

The CIA always kept its alleged efforts to assassinate Castro very quiet and hidden from the American public. After the assassination of President Kennedy, CIA's Dulles[27] and Angleton kept the records hidden from the Warren Commission as well. The CIA's memory lapses before the Church Committee were remarkable, because spymaster Allen Dulles, then the Agency's Director, sat on the panel. Senator Richard Schweiker, who as a member of the Church Committee listened to all the witnesses on the subject, was puzzled by the CIA's forgetfulness, and raised the possibility that Kennedy had been killed in retaliation for his attempts to assassinate Castro.

But, strange bedfellows, both American liberals and their arch enemy CIA have always been at pains in their efforts to hide the existence of any connections between Fidel Castro and the assassination of President John F. Kennedy. For example, in an article in which sixty different versions of the Kennedy assassination are mentioned and where all types of theories about the *who* and *why* are given, author Edward Jay Epstein, whose close CIA links have been suggested, mentions only one in which Castro appears implicated with the assassination. In this only case, it happens to be a theory proposed, of all people, by famous psychic Jeanne Dixon.[28]

In the same fashion, Russian author Igor Efimov gives a list of eight probable connections to the Kennedy assassination, and lists them in order of importance: 1. the Mafia; 2. LBJ; 3. J. Edgar Hoover; 4. right wing extremists; 5. anti-Castro Cubans; 6. the military-industrial complex; 7. Nikita Khrushchev; and 8. Fidel Castro.[29]

Likewise, sociologist David Simone, working on a study of the books dealing with the Kennedy assassination, compiled about six hundred titles and found that 20 percent of them blamed either a lone assassin or the media or the anti-Castro Cubans or the Russians. The other 80 percent blamed the CIA.[30] However, not a single book published at the time pointed to Fidel Castro as the instigator of the assassination.

Similarly, although there was a large amount of evidence pointing to the possibility of a Castro connection to the assassination of President Kennedy, the American investigative agencies, for some strange reason, choose to look the other way. The fact is explicitly mentioned in the Schweiker report,

> Despite knowledge of Oswald's apparent interest in pro-Castro and anti-Castro activities and top-level awareness of certain CIA assassination plots, the FBI made no special investigative effort into questions of possible Cuban government or Cuban exile involvement in the assassination independent of the Oswald investigation. . . . [This] failure to follow significant leads in the Cuba area is surprising. These leads raise significant questions.[31]

To some extent it is understandable that CFR agents in the CIA, President Johnson, and some other CFR-controlled U.S. Government agencies, were apprehensive about the possibility of either a Kremlin or a Castro connection. Any link between Castro and the Kennedy assassination, they allegedly feared, might bring up a situation potentially as dangerous as the Cuban missile crisis.[32] It is more difficult, however, to understand the American liberals' interest in ignoring the possibility of any Castro-Kennedy connection. An explanation that has been advanced for this behavior is that they feared finding themselves in the end pointing a finger at their usual example of assassination attempts by the evil CIA: Fidel Castro.[33]

Some Castro-friendly authors have made an extraordinary effort trying to prove that, far from hating Kennedy, at the time of the assassination Castro actually had begun an effort to seek an accommodation with the U.S.[34] A typical example of this type of asinine argument is Peter Kornbluh's article "JFK & Castro: The Secret Quest for Accommodation."[35] To support his thesis, Kornbluh brings a series of declassified documents showing that, unbeknownst to all but his brother and a few close advisors, President Kennedy had begun in 1963 a secret path towards a rapprochement with Castro. Kornbluh also mentions some declassified documents proving that Castro had made some overtures in the same direction.

Nevertheless, apart from the inconsistencies between those documents and the actual behavior of Castro and the Kennedys, Kornbluh's article is too close for comfort to the official Castroist line developed by the Cuban intelligence services. Both Carlos Lechuga, a former Cuban ambassador to the U.N., and Fabián Escalante, a senior Cuban counterintelligence officer, produced exactly this same type of disinformation for many years.[36]

In his article, Kornbluh reluctantly admits that "John F, Kennedy would seem the most unlikely of presidents to seek an accommodation with Fidel Castro." The reason for this unlikeness, which Kornbluh seems to ignore, is because at the time of his alleged moves to rapprochement, JFK and his brother actually were aggressively planning the assassination of Fidel Castro, a fact that not even a thousand dubious declassified documents can deny.

Most of the arguments developed by these authors follow this line: After the Cuban missile crisis Kennedy made up his mind to tolerate Castro. Kennedy refused to invade Cuba, and was preparing to normalize relations with the Cuban leader. During the Cuban missile crisis, the argument goes, President Kennedy reached an agreement with Soviet Premier Nikita Khrushchev that included his promise to stop the secret war against Cuba and the assassinations attempts against Castro.

But these arguments don't ring true. In the first place, there is no evidence that such an agreement between Kennedy and Khrushchev ever took place. Henry Kissinger, for one, once tried to find it when he was Secretary of State, but was not successful in his search. Other attempts to find the document have failed as well. Consequently, it is safe to surmise that it never existed. Secondly, there is strong evidence that after the Cuban missile crisis the Kennedy brothers persisted in their anti-Castro policies. Close friends and associates have recorded the visceral hatred Kennedy and his brother felt for Castro before, during, and after the missile crisis. Ted Sorensen reported that, after the missile crisis, President Kennedy continued his efforts to isolate the Castro regime, and remained committed to "harass, disrupt and weaken Cuba politically and economically."[37]

A report by the CIA inspector general of August 25, 1967, stated, "We cannot overemphasize the extent to which responsible agency officers felt themselves subject to the Kennedy administration's severe pressures to do something about Castro and his regime."[38] Former CIA director Richard Helms shared the same opinion. Talking to Ronald Kessler, Helms said, "All I know is Jack Kennedy and his brother were bound to have us take on this effort [to get rid of Castro]."[39]

Through David Rockefeller's CFR agents at the highest levels of the CIA, Castro knew of this. He had, therefore, no reason to believe that the Kennedys had changed their minds about him so fast. Out of personal experience, Castro may have guessed that, as it happens with most politicians, President Kennedy's words for public consumption were in sharp contrast with his actions. But, even if the Kennedys had changed their minds, even if their hatred for Castro had suddenly and inexplicably turned into love, it would have made no difference at all, at least to Castro's vengeful, never forgetful eyes.

As his close friends have testified over and over, Castro is a very vindictive person.[40] He never forgets a personal offense, real or imagined, particularly when he feels he has been humiliated. There is evidence that he felt deeply humiliated with the outcome of the missile crisis. Witnesses recall his furious temper tantrum when he got the news that Khrushchev and Kennedy had solved the crisis behind his back, fully ignoring him.

I witnessed myself first hand Castro's rage when, a few days after the end of the crisis, an angry Castro told a group of students at the University of Havana that Nikita Khrushchev was *"un maricón"* (a faggot),[41] and John F. Kennedy *"un millonario come mierda y un hijo de puta"* (lit. a shit-eating millionaire and a son of a bitch).[42] Actually, Castro had enough reasons for feeling that Kennedy had tried to humiliate him. Sorensen recalls that some of the measures suggested by the Ex-Comm[43] to President Kennedy, like low-level flights over Cuba, for example, were intended not only to improve reconnaissance but also to harass and humiliate Castro.[44]

Castro's Version of the Kennedy Assassination

On November 22, 1963, Fidel Castro was engaged in a friendly conversation with French journalist Jean Daniel when the news came that President Kennedy had been assassinated. Daniel told the story in detail.

It was around 1:30 in the afternoon, Cuban time, wrote Daniel. We were having lunch in the living room of the modest summer residence that Fidel Castro owns on magnificent Varadero Beach, 120 kilometers from Havana. The phone rang, and an aide told Fidel that President Dorticós had an urgent message for him. Fidel picked up the phone and I heard him say: *"¿Cómo? ¿Un atentado?"* ("What? An assassination attempt?") Castro then told Daniel that Kennedy had been shot in Dallas.

According to Daniel, Castro's initial reaction was of surprise and shock. He came back, wrote Daniel, sat down, and repeated three times the words: *"Es una mala noticia."* (That's bad news). Then, he asked Daniel, "But tell me, how many Presidents have there been in the United States? Thirty-six? And four of them have been assassinated. That's disturbing. Here in Cuba there has never been a President assassinated. You know, when we were in the Sierra, there were people (not in my group, but another) who wanted to kill Batista. They believed that they could put an end to the regime by cutting off his head. As for myself, I was always furiously hostile to such methods."[45]

Only three days earlier, in November 19th, *l'Express* had published Daniel's previous interview with Castro, in which the Cuban leader had said that, although he considered Kennedy was to blame for most of the Bay of Pigs incident, "I believe that in the last few months he has come to a better understanding of the situation and, in any case, I am convinced that anyone who might replace him would be worse." Daniel attributed to Castro the assertion that if peace in North and South America were to be won, "there must arise in the United States a man with the capacity to understand and to adapt himself to the explosive reality of Latin America." To Castro, Daniel pointed out,

> . . . this man might, even now, be Kennedy. He still has the full opportunity of becoming, in the eyes of History, the greatest President of the United States — the one who would at last come to recognition of the fact that there can be coexistence between capitalists and socialists, even in the American hemisphere. He would

then be even a greater President than Lincoln. I know that Khrushchev, for example, considers Kennedy a man with whom it is possible to have discussions. . . Other people tell me that, before discussions can take place, it will be necessary to await his second term. . . if you see him again, you can tell him that, if it helps him to win his re-election, I am ready to announce that [presidential candidate, Senator Barry] Goldwater is a friend of mine![46]

Daniel had an interview scheduled to see Kennedy a short time after his return from Dallas. He already had had an interview with Kennedy on October 24th, before going directly to Havana to interview Castro. Daniel promised Castro that he would go back to the United States to deliver his confidential message to Kennedy before either interview were published.

Liberal journalists have interpreted Castro's message to Kennedy as an effort through non-diplomatic channels to explore the possibility of normalizing U.S.-Cuban relations. An affirmative response by the American President, they claim, would have paved the way to an eventual top-level meeting with Kennedy — a meeting much less likely to be held with his successor — one which might have stabilized the Castro Government, enabling it to channel funds and labor, now invested in national defense and weapons, to economic projects desperately needed by the Cuban people. That was not the right moment, they reasoned, Castro would have chosen to kill President Kennedy.

Between July and October of 1974, Castro-friendly American journalists Frank Mankiewicz and Kirby Jones visited Cuba three times and recorded a series of interviews with Fidel Castro. In an introduction to the book they published later, the authors mentioned how, among dozens of requests from all three American TV networks and newspapers and many foreign countries, Castro rejected all others and selected them. It seems that Castro's intelligence officers did their homework, because the questions drawn up by Mankiewicz and Jones were designed to allow Castro to show his best colors — not necessarily the true ones. In one of the interviews the subject of John F. Kennedy was brought up.

Contrary to what some people may think, Fidel Castro knows Americans very well. His answers to Mankiewicz and Jones mentioned all the nice things about Kennedy American liberals loved to hear. In typical Castro fashion, like when he was trying to mesmerize his audience, he lowered his voice, looked Mankiewicz and Jones in the eye, and told them about Kennedy's courage and decisiveness and how unpleasant it was for him to learn about the President's death.

Then, Castro approached the subject of the assassination and, after expressing some ideas that seemed to have been taken directly from the Warren Commission report, he ended up by stating, categorically, "We have never believed in carrying out this type of activity of assassination of adversaries." Not even during the early stages of your revolutionary fight? — he was asked. "Never. And our revolutionary background proves it."[47]

In mid-1975, Democratic Senator George McGovern (CFR) visited Cuba. While he was talking to Castro during a long drive back to Havana from the provinces he raised the question of Kennedy's assassinations. McGovern recalls that Castro answered in disbelief:

> We had troubles with the Kennedy administration, but it is monstrous even to contemplate that we might murder the head of state of any nation, to say nothing of being so foolish as to incur the wrath of a great power like the United States.

Senator McGovern said that he was impressed by Castro's sincerity and rational, logical arguments.[48] Apparently the good, leftist senator ignored that, notwithstanding his constant claims for truthfulness, Fidel Castro was a consummate liar, and a very convincing one. Over the years, he proved to be a master of saying one thing while having in mind something totally different.

Fidel Castro was a compulsive, pathological liar. He lied not only for political reasons about things of cardinal importance, but also gratuitously, over matters of little relevance. But, as it happens with most compulsive liars, he had a strong concern about keeping his image of a sincere, truthful person.

Just a perfunctory reading of Castro's speeches shows dozens of instances in which he admitted *a posteriori* that he had lied. An analyst of Castro's political behavior pointed out that "the Cuban dictator is a liar who confesses the truth — retroactively."[49] The fact explain why, writing about Castro's unbroken record of deceit, Cuban exile Mario Lazo, who knew him well, called Fidel Castro "the great dissembler."[50]

On April 3, 1978, some members of the House Select Committee on Assassinations traveled to Havana and managed to get an interview with Fidel Castro. In all, they spent more than four hours with the Cuban leader, in which many topics related and unrelated with the Kennedy assassination were discussed. Castro expressed his reaction to allegations of his complicity in the Kennedy assassination in this way:

Who here could have operated and planned something so delicate as the death of the United States president? That was insane. From the ideological point of view, it was tremendous insanity. That would have been the most perfect pretext for the United States to invade our country, which is what I have tried to prevent for all these years.[51]

Though some members of the group were not fully satisfied with Castro's explanation, most of them agreed that what he had said made sense. But, by unconsciously applying the mirror image theory that implies that whatever makes sense to them must make sense to everybody, the members of the Committee made a big mistake.

Adding insult to injury, a relatively recent book revealed that the Warren Commission had questioned Castro.[52] The story of Castro's questioning was told in *A Cruel and Shocking Act: the Secret History of the Kennedy Assassination*, a book by Philip Shenon, a former investigative reporter for the CFR-controlled *New York Times*. Not surprisingly, Shenon does not dispute the Warren Commission's conclusion that Lee Harvey Oswald was the lone gunman. In fact, he, again, underlines that there is no evidence to suggest there was a conspiracy or anybody else involved.

Senator McGovern asking Castro face to face if he had ordered the Kennedy assassination may have been an example of naïveté or stupidity, but I don't think McGovern was naïve or stupid. Then, how can we explain such foolish behavior?

First of all, if something characterized Castro's behavior it is his irrationality and lack of common sense. The fact has been extensively documented, mostly under a positive light, to explain some of Castro's successes. Secondly, contrary to his claims, the evidence shows that practically since he took power in Cuba in 1959, Fidel Castro actually tried, by any means available, to provoke the United States into invading Cuba. Finally, given Castro's long history of insanity and irrationality and the way his convoluted mind worked, the fact that he so emphatically stated that it would have been insane for him to order the Kennedy assassination is in itself a strong indication that he may well have been involved in it.

As we have seen above, sometimes Castro's photographic memory works selectively. His claims to Mankiewicz and Jones that "We have never believed in carrying out this type of activity of assassination of adversaries. Never," were highly misleading.[53] Moreover, contrary to what he said to Jean Daniel when he heard the news of the Kennedy assassination, Fidel Castro's background actually shows that, far from being "furiously hostile" to political assassination, he actually was always very fond of it.

The information I have provided above summarizes most of the American scholars' and journalists' Castro-friendly version of Castro's version of the Kennedy assassination. Notwithstanding his claims, however, the available record by far contradicts his words. First of all, Castro never felt much respect for John F. Kennedy. In his speech to the U. N. General Assembly in 1960, Castro called Kennedy "an illiterate and ignorant millionaire," a characterization that perhaps was not too far off the mark.[54]

In September 1963, Castro showed up unexpectedly at a Brazilian Embassy reception in Havana and launched into a tirade against JFK. Castro called President Kennedy, "the Batista of his time, and the most opportunistic American president of all times," and ended by calling JFK *"un cretino"* (an idiot).[55]

Secondly, just a little digging into his early history shows that Castro's claim that he had always been furiously hostile to the assassination of adversaries, including presidents, was in strong contradiction with the facts. Contrasting with the Kennedys, who were just *aficionados* in the art of political assassination, Castro had a lot of hands-on experience.

There is abundant circumstantial evidence indicating that Castro knew in advance about the CIA's plans to assassinate President Kennedy the same way he knew in advance about the upcoming invasion at the Bay of Pigs.[56] Now, because of the size of the operation, the invasion plans were known by dozens, even hundreds of people and Castro's foreknowledge may be explained by the possibility that he had spies infiltrated among the invaders and the anti-Castro community in Miami.

In contrast, however, the JFK assassination operation was a top-level secret operation, known only by a few CFR agents at the highest levels of CIA. Even more, in the case of the CIA, as in every intelligence agency in the world, all operational information about top-level operations is strictly kept under the terms of need-to-know and compartmentation. This means that information about an operation is given only to the people who need to know and only the part they need to know to carry out their part in it. Moreover, like in the Indian parable of the six blind men and the elephant, the participants in an operation are compartmentalized to the point that they only know about the specific part of the operation they are going to play a role in, but don't need to know about parts of it in which they have no direct participation. This forbids that, not even by applying any type of logic, they may guess what the operation is all about.[57]

So, because of this, one can safely assume that Castro knew about the assassination not because some of his secret agents allegedly infiltrated into the CIA had informed him, but because he was part of the operation.

But, some may ask, how come Castro would be a CIA asset when the CIA tried to assassinate Castro several times.[58] According to the 2006 British documentary *638 Ways to Kill Castro*, "More people have tried to murder the world's most famous socialist than any man alive."

The source of this information is *Executive Action: 634 Ways to Kill Fidel Castro*, a book by former chief of Cuba's counterintelligence Fabián Escalante.[59] There are many stories about how dozens of CIA-planned attempts to assassinate Castro ended in failure. In its investigations about the allegations, the Senate Committee on assassinations, chaired by Senator Frank Church, found "concrete evidence" of eight assassination plots involving the CIA against the Cuban leader. On the other hand, in August 1975, Castro complained to Senator George McGovern that the actual number was, in fact, twenty-four.[60]

This paints the CIA as sort of gang that couldn't shoot straight. Other sources, however, indicate that the CIA was actually the gang that shouldn't shoot straight.[61] It is very difficult to believe that the CIA, who failed to kill Castro after so many assassination attempts, managed to assassinate Kennedy on the very first attempt. Only the must gullible can accept this.

The conspiracy theory that the CIA ever tried to assassinate Castro is even more farfetched than the one created by the Warren Commission about Oswald being the lone nut assassin. Contrary to what die-hard Castro admirers claim, far from trying to kill Castro the CIA always protected him. The best evidence of this is that the CIA, so expert in assassinating people abroad and in the U.S., never killed Castro, and that is an easily verifiable, incontrovertible fact.

Nevertheless, a not well-known interesting detail is that all the failed alleged assassination attempts on Castro, even the ones in which some anti-Castro Cubans in the U.S. participated, were all conducted by the CIA or under CIA supervision. On the other hand, the CIA was very careful in not allowing anti-Castro Cubans to attempt the assassination by themselves alone. Actually, when some of them tried to assassinate Castro free-lance, the FBI acted against them to prevent the operation. A logical explanation is that, far from trying to kill Castro, the CIA was actually protecting him, and the assassination attempts were just acting, which explains why all of them failed.

It seems that at least some anti-Castro Cubans who really wanted to assassinate Castro, at some time arrived at a similar conclusion. Anti-Castro physician Orlando Bosch, for one, who actively fought Castro since the mid-Sixties, always cautioned Cubans in Miami about not trusting the CIA in their war against Castro.[62] This cautious behavior may explain why Bosh survived the anti-Castro war and died of old age in his eighties and his friend Luis Posada Carriles is still alive.

Another who discovered that the Castro-CIA combination was extremely unhealthy was Nicaragua's guerrilla leader Edén Pastora, the famous "Comandante cero." In 1986 Pastora gave up his four-year struggle fighting both the Somoza dictatorship and the CIA, surrendered his guerrilla group to the Costa Rican government and asked for political asylum in that country.[63]

A Different Version of Castro's Role in the Kennedy Assassination

When Senator George McGovern took at face value Castro's answers to his questions, he was either too naïve, or just another victim of Castro's powers of fascination.[64] Any intelligence analyst would agree that an evaluation of Fidel Castro's version of the Kennedy assassination should be that the source was unreliable and the accuracy of the information doubtful. (See Appendix II, The Evaluation of Information.)

The fact that the Kennedy brothers were out to get Castro has been extensively documented. Also, the evidence indicates that Castro knew all the time of the assassination attempts. On September 7, 1963, two months before the Kennedy assassination, Castro referred to the assassination attempts against him in a speech, adding that Kennedy and his brother would take care of themselves, since they, too, might become targets.[65]

After Kennedy was killed in Dallas, the CIA engaged in an extraordinary cover-up operation. Though many facts pointed to a Castro connection, the CIA literally erased all links between Castro and the Kennedy assassination. Facts like Oswald's arrest in New Orleans while distributing pro-Castro pamphlets, his presentation on a New Orleans radio program defending Castro, and his visit to the Cuban consulate in Mexico City, were ignored, interpreted as disinformation or treated as non-relevant. Following Allen Dulles' orders, CIA's counterintelligence Chief James J. Angleton even went to the point of calling Bill Sullivan of the FBI and rehearsing with him the answers they would give to the Warren Commission investigators.[66]

Both Castro's reaction to the assassination and the American liberal media's explanation of the rationality of his position are in total contradiction with Castro's previous behavior. First of all, contrary to American wishful thinking, Castro never sought the normalization of his relations with the United States. An incident, in which in 1996 he ordered his air force to shoot down two civilian airplanes of the Brothers to the Rescue organization at the same time President Clinton was trying to normalize relations with Cuba, is evidence of this. Castro's anti-American vendetta was his main *raison d'être*, so it doesn't make any sense that he was going to change precisely at that time. Secondly, the normalization of relations with the United States would have had no effect on the stabilization of the Castro regime, for the simple reason that the main destabilizing force in Cuba was never the United States, but Castro himself.

Moreover, it doesn't make any sense either, as some have indicated, that the normalization of relations with the U.S. would have allowed Castro to channel funds and labor he was investing in weapons, to economic projects desperately needed by the Cuban people. Living himself and his clique in opulence, Castro has never cared much for the desperate needs of the Cuban people. Investing in weapons and other means of mass destruction was his main hobby. No wonder Cubans used to call him, among many other nicknames, *"Armando Guerra,"* a common Hispanic name that is also a pun for "making war."

On several occasions Fidel Castro categorically denied any knowledge or participation in the Kennedy assassination, but the facts point to the contrary. For a long time there have been rumors in the media that, during his visit to the Cuban Consulate, Lee Harvey Oswald expressed his intentions to kill President Kennedy. Cuban Consulate employees Eusebio Azcue and Rubén Durán, the ones who talked to Oswald during his visit, claimed that they heard no such threat, and so the fact remains a mystery. But there is at least one important person who believed they were not telling the truth. Clarence Kelley, Hoover's replacement as FBI Director, was convinced that Oswald actually made such a threat.[67]

The story of Oswald's visit to the Cuban Consulate in Mexico City has always been surrounded by mystery. The CIA claimed that it did not know that Oswald had visited the Cuban Consulate until after the assassination. An explanation given *a posteriori* by CFR agent Richard Helms was that CIA denials were intended to protect the Agency's sources there. But some people believe the denials were actually intended to cover something even more damaging than the fact that the CIA knew about Oswald's threats to kill Kennedy.

FBI's Director J. Edgar Hoover told the Warren Commission that Castro mentioned Oswald's threats to a Bureau's source known by the code name "Solo," but this fact was withheld from the American public. The National Archives released Solo's file in early 1995, and there are clues in it to suggest that "Solo" was probably Morris Childs.[68] The file shows that Solo-Childs informed the FBI about Castro's knowledge of Oswald's threats.

Kelley was convinced that during his visit to the Cuban Consulate, Oswald "definitely offered to kill President Kennedy." He added that the "Solo" source in Cuba "verified that Oswald had offered to kill the American president." Kelley's use of the word "verified" instead of "discovered" seems to be hinting that the CIA knew about this and did not inform the FBI. Also, there are indications that, at some time before the assassination, the Cuban bureau at the CIA had developed a keen operational interest in Oswald.[69]

But this is not the only disturbing fact linking Fidel Castro to the assassination of President Kennedy. In January 8, 1959, just a few days after Castro's victory over Batista's forces, Jack Ruby made a contact with Robert (Dick) McKeown, a gunrunner who had been supplying Castro with arms. A few weeks later, on February 1, Ruby met McKeown in Kemah, Texas, and offered him $15,000 for a personal introduction to Castro.

On April 27, 1959, after concluding his first trip to the United States following his victory, Castro traveled to Houston. Next day, he met with McKeown and offered him a job in the Cuban government. McKeown turned Castro's offer down.

On July 8, 1959, Castro ordered that an important CIA asset, Santo Trafficante, Jr., Florida numbers-racket boss and key man in the Meyer Lansky gambling empire in Havana, be detained and eventually expelled from Cuba. In the meanwhile, Trafficante was held in a jail not far from Havana. Some witnesses claim, however, that Trafficante's conditions in Castro's jail were privileged — his jail resembled a hotel room, with air-conditioner and a TV set.

On September 5, 1959, Jack Ruby flew to Havana where he spent several days. There is evidence that he visited Trafficante in his cell more than once. On September 12 Ruby flew again to Havana from Miami, returning the same day. U.S. Immigration and Naturalization records about Ruby's first visit to Havana are nonexistent or missing, although they show that he did fly from Miami to Havana, and then from Havana to New Orleans on

September 13.[70]

But there is more than meets the eye in the Castro-Trafficante connection. Some people, including some CIA officers, suspected that Castro had managed to turn Trafficante into his agent. According to them, it was Trafficante who had been providing Castro with inside information about CIA-Mafia attempts to kill him. There were rumors at the time among Cuban exiles in Miami, that when Castro ran the Mafia racketeers out of Cuba and seized the casinos, he put Trafficante in jail to cover up the fact that Trafficante was working for him.[71]

Even more, there is strong evidence that, in September of 1962, Trafficante hinted that Kennedy was going to be assassinated. In a conversation with José Alemán, a wealthy Cuban exile, Trafficante said, "Mark my words, this man Kennedy is in trouble and he will get what is coming to him." When Alemán suggested that Kennedy would probably get reelected, Trafficante replied, "No, José, he is going to be hit."[72] Some people interpreted this conversation as evidence that the Mafia was behind the president's assassination. However, if it is true, as the evidence seems to indicate, that at the time Trafficante was in fact a Castro asset, Trafficante's words take on a totally different meaning.

Alemán was convinced that Trafficante had ties with Cubela, and that both Trafficante and Cubela were working for Castro. Though Alemán did not know at the time that Trafficante was the point man for the CIA's attempts to kill Castro, or that the CIA had recruited Rolando Cubela to do the job, he had a strong suspicion that Trafficante and Cubela were "linked", and that "something was wrong in some way." Alemán's suspicions were based mainly on the fact that he believed Cubela was a Castroist agent, and that Trafficante's *bolita* (numbers racket) revenues were used to pay off Castro's secret agents in the U. S.[73]

Even though he was unaware of it, Alemán's suspicions had been expressed in a very similar way on a Federal Bureau of Narcotics memo dated July 21, 1961, reporting rumors that Castro had put Trafficante in jail merely "to make it appear that he had a personal dislike for Castro, when in fact Trafficante is an agent of Castro," and his "outlet for illegal contraband in the country." The memo went on to confirm Alemán's suspicions about the *bolita* scheme, stating that, "Fidel Castro has operatives in Miami making heavy bets with Santo Trafficante Jr.'s organization."[74]

On March 16, 1977, Santo Trafficante was summoned before the House Assassinations Committee and asked if he had known or discussed with anybody information that President Kennedy was going to be assassinated. Trafficante refused to answer, citing his Constitutional right to avoid self-incrimination.[75] He likewise remained silent when asked if Jack Ruby had visited him in Cuba in 1959. The Committee reported that there was "considerable evidence" that such an encounter "did take place."[76]

There are even more loose ends pointing to a Castro connection to the JFK assassination. First, there is information that on November 22, 1962, the very same day Kennedy was shot in Dallas at 12:30 p.m., a "mysterious passenger" departed from Mexico City to Havana after having arrived from the United States in a highly irregular way. According to the Senate Committee report,

> On December 1, 1963, CIA received information that a November 22 Cubana Airlines flight from Mexico City to Cuba was delayed some five hours, from 6:00 p.m. to 11:00 p.m. E.S.T., awaiting an unidentified passenger. This unidentified passenger arrived at the airport in a twin-engine aircraft at 10:30 p.m. and boarded the Cubana Airlines plane without passing through customs, where he would have needed to identify himself by displaying a passport. The individual traveled to Cuba in the cockpit of the Cubana Airlines plane, thus again avoiding identification by the passengers.[77]

Moreover, in June 1976, the Church Committee disclosed that CIA and FBI files relating to the assassination of President Kennedy contained references to the mysterious movements of a "pro-Castro Cuban-American" who flew to Cuba shortly after the events in Dallas.[78] According to the Senate Committee Report, at least one source told the CIA that this Cuban-American might have been involved in the assassination of President Kennedy. It is also believed that he was a member of the Tampa, Florida branch of the Fair Play For Cuba Committee, to which Lee Oswald had once written. Evidence surfaced some years later shows that the mysterious passenger was Miguel Casas Sáez, a close associate of Raúl Castro. Casas, who was fluent in Russian, had been in Dallas from early November to the 22nd.[79]

Apparently, Casas was not the only Castro agent in Dallas the day of the assassination. James Johnston, a Washington lawyer who has studied the assassination in detail, wrote about the strange behavior of an alleged Cuban-American named Gilberto Policarpio López, a sort of Oswald's double. "Like Oswald," wrote Johnston, "he had recently applied for a Cuban visa but it had been denied. Like Oswald, he was living alone because of alleged marital problems. Like Oswald, he had contacts with the

Fair Play for Cuba Committee."[80] After getting a Mexican visa, López flew from Tampa to Texas on November 20th, and entered Mexico the day after the assassination. According to Johnston, López was the only passenger on board on a Cubana Airlines flight to Havana on November 27th.

Nevertheless, for some strange reasons the FBI failed to follow up on information received by CIA headquarters from its Mexico Station on December 3, 1963, about the suspicious activities of Casas and López. Though López' itinerary was confirmed by several sources, the FBI failed to investigate him. Even more, there is a March 20, 1964, memo from Mexico Station to the CIA Director, stating that one of their sources heard that "Gilberto López, U.S. citizen, was involved in President Kennedy's assassination."[81]

Finally, there is the undeniable fact that Castro *did* threaten to kill President Kennedy. In an impromptu interview with Associate Press correspondent Daniel Harker while attending a reception at the Brazilian Embassy in September 7, 1963, Castro delivered a very clear warning to the Kennedy brothers. Talking about the attempts by the Kennedys to "get" him, he said that the members of the Kennedy administration would find themselves in danger if they persisted in their behavior, bitterly adding,

> We are prepared to fight them and answer in kind. United States leaders should think that if they are aiding terrorist plans to eliminate Cuban leaders . . . they themselves will not be safe.[82]

Castro's words to Harker, including his warning to the Kennedys, initially appeared on September 9, 1963, in the New Orleans *Times-Picayune*. The *New York Times* published the interview, but cautiously deleted the most important portion of Castro's warning. Castro ended his message with a threatening note: "Let Kennedy and his brother Robert watch out, . . . they, too, could become targets of assassination." [83]

The timing of Castro's threat is revealing because it happened the very same day CIA headquarters was informed of the first attempt to recruit Rolando Cubela, a senior official in the Castro government, with the intention of inducing him to assassinate Castro. The operation is referred to in official CIA documents by its cryptograph, AM/LASH. But there is evidence indicating that Cubela was actually a double agent working for Castro.[84] Therefore, it seems that Castro knew of the CIA's plan, either through Cubela or through some other CFR agent right in Langley.

Though many authors have tried to downplay or completely ignore the importance of Castro's words, there is evidence that his threat of reprisals against American leaders was considered serious enough as to trigger some reaction from the Kennedy Administration. The Special Group in the National Security Council, augmented by Attorney General Robert Kennedy and General Maxwell Taylor, which supervised the CIA's covert activities against Cuba, discussed Castro's words and designated a special committee to weigh the risks of continuing with their anti-Castro activities. The committee met on September 12 at the Department of State. According to a memorandum of the meeting, the members agreed that "there was a strong likelihood that Castro would retaliate in some way . . ." But they concluded that the specific possibility of "attacks against U.S. officials" was "unlikely."[85] It seems that, as it happened most of the time, CFR agents in the National Security Council made an effort to deviate the attention from Fidel Castro.

On October 7, just a few weeks after the incident at the Brazilian embassy, Castro repeated his threat. After he had delivered a long speech, Castro answered questions from foreign reporters. He accused the U.S. as the perpetrator of an undeclared war against Cuba, and blamed Kennedy for the responsibility. Then, in another direct threat, Castro stated emphatically, "They [the Kennedys] are our enemies, and we know how to be their enemies."[86]

Knowing Castro's long history of using assassination as a political tool one may safely surmise that this was not an empty threat. Colonel Antonio (Tony) de la Guardia, Castro personal hit-man, boasted that, following Castro's order, he had assassinated more than 60 people, some of them in the U.S.[87]

To the evidence I have provided above I would like to add one from my own personal experience. The day Kennedy was assassinated I was working at one of the enterprises of the Cuban Ministry of Foreign Trade, after being released from active duty in the Army just a few weeks before. As it was customary, as soon as I left the Army I had to join the Reserve. As soon as Castro allegedly heard the news of the assassination, he ordered a full mobilization of the Cuban military, including the reserve and the militia. Half an hour after I heard the news on the radio I got a phone call from my reserve military unit ordering me to present myself immediately for active duty. Less than three hours later we were in the trenches, ready to fight an American invasion.

With the benefit of hindsight now I see that some things were not quite right. When I arrived at my unit, about an hour after Castro ordered the mobilization, the trucks were ready, waiting to bring us to our positions.

How had they managed to get the drivers, who were also reservists like myself, so quickly to the unit? Normally, giving the state of combat readiness of Cuban reserve units at the time, this type of mobilization normally took no less than twelve hours to bring the men to the field. How come it worked so fast this time? When we reached our positions in the field even the cooks were already there, apparently waiting for us to arrive. I participated in many mobilizations, before and after, and none of them worked as well as this one.

In August 1997, almost 34 years after the assassination of president Kennedy, the Assassination Records board, a special committee appointed by Congress to facilitate the release of records on the incident, released 84 formerly classified documents of the National Security Agency (NSA). The NSA's specializes in "signals intelligence" — the global interception, collection and analysis of telephone and radio conversations. Some of the released intercepts refer to defensive measures ordered by Castro.

According to some of the documents, the very day Kennedy was killed, Cuban military units hit the trenches on Cuba's northern coast, waiting for an American invasion. In a speech broadcast on Cuban radio and TV on November 23, Castro said that JFK's death "may have very negative repercussions with regard to the interests of our country." Moreover, an intercepted message a European intelligence officer cabled home from Havana mentions: "Although it was only the third time I had witnessed a speech by Fidel, I got the impression that on this occasion he was frightened, if not terrified." [88]

The question that came to my mind is, was Castro aware that something would come up? Had the armed forces already been prepared beforehand for some upcoming military action? Now I am pretty sure he knew about the Kennedy assassination, and not because his agents infiltrated in the U.S. told him, but because, as a key part of the operation, he had been informed beforehand by top level members of the Invisible Government of the United States.

Castro was terrified because he knew that, had the American people discovered his participation in the JFK assassination, his days would have been numbered. But he had no reasons to be frightened. David and his CFR agents were doing a good job erasing all traces of Castro's participation in the JFK assassination.

Chapter 12

The CIA and the Kennedy Assassination

> *The past telescopes into the future.*
> — James Jesus Angleton.

As I explained in Chapter 8, the Rockefellers were the true creators of the Central Intelligence Agency and, continuing the family tradition, one of the CIA's functions was to eliminate the Rockefeller family's real or imagined enemies. Since its very creation, the Rockefellers' key man inside the CIA was Allen Dulles, and Dulles' most trusted man inside the CIA was James Jesus Angleton, the man in charge of CIA's assassination teams.

Several books about Oswald's links to the CIA have been written. Among the best are John Newman, *Oswald and the CIA*[1] and Philip H. Melanson, *Spy Saga: Lee Harvey Oswald and U.S. Intelligence*.[2] Most of them, however, barely mention or outright ignore Angleton's key role in the Kennedy assassination, and the few who have studied Angleton's role seem to have done it for the sole purpose of disinformation.[3]

Angleton and Oswald

James Jesus Angleton, the CIA's legendary chief of counterintelligence, is without a doubt one of the most colorful characters in the dark gray, paranoid netherworld of intelligence and espionage. His life and career has been the subject of many books and articles,[4] as well as at least three spy novels,[5] and two spy films.[6] Angleton's life was the classic mystery wrapped inside an enigma protected by a bodyguard of lies.[7] Privately, Richard Helms called him a "strange, strange man."[8]

On the other hand, authors John Loftus and Mark Aarons are convinced that Angleton was not a hero but a villain. Among his many treacherous and criminal activities, Angleton "laundered Nazi money and built a Vatican escape route for the fugitives of the Third Reich."[7]

Allen Dulles and James Jesus Angleton became friends when both were doing dirty jobs for the OSS in Europe on behalf of the Rockefellers and other international bankers. In 1954, CIA Director Allen Dulles (CFR) appointed James Jesus Angleton chief of the CIA's counterintelligence section.[9] Two years later Angleton had the greatest success of his career when he obtained a transcript of Nikita Khrushchev's 1956 speech to the Soviet Party Congress denouncing Stalin's crimes. After that, Angleton faded into anonymity until the CIA "family jewels" scandal about the Agency's outrageous misbehavior brought him to public attention.[10]

Among the many things the "family jewels" revelations brought to light was that the CIA, in violation of its charter that expressly prohibited the Agency from operating on American soil, had conducted in 1967 an extensive operation, codenamed Chaos, to spy on American citizens who lawfully protested against the war in Vietnam. The CIA officers in charge of Chaos were Angleton and his counterintelligence staff.[11]

One of the most intriguing aspects of Oswald's life is his defection to the Soviet Union in October 1959. It seems, however, that Oswald was not a true defector. There are indications that, like several other young men similar to him,[12] Oswald was part of Angleton's "false defector" program, one of CIA's best-kept secrets.

Granted, until now no CIA document has been found that mentions a "false defector" program, but that does not mean such a program did not exist. CIA Director Allen Dulles (CFR) personally selected CIA's counterintelligence chief James Jesus Angleton to run that program.[13]

In fact, Oswald's "defection" to the Soviet Union was a key element of an important CIA operation to derail Khrushchev's efforts to end the Cold War: the shooting down of a U.S. U-2 plane deep inside Soviet territory.

A summit meeting between Soviet Premier Khrushchev and President

Eisenhower had been scheduled to take place in Paris on May 16, 1960, and the Soviet Premier planned to convince the American President that peaceful coexistence, not nuclear war, was the right and only course to follow. But the Soviet hawks used the U-2 incident as a pretext to force Khrushchev to cancel the meeting.

It was also used by American warmongers, most of them CFR members, to justify the raising of war budgets, which directly benefited the Rockefellers and the military-industrial-banking complex. And CFR secret agent Angleton played a key role in this despicable act of betrayal of the American people.

Just before he "defected" to the Soviet Union, Oswald had been a member of the U.S. military. He had worked for some time at the Atsugi Naval Air Force Base in Japan. Atsugi was used by some of the U-2 planes under CIA control that flew spy missions over the Soviet Union and Oswald was familiar with its operational capabilities. Everything indicates that Oswald's true mission consisted in telling the Soviets that the U-2 was just a sophisticated glider, with a lightly built airframe and big wings, and that just by exploding antiaircraft missiles as close as 300 feet from the plane would bring it down.

Apparently Oswald accomplished his secret mission, because on May 1st, 1960, just a few months after he defected, the Soviets shot down a U-2 plane the CIA had sent on an unauthorized flight deep inside Soviet territory. Proof that no missile actually hit the plane is that its pilot, Francis Gary Powers, was not killed, and the wreckage of the plane showed no signs of having been destroyed by explosives.[14]

Between June 1956 and April 9 1960, before Oswald's "defection," U-2s had flown 28 spy missions deep over Soviet territory without encountering any problems. After Oswald's "defection" a U-2 flight went unmolested, but the next, on May 1st, was shot down by Soviet SAMs [Surface to Air Missiles]. Powers himself suspected that Oswald told the Soviets the operational ceiling at which the U-2 flew.[15]

The Warren Commission interviewed some of Oswald's Marine colleagues who had worked with him at the Atsugi U-2 base in Japan. Not surprisingly, however, the members of the CFR-controlled Warren Commission did not question them about the U-2.[16]

Now, why did some Americans at the CIA want their enemies to shoot down an American plane? Simply because, as I explained above in this book, the Cold War was a hoax, though a very profitable one,[17] and the CFR conspirators who control the U.S. foreign policy and the CIA wanted to keep it hot. But Soviet Premier Khrushchev, with his new policy of peaceful coexistence, was threatening to cool it down.

Khrushchev had to be stopped, and David Rockefeller's agents in the CIA were eager to follow their master's voice. Oswald was just their tool to carry out their plans. Even more, some people suspected that, in order to guarantee that the U-2 was successfully shot down by the Soviets, apart from the information supplied by Oswald the CIA had sabotaged Powers' U-2.[18]

CFR agents within the CIA, from Director John McCone (CFR) on down, consistently denied that CIA had ever debriefed Oswald upon his return from the Soviet Union. Had Oswald been debriefed by the Agency, it would have been further confirmation that he was, indeed, a participant in Angleton's "false defector" program run by CIA counterintelligence.

Angleton's secretive counterintelligence empire employed over 200 people. Inside this large group was a small handful of Angleton's most trusted and close-mouthed men, called the Special Investigations Group (SIG). In 1959, when Lee Harvey Oswald defected to the Soviet Union, only about four or five people were part of SIG, which was headed by Birch D. O'Neal.[19] The Special Investigations Group was a very restricted operation and most CIA officers ignored its existence and the ones who knew about were denied access to it.

The SIG is a key element in the case of the Kennedy assassination because, for some unexplained reason, it was found that SIG held a 201 File (also known as a "Personality File") on Oswald prior to the assassination. Both the Church Committee and the United States House Select Committee on Assassinations' investigators noticed this strange fact, and they found no plausible explanation for the CIA's relationship with Oswald. Still today, nobody knows what SIG really did, and why Oswald's file would have been there.

Why wasn't this file opened in 1959 when Oswald — who had knowledge of the CIA's top secret U-2 program — defected, after he told the Consul at the U.S. Embassy in Moscow that he might have something of special interest to share with the Soviets?[20] Why didn't that set off alarm bells all over the place? Why was the 201 File on Oswald not opened for another year after his return? And why, when he, a "defector," returned to the States, did the CIA not debrief him? Or did they? These questions and more were raised by the House Select Committee on Assassination investigators, but were never adequately answered by the CIA.[21] Nevertheless, there is a possibility that, contrary to CIA's claims, Oswald had been debriefed by CIA officers after he returned from the Soviet Union.

Granted, CIA's debriefing Oswald in itself alone did not mean that he was a CIA asset. But the curious nature of his defection, with all its contradictions and CIA's attempts to hide their connection with him, combined with his possible debriefing by CIA, at least points to the possibility that Oswald was part of Angleton's false defector program.

Moreover, there is at least one documentary piece of evidence pointing to Oswald as a CIA plant in the Soviet Union. The opening document in Oswald's 201 File reflected Oswald as still being in the Marine Corps as of December 1960, even after his defection to the Soviet Union, suggesting that his "defection" did not bother them. The CIA index card indicated that "as of 1960" Oswald was still in the Marines.

Also, there is the question: Why did Angleton withhold this potentially crucial information about Oswald's contacts with the Castro government from the Warren Commission investigators? Was he concerned where it might lead? Why did Allen Dulles make an extraordinary effort to avoid the Warren Commission investigating Oswald's ties to the CIA.[22]

According to a widely-accepted explanation, the biggest fear among members of the Warren Commission and new President Lyndon Johnson was that, if they would discover an explosively dangerous truth, it would lead to a third world war.

If it had been found out that the KGB or the DGI [Cuban intelligence service] was complicit in the Kennedy assassination, the theory went, the U.S. may well have been provoked to invade Cuba, leading to a clash with the Russian troops still stationed there, leading to ... who knows. The price of revenge might have been too high.

This, however, was just CIA disinformational hogwash produced in an effort to explain the unexplainable.

Angleton and the Assassination of Gaitán

Confirming the forensic principle that every contact leaves a trace,[23] many years later an important piece of this historical puzzle called the Bogotazo appeared in the most unexpected place. In his autobiography *Vivir para contarla*, Colombian Nobel Prize writer Gabriel García Márquez, who was a young man in Bogotá during the riots, wrote that he witnessed first hand the killing of Roa Sierra, Gaitán's alleged assassin, who had taken refuge from the mob in a nearby pharmacy. According to García Márquez,

> Fifty years later it is still fixed in my memory the image of the man who seemed to be instigating the mob in front of the pharmacy, of whom I have not found any reference in any of the testimonies given by the witnesses. I saw him from very close by, very well dressed, with a skin like alabaster, and a millimetric control over his actions. He called my attention so much that I kept watching him until a brand new car picked him up soon after the mob took away the assassin's cadaver and, since then, it disappeared from history's memory — even mine. Only many years after, in my times as a journalist, it occurred to me that the man might have been instrumental in the killing of a false assassin to protect the identity of the true one.[24]

Until now nobody had found who the mysterious man was, but García Márquez' suspicion that the man was part of the assassination makes sense. Moreover, I have the suspicion that the elegantly dressed mysterious man who accompanied the alleged assassin Roa Sierra to Gaitán's office and later instigated the crowd to beat Roa to death was none other than CIA's future counterintelligence chief James Jesus Angleton in charge of assassination teams.

I base my suspicion on five things. First, the fact that Angleton fits to a large degree the physical description of the individual mentioned by the witnesses, the one who incited the rioters to kill Roa Sierra. Moreover he also fits the description Gaitán's secretary made of the man who in two occasions accompanied Roa during his visits to the office.

According to Gaitán's secretary, in the few days before the murder, Juan Roa Sierra came several times to her office, which gave entrance to that of Dr. Gaitán, with a request to see Dr. Gaitán. She also remembered that, at least in two occasions, Juan Roa Sierra was accompanied,

> . . . by another man, thin, tolerably well dressed but of a wild appearance, with bulging eyes and an aggressive manner. On these occasions, the latter, and not Juan Roa Sierra, acted as spokesman in the attempt to obtain an interview. [25]

Secondly, because this mysterious man was playing a key part in a very secret and important operation, and Angleton was one of Allen Dulles' trusted men. One of the few of Angleton's photographs ever published[26] show him carrying the urn containing Dulles' ashes, an honor granted only to one of the deceased's closest friends. Moreover, Allen Dulles was a Rockefeller key man.

Third, because Angleton's mother was Mexican and he, though not fully fluent in Spanish, knew enough of the language to briefly pass as a native. Angleton was the son of an American cavalry officer, James Hugh Angleton, who rode into Mexico with General Pershing in pursuit of Pancho Villa. He fell in love with a Mexican beauty he met at the border city of Nogales, Carmen Mercedes Moreno.[27] As proof of her Catholic faith, she gave her son the middle name Jesus, pronounced *Jesús*, Spanish style.

In an interview with Tom Mangold, Carmen mentioned James' close ties with his maternal grandmother, Mercedes, who spoke no English. This is another item of evidence indicating that Angleton was fluent to a certain degree in the Spanish language.[28]

Fourth, there is some unaccounted time in Angleton's life that, strangely, coincides with the Bogotazo events. In July, 1947, Angleton accepted a senior position at CIA as the top aide to the director of the Office of Special Operations (OSO) and the family moved to Washington, D.C.[29] The only source for this information, however, is Cicely Angleton herself, in an interview she had with Jeff Goldberg on March 3, 1989.[30]

But, and this is sort of strange because, according to Angleton's CIA personnel records, though he officially joined the Agency on December 30, 1947, he was granted a seven-month leave of absence to live in Tucson with his family before assuming his position at CIA.[31] Consequently, Angleton had enough time and opportunity to move secretly to Colombia under a false name and passport, accomplish his first CIA assassination mission there, and come back to Tucson unnoticed before moving to Washington D.C.

Finally, it is known that, first at the OSS and later at CIA, Angleton had direct participation in two early secret projects on mind control: BLUEBIRD and ARTICHOKE.

In conclusion, Angleton had the motive, the ability, the means, and the opportunity to have participated in the Bogotazo operation. Even more, like most experienced criminals, he was clever enough to create an alibi, backed by a respectable, though not fully impartial witness: his wife.

Nonetheless, we can only conjecture about Angleton's role in the JFK assassination, because he was a true master in hiding his participation in key operations. There are, however, two events we know for sure linking him to the Kennedy assassination. In 1964, a few hours after Mary Pinchot, a Washington D.C. area artist was mysteriously gunned down in Georgetown, Angleton broke into her house and stole her diary.[32] Pinchot was one of President Kennedy's secret lovers, and apparently she kept a diary of the affair. The conspirators who carried out the Kennedy assassination most likely feared that Pinchot's diary might contain incriminating evidence of their treachery.

Moreover, according to some sources, Angleton also personally stole papers of Mexico City CIA's station chief Winston Scott who had interacted with Oswald. When Scott suddenly died, Angleton rushed to Mexico City and seized Scott's unpublished memoir. In the memoir, Scott disputed a key finding of the Warren Commission.[33] The CFR conspirators feared that both Pinchot's diary and Scott's memoir may contain evidence linking them to the President's assassination, and they sent their trusted secret agent James Jesus Angleton to destroy it at all costs.

Still, as late as 1972, Angleton kept muddying the waters in relation to Oswald's ties to the CIA. On April 5, 1972, CIA counterintelligence chief James Angleton, backed by director Richard Helms (CFR), issued a blanket order: "The Agency was not, under any circumstances, to make inquiries or ask any source or defector about Oswald."[34]

Roa Sierra and Lee Harvey Oswald: Manchurian Candidates?

The available record strongly suggests that both Juan Roa Sierra and Lee Harvey Oswald were patsies — the fall guys whose only role was taking the blame for the assassinations. When the Dallas police interrogated him, Oswald told them "I am a patsy." Similarly, Roa Sierra never confessed to having killing Gaitán, and it is obvious that he was not the person who pulled the trigger. Anyway, the question remaining is: were both of them also Manchurian Candidates?

According to Roa's mother, Encarnación Sierra, in the weeks previous to the assassination of Gaitán his son had visited at least nine times the office of Johan Umland Gert, a German astrologer.[35] Umland not only divined Roa's future, but also gave him some money.[36]

Roa's mother also said that, some time before Gaitán's assassination, her son told her that at times he was having tremors in his whole body, a knot in the pit of his stomach, and something strange in his brain.[37] She also mentioned that, since a few months before the assassination, she had noticed that her son began behaving a little strangely. He frequently laughed to himself, quit his job and looked too thoughtful. He had fainting fits and suffered from severe headaches, saying that he felt as if corn was popping inside his head.[38]

Most likely Roa was mentally conditioned by Umland, who may actually have been a CIA psychiatrist specializing in mind control, or have collaborated with the CIA psychiatrists in the process. Adding to my suspicion is the fact that Umland was German and it is known that, through Project PAPERCLIP, the CIA brought to the U.S. many Nazi scientists, including many of the ones who had been working on mind control research for the Nazis.

In his 2003 book *Case Closed: Lee Harvey Oswald and the Assassination of JFK*, Gerald Posner describes Oswald as a psychologically disturbed malcontent.[39] Nevertheless, though Oswald was no fool — he was a quick learner and his IQ tests showed his intelligence was above average — there is some truth that he was emotionally disturbed, which made him a good candidate for mind control.

Similarly to Roa Sierra, Oswald was known to have visited David Ferrie, a known CIA asset. Ferrie claimed to be a psychologist and a hypnotist.[40]

When the FBI contacted Jack Martin, who worked for New Orleans private investigator Guy Banister, in relation to the JFK assassination, he told the FBI that Ferrie might have hypnotized Oswald into assassinating Kennedy. Of course, the FBI considered Martin's evidence unreliable. Nevertheless, FBI agents interviewed Ferrie twice about Martin's allegations.[41] With the benefit of hindsight, however, one can conclude that Ferrie may have collaborated in the process of turning Oswald into a Manchurian candidate.

Moreover, Dick Russell, a decorated Korean War veteran, wrote *The Man Who Knew Too Much,*[42] a book about the Kennedy assassination. In it he uncovered evidence that supports the theory that Lee Harvey Oswald was a product of MK-ULTRA. One of the CIA's overseas locations for LSD and mind-control experiments was Atsugi Naval Air base in Japan where Oswald served as a Marine radar technician. Russell says that after his book was published, a former CIA counterintelligence expert called him and told Oswald had been "viewed by the CIA as fitting the psychological profile of someone they were looking for in their MK-ULTRA program," and that he had been mind-conditioned to defect to the USSR.

In the case of Roa Sierra, two main things can be inferred from the stories told by the witnesses. First, that there were two men involved in the assassination. Secondly, that just seconds after the assassination, Roa changed his behavior dramatically, passing without transition from an emotional violent state to one of depression and inaction — he changed from a tiger into a mouse in a split second. But, though puzzling to the untrained eye, these apparently unexplainable things are easy to explain if one has a key: mind control.

William Turner, an author who studied the assassination of Robert Kennedy and the possibility that his alleged assassin may have been a Manchurian Candidate acting under posthypnotic suggestion,[43] studied the symptoms of hypno-conditioning. Cardinal among these symptoms are a dramatic personality change before the actual event, and a state of peaceful tranquility while committing of the action, particularly evident in the subject's eyes.

Then, after committing the action, signs of withdrawal from the hypnotic state appear: the individual seems disoriented, without a clear idea of what just has happened. This state is the results of posthypnotic amnesic blocks implanted by the programmer in the subject's mind.[44] If one is to believe the witnesses' accounts, both Roa Sierra and Oswald evidenced most of the disorientation symptoms mentioned by Turner.

It seems that Roa Sierra actually was a Manchurian Candidate.[45] He was a predecessor of Lee Harvey Oswald, Sirhan Sirhan,[46] James Earl Ray, Mark David Chapman and John Hinckley, Jr., the ones who years later were used as patsies in the assassinations of President John F. Kennedy, his brother Robert, Martin Luther King, Jr., and John Lennon, as well as the one who tried to kill President Reagan — placing CFR agent George H. W. Bush just one step from becoming U.S. President.

The term Manchurian Candidate to indicate a brainwashed, mentally-controlled assassin came into use in 1959, when author Richard Condon made it the title of his best-selling novel, later made a popular movie starring Frank Sinatra, and, more recently, a remake starring Denzel Washington. In the novel, a person is hypno-conditioned to unwittingly commit a crime.[47] In the cases of Roa, Oswald and Sirhan, however, most likely they were brainwashed to *believe* they were committing a crime, while the true assassin committed it. This casts them in the double role of decoy and fall guys or patsies, which is the core of my theory that Roa and Oswald were both Manchurian Candidates and patsies.

The CFR, the CIA and the Assassinations of Gaitán and Kennedy

There are enormous parallels between the *modus operandi* used in the assassinations of Colombia's leader Gaitán in 1948 and President Kennedy in 1963. Namely:

Gaitan's assassination, 1948	Kennedy's assassination, 1963
Gaitán loved his country and wanted to change politics as usual. He believed that the role of the government was to protect the common people, not the big banks and corporations.	John F. Kennedy loved his country and wanted to change politics as usual. He believed that the role of the government was to protect the common people, not the big banks and corporations.
There was a strong possibility that Gaitán would have been elected Colombia's president in the coming elections. Had Gaitán become Colombia's president, most likely he would have reopened the investigation of the massacre of the United Fruit workers in 1928. The Rockefellers and their CFR minions were not pleased with that possibility	In 1960, John F. Kennedy won the presidency in an extremely close election against the Rockefeller-backed Presidential candidate Richard M. Nixon. Kennedy's election as U.S. President took the CFR conspirators by surprise. As soon as he was sworn into office, JFK began clashing with Rockefellers' interests. The Rockefellers and their CFR minions were not pleased.
Everything indicates that Gaitán's alleged assassin Juan Roa Sierra, was a patsy.	Everything indicates that JFK's alleged assassin Lee Harvey Oswald, was a patsy.
It seems that Roa Sierra was a Manchurian candidate who had been psychologically programmed to commit a murderous act against his will.	It seems that Oswald was a Manchurian candidate who had been psychologically programmed to commit a murderous act against his will.

Most likely Roa was under the effect of hallucinogenic drugs like LSD. He had an unstable personality, which made him susceptible to an especially deep form of hypnotism.

In the weeks before the assassination of Gaitán, Roa Sierra had been visiting a German "astrologer" who apparently put some ideas in his mind. Roa's mother mentioned that, since a few months before the assassination, she had noticed that her son began behaving a little strangely. He frequently laughed to himself, quit his job and looked too thoughtful.

The original plan was to mentally condition Roa to make him believe he was to assassinate Gaitán while the true assassins would commit the crime and also kill Roa. But he managed to escape and Angleton had to incite the rioters to kill him.

After the assassination, Roa was called a loner, secretive, "psychological misfit, having delusions of grandiosity." In the post-assassination cover-up, he was called a "lone nut" who acted alone and was not part of a conspiracy.

Roa never confessed to have assassinated Gaitán. When somebody asked him why he had assassinated Gaitán he answered: "Oh, sir, powerful things I can't tell you."

Most likely Oswald was under the effect of hallucinogenic drugs like LSD. He had an unstable personality, which made him susceptible to an especially deep form of hypnotism.

It is known that Oswald had spent some time at the Atsugi military base in Japan, a place known to be used for carrying out experiments with LSD on military personnel.[51] Moreover, while in New Orleans, Oswald visited on several occasions David Ferrie, a CIA asset who advertised himself as a "psychologist" and claimed to be a hypnotist.

The original plan was to mentally condition Oswald to make him believe he was to assassinate Kennedy while the true assassins would commit the crime and police officer J. D. Tippit kill Oswald. But he managed to escape and Ruby had to kill him.

After the assassination, Oswald was called a loner, secretive, "psychological misfit, having delusions of grandiosity." In the post-assassination cover-up, he was called a "lone nut" that acted alone and was not part of a conspiracy.

Oswald never confessed to have assassinated Kennedy. When the Dallas police interrogated him why he had assassinated Kennedy he answered: "I am a patsy."

After Gaitán's assassination, several witnesses mentioned the presence of more than one assassin

After Kennedy's assassination, several witnesses mentioned the presence of more than one assassin

Roa's old revolver could no have been the weapon used in the assassination.

Oswald's old rifle could not have been the weapon used in the assassination.

CIA's James Jesus Angleton played an important role in the Gaitan assassination.

CIA's James Jesus Angleton played an important role in the JFK assassination.

Several CIA and ex-OSS officers were in Bogotá during the assassination: Norman Armour (OSS), John C. Wiley (OSS), John Mepples Spiritto (CIA, had worked project Artichoke), CIA asset William Pawley, Fidel Castro and Rafael del Pino (CIA agents).

Several CIA officers were in Dallas during the Kennedy assassination, among them E. Howard Hunt, George H.W. Bush, Cord Meyer, Edward Lansdale and Frank Sturgis, as well as CIA asset William Pawley.

Several CFR members were in Bogotá during Gaitán's assassination, among them Secretary of State George Marshall, Averell Harriman, Norman Armour and John C. Wiley. All of them, together with the U.S. mainstream press, played a role in the cover-up by blaming the local Communists and the Soviet Union for the assassination.

CFR members in the Warren Commission, Allen Dulles, John McCloy and Gerald Ford, as well as CFR members in the U.S. Government and the mainstream press, played a key role in the cover-up to hide the true perpetrators of the Kennedy assassination.

By assassinating Gaitán, the Rockefellers and their CFR conspirators killed several birds with a single stone. In the first place, they got rid of a nationalist leader, a potential enemy they feared. Secondly, they used Gaitán's assassination as a tool to incite the masses to join a revolt they

By assassinating John F. Kennedy, the Rockefellers and their CFR conspirators eliminated the main obstacle to their plans of warming-up the Cold War and increasing the U.S. participation in the profitable and eugenistically useful Vietnam War. Moreover, they got rid of a national-

had prepared way in advance. Finally, blaming the Communists and by implication the Soviet Union for the assassination and the riots, they created an excellent ideological pretext to justify the quick start of the Cold War in Latin America.

ist leader who was becoming a big threat to their secret plans of destroying America's economy and culture and fusing it into an amalgamation of countries under the so-called New World Order under their control.

CFR agents in the academia and the mainstream press made an inordinate effort to hide Fidel Castro's true role in the assassination of Gaitán.

CFR agents in the academia and the mainstream press made an inordinate effort to hide Fidel Castro's true role in the assassination of President Kennedy.

The assassination of Gaitán and the Bogotazo riots were the pretext used by CFR conspirators and the mainstream media under their control to launch in full force the Cold War.

After the assassination of President Kennedy, the CFR conspirators and their minions in the mainstream media pushed the U.S. again into the Cold War.

The extraordinary similarities between the *modus operandi* carried out by CFR agents and CIA officers in both the assassinations of Gaitán and Kennedy indicate that this was not the product of a coincidence, but just the repetition of an assassination methodology considered practical and efficient. Even more important, for these and other reasons explained above in this book, one may safely conclude that in any assassination where the CIA has played a key role and CFR agents have actively participated in the cover-up the orders must have come from the same source.

Chapter 13

Who Killed President Kennedy?

> *Political language... is designed to make lies sound*
> *truthful and murder respectable, and to give an*
> *appearance of solidity to pure wind.*
> — George Orwell.

On Chapter Eleven, I dealt in some detail about the possibility that Castro may have played an important role in the assassination of President Kennedy, not because I think he was the mastermind behind the assassination but because there has been a sort of conspiracy of silence designed in an effort to ignore Castro's role in the event. Even so, I don't think that Castro, the Mob, the Mossad, anti-Castro Cubans,[1] right wing extremists, LBJ, J. Edgar Hoover or the military-industrial-complex, not even the CIA and much less the KGB or Nikita Khrushchev, had the absolute power over the U.S. Government, the mainstream media and the academia necessary to carry out such of a complex operation as the JFK assassination and its cover-up.

Did the U.S. Government Kill President Kennedy?

None of the entities I mentioned above had the power to order the Secret Service to retire its protection to President Kennedy just a few minutes before the shooting. None of them had the power to change the route of the motorcade to pass near the book depository. None of them had the power to tell Oswald to apply for a job at the book depository weeks before the route of the motorcade was known. None of them had the power to allow Oswald, a potential security risk, to come back from the Soviet Union uncontested, much less to carry out the pervasive cover-up operation that followed the assassination. Only the U.S. Government had the power to do this.

But this is not new. Many serious researchers who have studied the assassination have arrived at the unavoidable conclusion that the U.S. Government was behind the assassination. I am aware, however, that Professor Donald Gibson, who wrote what I consider one of the best books on the Kennedy assassination, in another book he wrote on the subject, criticized the authors who blamed the U.S. Government for the assassination. According to Professor Gibson,

> The "government" did not hate the President. Most likely most of the government liked him. "The government" did not have men at the top of the Establishment media. "The government" did not order Alsop, Rostow, Acheson, McCloy, Dulles, and James Reston to do what they did. Groups within the Establishment did hate Kennedy. They did have their people at high levels of certain parts of the government. The Establishment interests did close the case within hours of the assassination. Establishment people did create and control the so-called Warren Commission.
>
> John Kennedy headed the United States government, a government made up mostly of loyal, average Americans. The opposition within the government to Kennedy's policies did not come from those people. . . . To blame "the government" is, in a sense, to blame Kennedy, who was the government, who believed in the positive potential of government. To blame "the government" is, in a sense, to attack Kennedy a second time.[2]

The problem with that view, however, is that when I say that the U.S. Government did it, I am not talking about the fake U.S. Government in Washington D.C., but about the true Invisible Government of the United States[3] whose visible head is in the Harold Pratt House in Manhattan, headquarters of the Council on Foreign Relations — which is quite different from what Gibson calls 'the government," or "the Establishment."[4] Actually, all of the persons Gibson mentions in his criticism as part of a government made up mostly of loyal, average Americans — Stewart Alsop, W.W. Rostow, Dean Acheson, John McCloy, Allen Dulles, and James Reston, as well as Dean Rusk, Arthur Schlesinger Jr., Robert McNamara, Douglas Dillon, Theodore Sorensen, McGeorge Bundy — were not loyal Americans but traitors, because thery were directly or indirectly linked to the Invisible Government through their membership to the Council on Foreign Relations. You cannot be a loyal American and at the same time be a member of an organization that systematically advances the notion that the U.S. should abolish the Constitution, end its sovereignty, open its borders and fusion itself to the rest of the countries on this planet in what they call a New World Order under the control of a bunch of international bankers.

Contrary to what Professor Gibson believes, John F. Kennedy did not head the U.S. Government. Actually, one of his biggest mistakes was believing that he was the head of the real U. S. Government, and he paid dearly for his mistake.

Over the years, and particularly after the popularization of the Internet, a medium the CFR conspirators do not fully control, even the most gullible American citizen has suspected that there must be a secret reason why more often than not our government ends up acting against the best interests of the American people, as well as helping our enemies and betraying our friends. Just a handful of scholars, though, have seriously studied the phenomenon. The ones who have done it concluded that the U.S. Government has been hijacked by a cabal of rich, powerful individuals, who have been using it to advance their own private interests.

This supra-elite of a few dozen immensely wealthy and powerful individuals has been called different names: the Power Elite, the Eastern Establishment, the High Cabal, the Group, the Order, the Deep State, the Secret Team, the Secret Empire, the Secret Government, the Insiders, the Conspirators, the Imperial Brain Trust, the Usurpers, and the Invisible Government.

Probably the first author who rightly pointed to the Council on Foreign Relations as the true source of the invisible Government of the United States was Emanuel Josephson in his 1952 book *Rockefeller "Internationalist" : The Man Who Misrules the World*.[5] Josephson titled Chapter XIII of his book, "The Council on Foreign Relations: 'Foreign Office' of the Rockefeller Empire. The Invisible Government."[6] A few pages below he added,

So consistently have high, policy-making positions in the government been filled from the ranks of the Rockefeller's Council that it can be called the invisible government of the United Sates.[7]

Another author who identified the CFR as the center of the Invisible Government of the United States was Dan Smoot in his 1962 book *The Invisible Government*.[8] Smoot, a former member of the FBI Headquarters staff in Washington, D.C., expressed his conviction,

> I am convinced that the Council on Foreign Relations, together with a great number of other associated tax-exempt organizations, constitutes the invisible government which set the major policies of the federal government; exercises controlling influence on government officials who implement the policies; and, through massive and skillful propaganda, influences Congress and the public to support the policies.
>
> I am convinced the objective of this invisible government is to convert America into a socialist state and make it a unit in a one-world socialist system.[9]

Some years later, John Stormer in his book *None Dare Call it Treason*,[10] Gary Allen in *None Dare Call it Conspiracy*,[11] and Phoebe Courtney in her *The CFR, Part II*,[12] further identified the CFR as the center of the Invisible Government of the United States.

Nevertheless, the existence of this Invisible Government of the United States hiding in the shadows is not new. As early as 1931 President Woodrow Wilson made a confession in his book *The New Freedom*:

> Since I entered politics, I have chiefly had men's views confided to me privately. Some of the biggest men in the United States, in the field of commerce and manufacture, are afraid of somebody, are afraid of something. They know there is a power somewhere so organized, so subtle, so watchful, so interlocked, so complete, so pervasive that they had better not speak above their breath when they speak in condemnation of it.[13]

Evidently, what Wilson is talking about is not a simple "Establishment," but a quite different creature. Anyway, what really is the "Establishment"?

According to most dictionaries, the Establishment (often written with initial capital letter) is the existing political power structure in society; the dominant groups in society and their customs or institutions; the institutional authority.

Most members of the Establishment in democratic, and even in autocratic countries, belong to old, wealthy families, whose ancestors were linked to the initial struggles in the formation of the country. As members of the Establishment, their main objective is protecting their interests, most likely by supporting the *status quo* and advancing the country's economic independence and protecting its sovereignty and culture. The Establishment has been described with some accuracy in academic books such as C. Wright Mill's *The Power Elite* and G. William Domhoff *Who Rules America?*

Members of the Establishment are nationalists, not globalists. They don't open their countries' borders to illegal aliens. They don' work hard to destroy their countries' economies. They don't want to destroy their countries' culture, religion, and social and sexual mores. They don't hate their countries. Moreover, they don't plan for population extermination through eugenics. They don't want to fuse their countries to other countries into a world government. Establishment people are traditionalists, not revolutionaries.

In contrast, the ultimate goal of the Invisible Government of the United States is destroying the *status quo* by destroying the country's economic independence, sovereignty, culture and social and sexual mores. This Invisible Government has been described in great detail not only in Dan Smoot's *The Invisible Government*,[14] but also in James Perloff's *The Shadows of Power* and, more recently, in my own *Psychological Warfare and the New World Order*.

People such as Henry Kissinger, Zbigniew Brzezinski, Fareed Zakaria, Madeleine Albright, Dick Cheney, Bill and Hillary Clinton, John McCain and Barack Obama did not reach their positions of power in the U.S. because they were part of the Establishment. They did so because they had willingly accepted their assigned role as obedient tools of the Rockefellers' Invisible Government.

Actually, the Invisible Government of the U.S. has always been anti-Establishment. Proof of it is that the Rockefellers and their minions have always secretly supported anti-Establishment movements. The American Left has always been secretly bankrolled by the most reactionary elements, particularly the Rockefellers, who have used their non-profit, "philanthropic" foundations as cut-outs to hide from public scrutiny the true source of the money.[15] This explains why CFR member George Soros is secretly funding Antifa, a Fascist terrorist organization.[16]

Obviously, the Invisible Government of the United States cannot be called an Establishment by any stretch of the imagination. Calling the Invisible Government of the U.S. "the Establishment" is a gross misrepresentation. Actually, it seems that the term "the Establishment" has become a smoke screen to hide the Invisible Government from public scrutiny.

Did the CIA Kill President Kennedy?

As we saw above in Chapter 3, as soon as the Rockefellers and their minions realized that President Kennedy had his own agenda, quite different from the CFR's secret agenda, CFR members infiltrated in the media and the U.S. Government carried out a veritable war of attrition against the new President — quite similar to the war of attrition they began carrying out against President Trump as soon as he got elected. This, however, is not the product of a coincidence.

The Council of Foreign Relations has been for almost a century the true and only visible head of the Invisible Government of the United States. The Invisible Govenment saw Kennedy as a serious threat to its power and reacted accordingly. Proof of this is that most of the people who openly or covertly fiercely fought President Kennedy — David and Nelson Rockefeller, Henry Luce, Dean Rusk, John Foster Dulles, Allen Dulles, George Marshall, Henry Cabot Lodge, Douglas Dillon, Adolf Berle, McGeorge Bundy, John McCloy, Robert Lovett, Richard Helms, Adlai Stevenson, Richard Bissell and Robert McNamara, just to mention a few of the most notorious ones, were influential CFR members.

At some time, leaders at the highest levels of the Invisible Government realized that JFK could not be controlled and concluded he had to be terminated with extreme prejudice.[17]

The only U.S. Government organization that has the manpower and expertise to carry out a covert operation of that magnitude — the assassination of an American President — is not the FBI, nor the Secret Service, nor the State Department, not even the Pentagon. The only U.S. Government organization that could do it is the Central Intelligence Agency. No wonder most theories about the JFK assassinations that involve domestic actors mention the CIA as possible perpetrator.

As we have seen in this book, however, the CIA was created, and has always worked for the Invisible Government. On the other hand, it would be unfair to blame the CIA as a whole for the Kennedy assassination. Actually, the CIA is not a homogenous entity. Like Russian Matryoshka dolls, there are CIAs within CIAs, within CIAs, most of them quite different.[18]

The main reason given to the American public for the creation of the CIA was to avoid Pearl Harbor-like "surprises." Yet, if one is to believe CIA's critics, over and over, since its very creation, the CIA has been taken by surprise by events it didn't foresee.

The Bogotazo riots in Colombia in 1948, the Soviets launching the Sputnik in 1957, Castro grabbing power in Cuba in 1959, the Bay of Pigs debacle in 1961, the Cuban missile crisis in 1962, the coup that deposed Nikita Khrushchev in 1964, the Soviet invasion of Czechoslovakia in 1968, the attack launched by Egypt and Syria against Israel in 1973, Castro's invasion of Angola in 1975, the fall of the Shah in Iran in 1979, the fall of the Berlin Wall in 1989, the collapse of the Soviet Union in 1990, India's testing of a nuclear bomb in 1998, and the events of September 11, 2001,[19] just to mention a few, are cases in which the CIA was apparently caught asleep at the wheel.

But, if one studies in detail every single one of these cases where the CIA allegedly failed to alert the U.S. Government about the possibility of an important act of aggression against the American people, one can find that, on the contrary, CIA analysts did their job right, but nobody at the highest levels of the CIA paid attention. The excuse developed by the CFR conspirators to justify these failures is that, though the CIA and other intelligence agencies provided the intelligence, they failed to connect the dots.

But a simple analysis of the CIA's intelligence "failures" shows that they seamlessly dovetail with the CFR conspirators' successes. Indeed, most of the international political goals of the CFR conspirators have been reached thanks to CIA's alleged "intelligence failures." This may be the reason why after every alleged "failure" nobody in the CIA is ever disciplined, let alone fired.[20] Consequently, one can safely surmise that people at the higher levels of the U.S. Government failed to connect the dots because the lines connecting the dots pointed to CFR treason and, as we well know, the CFR and its Rockefellers masters are untouchables.

This is not new and at least somebody has noticed it. As former CIA analyst Melvin A. Goodman has pointed out, after every "intelligence failure," some of the analysts directly responsible for the failure are given big cash bonuses and promotions[21] and the CIA's budget is increased.

So, contrary to the disinformers' claims, far from accumulating failures, the CIA has always been one of the most successful tools used by the conspirators entrenched in the Council on Foreign Relations in the pursuit of their hidden goal: the creation of a communo-fascist global government controlled by Wall Street bankers, oil magnates and multinational corporations — what they euphemistically call the New World Order.

There were several CIA officers in Dallas at the time of the Kennedy assassination, and everything indicates they had a direct participation in it. The known ones are James Jesus Angleton, E. Howard Hunt, George H.W. Bush, Cord Meyer and Frank Sturgis. They, however, were not working for the CIA properly, but for their boss Allen Dulles, and Dulles' true boss was David Rockefeller. So, why blame the CIA for the Kennedy assassination when at least 99.9 percent of its employees had nothing to do with it?

Actually, even before the assassination of President Kennedy, these and other Rockefeller agents in the CIA had already been doing this type of job abroad. According to William Blum, one of the authors who has better studied the subject, after the Kennedy assassination they may have played a key role in the assassination of opposition leader Recto of the Philippines, Prime Minister Indira Gandhi of India, President Nasser of Egypt, Prince Sihanouk of Cambodia, President Duvalier of Haiti, President Trujillo of the Dominican Republic, and President Diem of South Vietnam.[22] Evidently, in 1963 the CIA already had the capability and the expertise to carry out such type of covert operations.

Nevertheless, the assassination of Colombia's leader Jorge Eliécer Gaitán in 1948 was a sort of dry run for the assassination of President Kennedy in 1963. Most of the techniques and procedures the CIA's covert operations team tested in Gaitán's assassination were closely followed in the JFK assassination.

So, to the question, did the CIA assassinate Kennedy, my answer is, definitively not. Just a handful of CIA officers played a role in the JFK assassination, but they actually were CFR double agents infiltrated inside the CIA. Some of them may have fooled themselves into believing that they were true patriots who assassinated Kennedy to save America from a Communist, but Allen Dulles, James Angleton, Richard Bissell and Richard Helms knew very well were actually betraying the American people.

Liberal "progressive" admirers of Castro who have written about the Kennedy assassination never fail to mention "anti-Castro Cubans" among the main suspects. I have always asked myself why not even their strongest critics have ever called Kissinger an "anti-Castro German," Bzrezinski an "anti-Castro Polish' or Obama a "pro-Castro Kenyan." I see a clear element of racism in the systematic pegging of this deprecative tag to those Cuban-born American citizens who firmly opposed the Cuban tyrant.

Proof of this is that such "progressive" Castro admirers never mention that President Batista, the man Castro overthrew in 1959, was a mulatto whose skin was darker than Obama's — allegedly the first black American President. But be warned: this is a politically incorrect fact you can mention in the People's Republic of Berkeley only at your own risk.

My personal opinion is that the survivors of the Bay of Pigs betrayal should have openly killed Kennedy when he went to Miami to receive the Brigade's flag. Killing the man who knowingly sent them to their death would have been a just act of retribution.[23] Nevertheless, they didn't kill Kennedy, but most people in the U.S. still blame them for it and don't respect them. Had they killed Kennedy, most Americans would have blamed them the same, but at least those Cubans would have gained their respect.

But they didn't kill Kennedy because they loved America and respected its laws. It would have been inconceivable for them to attempt on the life of an American President. On the contrary, many of them joined the U.S. military and honorably served their country of adoption for many years.

As I have shown in chapters Seven and Eight of this book, the Rockefellers, a family of sociopathic criminals with a flair for eliminating their enemies, were the true creators of the CIA, and the Agency has always worked to protect and advance the interests of the Rockefellers and their fellow bankers, not the interests of the American people. President Kennedy's plans in national and international politics were diametrically opposed to the Rockefellers' globalist plans. Soon after he was sworn into office, it became evident that they would never be able to convince, co-opt, coerce, or threaten JFK into changing his policies. Consequently, the only way open for the Rockefellers was to use their CIA — most likely with the help of their secret agent Fidel Castro — to terminate JFK with extreme prejudice.

Did Castro Kill President Kennedy?

Historians believe in synchronicity and coincidences, intelligence officers don't. To any intelligence officer it would have seemed a strange coincidence that, just a few days before the Kennedy assassination, Castro had given, following his own suggestion, an interview to French journalist Jean Daniel. It was an even stranger coincidence that, at the very moment in which Kennedy was assassinated and a few hours after a senior CIA officer had a secret meeting with double agent Rolando Cubela to discuss Castro's assassination, Castro was engaged in a friendly conversation with Daniel in which Castro said many rosy things about the American President.

The meeting with Daniel was very handy, because it allowed for Castro's friendly feelings toward Kennedy to be recorded for posterity by a respectable, easily verifiable independent source. But one must keep in mind that the Fidel Castro who told Daniel so many nice things about Kennedy was the very same Fidel Castro who never lost an opportunity to berate the American President. He was also the one who, just a few weeks earlier, had several times publicly threatened both John and Robert Kennedy with retaliation in kind for their attempts to assassinate him.

Some Kennedy assassination researchers who studied the Warren Commission documents have noticed the way Allen Dulles consistently blanked out whenever the discussion touched Castro. The only logical explanation they found out to explain Allen's strange behavior is that any mentioning of Castro might bring out the CIA's plans to assassinate the Cuban leader.[24]

This, Warren Commission members might feared, would have encouraged doubts that Oswald acted alone, implicate Castro and perhaps even the Soviet Union, which might have brought a confrontation much worse than the Cuban missile crisis.[25]

This, however, is pure hogwash, because one of the few people at CIA who knew for sure that Castro was a CIA asset was Allen Dulles. He and his Rockefeller masters did not fear the Soviet Union, but the American people. Just the suspicion that Castro, acting on behalf of the Rockefellers, had assassinated Kennedy would have unleashed the biggest scandal in American history.

The theory that Castro had absolutely nothing to do with the assassination of President Kennedy cannot stand a serious analysis. Castro had the motive, the ability, the means, the opportunity and the expertise to have ordered the assassination of President Kennedy. Even more, like many experienced criminals, he was clever enough to create a perfect alibi, backed by a respectable, impartial witness.

In the first place, as I have shown above, Castro had sufficient motives to order President Kennedy's assassination. When the Church Committee developed the details of the Kennedy plots to kill Castro — which Kennedy admirers disingenuously refer to as the "CIA-Mafia plots" — it established that Castro had ample reason to retaliate and seek the death of the American President. Even more, Kennedy had humiliated Castro, something that the Maximum Leader, a very spiteful person, never took lightly or ever forgot.

Perhaps President Kennedy believed that Fidel Castro was just another Diem, easy to get rid of. But Fidel Castro was no Diem. Political assassination was never alien to Castro, and his activities as a gangster at the University of Havana have been widely documented, as well as the fact that he was an expert in retaliating in kind.

Secondly, Castro had the ability to commit that type of crime. Very early in his political career he initiated himself in the art of political assassination and at the time of the JFK assassination he already had been practicing it for many years. Also, as I have shown above, he was very good at it, because he was never caught. But, perhaps blinded by the arrogance of power that seems to emanate from the White House, President Kennedy failed to notice that he and his brother were amateur assassins dealing with a professional.

The fact that Castro was a professional assassin was acknowledged by a qualified colleague. It is known that Sam Giancana warned his associate Johnny Rosselli to be very careful with Castro because, "He's an assassin. He knows all the tricks."[26] But President Kennedy, like many others, ignored Castro's warning signs and paid with his life for his gross mistake.

Thirdly, Castro also had the means to carry out an assassination attempt on President Kennedy. The sophistication and efficiency of Castro's secret services and his network of agents operating freely among the thousands of Cubans in the United States has been documented. It would have been very easy for Castro to use his agents in place or infiltrate one or several hit teams into the United States to carry out his wet affairs.[27] It is well known that Castro's hit men were operating in the U.S. As *UPI* reporter Edward McCarthy revealed, at the moment President Kennedy was killed, four hit teams of Castro's assassins were already in the United States.[28]

Finally, there is no doubt that Castro had the opportunity to order the assassination. We will never know, for sure, because there is no way we can check his whereabouts during the days prior to the assassination, but his repeated threats were plain and clear.

It has been amply documented that Castro had the motive, the ability, the means and the opportunity, though perhaps not to the extent it deserves.[29] What has remained unknown to the American public, however, is the fact that, as explained in detail in Chapter 11, Fidel Castro always has shown a strong tendency to commit this particular type of crime.

There is evidence that he was involved in the 1979 assassination of ex-President Somoza of Nicaragua by a Sandinista hit team trained in Cuba. Moreover, there are suspicions that in 1976 he planned to assassinate both President Gerald Ford and his contender Ronald Reagan.[30]

Fidel Castro has always felt an irrational, visceral hatred for democratically elected presidents. It seems that these strong feelings were not tempered with age. Sources close to the Cuban leader have commented that, since late 2000, Castro expressed on many occasions a strong hatred for Presidents Francisco Flores of El Salvador, Vicente Fox of Mexico, Fernando de la Rúa of Argentina, and U.S. President George W. Bush.

Even more, after the 2009 condemnation in Geneva of his regime's gross violations of human rights,[31] the list of presidents he wanted to assassinate grew considerably. According to sources close to Castro, Costa Rica's President Miguel Angel Rodríguez, Panama's Mireya Moscoso, Guatemala's Alfonso Portillo, Uruguay's Jorge Batlle, and Canada's Prime Minister Jean Chrétien and even President Vaclav Havel of the Czech Republic were added to Castro's hit list.[32]

Given his previous efforts to kill presidents, one can state without any shadow of a doubt that Castro not only had the motive, the ability, the means and the opportunity, but also the inclination to order such an incredible thing as the assassination of an American President. Moreover, given the fact that most people act consistently with their past behavior, one can safely assume that Castro at least planned to assassinate President Kennedy.

In any event, overwhelming circumstantial evidence indicates that Castro at least played a role in the assassination of President Kennedy. So, how can we explain that most American authors who have written about the assassination have managed to keep Castro out of the picture?

The most blatant omission was committed by the CFR-controlled Warren Commission, which carefully avoided mentioning Castro as a possible suspect of participating in the assassination. The reason for this notable omission is because, though Castro was the one of the executors, as a secret CFR agent, he may have just followed orders.

Because of this, covering Castro's tracks was a priority of the Commission members. This explains why senior CFR agent Allen Dulles, the man Kennedy had fired as CIA director, was one of the main members of the Commission. This explains why the Commission's conclusions were a travesty of justice and a cover-up.

On the other hand, after knowing of John Kennedy's attempts to assassinate Castro, as well as Kennedy's role in the 1963 assassination of President Ngo Dinh Diem of South Vietnam, not to mention the assassinations of Trujillo and Patrice Lumumba,[33] one may well say that both Mafia capos, Castro and Kennedy, had a penchant for assassinating presidents. Castro, however, was by far the best.

As I mentioned above, like all professional criminals, Castro created a perfect alibi when he called Jean Daniel for an interview at exactly the time the assassination of President Kennedy was taking place. It is a common practice in intelligence business to use journalists as unwitting vehicles to pass disinformation. Castro's use of Jean Daniel is very similar to Kennedy's use of Tad Szulc, then a *New York Times* correspondent, when the President called Szulc to the White House on November 9, 1961, and asked him, "What would you think if I ordered Castro to be assassinated?"

Szulc replied that he did not foresee Castro's killing necessarily leading to any change in Cuba, and that he did not think that the United States should be party to political assassinations. To this Kennedy replied, "I agree with you completely." And then he continued for several minutes duplicitously stating that he and his brother felt "the United States for moral reasons should never be in a situation of having recourse to assassination."[34]

In a speech he gave on November 16 at the University of Washington, Kennedy elaborated upon the subject. He shamelessly declared, "We cannot, as a free nation, compete with our adversaries in tactics of terror, assassination, false promises, counterfeit mobs and crises."

David Rockefeller, the CIA and Fidel Castro

In his 2002 *Memoirs*, David mentions how he "confronted Fidel Castro during his 1996 visit to New York."[35] In another part, he made an effort to explain the reason why he appears effusively smiling in a photo with Fidel Castro. According to David, on October 23 1995, the Council on Foreign Relations profited from the opportunity that the U.N. was celebrating its fiftieth anniversary that attracted two hundred heads of state to New York and invited many of them to speak at the Council — Castro among them.

David mentions that Castro wanted especially to meet him, but a convenient time had not yet been found. But, according to David, at the formal reception hosted by UN Secretary-General Boutrous-Ghali,

Castro spotted me, charged across the delegates' lounge, and grabbed my hands, shaking it warmly. I was chagrined, sensing the photo frenzy about to erupt. But I smiled as the paparazzi snapped away. Predictably, the photo of "the Capitalist and the Communist" appeared on the front page of newspapers from Ankara to Zanzibar; and just as predictably I was criticized for appearing with a man considered one of our nations bitterest enemies.[36]

As usual, David was disingenuous. His description of the event makes us think that this was the first time he met with Fidel Castro, but is was not. Actually he had met him many years before.

In April 1959, just four months after he had grabbed power in Cuba, Castro accepted an invitation from the American Society of Newspaper Editors to visit the U.S. During the visit, he gave a talk a the Harold Pratt House in Manhattan, headquarters of the Council of Foreign Relations. After his talk, he had a long private meeting with David Rockefeller.[37]

We don't know what they talked about — the meeting was conveniently ignored by the mainstream press — but we can safely guess that this was the moment Castro, who is no fool, realized where the true power was and decided to bypass the CIA from that moment on and begin dealing directly with the CIA's boss. Nevertheless, after meeting with Castro, former Secretary of State Dean Acheson (CFR) called him "the first democrat of Latin America."[38]

On the other hand, David Rockefeller's actions showed that, like Fidel Castro, he had a low respect for human life. This may explained his appreciation for mass assassins such as Stalin, Mao and Hitler. When David finally met Castro personally he most likely realized he had found his mirror soul; a psychopath who would not vacillate in carrying out his orders.

It was not by chance that, just a few weeks after returning from this trip to the U.S., Castro began implementing David's orders: a carefully designed two-pronged plan whose goal was both the destabilization of Latin America as a way to maximize the fear of communism and the penetration of the Soviet leadership by an agent provocateur who would push the Soviets into unwanted military adventures all around the globe.

In order to survive, the military-industrial-banking complex under Rockefeller's control needed long, unwinnable wars and revolutions, and Dr. Castro was ready to give them the medicine David and his minions craved. To this effect, as soon as he grabbed power in Cuba, Castro began sending military expeditions to Santo Domingo, Panama, Venezuela, and other Latin American countries as well as aggressively approaching the Soviets to accept him as a *bona fide* member of the communist camp.

The fact was acknowledged by authors Peter Collier and David Horowitz. According to them,

> Far from being driven reluctantly into waiting Soviet arms, Fidel actively *provoked* and escalated the confrontation with Washington in *order* to force a cautious, apprehensive and recalcitrant Kremlin to grant that embrace.[39] [Emphasis in original]

Nevertheless, this was not the only time David had a long conversation with his secret agent Fidel Castro. In February 2001, a high-level delegation of the Council on Foreign Relations led by David Rockefeller visited Cuba and held a long meeting with Castro. After the meeting, David advised Cuba as the economic and social model to follow and CFR chairman Peter Peterson praised the Cuban leadership's passionate commitment to providing high education and health standards for its people and told the press: "I suspect that Cuba is among the best educated countries in the entire hemisphere."[40]

Robert Kennedy visited Peru in 1965. During the visit, some locals complained about American imperialism and the abuses of the Rockefeller-owned International Petroleum Company. Kennedy finally said:

> Well, why don't you just go ahead and nationalize the damn thing. I mean nothing's going to happen. . . . The United Stated government isn't going to send destroyers or anything like that. Why don't you just do it?[41]

The Peruvians were appalled. According to them the Rockefellers ran the U.S. policy and would not permit it. "Oh. Come on," said Robert. "In our country we eat Rockefellers for breakfast.[42]

Bobby Kennedy was dead wrong. Actually, the Rockefellers are the ones who have been having Kennedys for breakfast, lunch and dinner . . . and they seemingly enjoyed the dish.

Who Was the Mastermind?

It is a common occurrence that the jury at a murder trial may find abundant accumulated circumstantial evidence so overwhelming that a guilty verdict is expected — even though there may be no witness to the crime. In the case of the CFR, the evidence that this organization has planned and carried out many crimes against the American people is so overwhelming that a guilty verdict is unavoidable.

Dozens of books, films and TV serials have been made depicting the criminal activities of the Italian Mafia — of which the novel and film *The Godfather* and the TV series *The Sopranos* are perhaps the most widely known — to the point that the word "Mafia" became a synonym for organized crime. Just a few have been made, however, about the Irish and Jewish Mafias, who also played an important part in the history of organized crime in America. In contrast, nothing has been ever written about the best organized, most powerful, most important, ruthless and successful of all American Mafias: the CFR Mafia.

Hiding behind an institutional cover of respectability, the Council on Foreign Relations is basically a criminal organization, the cover for a Mafia of Wall Street bankers, oil magnates and CEOs of transnational corporations, composed of ethically and morally challenged individuals, associated to carry out criminal activities sanctioned by David Rockefeller. The criminal activities of this Council on Foreign Relations Mafia have caused more death and suffering than the ones committed by all the other Mafias together.

Why do the American people totally ignore the existence of this dangerous crime syndicate? Because, contrary to the other minor Mafias, the CFR Mafia exerts an almost total control not only over the U.S. Government, but also over the mainstream media, particularly TV, national newspapers and magazines, and the book and film industries.[43]

The CFR Mafia also managed to get control of the U.S. intelligence services. Most officers of the Office of Special Services (OSS), the U.S. WWII intelligence agency, were Wall Street lawyers and bankers, and most of them were CFR members. There is abundant evidence indicating that CFR members were instrumental in helping Hitler to grab power in Germany, and later did business with Nazi Germany before and during the war.[44] Therefore it makes sense to think that the ones who joined the OSS didn't do it out of patriotism or altruism, to fight the Nazis or to protect the interests of the American people, but to protect their own narrow interests. Actually, one of the OSS's main secret missions during WWII was helping senior Nazi war criminals to escape with their gold and to protect German corporations like I.G. Farben, which had been collaborating with the Nazis while associated with Wall Street banks.

The Council on Foreign Relations *is* a criminal organization. Just a cursory view at the criminal activities of a few of the most prominent members of the CFR Mafia shows that perhaps it is easier to find more candor, honesty and purity in San Quentin than at the CFR. The Rockefellers, particularly Nelson and David, were first-class sociopaths[45] who surrounded themselves with a group of second-line sociopathts such as the Dulleses, Kissinger, Brzezinski, the Bushes and the Clintons. Those sociopaths recruited psychopaths such as Castro, Wisner and Angleton whose job was carrying out the Rockefellers' dirty work of theft, subversion and assassination. Like in a criminal Mafia, since he appointed himself in 1941 Chairman of the Board of the Council on Foreign Relations until his death in 2017, David Rockefeller was its Godfather.

One has to be very naïve to believe even for a second that the CIA would try to kill a foreign, much less a U.S. leader, without an express, or at least implied, order from the highest levels of the U.S. Government — that is, from the true President of the Invisible Government of the U.S., David Rockefeller himself. Contrary to Senator Frank Church's claims, the CIA has never been a "rogue elephant." On the contrary, the CIA has always been the hidden arm of President David Rockefeller, and he used the Agency to its fullest.

Following orders from David Rockefeller, CFR psychopaths inside the CIA actively participated in the assassination of foreign leaders all around the world. They also planned and carried out the assassination of American leaders, such as General Patton, Admiral Forrestal, U.S. Senator McCarthy, civil rights leader Martin Luther King and, last but not least, President John F. Kennedy and his brother Robert.

They have carried out the assassinations of people who, for one or another reason, they have considered a threat to their evil plans. CFR sociopaths in the U.S. Government and the mainstream media have also had an active part in the cover-up of those crimes.

This way of getting rid of their potential enemies never stopped. The justification for some of these acts was that those leaders were communists — the secret operating principle is that a communist is anybody who becomes a threat to the Rockefeller's interests.

CFR psychopaths in the CIA and the U.S. military have also had an active participation in mass murder in Latin America, Asia, Africa and the Middle East.

Acting on behalf of the CFR sociopaths, CFR psychopaths inside the CIA, the U.S. military and the U.S. Government have committed massive genocide and assassination,[46] waged unprovoked wars, performed psychological warfare operations against the American and other peoples around the world, and overthrown legitimate government leaders through coups d'état and assassinations, including American presidents. They have systematically committed fraud and stolen money, property and natural resources from the American people and the peoples of the world.

Their ultimate genocidal goal is the elimination of no less than 85 percent of the population of this planet — the "useless eaters" who are destroying Gaia's natural resources— and reducing the survivors to pre-industrial, feudal levels of consumption, after they have fully implemented the global totalitarian communo-fascist dictatorship they call the New World Order, which, of course, they plan to control.

Most sociopaths with a criminal mind have found refuge in the Rockefeller-controlled Council on Foreign Relations. This is the place where they can associate with other sociopaths like themselves as well as the psychopaths ready carry out their criminal orders.

Most likely, neither David Rockefeller nor any his sociopathic minions such as Henry Kissinger, Robert McNamara or Bill Clinton, have ever killed anybody with their own hands. But they are the ones who have given the orders to some of their trusted psychopaths who do the actual killings.[47]

In his book *Without Conscience*, Dr. Robert Hare explains that, in addition to being "slick," liars, and fast talkers, sociopaths are unable to alter their behavior even when caught. They are,

> ... social predators who charm, manipulate, and ruthlessly plow their way through life, leaving a broad trail of broken hearts, shattered expectations, and empty wallets. Completely lacking in conscience and in feelings for others, they selfishly make what they want and do as they please, violating social norms and expectations without the slightest sense of guilt or regret.[48]

The above description accurately fits the behavior of most CFR members, particularly the ones in its core nucleus and the inner circle around David Rockefeller.

Through his agents infiltrated in the U.S. Government, David was in command of the Department of Defense, the National Security Council, the CIA, the Department of State, the Department of the Treasury, the Department of Education, and the rest of all key organization in the U.S., perhaps with the exception of the FBI while J. Edgar Hoover was its director.

None of the usual suspects — the Mafia, anti-Castro Cubans, Lyndon Johnson, the South Vietnamese, J. Edgar Hoover, just to mention a few — had the power to carry out the full operation. Actually, though I am convinced that both Castro and the CIA played a key role in the operational part of the JFK assassination, neither Castro nor the CIA had the power to control the Secret Service or the doctors who performed the autopsy, much less the people who carried out the cover-up and the post-cover-up. Only a person who controlled Castro, the CIA, the U.S. Government and the mainstream media had the power to do it, and that person was David Rockefeller.

While far from being a perfect man, Kennedy was a patriot who loved his country and he clashed against America's worst domestic enemies: the Rockefellers and their minions in the Council on Foreign Relations. Almost everything he did threatened the CFR conspirators' plans.

He began withdrawing CIA "advisers" from Vietnam; fired CIA's trusted CFR agents Allen Dulles and Richard Bissell, signed orders to pass the control over covert operations from the hands of the CIA and passed them to the military, and ordered the Treasury to print government currency as a first step to break the Federal Reserve Bank's monopoly.

Whoever ordered the assassination of President John F. Kennedy had to be a person of immense power and, particularly in the United States, immense power has always been linked to immense wealth. Therefore, the only person who could have ordered to assassination of President Kennedy was his worst enemy, the *capo di tutti capi* of the CFR Mafia, David Rockefeller.

Key men who participated in the planning and execution of the operation and had full knowledge about it were his brother Nelson, Allen Dulles, James Jesus Angleton, Richard Bissell, Richard Helms and George H.W. Bush — all of them CFR members or assetts. Others who played a secondary role were E. Howard Hunt, Bill Harvey, Frank Wisner, Frank Sturgis and Tracy Barnes.

Last, but not least, Fidel Castro played a key role in the operation. David may have included Castro after his own request, just to give the Cuban psychopath the opportunity to quench his insatiable thirst for revenge.

By the way, just recently somebody reached my same conclusion that David Rockefeller was the mastermind behind the JFK assassination. According to Kevin Barrett, Editor of the website *Veterans Today*,

> David Rockefeller was such an important figure that he had to "give the nod" to the JFK assassination. On the night of November 21, 1963, Rockefeller's right hand man and emissary John J. McCloy, along with J. Edgar Hoover and his "wife" Clyde Tolson, ultra-corrupt Vice President Lyndon Johnson, mafia hit man Jack Ruby, future president Richard M. Nixon, George Brown (of Brown and Root), and other Deep State kingpins gathered at mafia lynchpin Clint Murchison's house in Dallas. Johnson emerged from the meeting to tell his mistress Madeleine Duncan Brown that "after tomorrow, those goddamn Kennedys will never embarrass me again."[49]

Epilogue

It is tough to make predictions, especially about the future.
— Yogi Berra.

The End of the American Dream

The JFK assassination marked the beginning of the overthrow of the American Republic and the beginning of the implementation of the CFR conspirators' totalitarian global society they call the New World Order.

The assassination of President John F. Kennedy in 1963 was a dagger stuck in the very heart and soul of America. It was the day Americans began losing their country. It marked the end of the American Dream and the beginning of the American Nightmare.

This nightmare, quite similar to the nightmare Fidel Castro implemented in Cuba following David Rockefeller's orders,[1] opened the doors for the Vietnam War, the total destruction of the U.S. industrial base, the impoverishing of farmers and workers, the growing mass of unemployed, and the planned decline of the country's energy and transportation infrastructure. The American nightmare worsened during the calamitous 20 years of Bushes and Clintons and, after the 9/11 events and the so-called War on Terror, marked a sharp turn to a totalitarian police state that culminated in the eight disastrous Obama years.[2]

At the same time, while a large majority of the American people were becoming dirt poor, a very small minority was turning filthy rich. From a rich, powerful country with a large middle class, America had rapidly turned into an economic and social disaster. For the first time since the end of WWII, Americans were experiencing the new reality that their children were going to be poorer than their parents.

In the Introduction to this book I pointed to the Central Intelligence Agency, Fidel Castro and David Rockefeller as the three main suspects in the assassination of President John F. Kennedy. Now, however, after providing all the information I gathered to support my claims, I have to fine-tune my initial assertion.

Following implicit or explicit orders from David Rockefeller, President Kennedy was assassinated by a cabal of traitors infiltrated in the U.S. Government, the CIA and the military, with the support of traitors in the academia and the mainstream press. The great majority of these traitors were members of the Rockefeller-created Council on Foreign Relations. Most likely, David's secret agent Fidel Castro played an important role in the assassination.

As he told the American people in his Inaugural Address, President Kennedy wanted to re-establish a Republic of the people, by the people, for the people, but David Rockefeller and his CFR minions had a very different idea for America.

In June, 1991, during a secret meeting of the Bilderberg Group, CFR chairman David Rockefeller clearly expressed his idea for the future of America and the world and thanked the media for keeping secret his evil plan for America and the world:

We are grateful to the *Washington Post*, the *New York Times*, *Time* magazine and other great publications whose directors have attended our meetings and respected their promises of discretion for almost forty years. It would have been impossible for us to develop our plan for the world if we had been subject to the bright lights of publicity during those years. But the world is now more sophisticated and prepared to march towards a world government. The supra-national sovereignty of an intellectual elite and world bankers is surely preferable to the national auto determination practiced in past centuries.[3]

Contrary to JFK, David was secretly working hard to establish a totalitarian dictatorship of the bankers, by the bankers and for the bankers. Unfortunately, CFR conspirators working in the shadows sabotaged JFK's dream and, after his death, David's nightmare has been fully implemented.

David was extremely upset at having in the White House a true American patriot who refused to play the usual puppet role he, the true President of the United States, had assigned to American Presidents. So, he let his CIA psychopaths know how frustrated he felt, and they got the hint. Afterwards, the Dulles-Angleton executive action[4] team went to work full time on the planning of JFK's assassination.

In the closing speech at the trial of Clay Shaw on February 28, 1969, New Orleans District Attorney Jim Garrison told the jury:

> The government's handling of the investigation of John Kennedy's murder was a fraud. It was the greatest fraud in the history of our country. It probably was the greatest fraud ever perpetrated in the history of humankind. That doesn't mean that we have to accept the continued existence of the kind of government which allows this to happen. We can do something about it. We're forced either to leave this country or to accept the authoritarianism that has developed — the authoritarianism which tells us that in the year 2029 we can see the evidence about what happened to John Kennedy.[5]

Of course, Garrison said this before the 9/11 events, which, as of today, is the greatest fraud in the history of this country. As a direct consequence of these two frauds, currently more and more Americans are afraid of their future. They see little hope for themselves, their children and their country. The appearance of democracy remains, but people no longer believe they have the power to change the wrong policies, much less the state of things.

After the successful assassination of President John F. Kennedy, the one percent elite has grown more obtuse and unresponsive to the seething anger that lies just below the surface of a seemingly dormant society. The economic chasm separating the rich and the poor keeps growing and, as the election of Donald Trump as U.S. President in 2016 clearly evidenced, it has begun to fuel populist anger.

Currently, most Americans are convinced that the two parties are a hoax and elections are no longer an instrument for change. Political impotence has led to frustration, depression and rage. The direct result of this is that new movements such as the alt-right that embraces more extreme remedies to the present state of things have emerged because the traditional parties no longer represent the will of the people.

In its April, 1972, issue commemorating the 50th anniversary of its creation, *Foreign Affairs*, the CFR's organ, published a revealing article by Kingman Brewster Jr., "Reflections on Our National Purpose."[6] The title is purposely misleading, because the "our" in it does not refer to *us*, the American people, but to *them*, the CFR members. So, translated into plain English, the article's title should have been "Reflections on the CFR's National Purpose," and their purpose is none other than to abolish America's sovereignty.

According to Brewster, *our* purpose should be to do away with our nationality, to "take some risks in order to invite others to pool their sovereignty with ours…", adding:

> It is hard to see how we will engage the youth, and stand any chance of competing for the respect of mankind generally, if we continue to be more concerned with the sovereignty of nations than with the ultimate sovereignty of peoples.[7]

Nevertheless, while researching for the writing of this book I discovered an extraordinary parallel between John F. Kennedy's and Donald Trump's national purpose for America. Even their electoral campaign mottos were quite similar: "Get America moving again," (Kennedy), "Make America great again," (Trump). No wonder the CFR globalists got rid of Kennedy and now are doing everything they can to get rid of Trump.

Unfortunately, however, John F. Kennedy never fully realized who his true enemies were and Donald Trump seems clueless about who they are.

Will the CFR Conspirators Allow President Trump to Accomplish JFK's Dream?

On January 20, 1961, John F. Kennedy was inaugurated as the Thirty-Fifth President of the United States. His inaugural address was a patriotic call for advancing America socially and economically. In it, he challenged the Soviets to use the "wonders of science" for economic progress and space exploration instead of militarism.

President Kennedy's inaugural address was a true harbinger of the big changes he planned to make in American foreign policy. In the first part the new president clearly expressed his intention to end the ongoing U.S. imperial policies:

> To those new states whom we welcome to the ranks of the free, we pledge our word that one form of colonial control shall not have passed away merely to be replaced by a far more iron tyranny. We shall not always expect to find them supporting our view. But we shall always hope to find them strongly supporting their own freedom.[8]

The second part of his speech was a clear reference to the futility of the Cold War policy and the risks to mankind it involved,

> Finally, to those nations who would make themselves our adversary, we offer not a pledge but a request: that both sides begin anew the quest for peace, before the dark powers of destruction unleashed by science engulf all humanity in planned or accidental self-destruction.[9]

Soon after, Kennedy began an aggressive program to make a reality his promise to "get America moving again," and declared that the 1960s would be the decade of development for America. He stressed the importance of creating an abundant and growing supply of cheap energy. Unfortunately, however, Kennedy was not aware that the CFR conspirators had already decided that the 1960s would be the decade that would mark the beginning of energy scarcity, deindustrialization and nondevelopment in America.

JFK was aware that, for some reason he may not have fully understood at the time, America had stopped in its tracks toward progress. Therefore, economic growth was Kennedy's main goal of his domestic agenda. He expressed this concern in a speech to the Congress on February 2, 1961, where he presented his Program to Restore Momentum to the American Economy.[10]

Like Trump's, Kennedy's inaugural address was a clear defiance of the traditional CFR-created American foreign policy. It marked the beginning of a new type of foreign policy seeking a peaceful solution to the unproductive, dangerous Cold War against the Soviet Union and changing the world's future direction. Kennedy wanted to make clear to Soviet chairman Nikita Khrushchev that he did not prefer a Cold War, much less a nuclear war, but a genuine peace based on negotiations and mutual cooperation.[11] He also wanted to put and end to the U.S. imperial foreign policy, which only benefited a small group of bankers and transnational corporations, not the American people, and begin a new approach of U.S. policy toward Latin America and the Third World.

In foreign policy, Kennedy also took some initiatives that indicated he was going to carry out the promises he had made as a candidate. The measures he had in mind indicated a radical change from traditional U.S. foreign policy. Among these were respect for the sovereignty, autonomy and independence of other nations, as well as promoting expanded opportunities and higher standards of living.

Kennedy was opposed to foreign policies based on the domination of weak, poor nations by powerful ones, conducive to perpetuating economic backwardness and exploitation of natural resources. He expressed this clearly in a message he sent to Congress just two months after he was sworn into office in which he stated that the, "1960s can be — and must be — the crucial decade of development for Latin America, Africa, the Middle East, and Asia."[12]

On February 1959, in a speech to the Senate, Senator Kennedy had strongly criticized what he saw as a gap more dangerous than the missile gap. It was precisely in that speech where Kennedy clearly expressed his critical view of what was wrong with U.S. foreign policy:

> As a nation, we [should] think not of war but of peace; not of crusades of conflict but of covenants of cooperation; not of the pageantry of imperialism but of the pride of new states freshly risen to independence.[13]

Kennedy's mention of what he defined as "the pageantry of imperialism," was a direct attack on the architects of the so-called "American imperialism" — which was actually the imperialism of the oil magnates, Wall Street bankers and CEOs of transnational corporations ensconced at the Council on Foreign Relations. Proof of this was that, soon after Kennedy began implementing his policies, the CFR-controlled media, particularly the *New York Times*, the *Wall Street Journal*, *Time*, *Life*, *Fortune* and the emerging TV news, launched a systematic stream of criticism, very similar to what they are now doing to Donald Trump.

Unfortunately, Kennedy was not aware that the negative trend of the American economy he was trying to stop and reverse had not been the result of chance or incompetence, but of a carefully-conceived plan to destroy the U.S. economy and change America into a third world country. Many years before, the globalist conspirators at the Council on Foreign Relations had already decided that, far from being the decade of development, the 1960s would be the decade devoted to lowering the levels of education by turning it into indoctrination as well as lowering American standards of living and increasing poverty levels by systematically destroying the U.S. industrial and economic base.

On June 10, 1963, in the commencement address at American University in Washington, D.C., President Kennedy took another step forward and announced that the Soviets had expressed a desire to negotiate a nuclear test ban treaty and that the U.S had postponed some planned atmospheric nuclear tests.[14] An interesting detail is that President Kennedy's efforts to end the Cold War closely resembled Soviet Premier Nikita Khrushchev's doctrine of Peaceful Coexistence.[15]

One of the fateful steps taken by Kennedy after he was sworn in as President was to scrap the National Security Council mechanism. Being statutory, he could not abolish the NSC unilaterally, but he simply ignored it.[16] Then, after the Bay of Pigs debacle — which, as I have shown above in this book, actually was a very successful PsyOp carried out by the CFR conspirators — he fired CIA Director Allen Dulles, a senior CFR conspirator closely associated to the Rockefeller gang, as well as Richard Bissell, the man in charge of CIA's covert operations and also a CFR member, and told some close friends that he wanted to "splinter" the CIA "into a thousand pieces and scatter [it] to the winds."[17] Unfortunately, the CFR conspirators already had a counterplan to prevent JFK from carrying out his plan.

Many Americans who gave their votes to Trump were confused trying to understand the logic of his ordering a missile attack on Syria, a sovereign state with which we are not at war with. Even if the sarin gas attack on civilians was real — which I doubt, because it has all the characteristics of a false flag operation — the U.S. has no right whatsoever to continue acting as the policeman of the world. Actually, to stop these foreign entanglements the Founder Fathers advised against was one of the reasons why most people gave their votes to Trump.

Moreover, the fact that Hillary Clinton, Nancy Pelosi, John McCain, Lindsey Graham, Chuck Schumer, the Neocons, the *New York Times*, the *Wall Street Journal* and other CFR-controlled media praised Trump's illegal military action against Syria is a clear indication that his decision was wrong.

I hope that, after President Trump realizes that his advisors lied about Syria[18] exactly as JFK's advisors lied about the Bay of Pigs operation, he admits his mistake, gets rid of the traitors around him and corrects the course of the ship of state according to what he solemnly promised the American people in his inaugural address.

Will the CFR Conspirators Overthrow President Trump?

If you believe what the mainstream media and the disinformers of both sides of the Repucratic coin are trying to make us believe, the past election was a victory for Republican candidate Donald Trump over Democratic candidate Hillary Clinton, and that it was a victory for conservative Americans in their fight against liberal "progressives."

Nothing can be farther from the truth.

The result of the past election was not a victory for Donald Trump. Actually, it was a calamitous defeat for the forces behind the New World Order, particularly the CFR conspirators and their minions. Evidence of this is that just recently former President George H.W. Bush, a key CFR member who mentioned the New World Order in every speech, strongly criticized President Trump, calling him "a blowhard," and that "This guy doesn't know what it means to be president."[19]

Donald Trump made clear his opposition to the New World Order in his first post-victory rally in Cincinnati, Ohio on December 1, 2016. There he clarified his "America First" policy. He said that attempts to "separate us by race, by age, by income, by place of birth, and by geography" were over. "Now is the time to embrace the one thing that truly unites us. You know what that is? America." . . . "We hear a lot of talk about how we are becoming a 'globalized world.' But the relationships that people value in this country are local."

He continued his speech with a strong attack on the CFR conspirators' New World Order:

> There is no global anthem. No global currency. No certificate of global citizenship. We pledge allegiance to one flag and that flag is the American flag . . . From now on it is going to be: America First

... Never anyone again will any other interests come before the interest of the American people. It is not going to happen again.[20]

To top it off, Trump's election by the American people coincided with the Brexit, the growing collapse of the European Union, Russia's strong opposition to the New World Order, the CFR's failure to overthrow Assad in Syria to give control of the whole Middle East to extremist Muslims, the refusal of Philippine's President Duterte to play their game, and the Colombian people's rejection of a Peace Accord with the murderous, corrupt FARC guerrilla.[21]

No wonder the CFR conspirators are so nervous and concerned about their future. It seems, though, that they still refuse to accept the reality of their defeat and are planning to avoid at all costs that Donald Trump carries out his promises to the American people and becomes a successful president of the United States — even if to avoid it they have to push America into a nuclear Armageddon. This explains why the CFR, the CIA, Obama, and their lapdog John McCain, one of the most despicable characters in American politics, are desperately trying to push America into new wars.

Currently, the same people who told us that Saddam Hussein was stockpiling weapons of mass destruction in Iraq are now desperately trying to delegitimize Trump by claiming that the Russian government influenced the results of the election. Moreover, impostor Barry Soetoro declared that he planned to stay in Washington D.C. in order to create a "shadow government" to fight President Trump.[22] Now, given the fact that Soetoro is a mentally-retarded imbecile who cannot produce ideas of his own, one has to conclude that his "shadow government" will be fully under the control of the Invisible Government controlled by Wall Street bankers, oil magnates and CEOs of transnational corporations in the Council on Foreign Relations in Manhattan.

Nevertheless, we should not be surprised by the globalist conspirators' knee-jerk reaction. They have plenty of reasons to be scared to death.

It is evident that one of Trump's goals is to disassemble the New World Order machinery that the globalist conspirators have so carefully been assembling during the past hundred years. An investigation of Obama's true place of birth may bring the impostor to a long vacation in a federal prison and will automatically invalidate all his executive orders and maybe even his nominations to the Supreme Court. An investigation into Hillary's shady deals through her foundation may send her to join Obama. An investigation of McCain's activities at the Hanoi Hilton may uncover his dirtiest secrets.[23] An investigation of the roles of George W. Bush, Dick Cheney and other CFR members in the 9/11 events may bring stiff penalties to them and their accomplices. Even worse, an investigation of the treacherous role of the Council on Foreign Relations may result in its destruction.[24]

Obviously, the CFR conspirators cannot risk these possibilities. For them, preventing the success of Trump's presidency is a matter of life or death.

During a 1992 interview with Sarah McLendon, at the time a senior journalist of the White House press corps, George H.W. Bush told her: "Sarah, if the American people ever find out what we have done, they would chase us down the street and lynch us."[25] Well, currently a large majority of the American people has found out, and apparently the CFR conspirators have not yet realized that the only person who stands between them and the lynching mobs is Donald Trump. He is their only chance they have to solve this problem in a legal, civilized way.

So, the traitorous CFR conspirators should tread carefully, and not underestimate Trump and his allies. The best thing they should do is to accept their defeat, keep their agents and puppets under a tight leash, and avoid an incident that may bring them dire consequences.

To Make America Great Again, President Trump Must Destroy the Alien Queen

It is evident that Donald Trump does not care much about ideology. Apparently he thinks that just by fixing the U.S. economic, political and social problems he will make America great again. Unfortunately, he is wrong. The problem America is currently facing is not just economic, political or social: it is an ideological problem.

The American Republic is in grave danger, and we are past the time for Band Aid cures. In order to produce major changes, President Trump needs to find the true source of the problem — who the true enemies of America are — and strike at it hard.

In the film *Aliens*, the spaceship's crew under attack finally notices that just taking out the aliens one by one is an exercise in futility and frustration, because they reproduce faster than the crew can kill them. Then a member of the crew realizes that in order to solve the problem they must begin by taking out the Alien Queen.

In the same fashion, taking out the CIA will not solve the problem. To eliminate the cause of evil, we most strike at the root. Unless we get rid of the Alien Queen, we will not solve the problem.

This Alien Queen is the one who hatched not only the CIA, but also the Fed, the DHS, the IRS, NSC, NSA, FEMA, TSA and the rest of the alphabet soup of aberrations working hard to destroy the freedoms guaranteed by our Constitution. The Alien Queen is currently hatching dozens of eggs that will provide replacements for the new generations of Kissingers, Brzezinskis, Carters, Soroses, Strongs, Clintons and Bushes. And the evil Alien Queen's nest is at the Harold Pratt House in Manhattan, headquarters of the Council on Foreign Relations and center of the Invisible Government of the United States.

It has become evident that the people who control the Invisible Government of the United States want to destroy this country — this is basically what the New World Order is all about. This is difficult to understand, because not even most of the worst dictators and tyrants the world has known wanted to destroy their own countries. Perhaps an explanation for this is that, with the exception of the Rockefellers and the Morgans, the rest of the people who constitute the Invisible Government of the United States — the Warburgs, the Rothschilds, the Schiffs, the Lehmans, the Kuhns, the Loebs — are not even Americans and don't care a rat's ass about this country, its Constitution and its people

For close to a century, the CFR has been the main source of anti-American activity in the world. The main goals of this group of international bankers have been the elimination of the U.S. sovereignty, the opening of the borders and the cancellation of the Constitution, as well as the elimination of 85 percent of the planet's population and the reduction of the survivors to pre-industrial levels of consumption in a global government under their control.

CFR members have openly spoken about their agenda on innumerable occasions. In 1942, the chairman of the National Council of Churches and CFR founder John Foster Dulles, issued a report claiming that "a new order of economic life is both imminent and imperative," and called for,

> . . . a world government, strong immediate limitation of national sovereignty, international control of all armies and navies, a universal system of money, world-wide freedom of immigration, progressive elimination of all tariff and quota restrictions on world trade and a democratically controlled world bank.

In his 1945 book *Modern Man is Obsolete*, CFR member Norman Cousins stated:

> We even debate the question of "surrendering" some of our sovereignty — as though there is still something to surrender. There is nothing left to surrender. There is something to gain. A common world sovereignty ... would mean that no state could act unilaterally from the central authority as a method to achieve its aims. . . . There is no need to discuss the historical reasons pointing to and arguing for world government.

In September 1946, in an address to the UNESCO, Assistant Secretary of State William B. Benton (CFR), declared:

> You are expected to help carry out the UNESCO program within the United States. . . . We are at the beginning of a long process of breaking down the walls of national sovereignty.

The CFR's concerted attack on the U.S. sovereignty didn't pass unnoticed by the American people and many Americans expressed their distaste for this treacherous organization. As a result, in 1952, in response to growing concern about the illicit, conspiratorial activities of the CFR, the U.S. Congress created a Special Committee on Tax Exempt Foundations (commonly referred to as the Reece Committee). The final report in 1954 stated that the Committee had found that the CFR controlled most of these Foundations and its aim was to abolish national sovereignty and that the CFR "overly propagandizes the globalist concept." Its two main objectives are world government and global banking.

Unfortunately, nothing came out of the Reece Committee. But, in 1956 the Director of the Federal Bureau of Investigation (FBI) J. Edgar Hoover (not a CFR member), received hundreds of letters from concerned citizens and members of Congress, accusing the Council on Foreign Relations of treason and promoting communism through its agents infiltrated into the U.S. Government. Hoover ordered an investigation but, soon after, President Eisenhower (CFR) signed an executive order prohibiting the FBI from investigating federal government employees.

You don't need to be a "conspiracy theorist" to reach the conclusion that an anti-American, internationalist organization, whose goal is the elimination of the U.S. national sovereignty and borders as a first step to create a one-world government, has infiltrated and is now in control of the U.S. Government.

As an American, you should be concerned after knowing that the CFR, an organization whose members have not been elected by the American people, has successfully penetrated the three branches of the American government, particularly the executive branch. Since its creation, the CFR has also penetrated the U.S. diplomatic corps and intelligence services. It is now in an accelerated process of getting full control over the U.S. military.

The darkest characters of American politics in the recent history of the United States — Col. Edward Mandell House, Sumner Welles, Henry Stimson, John Foster and Allen Dulles, Dean Acheson, John McCloy, George Marshall,[26] Dwight D. Eisenhower,[27] Dean Rusk, Robert McNamara, Bush Sr. and Jr., Bill and Hillary Clinton, Henry Kissinger,[28] George Soros, Maurice Strong, Zbigniew Brzezinski, Jeane Kirkpatrick, Dick Cheney, Madeleine Albright, John McCain, Richard Nixon, Barack Obama and Dianne Feinstein, just to mention a few of the most notorious — have been directly or indirectly linked to the Rockefellers and the Council on Foreign Relations.

The treasonous activities of these individuals have caused irreparable damage to the American Republic. Acting under a false façade of patriotism, their actions have cost thousands of precious American lives, loss of jobs and property, and diminishing freedom. Adding insult to injury, they don't fear retribution because they know they are above the law.

During the administration of George H. W. Bush, most Cabinet members were also CFR members. Nevertheless, we should be even more concerned after knowing that the number of CFR members in the Clinton, George W. Bush and Obama administrations was even higher. In these four administrations, most members of the powerful National Security Council have been also CFR members. The number of CFR members in the Obama administration broke all previous records.

Given the fact that, like horse whisperers, members of the Cabinet and the NSC are the ones who tell American presidents what to do, it happens that the list of the people who have had a cardinal role in the revolutionary changes America has experienced in the past 50 years reads like a membership roster of the Council on Foreign Relations. This cannot be the product of a coincidence.

Actually, behind every act of treason to the American people and aggression against the peoples of the world, you will find, hiding in the shadows, one or more members of the Council on Foreign Relations. Of course, the assassination of President John F. Kennedy is not an exception to this rule.

Most books about the JFK assassination written by well intentioned, honest authors point to the Central Intelligence Agency as the main culprit. Others believed it was the "deep state" that killed Kennedy. A few have concluded that the Wall Street and military-industrial-complex were behind it. Granted, those authors have been very close to the truth. Nevertheless, in this book I have tried to be more specific.

Overwhelming circumstantial evidence indicates that the assassination of President Kennedy and its cover-up was a joint Castro-CIA-CFR operation following orders from their master, David Rockefeller.

Nonetheless, we must keep in mind that by blaming abstract entities such as the military-industrial-complex, Wall Street, the Establishment, and even the CIA or the CFR, wittingly or unwittingly we are helping the perpetrators of crimes against America hide behind a curtain of anonymity.

In *Fuenteovejuna*, a famous play by 17th Century Spanish playwright Lope de Vega, some people in the small village of Fuenteovejuna, angry at a commander who mistreated them, ambushed and killed him. When the King's Magistrate and soldiers arrived at the village to investigate the crime he called the villagers to the main square and asked them: *"Quién mató al Comendador?"* [who killed the commander?] and they all answered *"Fuenteovejuna, Señor."* [Fuenteovejuna did it, Sir.]. Faced with the impossibility of punishing the whole village, the magistrate left the village leaving the villagers unpunished.

In the same fashion, faced with the impossibility of investigating and, if found guilty, sentencing to death in the electric chair the CIA, the CFR, the military-industrial-complex or the Establishment, by blaming these collective, abstract entities, not specific persons inside these organizations, we are helping the guilty to keep their crimes unpunished. That is why in this book I have made an effort to put the blame on specific persons.

Nevertheless, as you have seen in this book, most of the people connected in any way to the JFK assassination, its cover-up and its post-cover-up, have been members of the Council on Foreign Relations

Of course, the CIA played a role in the JFK assassination, but who in the CIA was part of it? The old lady who cleans the toilets in the second floor of the CIA building at Langley? Of course not. The intelligence analysts working in the Directorate of Intelligence? None of them. Not even all CIA officers working in the covert operations branch took part in the operation. For sure, the ones involved were CIA Director Allen Dulles, Deputy Director for Plans Richard Bissell, and Richard Helms, also in the Directorate of Plans (covert operations), as well as Chief of Counterintelligence James Jesus Angleton and probably George H.W. Bush.[29] Other CIA officers such as E. Howard Hunt, David Atlee Phillips, Frank Sturgis, William Harvey, David Sánchez Morales, Antonio Veciana and Cord Meyer probably played a subordinate role in the operation.

Contrary to what some authors have written, however, these people were not part of a "rogue faction" of "disgruntled" CIA officers.[30] Actually, they were the real CIA. They were working on the CIA's real mission, the true and only purpose for what it was created: protecting and defending the interests of the Rockefellers and their fellow bankers. The rest is smoke and mirrors, disinformation created and advanced by the CFR conspirators to hide their treachery.

Most likely, Gen. Maxwell Taylor and Secretary of State Dean Rusk knew about the Kennedy assassination plan, even though they didn't have a direct participation in it. It is not a coincidence that all of them were trusted CFR members.[31] Another one who knew for sure was FBI Director J. Edgar Hoover, though he discovered it by his own means, and didn't act to stop it because he hated the Kennedys. Apparently, a few days before the assassination LBJ was told about the operation and he did nothing to stop it because he had enough reasons to hate the Kennedys and also because he had been promised that he would become the next President.

Also, Warren Commission members Allen Dulles (CFR), John McCloy (CFR) and Gerald Ford (CFR) participated in the initial cover-up, with the full support of the *New York Times, The Wall Street Journal, Time* magazine and other CFR-controlled media.

In 1949 David Rockefeller appointed himself CFR Director. At the time of the JFK assassination he was fully in control of the CFR and, through his agents at the highest levels of the Agency, he was also in control of the CIA. Therefore, it is safe to conclude that David Rockefeller must have been the mastermind behind the JFK assassination.

Moreover, the person who ordered the assassination of President Kennedy must have been somebody with an enormous fortune and enormous power. Granted, David Rockefeller was not the only American who owned an enormous fortune, but none of the others had his power.[32]

Actually, this is nothing new, much less surprising to anyone who has studied American politics, because, as I have mentioned over and over in this book, behind every act of treason to this country you will find hiding in the shadows one or several CFR members. What is really surprising, though, is that just a few of the authors who have written the more than two thousand books about the JFK assassination have mentioned the CFR's and Castro's role in it, and none of them has pointed at David Rockefeller as the mastermind of the operation.

It is not a coincidence that most people fiercely opposing President Donald Trump, such as the Clintons,[33] the Bushes, the Neocons, George Soros, Barack Obama and John McCain, just to mention a few, are either CFR members of under CFR control.

I think that one of the things President Trump should have done as soon as he was sworn as President was to reopen the investigation of the CFR's treacherous activities. If what we suspect is confirmed by the facts, this anti-American terrorist organization must be dissolved and its members banned to run for office or occupy government positions. The main culprits must be charged with treason and, if found guilty, sent to prison. Unfortunately, President Trump seems oblivious to the CFR's treachery.

Also, the more than a hundred of senior members of the U.S. military who have betrayed America by joining this treacherous organization must be dishonorably discharged and tried for high treason. The ones already retired must lose their retirement benefits. As Commander-in-Chief, President Trump should have got rid of those traitors as soon as he moved to the White House. Unfortunately, it seems that doing this is not among his immediate plans.

One of the few members of the Trump administration who seemed to know the true source of the problem America is facing was Stephen Bannon. Since the very beginning I saw Bannon as a sort of canary in the coal mine. Proof of it was that the CFR conspirators and their minions concentrated their attacks on him. So, when Trump fired him, it was a very bad sign.

The CFR is mainly an organization of the bankers, to the bankers and for the bankers. Those international bankers are the ones who own the U.S. national debt, that already has surpassed $20 trillion. This means that, as December, 2017, every American citizen owes $62,969.00 to the international bankers who own the debt. By the end of Fiscal Year 2018 it is expected to reach $24 trillion.

This humongous debt is unpayable. It is the greatest threat to the national security of the United States. Moreover, it is morally repugnant and unethical that American taxpayers need to work so hard to feed the banking leeches by paying every year the interests of this debt. Usury must end. The U.S. debt must be terminated!

So, one of the first things President Trump should have done was to cancel the U.S. national debt. He could have done this very easily by sending, delivered by military courier, a letter to every loan shark banker who owns the Fed containing a $1.00 bill as final payment for the debt, politely reminding them that the U.S. has the most powerful military forces in the world and would not tolerate any reprisals. Next, he should have gotten rid of the Federal Reserve Bank and ordered the Treasury Department to print U.S. dollars backed by gold and silver. Unfortunately, he didn't.

I have mentioned above some of the reasons why David Rockefeller ordered his hit men inside the CIA to terminate President Kennedy with extreme prejudice. The main reason, however, was because, most likely unknowingly, JFK was fighting against the Rockefellers' New World Order, which, by the way, is exactly the same reason why the CFR conspirators and their minions are now working hard to overthrow President Trump by any means necessary.

The assassination of President Kennedy was neither the first, nor the last, of many CFR, CIA, and Castro joint operations following orders from the President of the Invisible Government of the United States David Rockefeller. The assassination of Colombia's leader Gaitán, the Bay of Pigs invasion, the capture and killing of Chef Guevara, the creation of anti-U.S. guerrillas in Latin America and the invasion of Angola in 1975,[34] just to mention a few, were well-coordinated CFR, CIA, Castro covert joint operations.

If something has been evidenced, however, it is that the Rockefellers and their minions in the CFR and the CIA lack imagination and creativity. The pretext they used to justify their assassination of President Kennedy, accusing him of being soft of communism, is a carbon copy of the pretext they are currently using to justify the overthrowing of President Trump, his alleged collusion with Russia.[35]

Though evidently farfetched, it is somehow working not only because "progressive" Democrats will resort to any argument to get rid of President Trump, but also because most "conservative" Republicans[36] have been so thoroughly brainwashed that they are convinced that the fall of the Soviet

Union was a hoax, communism is still alive and well in Russia, and Vladimir Putin is a Communist in the closet.[37]

Donald Trump's election indicates a broad rejection by the majority of the American people of the country's political class, its media, its economic system and its primary institutions. It has become evident, however, that the CFR conspirators and their minions are not going to accept their defeat peacefully.

Sun Tzu, a Chinese general who lived in 544-496 B.C., wrote that only the general who knows his enemy like himself would win all the battles. Unfortunately, every day is becoming more and more evident that President Donald Trump has no idea of who the true enemies of America are.[38] So, either the same people who killed Kennedy will co-opt Trump or they will assassinate him. The globalist conspirators will not tolerate Donald Trump dismantling the machinery of treason in pursuit of their communo-fascist New World Order that took them close to a century to assemble.

Nevertheless, as the saying goes, hope for the best, prepare for the worst, and don't be surprised by anything in between.

In the meantime, there is something very important you can do: send letters and e-mails to the President, the Vice President, the Attorney General and the Director of the FBI, *demanding* them to open an investigation on the treasonous anti-American activities of the Council on Foreign Relations.[39] Encourage your friends to do the same.

Appendix I

Fidel Castro: A Rockefellers' Eugenic Tool?

I felt an incredible love for the nuclear missiles.
— Fidel Castro.

The Rockefellers and Eugenics

Since the beginning of the past century the Rockefellers, a family of sociopaths, became obsessed with population control. They were convinced that the world was overpopulated and that population must be reduced by any means necessary. In order to hide these irrational beliefs under a cover of science they found a good ally in the proponents of the eugenics "science."

As early as 1915, John D. Rockefeller, Jr. said:

> For the first time in dramatic history the perplexing problem of the limitation of undesirable offspring which has been engaging the attention of thoughtful eugenists and sociologists the world over is dealt on the stage in the play we are to produce.[1]

In the early 1900s, biologist Charles Davenport and former teacher Harry Laughlin founded with money provided by the Rockefellers[2] the Eugenics

Record Office at Cold Spring Harbor Laboratory on Long Island.[3] It remained active for close to three decades.

Contrary to the English eugenics movement, which promoted eugenics through selective breeding for positive traits, the American eugenics movement was focused on eliminating negative traits. Key among those "negative" traits were poverty and lack of education in minority populations. In an effort to eliminate those "negative" traits, American eugenicists helped drive legislation for their forced sterilization.[4]

California's eugenics program was so advanced that the Nazis turned to California for advice in perfecting their own efforts. Hitler proudly admitted to following the laws of several American states that allowed for the prevention of reproduction of the "unfit."[5]

The Eugenics Record Office closed its doors in 1939, but the Rockefellers did not end their dreams of global depopulation.

On May 5th, 2009, some of the most notorious members of the "billionaires club" — David Rockefeller, Bill Gates, Ted Turner, Oprah Winfrey, Warren Buffett, George Soros, Eli Broad, Peter G. Peterson, Patty Stonesifer, John Morgridge, Michael Bloomberg and a few other billionaires — most of them CFR members — secretly met at the Manhattan residence of Sir Paul Nurse, president of Rockefeller University.

As expected, the U.S. mainstream media was very careful not to inform the American people about the billionaires meeting in Manhattan, but some details eventually were known. Quoting an anonymous person who attended the meeting, a major U.K. newspaper reported, "a consensus emerged that they would back a strategy in which population growth would be tackled as a potentially disastrous environmental, social and industrial threat."

According to other sources, the billionaires who attended the secret meeting convened on the initiative of Bill Gates. Giving credibility to this is the fact that Gates had made similar points at a conference he attended on February 18, 2010, in Long Beach, California. Gates said,

> Official projections say the world's population will peak at 9.3 billion [up from 6.6 billion today] but with charitable initiatives, such as better reproductive healthcare, we think we can cap that at 8.3 billion.

Translated into plain English, "reproductive healthcare" actually means that Mr. Gates was planning to provide the funds for the killing of more than a billion human beings through wholesale abortion.

Also present at the meeting in Manhattan was media czar Ted Turner, a billionaire founder of *CNN*, who stated in a 1996 interview for the *Audubon* nature magazine that a 95% reduction of world population to between 225-300 million would be "ideal." In a 2008 interview at Philadelphia's Temple University, Turner fine-tuned the number to 2 billion, a cut of more than 70% from today's population.

The Rockefeller family is known for their generosity in contributing, through their non-profit, "philanthropic" foundations, to all causes whose goal is population control. They were instrumental in the creation of the eugenics movement in the U.S., which later was exported to Germany where the Nazis brought it to its highest development. Since the early 1920s, the Rockefeller Foundation began funding the eugenics research in Germany through the Kaiser-Wilhelm Institutes in Berlin and Munich. Beginning in the 1950s, John D. Rockefeller III used his foundation money to create a population reduction neo-Malthusian program through his private Population Council in New York.

In early 2011, enviro-journalist Bryan Nelson wrote a *Mother Nature Network* report entitled "Was Genghis Khan History's Greenest Conqueror?,"[6] that gives a quite accurate vision of what the eugenicists have in mind. In it, Nelson claimed that Genghis Khan's invasions of the 13th and 14th centuries were so sweeping, it "may have been the first instance in history of a single culture causing man-made climate change." According to Nelson, Genghis Khan contributed to cooling the environment through his massive killing of human beings, by "effectively scrubbing around 700 million tons of carbon from the atmosphere."

It is not a coincidence that all the billionaires who attended the Manhattan meeting are strong supporters of the creation of a New World Order. The NWO they envision is the global, communo-fascist totalitarian regime that will be implemented after they have killed no less than 85 percent of the current world's population and reduced the survivors to pre-industrial level of consumption. This will be the New World Order they envision: a techno-fascist medieval society with no middle classes, with only the dirt poor surviving serfs confined to decaying cities and the one-percent billionaire masters living in fortified castles, enjoying latest technological advances and the beauty of a depopulated Gaia.

Nevertheless, cognizant of the conclusions of the *Report on Iron Mountain*, the Rockefellers and their globalist minions knew that the best tool for population reduction is war, and the most efficient type of war to kill billions of people is nuclear war. So, they were not pleased when they discovered that both President Kennedy and Soviet Premier Khrushchev abhorred nuclear war. But then good Fidel came to their rescue.

As I mentioned in Chapter Four, at the most critic moment of the Cuban missile crisis, Castro sent a message to Soviet Premier Khrushchev asking him to launch a preemptive nuclear strike upon the United States. A scared-to-death Khrushchev promptly answered back, reminding the trigger-happy Cuban madman that such action would start a worldwide thermonuclear war.

For many years I had sort of shared Khrushchev's view that Fidel Castro was just a madman. Recently, however, I have changed my opinion.

I already mentioned, a October 11, 1987, article by Seymour Hersh in the *Washington Post*, titled "Was Castro Out of Control in 1962?" But there is, however, even a more frightful possibility: that, contrary to all logic and common sense, Castro was *not* out of control in 1962, but he was following orders from his Rockefeller masters when he tried hard to push the U.S.S.R. and the U.S. into a nuclear global holocaust.

Castro's Extraordinary Love for Nuclear Missiles

In December 1962, the Hearst-owned *San Francisco Chronicle* and *News Call Bulletin* published a *UPI* cable claiming that Ernesto "Che" Guevara told a reporter in Havana that "to defend [himself] against aggression" Fidel Castro had planned a nuclear attack on key U.S. cities, including New York. Though the *Chronicle* buried the story on page 16, the *News Call Bulletin* ran a dramatic front-page headline in big, bold letters: "How Castro Plotted Atomic Attack on US!" The *Chronicle* added, "Secretary of State Dean Rusk called Guevara's remark about a nuclear attack 'just talk'."[7]

But Mr. Rusk, a trusted CFR member, was just protecting David's secret eugenics agent. Guevara's remarks were not 'just talk.' In an interview Guevara gave a few weeks after the crisis to Sam Russell, a British correspondent for the *Daily Worker*, Guevara said that if the missiles had been under Cuban control, they would had fired them off.[8]

Moreover, in an editorial he wrote after the missile crisis for *Verde Olivo*, the Cuban Armed Forces weekly magazine, Guevara made his point even more clear, exhorting the Soviets to stand by their commitment to Cuba, no matter what the cost:

> What we contend is that we must walk by the path of liberation even when it may cost millions of atomic victims, because in the struggle to death between two systems the only thing that can be

considered is the definitive victory of socialism or its retrogression under the nuclear victory of imperialist aggression.[9]

As in many other occasions, Guevara was acting as Castro's mouthpiece. It is a matter of public record that Castro was extremely dissatisfied with the peaceful solution to the Cuban missile crisis. The fact that nuclear war had been averted, and the Russians had allegedly received from the American government a pledge for the non-invasion of Cuba, was apparently not important for Castro. For him the kind of political solutions possible within the parameters of peaceful coexistence were not real solutions. They merely postponed what he believed was an inevitable final confrontation with American imperialism. As always, Castro was itching for a fight — in this case the definitive fight, a nuclear one.

Castro's bellicose position during the crisis was later revealed by two of his closest associates. A year after the missile crisis, Che Guevara wrote: "There can be no bargaining, no half measures, no partial guarantees of a country's stability. The victory must be total."[10] A month later, Raúl Castro, at the time head of Cuba's armed forces, reiterated his brother's militant opposition to peaceful coexistence, saying, "We must never establish peaceful coexistence with our enemies."[11]

According to documents made public in Cuba in August 1997, six years after the missile crisis, in a speech to the Central Committee of Cuba's Communist Party in 1968, Castro said he felt "an incredible love" for the nuclear missiles that brought on the crisis, and wanted to keep them even after the Soviets agreed to remove them. Castro admitted to laughing with his advisers even as the possibility of nuclear war loomed, as documents published by the French daily *Le Monde* show.[12]

Le Monde reported that Castro's account of the crisis was provided to the newspaper by Vincent Touze, a French academic and expert on the missile crisis. A few days after the crisis began, at the crucial point when allegedly it had brought the two superpowers closer to a nuclear confrontation than at any other time during the Cold War, Soviet leader Nikita Khrushchev agreed to withdraw the missiles. Castro, who had little control over the situation, said he dearly wanted to keep the missiles, which he saw as a super weapon for any battle against the United States.

We defended these missiles with affection, with an incredible love. We were fighting for the first time almost on equal terms with an enemy that had threatened and provoked us unceasingly.

Castro said in his report to the Central Committee of his "Communist" Party.[13]

According to Cuban documents, when Soviet advisers came to Cuba in the summer of 1962 to discuss the installation of the missiles, Castro asked the Kremlin to deploy 1,000 missiles, and became upset when told that only about 40 would be installed.

The documents quoted Castro as telling members of the Central Committee of his "Communist" Party:

We didn't envisage lightly the idea we could disappear . . . It was a very interesting fact because we were in the antechamber of the holocaust and we were telling jokes. . . . Evidently, we knew that we were going to be made to play the role of death, but we were determined to play it.

Castro added that he had placed great faith in the Soviets but soon lost confidence in its ally. He said the Kremlin had botched the situation, which he called a "disaster."

He also said he had wanted to inform the United States about the missiles before reconnaissance planes spotted them, but was overruled by Khrushchev. However, Castro admitted his government had been naïve, confessing that nobody in the Cuban leadership even knew what nuclear missiles looked like,[14] although he accepted the weapons "without hesitation."[15]

The Rockefellers and Nuclear War

Evidence indicates that the Rockefellers not only wanted to kill most of the people on this planet through a nuclear holocaust, but also actively planned to survive it.

In the early 1960s, when nobody dreamed about a Cuban missile crisis, CFR honcho Nelson Rockefeller began frantically selling the idea of building nuclear shelters in every American building, and American schoolchildren began rehearsing for a coming nuclear attack by hiding under their desks.

Americans saw photographs in *Life* magazine of Governor Nelson Rockefeller, a messianic proponent of fallout shelters, sitting in a mockup of the Concrete Block Shelter in a New York City bank in 1960. Rockefeller installed shelters in his homes in Pocantico, New York, Washington, D.C., and in the Governor's mansion in Albany, New York. He even tried, unsuccessfully, to pass a law that would have required every New York State resident to have a family fallout shelter.

In November 1961, an article by Gilbert Burck appeared in *Fortune* magazine outlining the plans of Nelson Rockefeller, Edward Teller, Herman Kahn, and Chet Holifield for an enormous network of concrete lined underground fallout shelters throughout the United States sufficient to shelter millions of people to serve as a refuge in case of nuclear war.[16]

As I mentioned in Chapter 1, the Iron Mountain is known to be the location where the first and the last meetings of a secret Study Group on global eugenics took place.[17] Iron Mountain in upstate New York, near the Hudson River, is very close to Rockefeller Family's compound at the Pocantico Hills.

Deep below Iron Mountain the Rockefellers built a huge underground bunker to be used as an emergency nuclear shelter to survive a nuclear Armageddon.[18] The bunker would also be used as the emergency headquarters for Shell, Standard Oil of New Jersey, Chase Manhattan bank, and other Rockefeller-controlled Wall Street firms and multinational corporations.

Apparently, Nelson Rockefeller was obsessed with nuclear war and nuclear shelters.[19] After a visit to India in 1973, Jawaharlal Nehru told some friends, "Governor Rockefeller is a very strange man. All he wants to talk about is bomb shelters."[20]

India's prime Minister was not off the mark. After Nelson became the Governor of New York, he ordered to be built, and paid for it with his own money, a nuclear shelter for the Executive Mansion, another for his apartment building on Fifth Avenue in Manhattan,[21] as well as the one I mentioned above at the Rockefeller's compound in upstate New York in the Pocantico Hills. He also ordered a giant nuclear shelter built in Albany, for an alternative seat of government, in case of nuclear attack.[22]

All these shelters were kept ready at all times, with canned food and water replaced periodically to ensure freshness. The Albany shelter was actually a bunker designed to withstand a direct nuclear blast and its radioactive residue, and was connected to the NORAD alert system through a sophisticated communications setup second only to the ones used by the Pentagon.

On his side, evidence indicates that Castro never stopped pursuing his cherished dream of a global nuclear Armageddon.

Shortly after the missile crisis of October 1962, the heads of state of seven Latin American countries called for hemispheric consultations to create a nuclear-free zone in Latin America. The agreement was finally signed in Tlatelolco, Mexico, in February of 1967. Cuba was among the countries invited to participate, but the Castro government refused, stating that it would not participate in the negotiation of an agreement to denuclearize Latin America because the U.S. deployed nuclear weapons and maintained nuclear bases in Latin America.[23]

Castro's position in relation with the Tlatelolco agreement was in sharp contrast to the policy of the Soviet Union. In retrospect, it seems that his reticence to sign both agreements was not the product of a passing mood, but of a carefully-designed plan directed at justifying the materialization of the nuclear dreams he shared with his Rockefeller masters.

Juan Vivés, a former Cuban intelligence officer who defected to France, claims that, for several years after the missile crisis, Castro tried unsuccessfully to build his own missile capable of carrying nuclear weapons. For the ultra secret project he recruited military engineers and professors from Cuban universities. The missile, a sort of primitive V-1 flying bomb similar to the one developed by the Nazis, would use a MiG-21 jet motor.

The testing of the prototypes of the Cuban missile, called *libertadoras* (liberators), suffered from a series of failures, but in 1977 the project was still active. According to Vivés, Castro said that the missiles were not intended as offensive weapons, but they would be used against the U.S. in case of an American attack on Cuba.[24]

After his missile development projects ended in failure, Castro's nuclear dream was postponed, but not forgotten. In 1989 General Rafael del Pino Díaz,[25] the highest-ranking Cuban defector, said that at the time of the U.S. invasion of Grenada in 1983, Castro ordered Cuban MiG-23 pilots to program their computers to attack targets in Florida. Among the selected targets was the Turkey Point nuclear plant, which Castro said had the potential of producing a nuclear disaster larger than Chernobyl.[26] According to Gen. del Pino, Castro's words were: "I don't have nuclear bombs, but I can produce a nuclear explosion."[27]

In another interview, Gen. del Pino claimed that, in 1968, when a group of Cubans were authorized to recover a MiG-17 taken to the U. S. by a defector, Cuban agents secretly took detailed photographs of Homestead Air Force Base in Florida. The base, Gen. del Pino said, had been targeted for an air attack by Cuban planes. The intention of the attack, Castro told the Cuban Air Force officers, would be to provoke the United States into an even stronger action "so the Soviet Union would become involved."[28]

Nevertheless, evidence of strange activities in Cuba long after the end of the missile crisis, indicated that Castro kept toying with the idea of a nuclear holocaust and was preparing himself for the event. *Newsweek* reported in early 1992 that Castro had been building a massive network of underground tunnels and concrete shelters in some cities, allegedly to protect the Cuban people from U.S. bombs. Later inquiries brought out that, at least since 1981, more than 10,000 Cuban troops were working 24 hours a day digging an intricate network of concrete-reinforced tunnels and bunkers beneath Havana and other parts of the Island.[29] It was believed that some of these tunnels could house an entire division of troops, plus tanks and equipment.[30]

The construction of tunnel continued uninterrupted for many years. As late as January 1999, the newspaper *Tribuna de La Habana* reported positive advances in tunnel construction in Havana during the previous year. Castro's estranged daughter Alina mentioned what had been a rumor running for many years in Cuba. Based on the fact that the tunnels had iron grills similar to jail cells, some people speculated that their real purpose was to trap the people and kill them using poison gas.[31]

There were indications, however, that Castro was not exactly preparing himself to survive, "some kind of final cataclysm," as *Newsweek* reported. Actually he was preparing to survive after a Castro-created cataclysm that will make Chernobyl look pale in comparison. That was, seemingly, his idea for a final solution to his "American problem."[32]

In late 2009, the *New York Times* published an incredible story, which shows that, twenty years after his failed attempts during the missile crisis, Castro was still dreaming about a nuclear Armageddon. According to document released later, in the early 1980s Castro tried again to convince the Soviets to launch a nuclear strike against the United States.[33] According to Andrian A. Danilov, a Soviet general staff officer from 1964 to the 1990s who wrote the Soviet Union's reference guide on strategic nuclear planning, in the early 1980s, Castro "pressed hard for a tougher Soviet line against the U.S. up to and including possible nuclear attacks."[34] According to another source, in 1981 Castro told the Soviet leaders to "seriously consider re-establishing the nuclear missile bases in Cuba dismantled after the missile crisis."[35]

On July 5, 2010, Cuba's state-run media published Fidel Castro's prediction that nuclear war will soon break out as the result of an U.S. conflict with Iran. A few days later, a happy, smiling Castro explained in greater detail his prediction on a taped interview aired on July 12 on Cuban television.

According to Castro, nuclear war would break out if the U.S. tried to militarily enforce sanctions against Iran for its nuclear program. "When they launch war, they're going to launch it there. It cannot help but be nuclear," he said. "I believe the danger of war is growing a lot. They are playing with fire."

On August 6, 2010, Castro brought the subject again when, in an address to the Cuban parliament that marked his first official government appearance since emergency surgery four years before, he hypocritically appealed to President Obama to avert global nuclear war.

Given the fact that most of Castro's predictions have become true, there were enough reasons to be alarmed. Was the Cuban tyrant a Caribbean Nostradamus, a soothsayer who had the ability to see the future?

Actually not. What Castro had, though, was a direct channel of communication with David Rockefeller, an immensely rich, powerful sociopath who had the ability to alter and change the future of this planet according to his will. Proof of this is that most of the events that Castro prognosticated, and soon after became reality, were made possible thanks to the efforts of CFR members infiltrated in the U.S. government.

Unfortunately, it seems that the Rockefellers and their CFR madmen are still craving a nuclear Armageddon as their preferred eugenic tool.

The January/February 2012 issue of *Foreign Affairs*, the Council on Foreign Relation's organ, published an article by Matthew Kroenig under the suggestive and appealing title "Time to Attack Iran. Why a Strike Is the Least Bad Option." Kroenig is one of the new ambitious madmen carefully nurtured by the CFR masters as substitutes for the aging Kissingers, Brzezinkis, McCains and Cheneys.

According to Kroenig, "skeptics of military action fail to appreciate the true danger that a nuclear-armed Iran would pose to U.S. interests in the Middle East and beyond." In the CFR conspirators' lingo, "U.S. interests" actually mean the interests of Wall Street bankers, oil magnates and transnational corporations. Now, given the fact that Russia and China most likely would not watch a U.S. direct attack on Iran sitting on their hands, one has to conclude that the conspirators' goal is not anymore war-for-oil but war-for-total-destruction of most of this planet.

This is not, however, the first time CFR agents have expressed the conspirators' wishes about the need to attack Iran. Way before Dr. Strangelove Kroenig encouraged itchy fingers in the Pentagon to push the red button, other CFR minions have repeatedly done it. As early as 2002,

neocon (neocommie?) Irving Kristol, acting as a CFR mouthpiece, expressed
the conspirators' idea that Iran was a rogue state whose threat against the
U.S. was too obvious to be ignored.[36]

Two years later, CFR member and Cold War enthusiast Graham Allison,
expressed a similar idea in an alarmist book he wrote about nuclear terrorism. According to Allison, "Iran today is the leading example of a country
that is simultaneously exploiting the current nonproliferation regime and
sneaking around it."[37] Currently, however, that assertion could easily be
applied to the U.S.

Despite all efforts, however, the Iran PsyOp has not worked as expected. So, the ever-resourceful warmongers at the CFR[38] have just brought
a new rabbit from their nuclear hat: North Korea's madman Kim Jong-
un.[39] Unfortunately, it seems that they have already co-opted President
Trump to help them play the nuclear game.

Two of the most cherished dreams of the Rockefellers are depopulation
and deindustrialization. That is precisely what the New World Order is all
about. According to the Rockefellers and their minions, the world is overpopulated, and they need to get rid of the excess baggage — that is, people
like you and me — which they think is no less than 85 percent of the current levels of population. Therefore, a long time ago, the CFR madmen
decided to resort to the best eugenics tool money can buy: total nuclear
war.

Actually, the Rockefellers and their minions at the CFR have been preparing for it since the 1960s, and apparently they have now concluded that
the time is ripe for a nuclear holocaust that will liberate them from us,
"useless eaters,"[40] so they can fully enjoy the Gaia's natural resources which
they believe belong to them.

Despite their efforts for many years of trying to kill the rest of us by
different means, which include conventional wars, artificially-created viruses, lethal prescription drugs and vaccines, and the poisoning of the air,
water, land and food, humans have proved to be extremely resilient. Therefore, it seems that the Rockefellers and their criminal associates at the CFR
may have concluded that only a nuclear Armageddon can do the job, and it
seems that they are working hard to spoil our day. Moreover, they are preparing to survive it.

Since the beginning of this century this select group of sociopaths have
been frantically buying huge tracts of land in Patagonia, the southernmost
region of Chile and Argentina.[41] Apparently they believe that this region is

the best location to survive a nuclear Armageddon that will destroy most of the northern hemisphere. Among the eugenicist billionaires[42] who have bought land in Patagonia are the Rockefellers,[43] Ted Turner, Bill Gates, Paul Allen, Fred Smith, George Soros, Warrent Buffett, the Bushes, the Castros,[44] Carlo and Luciano Benetton, Daniel Lerner, Joseph Lewis, Ward Lay, Henry Paulson and Mark Tercek, just to name a few.

Actually, this is not a new idea. Patagonia was the region chosen by the Nazis to hide after Germany's defeat. So, it doesn't come as a surprise that the American Nazis, some of which helped Nazi criminals escape to avoid justice, have chosen the area to survive.

I think it would be a great idea to suggest Russia's President Vladimir Putin that, instead of targeting American cities, he may target a few nuclear missiles to Patagonia. In case of an all-out nuclear war they have provoked, it would be an act of poetic justice to give the eugenicist rats a taste of their own medicine.

Appendix II

Information and Intelligence

The Value of Documents

People are expecting too much of the new batch of CIA's documents about the Kennedy assassination President Trump ordered to declassify and make available to the American public. As I mention in the Introduction, nothing new or revealing will come out proving that the JFK assassination was the result of a conspiracy at the highest levels of the U.S. Government.

If those documents exist, which I doubt, they will remain classified forever for reasons of national security — the handy pretext the CFR conspirators have used over and over to keep their treacherous activities out of the public's eye. We must keep in mind, however, that what they call "national security" is actually the personal security of the CFR conspirators.

Moreover, it is useful to keep in mind that declassified documents are as untrustworthy as any other source. The fact that a document was labeled classified, and it has been declassified after some period of time, does not guarantee that what it says is the truth, nor that its original intent had not been disinformation.

Intelligence analysts believe that all documents are suspect, particularly the ones purposely left as "historical evidence." Sir William Stephenson, the famous British spymaster, once said that nothing deceives like a document. As Daniel Ellsberg once put it, "The idea that official documents contain the real history of what transpires within the circles of power is a questionable assumption made by too many historians," adding that "So much of the official record is deception written as cover or justification for existing policy."[1]

Historians believe that there are just two types of documents: the real ones, in which everything is true, and the false ones, that everything in them is a lie. Intelligence analysts, however, add two more types to the list: real documents that tell lies and false documents that tell the truth. An example of the first is Robert Kennedy's efforts to produce a totally disingenuous official memo in order to leave a paper track proving that, contrary to his actions, he actually opposed the ongoing assassination attempts on Castro.[2] An example of the second is Dan Rather mentioning some documents critical of George W. Bush's service in the Air National Guard, which eventually it was found were forgeries. Nevertheless, the former secretary of the officer who signed one of the forgeries told Rather that though the document was not real, everything it said was true.[3]

Contrary to historians, intelligence analysts see all officially recorded information as potential disinformation. This includes official records, memos, letters, photographs, etc., including audio recordings and, particularly after the advent of computer generated imaging, film, video recordings and all types of computer data.

Not being trained in the black arts of intelligence and espionage, most scholars involved in the study of the JFK assassination have been accepting raw data, that is, information, — i.e., documents, interviews, etc. — as if it were what in the field of intelligence and espionage is called intelligence. They seem to ignore that intelligence is not just the product of the collection of information, but of the careful analysis of it and all types of data. It is not until the collected information has been thoroughly evaluated according to certain specific rules and criteria, that it becomes true intelligence.

An important element in the evaluation process is the verification that the information has not been intentionally created for disinformation purposes, that is, that the persons who created it have intentionally lied — probably the most obvious form of this is an aberration some CFR scholars created under the name of "oral history." A close reading of the books produced by these scholars, however, shows that the possibility that some of their sources may have intentionally lied for disinformation purposes seems to have been totally absent from their minds.

Most scholars believe that true history only comes out of the study of original documents. Scholars are apparently satisfied when they verify the authenticity of a document. In contrast, intelligence analysts go a step further and try to verify its reliability, which is mostly given by the reliability of the person or persons who created it in the first place. Therefore, the last thing they would do would be to trust documents produced by opposing intelligence services.

Intelligence analysts are aware that, particularly in recent history, some of the documents have been left for the sole purpose of disinformation. Moreover, most scholars apparently ignore that a great part of dirty politics is based on orders never put to paper or never spoken, but merely "understood" by subordinates. Therefore, an important part of modern history is systematically left out of the reach of scholarly work.

The Evaluation of Information

According to the Joint Chiefs of Staff's *Dictionary of Military and Associated Terms*, intelligence is the final product resulting from the collection, processing, integration, analysis, and interpretation of available information.[4] So, even though the term intelligence comprises something much more complex, we may safely accept the shorter definition that intelligence is just information after it has been properly evaluated.

In its advisory report to the U.S. Government, the 1955 task force on Intelligence Activities of the second Herbert Hoover Commission stated that: "Intelligence deals with all the things which should be known in advance of initiating a course of action."[5] A true expert gave a similar definition more than 2000 years ago. According to Sun Tzu, "the reason why the enlightened prince and the wise general conquer the enemy whenever they move and their achievement surpass those of ordinary men is foreknowledge [intelligence]."[6]

Though the definition of intelligence is very simple and straightforward, most authors dealing with the subject confuse it. Some of them use the terms information and intelligence as synonyms, when it is obvious that they are not. Others even have used the term "raw intelligence" as a synonym for information, but, as we will see below, contrary to information (which might contain misinformation and disinformation), intelligence is a very elaborated product; there is nothing raw in it.

The evaluation of information, also known as appraisal or assessment, has to do with the analysis of a piece of information in terms of credibility, reliability, pertinence and accuracy, to change it into intelligence. The evaluation of information is accomplished at several stages within the intelligence cycle[7] with progressively different contexts.

The evaluation or appraisal of a particular item of information is indicated by a conventional letter-number system.

Reliability of the Source	**Accuracy of the Information**
A Completely reliable	1 Confirmed by other reliable sources
B Usually reliable	2 Probably true
C Fairly reliable	3 Possibly true
D Not usually reliable	4 Doubtful
E Unreliable	5 Improbable
F Reliability cannot be judged	6 Accuracy cannot be judged

The evaluation of information simultaneously takes into consideration both the reliability of the source based on its previous performance and the credibility of the information itself. The process involves a check against intelligence already in hand and an educated guess as to the accuracy of the new information based on how well it dovetails with previous intelligence.[8]

Though independent, the two aspects cannot be totally separated from each other. The authoritativeness of the source, which may not necessarily coincide with its reliability, can never be ignored, though it is sometimes overrated in the light of the credibility of the information — something that has to do with the expectations of the people involved in the evaluation process. But people, including intelligence analysts, tend to believe what they suspect or expect to be true, or what better fits their personal needs, so there is always an element of bias in any evaluation of information.

It must be emphasized that both evaluations must be entirely independent of each other, and they are indicated in accordance with the system shown above. Thus, information judged to be "probably true" received from a source considered to be "usually reliable" is designated as "B2".

One must keep in mind that the question of what is authoritative and what is not is very relative. A highly authoritative source may produce credible information, but the intelligence officer must always ask himself the question "Why?" The higher the authoritativeness of the source, the higher the possibility that it may be biased or had been compromised and, therefore, the higher the danger of disinformation. Highly authoritative sources from totalitarian governments may not always tell the truth, to say the least, but highly authoritative sources from democratic countries may not be very reliable either. There is evidence that the CIA has been involved in recruiting scholars at the most prestigious American universities, and journalists in the most influential American media. Also, there is suspicion that the KGB, the Mossad, and even the Cuban intelligence services, among others, did a good job penetrating American universities and mainstream media.

From the point of view of intelligence and espionage, a stolen document is often more valuable than a gratuitously conveyed secret one from whatever source, since it diminishes, though not totally eliminates, the risk of deliberately misleading information. The "why?," however, applies not only to the danger of planted disinformation. It must also be asked of the source, even of the one whose *bona fides* is beyond question. The danger here is of an intelligence service believing what it wants to believe — a problem that has affected all the world's intelligence services at one time or another. The problem of the bias of the evaluator is one that is unavoidable in intelligence; it extends even to information of fullest credibility from the most reliable sources.

Bias in evaluation can never be fully eliminated in an intelligence service and, more importantly, in high government circles. Moreover, creating evaluators to evaluate the evaluators can only compound it. Within the intelligence establishment, the only effective safeguard lies in the individual competence and quality of its members. Even more important is their intellectual honesty and personal courage to face pressures from above.

One must always bear in mind that no source can ever be regarded as infallible and no single bit of information can ever be regarded as totally accurate. Whatever the case, the chances for error, misinterpretation, misunderstanding and deceit are too high to blindly trust any information.

Super patriots, doctrinaire partisans, court historians, bureaucratic climbers, people of provincial outlook, enemy moles — all of them are potential dangers to sound information evaluation. Perspective, perspicacity, worldliness, a soundly philosophical outlook, knowledge of History and perhaps a bit of skepticism and a sense of humor — these are the qualities of an intelligence analyst that minimize error in the analysis and evaluation of information.

Notes

Introduction

1. https://www.archives.gov/research/jfk/select-committee-report/
summary.html

2. Out of unavoidable oversimplification, most people usually refer to actions taken by intelligence services in collective terms such as "the CIA
knew," "the OSS thought," "the KGB acted," "the Mossad believed," etc.,
forgetting that intelligence services are not homogeneous entities. Moreover, due to the application of the principles of need-to-know and
compartmentation, common to all intelligence services, the right hand doesn't
know what the left hand is doing, and vice versa. The same principle applies to
entities such as the Military-Industrial Complex, the Council on Foreign Relations, the State Department, the U.S. Congress or the mainstream press.

   Therefore, when somebody says "the CIA knew," or mentions "a CIA
Report," it actually means "some people at CIA knew," or "some people at
CIA wrote a Report." This is why in this book I have made a conscious
effort to name the names of the traitors instead of blaming as a whole the
organization they belong to.

   Moreover, in the case of critical operations, like assassination attempts
on foreign leaders or using American citizens as unwilling guinea pigs to
test psychedelic drugs, it is likely that most people at the CIA, including
very senior officers, were left out in the dark about the operation.

3. The Directory of "Plans" was the innocuous name adopted by the CIA
to conceal its directory in charge of covert operations that included

assassinations.

4. Other Rockefellers' aberrant creations are the Council on Foreign Relations, the United Nations Organization, the Trilateral Commission, the World Trade Organization, the World Bank and the International Monetary Fund, just to mention a few.

5. For a succinct, factual introduction to the subject of conspiracies, the Council on Foreign Relations and its role in the destruction of America I suggest you to read my book *I Dare Call It Treason: The Council on Foreign Relations and the Betrayal of America*.

6. Jim Garrison, *On the Trail of the Assassins* (New York: Sheridan Square, 1988).

7. Robert Wilcox, *Target JFK: The Spy Who Killed Kennedy?* (New York: Regnery, 2016).

8. See Michael Scott Moore, "Did Castro Kill Kennedy?," *Der Spiegel*, January 4, 2006, http://www.spiegel.de/international/jfk-assassination-did-castro-kill-kennedy-a-393540.html

9. Brian Latell, *Castro's Secrets* (New York: Palgrave Macmillan, 2012), pp. 103, 215-216. By the way, Latell's book only shows that he is not a careful researcher because in my book *The Secret Fidel Castro* (Oakland, California: InteliBooks, 2001), I provided direct evidence that Castro knew in advance about the upcoming assassination attempt on Kennedy. See, p. 125.

10. Edward Jay Epstein, *The Annals of Unsolved Crime* (Brooklyn, NY: Melville House, 2012), pp. 316-318.

11. Clifford A. Pickover, *Surfing Through Hyperspace* (New York: Oxford University Press, 1999).

12. An indication that it didn't work, or the explanation given was a lie, is that, half a century later, the explanation for the CIA, the NSA and the rest of the alphabet soup intelligence agencies' failure to prevent the 9/11 events was a failure to connect the dots. As a result, instead of scrapping the CIA and the NSA, what the CFR conspirators did was creating new and more inefficient organizations such as the Department of Homeland Security and the Transportation Security Administration.

13. According to the Joint Chiefs of Staff's *Dictionary of Military and Associated Terms*, *intelligence* is the final product resulting from the collection, processing, integration, analysis, and interpretation of available information.

14. Even though the term intelligence comprises something much more complex, we may safely accept the shorter definition that intelligence is

just information after it has been properly evaluated.

The evaluation of information, also known as appraisal or assessment, has to do with the analysis of a piece of information in terms of credibility, reliability, pertinence and accuracy both of the information itself and its source, to change it into usable intelligence. The evaluation of information is accomplished at several stages within the intelligence cycle with progressively different contexts.

15. A typical example of this flat land, 2-D view of things is Christopher Andrew's book, *For the Presidents Eyes Only: Secret Intelligence and the American Presidency from Washington to Bush* (New York: Harper Perennial, 1996). Actually, the true purpose for the creation of the National Security Agency and the CIA was to filter and distort the information reaching American presidents.

16. For a clinical study of sociopathy and psychopathy see Robert Hare, *Without Conscience* (New York: Simon & Schuster, 1994).

17. Dr. Locard's principle quoted in Zakaria Erzinclioglu, *Every Contact Leaves a Trace: Scientific Detection in the Twentieth Century* (London: Carlton, 2001), p. 10.

18. *The Secret Fidel Castro; Psychological Warfare and the New World Order*; *La CIA, Fidel Castro, el Bogotazo y el Nuevo Orden Mundial*; *I Dare Call It Treason* and *American Inventors.*

19. Donald Gibson, *Battling Wall Street: The Kennedy Presidency* (New York: Sheridan Square, 1994).

20. "Termination with extreme prejudice," CIA euphemism for assassination.

21. Just recently, in a recent September 15, 20017, talk at a Geoengineeringwatch.org conference, Kevin Shipp, a whistleblower who held several high-level positions in the CIA, told the attendants: "The shadow government controls the deep state and manipulates our elected government behind the scenes." Adding, "The top of the shadow government is the National Security Agency and the Central Intelligence Agency." See Tyler Durden, "High-Ranking CIA Agent Blows Whistle On The Deep State And Shadow Government." *ZeroHedge*, Sep 16, 2017, http://www.zerohedge.com/news/2017-09-15/high-ranking-cia-agent-blows-whistle-deep-state-and-shadow-government

22. Agent provocateur (a.k.a. "provocation agent" and "tree-shaker" in CIA parlance). A person who penetrates a target organization to provoke and incite its members to do foolish things that go beyond their initial intentions and commit unlawful acts far beyond their original aims. As a

plant, the agent provocateur is ordered to associate himself with a certain target group or suspected person with whom he must pretend to sympathize. Usually, his goal is to incite the target (a person or an organization) into some action that will bring about apprehension, punishment or discredit to the person or the organization. For an excellent description of the job of an agent provocateur, see, William Norman Grigg, "The Manufactured Menace From Michigan, Take Two," *LewRockwell.com*, April 3, 2010, http://www.lewrockwell.com/grigg/grigg-w138.html.
23. See Jefferson Morley and Rex Bradford, "Donald Trump and the Kennedy Assassination: America's Most Powerful Conspiracy Theorist Will Decide Fate of Secret JFK Trove," *Newsweek*, June 21, 2017. Also Philip Shenon, "Will Trump Release the Missing JFK Files?," *Politico.com*, April 27, 2017, http://www.politico.com/magazine/story/2017/04/27/will-trump-release-the-missing-jfk-files-215079
24. Historians usually ignore evidence that contradicts their preconceptions. They just line up events that fit the pattern of their prejudices. When intelligence analysts find evidence that contradicts their preconceptions, they assume it is enemy deception until it has been corroborated and proved beyond any reasonable doubt.

Some cognitive theories state that there are two different ways by which human beings process information: the data-driven way and the theory-driven way. The first is (or, ideally, should be) the historian's approach, the second is the intelligence analyst's.
25. Melvin Beck, *Secret Contenders: The Myth of Cold War Counterintelligence* (New York: Sheridan Square, 1984), p. 85.
26. Walking back the cat is a counterintelligence term coined by author Robert Littell in one of his spy novels.
27. I already used this methodology in writing my book *Psychological Warfare and the New World Order.*
28. As a critic of the *ad causam* methodology when applied to the analysis of intelligence events, I will not fall in my own trap by using it in this book, which deals mostly with spies and espionage. Consequently, I am consciously using the *ad hominem* methodology as a valid, ethical, scholarly alternative. If some of the scholars I critically mention in this book feel upset because of my treatment, I would like to make it clear that I have no personal animosity against any of them. They should not expect, however, to delve into the spy world and be dealt with as scholars. If some of them feel hurt and complain about my treatment, it will be further proof that they are too naïve to be involved with spies. If they

cannot stand the heat, they should stay out of the kitchen.

Conversely, in the case of the spies I mention in this book, no disclaimer is needed. My approach is standard operating procedure in the trade, and they, as practitioners of the second oldest profession, not only are used to it but take it for granted. Moreover, they don't feel any professional respect for people who don't treat them the way they expect to be treated.

29. See Appendix II, The Evaluation of Information.

30. Tradecraft: the basic techniques, the *modus operandi* of a particular intelligence service in the conduct of its espionage activities. According to CIA veteran William Hood, tradecraft, though mysterious to outsiders, is just a " little more than a compound of common sense, experience, and certain almost universally accepted security practices . . ." William Hood, *Mole* (New York: Ballantine, 1982), p. xiv.

31. Sun Tzu, *The Art of War* - translated by Samuel B. Griffin (London: Oxford University Press, 1963), p. 66.

32. A phrase attributed to Henry II of England, expressing his frustration regarding his conflicts with Thomas Becket, the Archbishop of Canterbury. This was not a direct order, but after hearing this comment from their sovereign, four of his knights traveled to Canterbury and killed Becket. This phrase is now used to express the idea of how a ruler's wish can be interpreted as a command by his subordinates.

33. CIA's Office of Technical Services operates a printing plant and a team of graphic experts who can produce any type of high-quality forgeries of documents such as driver's licenses, passports and birth certificates. See Ronald Kessler, *Inside the CIA* (New York: Pocket Books, 1992), pp. 112-116. Most likely, Obama's fake birth certificate was produced at the CIA's OTS.

34. See Servando Gonzalez, *Psychological Warfare and the New World Order* (Oakland, California: Spooks Books, 2010), pp. 103-107.

35. Both Castro and the CIA collaborated in destabilizing the Allende government — the CIA by painting him as a radical leftist and Castro by openly criticizing him for not being radical enough. Moreover, if recently surfaced information is true, Allende did not commit suicide: his Cuban security chief, General Patricio de la Guardia, killed him, following Castro's direct orders. See Servando Gonzalez, "Fidel Castro: Asesino de Allende?," http:// 348 Servando Gonzalez, www.servandogonzalez.org.

36. Angleton was a highly educated and intelligent individual. Unfortunately, as I will show in this book, he chose to ally himself with

America's worse domestic enemies. See Servando Gonzalez,
"Deconstructing Angleton," *Paranoia* magazine, No. 53 (July 15, 2016).
37. Angleton quoted in Mark Riebling, *Wedge* (New York: Touchstone,
1994), p. 138.

Chapter 1

1. As a CFR critic put it graphically, "If every Secretary of State in the
U.S. Government, and every President, as well as the heads/producers/
editors of CNN, ABC, CBS, NBC, Gannet, yaddayadda, were all members of, say, the National Rifle Association or the John Birch Society, do
you think there'd be a shit-storm of protest? Damned straight there
would be." Alex Burns, "You Are Being Lied To. Disinformation Books
Roundtable," in Russ Kick, (ed.), *You Are Being Lied To* (New York: The
Disinformation Company, 2001), p. 338.
2. One of the Rockefeller sisters, Winifred, feared so much losing her
fortune and living in poverty that she committed suicide in 1951 at her
home in Deer Park, Greenwich, Connecticut, after killing her two
daughters.
3. The term *nutzlose Fresser* (useless eater) was coined by the Nazis.
4. See document "Vision for 2010," signed in February 1997 by General
Howell M. Estes III, Commander in Chief, North American Aerospace
Defense Command (CINCNORAD). The document is quoted in David
Ray Griffin and Peter Dale Scott, *9/11 and American Empire*
(Northampton, MA: Olive Branch, 2007), p. 14.
5. I have used the past tense, because currently, the United States of
America is a quite different country from the American Republic conceived by the Founding Fathers.
6. Cousteau's words may have carried some authority, because they
appeared in the UNESCO's *Courier* on November 1991. UNESCO is an
important part of the United Nations Organization, a creation of the
Rockefellers.
7. https://en.wikipedia.org/wiki/Bill_%26_Melinda_Gates_Foundation
8. Memorandum to Bernard Berelson (President, Population Council)
found in "Activities Relevant to the Study of Population Policy for the
U.S." 3/11/69 by Frederick S. Jaffe (Vice-president of Planned Parenthood - World Population), http://www.google.com/
url?sa=t&rct=j&q=&esrc=s&source-
content%2Fuploads%2F2012%2F09%2FJaffe-

Memo.pdf&usg=AFQjCNF1XKDeyCHCgsD10WURuGRiwCxLyA

9. Steve Weissman, "Why the Population Bomb Is a Rockefeller Baby," *Ramparts* Magazine, May 1970, p. 29; also Raymond B. Fosdick, *The Story of the Rockefeller Foundation* (New York: Harper & Row, 1952), p. 244.

10. John D. Rockefeller III, "People, Food and the Well-Being of Mankind", *Second McDougall Lecture 1961, Food and Agriculture Organization of the United Nations*, 1961, pp. 9, 16-18.

11. John D. Rockefeller III, *The Second American Revolution* (New York: Harper & Row, 1973).

12. This was a report that then-President Richard Nixon dismissed in a brief but stiff meeting with John D. Rockefeller III, adding to the long list of deliberate snubs Nixon directed at the Rockefellers, possibly to his ultimate political demise. For details of this incident, see Peter Collier and David Horowitz, *The Rockefellers: An American Dynasty*, (New York: New American Library, 1976), pp. 374-375.

13. Quoted in Steve Weissman, "Why The Population Bomb Is A Rockefeller Baby," *Ramparts,* May 1970, pp. 27-41.

14. David Rockefeller, "The Population Problem and Economic Progress," Vital Speeches of the Day, April 1, 1966, p. 367.

15. Among the critics advancing the wars-for-profit theory, probably the most prominent is Noam Chomsky, who has churned book after book strongly criticizing the U.S. as a warmongering imperialist nation. But there is something difficult to explain about Chomsky's books: despite the fact that most of them are about the U.S. policies toward Latin America, and that the Rockefellers have been major actors in these policies, they are barely mentioned, to the point that the name Rockefeller does not appear in the Index of most of Chomsky's books. No wonder some people suspect that Chomsky is actually a CIA asset.

16. Leonard C. Lewin, *Report From Iron Mountain: On the Possibility and Desirability of Peace* (New York: The Free Press, 1996).

17. See, Alan B. Jones, *How the World Really Works* (Paradise, California: ABJ Press, 1996), pp. 132-133.

18. See, G. Edward Griffin, *The Creature From Jekyll Island: A Second Look at the Federal Reserve* (Appleton, Wisconsin: American Opinion, 1994), p. 524.

19. Kissinger quoted in Leonard Lewin, "Report From Iron Mountain," The *New York Times Book Review,* March 19, 1972.

20. Herschel McLandress, "News of War and Peace You're Not Ready

For," Book World, in *The Washington Post*, November 26, 1967, p. 5.
21. Lewin, *op. cit.*, p. 63. But, as the current bogus war on terror has shown, turning a non-existing threat into a real one is not an easy task, and wars are not easy to maintain indefinitely. Despite great propagandistic effort and bogus attacks, the War on Terror never caught the fancy of the American people. This explains why McCain, the Neocons and other CFR-controlled warmongers have been desperately trying to revive the Cold War since Donald Trump became the U.S. President. But a large majority of the American people is not buying it
22. Lewin, *op. cit.*, p. 86.
23. George Kennan, "To Prevent a World Wasteland — A Proposal," *Foreign Affairs*, April 1970.
24. Curiously, while they keep pushing their anti-population agenda, the Rockefeller family keeps growing by leaps and bounds.
25. https://en.wikipedia.org/wiki/National_Security_Study_Memorandum_200
26. http://www.bibliotecapleyades.net/sociopolitica/master_file/global2000.htm
27. McNamara on Population Growth: The 1980s and Beyond [Robert S. McNamara] *Population and Development Review*, Vol. 5, No. 4 (Dec., 1979), pp. 736-739.
28. Al Gore, *Earth in Balance (*Boston, MA: Houghton Mifflin, 1992). Gore's book is a continuation of *Iron Mountain*'s ideas. See Tal Brooke, *One World* (Berkeley, California: End Run, 2000), p. 71.
29. Victor Navaski, Introduction to Leonard C. Lewin, *Report From Iron Mountain: On the Possibility and Desirability of Peace* (New York: The Free Press, 1996), pp. v, xiii.
30. Dennis L. Meadows and Donnella H. Meadows, *The Limits to Growth* (New York: Universe Books, 1972).
31. See H. S. D. Cole *et al.* (editors) *Models of Doom: A Critique of The Limits to Growth* (New York: Universe Books, 1973).
32. Gerald O. Barney, ed., *The Unfinished Agenda: A Task Force Report Sponsored by the Rockefellers Brothers Fund* (New York: Thomas Crowell, 1977). On March 16, 1979, *The China Syndrome*, a film starring Jane Fonda and Jack Lemmon, raised scary questions about how safe nuclear power plants really were.

In the film, a California nuclear plant nearly melts down and the company covers it up. The script had an eerie reference to a 1950s Atomic Energy Commission study that used Pennsylvania as a case study for a meltdown. As if on cue, on March 28, 1979, a strange China

Syndrome-like accident occurred at a nuclear plant in Three Mile Island, south of Harrisburg, Pennsylvania. After the TMI accident the CFR-controlled mainstream media fanned the public's opposition to nuclear plants and the nuclear industry went into a decades-long decline, with no new reactors built into the 21st century.

33. S. David Freeman et al., *A Time to Choose: America's Energy Future* (Cambridge, Massachusetts: J.B. Lippincott, 1974).

34. Laurance S. Rockefeller, "The Case for a Simpler Life-Style," *The Readers' Digest,* February 1976, pp. 2-6.

35. Jim MacNeill, Pieter Winsemius and Taizo Yakushiji, *Beyond Interdependence: The Meshing of the World's Economy and the Earth's Ecology* (A Trilateral Commission Book),www.40-beyond-interdependence-the-meshing-of-the-worlds-economy-and-the-earths-ecology-1991.pdf

36. Bob Adelmann, "The Legacy of Maurice Strong, the Head of the First Earth Summit," *The New American*, December 13, 2015.https://www.thenewamerican.com/tech/environment/item/22127-the-legacy-of-maurice-strong-the-head-of-the-first-earth-summit.

It is highly revealing that the new society Strong had in mind is eerily similar to the one Fidel Castro imposed upon the Cuban people in 1959.

37. Tom DeWeese, "Six Issues That Are Agenda 21," *DeWeese Report*, May 17, 216, http://deweesereport.com/2016/05/17/six-issues-that-are-agenda-21. For a critique of environmentalism as hoax see Larry Abraham, *The Greening* (Atlanta, Georgia: Soundview, 1993).

38. The American Left has always been secretly bankrolled by the most reactionary elements of the Right, using their non-profit, "philanthropic" foundations as cutouts to hide the true source of the money from public scrutiny. See, i.e., Evan Gahr, "Looking at Philanthropy The Gift of Giving: Paymasters of the PC Brigades," *The Wall Street Journal*, Jan 27, 1995; Bob Feldman, "Alternative Media Censorship: Sponsored by CIA's Ford Foundation?" *Disinfo.com*, September 18, 2002, http://old.disinfo.com/archive/pages/article/id2709/pg1/index.html; Joyce Price, "Media Give Liberal Causes Millions More, Study Says," *The Washington Times,* Nov. 14. 1993; Marshall Robinson, "The Ford Foundation: Sowing the Seeds of a Revolution," *Environment,* v. 35 n. 3 (April 1993) 10-20; Goldie Blumenstyk, "New Head of Ford Fund's Education Program is Champion of Women and Minority Students," *The Chronicle of Higher Education*, v. 39 n. 16 (Dec 9, 1992), A27; Daniel Brandt, "Philanthropists at War," *NameBase NewsLine*, No. 15 (October-December, 1996). The fact perhaps explains why the

American Left is perhaps one of the most reactionary Lefts in the world. Of course, they see themselves as "progressives." I call them "regressives."

Chapter 2

1. JFK took his Oath of Office just three days after President Eisenhower had warned in his Farewell Speech about the perils of the Military-Industrial-Complex. Nevertheless, Eisenhower was highly disingenuous. In the first place because when he made his speech, the Military Industrial Complex had already changed into the Military-Industrial-Banking Complex, with banks controlling the armament corporations. Secondly, because he owed his meteoric career to the MIC he was hypocritically denouncing. Thirdly, because he had been an accomplice both in obstructing the advances of Gen. Patton's 3rd Army during the war and in the assassination of Patton, who was killed because he opposed the CFR conspirator's plans to give Eastern Europe to Stalin. On Eisenhower's meteoric and treasonous career see Robert Welch, *The Politician* (Privately printed edition, 1963).

2. Starting in 1973, the CFR embarked upon a massive, nation-changing project named "Project 1980s." This project had at its core the policy of "controlled disintegration" of the U.S. economy and society. See Angie Carlson, "Project 80s: the CFR's Program for 'Controlled Disintegration,'" *NewsWithViews*, August 8, 2001, http://www.newswithviews.com/socialism/socialism1.htm

3. David Halberstam, *The Best and the Brightest* (New York: Random House, 1972), p. 60.

4. President John F. Kennedy, "Program to Restore Momentum to the American Economy," *House Documents, 87th Congress, 1st Session, Doc. No. 1*, Washington, DC: Government Printing Office, 1961.

5. James MacGregor Burns, *John Kennedy: A Political Profile* (New York: Avon, 1961), p. 254.

6. President John F. Kennedy, Washington, D.C. January 20, 1961, https://www.jfklibrary.org/Research/Research-Aids/Ready-Reference/JFK-Fast-Facts/Inaugural-Address.aspx

7. *Ibid.*

8. See Ted Sorensen, "JFK's inaugural address was world-changing" *The Guardian*, April 22, 2007, https://www.theguardian.com/theguardian/2007/apr/22/greatspeeches1

9. "Message to the Congress Presenting the President's First Economic Report," January 22, 1962, http://www.presidency.ucsb.edu/ws/ ?pid=8621

10. *Ibid.*

11. *Ibid.*

12. *Ibid.*

13. At the time, any big corporations already had begun the trend of closing their factories at home and moving them abroad in order to profit from low wages and local corruption. This was the birth of an economic aberration called the transnational corporations. Eventually these transnational corporations became so powerful that they began thinking about abolishing the nation-states and becoming themselves all-powerful political entities.

14. John F. Kennedy, "Foreign Aid," *House Documents, 87th Congress, 1st Session, Doc. No. 117*, Washington, D.C.: Government Printing Office.

15. Remarks of Senator John F. Kennedy, Democratic Dinner, San Juan, Puerto Rico, December 15, 1958, *John F. Kennedy Presidential Library and Museum*, https://www.jfklibrary.org/Research/Research-Aids/JFK-Speeches/San-Juan-PR_19581215.aspx

16. Remarks of Senator John F. Kennedy in the Senate, February 19, 1959, *John F. Kennedy Presidential Library and Museum*, https:// www.jfklibrary.org/Research/Research-Aids/JFK-Speeches/United-States-Senate-Economic-Gap_19590219.aspx

17. *Ibid.*

18. James MacGregor Burns, *John Kennedy: A Political Profile* (New York: Harcourt, Brace & World, 1961), p. 80.

19. *Ibid.*

20. Remarks of Senator John F. Kennedy in the Senate, Washington, D.C., June 14, 1960, https://www.jfklibrary.org/Research/Research-Aids/ JFK-Speeches/United-States-Senate-U-2-Incident_19600614.aspx

2.1 John F. Kennedy Inaugural Address, January 20, 1961, John F. Kennedy Presidential Library and Museum, https://www.jfklibrary.org/ Asset-Viewer/BqXIEM9F4024ntFl7SVAjA.aspx

22. John F. Kennedy Presidential Library and Museum, *New York Times Chronology*, September 1961, https://www.jfklibrary.org/Research/ Research-Aids/Ready-Reference/New-York-Times-Chronology/Browse-by-Date/New-York-Times-Chronology-September-1961.aspx

23. Laurence Burd, "Half Million Welcome. U.S. President Pledges

Help. Warns Rich to Pitch in and Uplift People," *Chicago Tribune*, December 18, 1961, p. 1, http://archives.chicagotribune.com/1961/12/18/page/1/article/half-million-welcome-kennedy-in-colombia#text. Nevertheless, It seems that actually the Alliance for Progress was a Rockefeller idea implanted in Kennedy's brain by his CFR advisors. See Chapter 8, Note 7. Most likely, however, the Rockefeller's idea of an Alliance for Progress was quite different from Kennedy's.
24. http://mikesbogotablog.blogspot.com/2011/12/kennedy-in-colombia.html
25. Henry Hurt, *Reasonable Doubt* (New York: Holt, Rinehart and Winston, 1985), p. 324.
26. http://www.presidency.ucsb.edu/ws/?pid=8448
27. *Banderilla*, literally, little flag. A dowel-stemmed dart, metal-tipped with a single barb. The wooden stem is decorated with colored paper strips.
28. Lyman B. Kirkpatrick, Jr., *The Real CIA* (New York: McMillan, 1968), p. 261.
29. Kennedy's words about splintering the CIA quoted in Taylor Branch and George Crile, "The Kennedy Vendetta," *Harper's*, August 1975, p. 50. The quote first appeared in the April 25, 1966 edition of the *New York Times*. According to the story, Kennedy, angry after the Bay of Pigs disaster, told it to a "trusted aide." Now, given the fact that most of Kennedy's "trusted aides" were CFR agents, most likely just a few minutes both later David Rockefeller and Allen Dulles got news of it.
30. G. Edward Griffin, a true expert in these matters does not agree with this. In his seminal book *The Creature From Jekyll Island: A Second Look at the Federal Reserve* (Westlake Village, California: American Opinion, 1994), Griffin mentions how JFK, a graduate of the Fabian London School of Economics, was an early advocate of socialism and how he advanced those ideas. (Griffin, pp. 109-110) To support this assertion, he quotes a speech delivered by JFK in September of 1963 at an IMF/World Bank meeting in which he praised the virtues of redistribution of wealth and social planning. (Griffin, p. 109.)

But we need to keep in mind that, like his doctoral dissertation and the book published under his name, most likely JFK, like most U.S. presidents before and after him, was actually reading a text written by one of his advisors, most of them CFR members. Nevertheless, despite of the fact that he had been trained at the Fabian-founded London School of Economics where he studied under the guidance of Harold Laski, JFK had been most of his life more interested in chasing girls and drinking than in ideology. This, however, seems to have changed in the last months of his presidency, with unexpected results.

Griffin also mentions that the bills either were never printed or, if printed, never circulated. (Griffin, p. 569.) But some people claim that some of these bills actually circulated, and photos of them have been posted in the Internet. Nevertheless, even if Griffin's is right about the bills, and most likely he is, there is the fact that, despite Kennedy himself telling that he was a CFR member, his name does not appear in any of the CFR's members lists.

31. See, National Security Memorandum No. 263, October 11, 1963.

32. Matthew Smith, *Say Goodbye to America* (London: Mainstream, 2001), p. 235-238.

33. Termination with extreme prejudice: CIA euphemism for liquidation or assassination.

34. As Professor Donald Gibson pointed out, by the early 1960s the Council on Foreign Relations, Morgan and Rockefeller interests, and the intelligence community were so extensively interbred as to be virtually a single entity. Donald Gibson, *Battling Wall Street: The Kennedy Presidency* (New York: Sheridan Square Press, 1994), p. 72.

35. Alan Yuhas, "JFK: declassified documents reveal a cunning and cagey president," *The Guardian*, Wednesday 7 October 2015, https://www.theguardian.com/us-news/2015/oct/07/jfk-kennedy-declassified-documents-reveal-a-cunning-and-cagey-president

36. Mentioning how some senior members of the military ignored JFK's orders about the missiles in Turkey, Robert Kennedy stated it clearly in his memoir of the Cuban missile crisis: "The President believed he was President, and that, his wishes having been made clear, they would be followed." Robert F. Kennedy, *Thirteen Days* (New York: W.W. Norton, 1969), p. 690.

Chapter 3

1. According to FBI records, JFK won the election thanks to the support of capo mobster Sam Giancana in return for protection from FBI investigation. Giancana's money and muscle was effectively used to bribe and coerce election officials into getting votes for JFK. See Thomas E. Woods, *The Politically Incorrect Guide to American History* (Washington, D.C.: Regnery, 2004), p. 213.

2. Arthur Schlesinger, Jr., *A Thousand Days: John F. Kennedy in the White House* (New York: Houghton Mifflin, 1965), pp. 128-129.

3. In their book *The Wise Men: Six Friends and the World They Made* (New York: Touchstone, 1986), about Robert Lovett, John McCloy, Averell Harriman, Charles Bohlen, George Kennan and Dean Acheson, authors Walter Isaacson and Evan Thomas paint a highly disingenuous picture of this group of traitors. With the exception of Lovett, all of them were CFR members. The damage these men did to the American Republic is incommensurable. As expected, both Isaacson and Thomas were trusted CFR members.

4. Arthur Schlesinger, Jr., *A Thousand Days: John F. Kennedy in the White House* (New York: Houghton Mifflin, 1965), p. 129.

5. Proof of this is that though National security adviser McGeorge Bundy had received the news by telephone the previous evening that a U-2 spy-plane photographs had revealed evidence of offensive missile sites under construction in Cuba, he waited until early Tuesday, October 16, 1962, to brief the president. Asked later about why he delayed telling the news to the President, he insisted that he had not wanted to disturb JFK's sleep. Well, the real reason for Bundy's behavior was because he informed first his true masters at the CFR.

6. In July 26, 1936, The *New York Times* had quoted Joseph Kennedy, JFK's father, as saying: "Fifty men have run America and that's a high figure." It seems that JFK either forgot, or never read his father's words.

7. See Matt Tibbi, "The Scam Wall Street Bankers Learned From the Mafia," *Rolling Stone*, June 21, 2012, http://www.rollingstone.com/politics/news/the-scam-wall-street-learned-from-the-mafia-20120620

8. Major General Smedley D. Butler, "In Time of Peace," *Common Sense*, Vol. 4, No. 11 (November 1935), pp. 8-12.

Butler joined the Marine Corps when the Spanish American War broke out. During his 34 years of Marine Corps service, Butler was awarded two Congressional Medals of Honor, the first one for the capture of Veracruz, Mexico in 1914, and the second one for the capture of Ft. Riviere, Haiti in 1917.

In addition, he was awarded numerous medals for heroism including the Marine Corps Brevet Medal (the highest Marine medal at its time for officers). He was one of only 19 people to be twice awarded the Congressional Medal of Honor.

9. For a view of how the CFR Mafia controls the media, see Denis W. Mazzoco, *Networks of Power: Corporate TV's Threat to Democracy*

(Boston, Massachusetts: South End, 1994); Michael Parenti, *Inventing Reality: The Politics of Mass Media* (New York: St. Martin's Press, 1986) Also, James R. Bennett, *Control of the Media in the United States: An Annotated Bibliography* (New York: Garland, 1992).

10. Congressional Record, Sixty-Fourth Congress, Second Session. Volume LIV, Part 3., From January 27, 1917, to February 12, 1917, pp. 2947-2948. This monopolistic control of the CFR globalist conspirators over the U.S. mainstream media has continued uncontested until very recently, when the new Internet-based media has destroyed their monopoly. Currently, Americans' distrust of the mainstream media is at an all-time high.

11. Kennedy referred to this in a speech he delivered in Tampa, Florida, at the 47th Meeting and Business Conference of the Florida Chamber of Commerce on November 18, 1963 https://www.jfklibrary.org/Asset-Viewer/Archives/JFKWHA-242.aspx

12. The similarities between the vicious attacks on Kennedy and the current frenzy of obfuscation, slander, vilification, disparaging and character assassination on President Donald Trump are not the product of chance or coincidences.

13. *Life*, February 10 1961, p. 26 "Kennedy Economics, Short-Term,"

14. "How to Put More Zing Into the Economy," *Life*, June 8 1962, p. 4.

15. Henry Luce (CFR), editor and owner of the influential *Time* and *Fortune* magazines, founded *Life* magazine in 1936. The Luce Empire grew fast thanks to loans from CFR members Dwight Morrow, Thomas Lamont, Harvey Firestone and Edward Roland Harriman.

16. Amazingly, these goals are quite similar to the ones advanced by Donald Trump during his presidential campaign.

17. "Why Kennedy's Tax Cut Trouble Gets Deeper," *Life*, March 29, 1963, p. 4.

18. *Time*, September 13, 1963 (Vol. 82 No. 11).

19. The monopoly capitalist's preferred way to raise productivity is by lowering workers' salaries and increasing work hours.

20. Remarks of Senator John F. Kennedy on Indochina before the Senate, Washington, D.C., April 6, 1954, John F. Kennedy Presidential Library and Museum, https://www.jfklibrary.org/Research/Research-Aids/JFK-Speeches/United-States-Senate-Indochina_19540406.aspx

21. Robert F. Kennedy Jr., "John F. Kennedy's Vision of Peace: On the 50th anniversary of JFK's death, his nephew recalls the fallen president's attempts to halt the war machine," *Rolling Stone*, November 20, 2013,

http://www.rollingstone.com/politics/news/john-f-kennedys-vision-of-peace-20131120

22. NSAM 263, http:
www.maryferrell.orgshowDoc.html?docId=945#relPageId=421&tab=page

23. In the CFR lingo, "national security" actually means the international security of the CFR conspirators' interests.

24. Donald Janson, "Rockefeller Says Kennedy's Policy Imperils Peace," the *New York Times*, November 17, 1963, p. 1.

25. "Press the War in Vietnam," *Life*, November 22, 1963, p. 4.

26. NSAM 273, http://www.maryferrell.org/showDoc.html?docId=945&relPageId=663

2.7 *Hilaire du Berrier Report*, September 1991. Hilaire du Berrier was the publisher of the Monte Carlo-based *Hilaire du Berrier Reports*. Mr. du Berrier closely followed and chronicled the activities of the Bilderberg and its overlapping groups, for over four decades.

Chapter 4

1. Soviet consensus about Castro's revolution living its last hours, Prof. Mikhail Bertram in conversation with the author in his office at Stanford University.

2. In 1954 the CIA overthrew Jacobo Arbez, the democratically elected President of Guatemala.

3. Castro's warnings in Tad Szulc and Meyer, *The Cuban Invasion* (New York: Praeger, 1962), p. 74.

4. *Ibid.*, p. 77.

5. Philip Bonsal, *Cuba, Castro, and the United States* (Pittsburgh: University of Pittsburgh Press, 1971), p. 183.

6. David Halberstam, *The Best and the Brightest* (Greenwich, Conn.: Fawcett Crest Books, 1972), p. 85.

7. *U.S. News and World Report,* September 17, 1962.

8. Daniel M. Rohrer, Mark G. Arnold, and Roger L. Conner, *By Weight of Arms: American Military Policy* (Skokie, Illinois: National Textbook Co., 1969), pp. 44-45.

9. Willauer's testimony in *Communist Threat to the U.S. Through the Caribbean*, 86th Congress, 1st Sess., Part. 3, Nov. 5, 1959, pp. 874-875.

10. *Ibid.*, pp. 875-878.

11. *The New York Times*, April 1, 1962, p. 40.

12. *St. Louis Post Dispatch*, April 22, p. 1961.

13. Juan Carlos Rodriguez, *The Bay of Pigs and the CIA* (New York: Ocean Press, 1999), p. 22.

14. "Inside Story of the Cuban Fiasco," *U.S. News and World Report*, May 15, 1961.

15. *National Review*, August 13, 1963, p. 106.

16. See Air Force Colonel Fred D. Stevens, "J.F.K. Muzzled Me," *The Miami Herald*, December 1, 1961.

17. Peter Wyden, *The Bay of Pigs* (New York: Simon and Schuster, 1979), p. 219.

18. *Ibid.*, p. 104.

19. Military officers have a saying: First time is happenstance, second time coincidence and third time enemy action. To counterintelligence officers, however, even the first time must be considered enemy action.

20. Wyden, *Op. Cit.*, p. 219.

21. Hugh Thomas, *The Cuban Revolution* (New York: Harper & Row, 1977), p. 585.

22. Quoted in Wise and Ross, *The Invisible Government* (New York: Bantam, 1962), pp. 201-202.

23. *Ibid.*, p. 202.

24. Tad Szulc and Karl E. Meyer, *The Cuban Invasion: The Chronicle of a Disaster* (New York: Ballantine, 1962), pp. 96-116. This insensitive disregard for the lives of military men is common among top CFR members. According to investigative journalists Woodward and Bernstein, Henry Kissinger, in the presence of CFR member Gen. Alexander Haig, pointedly referred to military men as "dumb, stupid animals to be used" as pawns for foreign policy. See Bob Woodward and Carl Bernstein, *The Final Days* (New York: Touchstone, 1994), pp. 194-195.

25. Theodore Sorensen, *Kennedy* (New York: Harper & Row, 1965), p. 296.

26. Christopher Andrew, *For the President's Eyes Only: Secret Intelligence and the American Presidency from Washington to Bush* (New York: Harper Perennial, 1996), p. 261.

27. Peter Kornbluh (ed.), *The Bay of Pigs Invasion: A Comprehensive Chronology of Events* (New York: New Press, 1998), p.305.

28. CFR agents present at the WH/4 meeting in Robert Pear, "The Pointing of Fingers at the Bay of Pigs," *The New York Times*, December 30, 1987, p. B-6.

29. Carol Rosenberg, "Bay of Pigs U.S. Invades Cuba Failure on Many Levels," *The Miami Herald*, August 11, 2005.

30. John F. Kennedy, *News Conference*, April 21, 1961, http://

www.presidency.ucsb.edu/ws/?pid=8077

31. Peter H. Smith, *Talons of the Eagle: Dynamics of U.S. – Latin American Relations*(New York: Oxford University Press, 1996), p. 167.

32. Dangle: intelligence lingo for an intelligence officer who is intentionally put into the path of an enemy agent in hopes that he will draw his attention. The idea is that the enemy agent eventually may try to recruit the dangle. Given the fact, however, that the basic rule of thumb of the intelligence job is to suspect anyone who takes the initiative in making an intelligence contact, "dangles" who make themselves too obvious trigger red lights flash and are usually not recruited.

33. Hugh Brogan, *Kennedy* (Harlow, England: Pearson Education, 1996), p. 447.

34. "Steel: The Ides of April," *Fortune* magazine, February, p. 97. *Fortune is* CFR corporate member.

35. Herbert S. Parmet, *JFK, The Presidency of John F. Kennedy* (New York: Dial Press, 1983), pp. 91-99.

36. Benjamin Bradlee, *Conversations With Kennedy* (New York: W.W. Norton, 1975), p. 76.

37. Richard Reeves, *President Kennedy: Profile of Power* (New York: Touchstone, 1993), p. 296.

38. Bradlee, *Ibid.*

39. President Kennedy's News Conference 30, April 11, 1962, https://www.jfklibrary.org/Research/Research-Aids/Ready-Reference/Press-Conferences/News-Conference-30.aspx

40. Roy Hoopes, *The Steel Crisis* (New York: John Day, 1963), p. 166.

41. *Ibid.*, p. 140.

42. President John F. Kennedy, Televised press conference of 11 Apr 1962,

4.3 Hoopes, *Op. Cit.*, p. 229.

44. *Ibid.*, p. 165.

45. *Ibid.*, p. 224.

46. The *Wall Street Journal,* April 19, 1962.

47. *U.S. News and World Report,* April 30, 1962.

48. For an in-depth analysis of the Cuban missile crisis see my book *The Nuclear Deception: Nikita Khrushchev and the Cuban Missile Crisis* (Oakland, California: Spooks Books, 2002).

49. *Russiapedia*, http://russiapedia.rt.com/on-this-day/april-18/

50. In July 1993, following a Freedom of Information Act request, the U.S. State Department declassified 21 confidential letters between Khrushchev and Kennedy. See *U.S. State Department, Foreign relations of the United States (FRUS), 1961-1963, Volume VI, Kennedy-*

Khrushchev Exchanges (Washington, D.C.: U.S. Government Printing Office, 1966).

51. *Ibid.*, p. 25.

52. Special National Intelligence Estimate number 85-3-62, "The Military Buildup in Cuba," September 19, 1962, in Central Intelligence Agency, *The Secret Cuban Missile Crisis Documents* (Washington, D.C.: Brassey's, 1994), p. 93.

53. See U.S. Congress, Senate Committee on Armed Services Preparedness Investigations Subcommittee, *Interim Report on Cuban Military Build-up*, 88th Congress, 1st. sess., 1963; Hanson Baldwin, "Growing Risks of Bureaucratic Intelligence, *The Reporter* (August 15, 1963); Roberta Wohlstetter, "Cuba and Pearl harbor: Hindsight and Foresight," *Foreign Affairs*, July 1965; "Intelligence Gap on Cuba? The Senate Gets the Report," *U.S. News and World Report*, May 20, 1963; Klauss Knorr, "Failures in National Defense estimates," *World Politics*, April 1964.

54. On the evening of October 15, 1962, CIA deputy director Ray Cline informed JFK's national security adviser McGeorge Bundy (CFR) that U-2 planes had discovered what appeared to be Soviet medium-range nuclear missiles bases on Cuban soil. But Bundy didn't tell the President immediately. Instead he told the news to his associates at the CFR. A few minutes later, while the President was kept in the dark, CFR members Dean Rusk, Paul Nitze and Robert McNamara were informed about the findings. See, Walter Isaacson and Evan Thomas, *The Wise Men: Six Friends and the World They Made* (New York: Touchstone, 1986), p. 619.

Bundy's behavior is not unusual. In 1968 CIA's Richard Bissell reported to his CFR masters at the Harold Pratt House about CIA's covert operations. The minutes of the Bissell report to a select group of CFR members on January 8, 1968, are reproduced in Victor Marchetti and John D. Marks, *The CIA and the Cult of Intelligence* (New York: Dell, 1974), pp. 358-376.

When the chips are down, the CFR conspirators' agents infiltrated in the U.S. government know perfectly well where the true center of power is located in this country — and it is not in Washington D.C.

55. Actually, Bundy had received the photos the day before, on the evening of October 15. He never explained satisfactorily why he waited to the next day to give Kennedy the important news.

56. ExComm, Executive Committtee of the National Security Council, created by Kennedy to include his brother Robert and other close collaborators.

57. Robert Kennedy, *Thirteen Days* (New York: W.W. Norton, 1971), pp. 5-6.

58. Ernest R. May and Philip D. Zelikow, *The Kennedy Tapes: Inside the White House During The Cuban Missile Crisis* (Cambridge, Massachusetts: Harvard University Press, 1997).

59. See, http://www.ourdocuments.gov/doc.php?flash=true&doc=94. The ever-lying *Wikipedia*, has published a U-2 photo claiming, "This U-2 reconnaissance photo showed concrete evidence of missile assembly in Cuba. Shown here are missile transporters and missile-ready tents where fueling and maintenance took place," (http://en.wikipedia.org/wiki/File:U2_Image_of_Cuban_Missile_Crisis.jpg). The photo, however, actually shows no evidence of strategic nuclear missiles on Cuban soil, but just a clearing in the ground and what looked like big, long crates covered by tarps. These resemble similar installations on Soviet soil appeared in photos taken by U-2 planes, which CIA photointerpreters guessed were strategic nuclear missile bases. At the time, however, the CIA had no agents in the field who were able to confirm the guess.

Even more important, how did the CIA know that fueling and maintenance of the missiles took place under the tents if it had no agents in the field to verify it?

60. Central Intelligence Agency, *The Secret Missile Crisis Documents* (Washington: Brassey's, 1994).

61. *Ibid.*, p. vi.

62. *Ibid.*, p. 71.

63. *Ibid.*, p. 140.

64. *Ibid.*, p. 155.

65. *Ibid.*, p. 255

66. *Ibid.*, p. 263

67. In my book *The Nuclear Deception: Nikita Khrushchev and the Cuban Missile Crisis* (Oakland, California: Spooks Books, 2002), I devoted a whole chapter (pp. 203-223) to prove that the so-called "National Security Archive," has nothing to do with national security and is not even an "archive" in the strict meaning of the word. Moreover, I have the suspicion that the "National Security Archive" is actually a CIA front.

68. See www.gwu.edu/~nsarchiv/nsa/cuba_mis_cri/photos.html.

69. Dino A. Brugioni, *Eyeball to Eyeball: The Inside Story of the Cuban Missile Crisis* (New York: Random House, 1991), p. 548.

70. *Ibid.*, p. 538.

71. *Ibid.*, p. 539.

72. *Ibid.*, p. 541.

73. *Ibid.*

74. *Ibid.*

75. *Ibid.*

76. *Ibid.*

77. *Ibid.*, p. 546

78. *Ibid.*, p. 547.

79. *Ibid.*

80. One of the most famous pictures by Surrealist painter René Magritte, *The Treachery of Images*, shows a very realistic picture of a pipe with the caption "This is not a pipe." Well, the same that you cannot smoke Magritte's picture of a pipe you can't fire pictures of nuclear missiles. Moreover, as Sun Tzu wisely stated "All warfare is based on deception."

81. For a good description of Kennedy's efforts to keep his own trigger-happy military under control, see James W. Douglass, *JFK and the Unspeakable* (New York: Touchstone, 2010), pp. 20-23, 29.

82. Nikita Khrushchev, *Khrushchev Remembers* (Boston: Little, Brown, 1970), pp. 497-498.

83. Document 45, Prime Minister Fidel Castro's letter to Premier Khrushchev, October 26, 1962, in Laurence Chang and Peter Kornbluh, eds., *The Cuban Missile Crisis, 1962: A National Security Archive Documents Reader* (New York: The New Press, 1992), p. 189. (Letter reprinted from the international edition of *Granma*).

84. Document 57, Premier Khrushchev's letter to Prime Minister Fidel Castro, October 30, 1962, in Laurence Chang and Peter Kornbluh, eds., *The Cuban Missile Crisis, 1962*, p. 243.

85. Daniel Ellsberg, "The Day Castro Almost Started World War III," The *New York Times*, October 31, 1987, p. A7.

86. Seymour Hersh, "Was Castro Out of Control in 1962?" in the *Washington Post*, October 11, 1987; Adrián Montoro, "Moscow Was Caught Between Cuba and U.S.," the *New York Times*, November 17, 1987; Rodríguez Menier in personal communication to the author, December 20, 1994. Menier claims he heard the story from Gen. José Abrahantes.

87. James Blight and David Welch, *On the Brink* (New York: Hill and Wang, 1989), p. 56.

88. Scott Armstrong and Phillip Brenner, "Cuba Crisis: No Hits But Many Errors," the *Los Angeles Times*, November 1, 1987.

89. Ricardo Rojo, *Mi amigo el Che* (Buenos Aires: Jorge Alvarez, 1968), p. 130.

90. In Cuba, *conga* is not the name of a percussion musical instrument (generically called *tumbadora*), but of a street dance usually performed

during *Mardi Gras*.

91. CIA, Office of Current Intelligence, "Readiness Status of Soviet Missiles in Cuba," October 23, 1962, NSF, Countries, Cuba, Kennedy Library.

92. President John F. Kennedy, Commencement Address at American University, Washington, D.C., June 10, 1963, http://www.presidency.ucsb.edu/ws/?pid=9266

93. *Ibid.*

94. John F. Kennedy, Address Before the 18th General Assembly of the United Nations, September 20, 1963, https://www.jfklibrary.org/Research/Research-Aids/JFK-Speeches/United-Nations_19630920.aspx

95. *Ibid.*

96. Early in July 1955, at a closed plenum of the Central Committee of the Communist Party, Premier Khrushchev laid out the new goals of Soviet policy. He solidified the concept of a new approach in Soviet foreign policy in 1956 at the 20th Congress of the Communist Party of the Soviet Union, and again at the 21th Congress of the Communist Party of the Soviet Union, held in Moscow from January 25 to February 5, 1959.

This was later was known as his "Doctrine of Peaceful Coexistence," accompanied by the slogan "To catch up and overtake the West" in economic well-being, and an improvement in the Soviet Union's internal affairs.

97. James K. Galbraith, "Exit Strategy: In 1963, JFK ordered a complete withdrawal from Vietnam," *Boston Review*, September 1, 2003, http://bostonreview.net/us/galbraith-exit-strategy-vietnam.

98. For a transcript of the film see http://www.errolmorris.com/film/fow_transcript.html

99. Jesse Ventura, *63 Documents the Government Doesn't Want You to Read* (New York: Skyhorse, 2011), pp. 48-49.

Chapter 5

1. Senator Joseph McCarthy and Ambassador Earl T. Smith firmly believed that a Communist cabal had infiltrated the State Department, and most members of the John Birch Society shared their belief. They were wrong. The traitors were not Communists but CFR members the Rcokefellers were using to advance their treasonous agenda .

2. The insistent push for democracy by CFR members and their allies is purposefully misleading. They would like to establish a democracy in the

U.S. because it is much easier to control the mob than the citizens of a representative republic, a fact the Founding Fathers of this country were aware of. Proof of this is that the word "democracy" does not appear in any of the three documents this Republic is based on: the Declaration of Independence, the Constitution and the Bill of Rights. In his *Republic,* Plato told that, as a rule, tyranny arises from democracy.

3. The Council on Foreign Relations is not a homogeneous group. Like most secret societies, the CFR consists of a central nucleus and several concentric circles. The people in the nucleus are the brains behind the CFR, and the ones who actually control the organization and fully know its secret goals. The CFR nucleus is formed by the Rockefellers, the Rothschilds, the Morgans, and a select group of oil magnates and Wall Street bankers. These people not only have immense fortunes, but also enormous power. For a detailed description of the CFR organizational structure see Servando Gonzalez, *Psychological Warfare and the New World Order* (Oakland, California: Spoks Books, 2010), 80-81.

4. The term Manchurian Candidate to indicate a brainwashed, mentally controlled assassin, came into use in 1959, when author Richard Condon made it the title of his best-selling novel, later made into a popular movie starring Frank Sinatra, and, more recently, a remake starring Denzel Washington. Though in the novel the person is hypno-conditioned to commit the actual crime, Roa Sierra, Lee Harvey Oswald and Sirhan Sirhan (Robert Kennedy's alleged assassin), most likely were cast in the double role of decoy and fall guy — a "patsy" — while the true assassin(s) committed the crime.

5. Mark Lane, *Plausible Denial* (New York: Thunder's Mouth, 1991), pp. 352-353.

6. In a *NOVA* documentary about the JFK assassination available on U-tube, a forensic "scientist" tried to prove that Kennedy's head moved so violently to the back because the bullet had hit him from the back — a conclusion as far-fetched as the explanation of the collapse of the World Trade Center's Twin Towers as the result of fires.

7. As a way of payment for his contribution to the cause of treason in America, CFR member James Reston was promoted as *NYT* associate editor in 1964 and to executive director in 1968.

8. *New York Herald Tribune*, 1963, p. 4.

9. *Dallas Morning News*, November 23, 1963, p. 14. One may guess that he either got the hint by reading the *New York Times* or through a call from his brother, former CIA Deputy Director Gen. Charles P. Cabell.

10. Katzenbach's memo is published at http://www.jfklancer.com/

Katzenbach.html

11. *The Wall Street Journal*, "President Kennedy," Editorial, November 25, p. 8.

12."The Early Assassins," *Time*, November 29, 1962, p. 28.

13. "The Moment of Tragedy," *U.S. News and World Report*, December 2, pp. 6, 32, 35.

14. "The Marxist Marine," *Newsweek*, December 2, p. 27.

15 .At the time, the editor-in-chief and publisher of the *Tribune* was John Hay Whitney, a member of the Council on Foreign Relations.

16. L. Fletcher Prouty, *JFK: The CIA, Vietnam, and the Plot to Assassinate John F. Kennedy* (New York: Birch Lane/Carol, 1992), pp. 306-309.

17. Donald Gibson, *The Kennedy Assassination Cover-Up* (San Diego, California: Progressive Press, 1999-2014), p. 25.

18. For an in-depth study of the Bogotazo riots and the assassination of Gaitán see Servando Gonzalez, *Op. Cit.*, pp. 153-179.

19. Servando Gonzalez, *Psychological Warfare and the New World Order* (Oakland, California: Spooks Books, 2010), p. 160

20. Information about *El Popular* in Angel Aparicio Laurencio, *Antecedentes desconocidos del nueve de abril* (Miami: Ediciones Universal, 1973), p. 39.

21. Mighty Wurlitzer. CIA's lingo fo a system or method of inserting a "news" piece in a small or cooperative newspaper or magazine, in hoping that larger papers, and eventually the big wire news services, would pick up this item of black information and disseminate it around the world. The supposed source, or originating paper, is quickly forgotten as the planted story works its way out to the front pages of the world's major papers.

22. *The Warren Report: Report of the President's Commission on the Assassination of President John F. Kennedy* (n.p.: Western Printing, n.d.), p. v. A final footnote to this book asserts that it is a transcript of the report of The President's Commission on the Assassination of John F. Kennedy, and that it was reproduced from the official text printed by the U.S. Printing Office and released to the public on September 27, 1964.

23. *Ibid.*, p. vii.

24. *Ibid.*, p. xi.

25. *Ibid.*

26. *Ibid.*, p. x.

27. Harry Elmer Barnes, "Revisionism and the Historical Blackout," in Barnes, ed., *Perpetual War for Perpetual Peace* (Caldwell, Id.: Caxton

Printers, 1953). In the same fashion, Spanish poet and writer José A. Valente criticized the rewriting of history in totalitarian societies and advanced his concept of "counterhistory" to oppose it. See Martha Acosta-Allento, "Time and Poetic Works of José A. Valente," *Confluencia*, Vol 4., No. 1 (Fall 1988).
28. Saturday Evening *Post,* October 4, 1947.
29. Rockefeller Foundation, *Annual Report*, 1946, p. 188.
30. A relatively recent example of deception and cover-up through historical blackout is the 2002 book *The Kennedy Tapes: Inside the White House During the Cuban Missile Crisis* (New York: W.W. Norton, 2002). Two CFR members, Ernest R. May and Philip D. Zelikow, supposedly listened to all of President John F. Kennedy audio tapes and wrote this book quoting all of the interesting facts so as to assure the public that there were no other important statements made on these tapes that the public would care to know about. There were two motives involved here: (1) to print only what the CFR wanted to be known about the JFK assassination, and (2) to throw any other potential researchers off the trail. This was a very grueling task of listening to hundreds of hours of taped conversations. Therefore, other researchers must just "take their word" that they had printed all of the interesting facts from these tapes. I suspect that two non-CFR researchers would have written an entirely different book. For a quite different view of the Cuban missile crisis, see Servando Gonzalez, *The Nuclear Hoax: Kennedy, Castro, Khrushchev and the Cuban Missile Crisis* (Oakland, CA: Spooks Books, 2002-216).
31. Warren Report, *Op. Cit.*
32. Peter Jennings' *Beyond Conspiracy*, http://www.imdb.com/title/tt0387490/
33. David Talbot, *Brothers: The Hidden History of the Kennedy Years* (London: Simon and Schuster, 2007), p. 281.
34. Michael Beschloss, "How the frenzied week after his murder led to 30 years of conspiracy theories," *Newsweek*, November 22, 1993, p. 62
35. Epstein, *Inquest: The Warren Commission and the Establishment of Truth* (New York: Bantam Books, 1966), p. 125.
36. *Ibid.*
37. *Ibid.*
38. *Ibid.*, p. 122. The three members of the Commission that supported the single bullet theory were Allen Dulles, John McCloy and Gerald Ford. At the time, both Dulles and McCloy were prominent CFR members. Ford does not appear in the CFR membership list until 1987 — maybe he won the invitation to join the CFR as a reward for his role in

the Commission.

39. Epstein, *Op. Cit.*

40. *Ibid.*, p. x.

41. *Ibid.*, p. xiii.

42. See Richard Belzer and D. Wayne, *Hit List: An In-Depth Investigation into the Mysterious Deaths of Witnesses to the JFK Assassination* (New York: Skyhorse, 2016)

43. Epstein, *Op. Cit.*, p. 2.

44. *Ibid.*, p. 30

45. *Ibid.*

46. *Ibid.*, p. 124.

47. *Ibid.*, p. 86.

48. *Ibid.*, p. xi.

49. David Robarge, "DCI John McCone and the Assassination of President John F. Kennedy," *Studies in Intelligence* Vol. 57, No. 3 (September 2013), p. 1.

50. Edward Jay Epstein, *The Assassination Chronicles: Inquest, Counterplot and Legend* (New York: Carroll and Graf, 1992). p. 11.

51. *Ibid.*

52. *Ibid.*, p. 12.

53. Agent: 1. A person who is recruited, trained, controlled, and employed to obtain and report information for intelligence or counterintelligence purposes from inside a target organization. Agents are the only members of the espionage system whose mission is actually spying. As a rule, intelligence services only rarely, if ever, employ fellow citizens as agents. The term, therefore, must never be confused with its lay use, as in "FBI agent" or "secret agent." In the interests of security, an agent acts independently from other agents and is under the control of a principal or a case officer. 2. Euphemism for a spy who is in your side.

54. Agent recruiting is basically based on the MICE formula: Money, Ideology, Compromise and Ego. These are the four basic human weaknesses exploited to convince or force a willing or unwilling target for recruitment into treachery and espionage. Most people believe that money and ideology are the most important things explaining why a person decides to become a traitor to his own country. Some tradecraft experts, however, are convinced that there is only a motivation that really matters, and that is ego. That is what ultimately leads someone to become a spy and betray his country.

The target for recruitment may see himself as serving a higher cause, or may think he wants all the money he has been promised. But these are merely conscious expressions of something deeper, and that is ego.

55. *Ibid.*, p. 14.
56. Edward Jay Epstein, *The Assassination Chronicles: Inquest, Counter-plot and Legend* (New York: Carroll and Graf, 1992).
57. See, Jim Garrison, *On the Trail of the Assassins* (New York: Sheridan Square, 1988).
58. Epstein, *Op.Cit,,* p. 182.
59. *Ibid.*, p. 250.
60. *Ibid.*, p. 267.
61. *Ibid.*, p. 250.
62. *Ibid.*, p. 278.
63. *Ibid.*, p. 291.
64. At the time I had pioneered the creation of multimedia hipertextual programs for the Apple Macintosh using their software development program HyperCard.
65. Edward Jay Epstein, *The Assassination Chronicles: Inquest, Counter-plot and Legend* (New York: Carroll and Graf, 1992).
66. Edward Jay Epstein, "Epitaph for Jim Garrison: Romancing the Assassination," *The New Yorker*, November 30, 1992.
67. *Ibid.* An interesting detail is that, since Donald Trump won the 2016 election, every issue of *The New Yorker* systematically publishes one or two articles furiously hostile to President Trump and his policies.
68. Servando Gonzalez, "A CIA Cock and Bull Story," April 27 2007, http://www.intelinet.org/sg_site/intelligence/sg_trento_review.html
69. A facsimile of the CIA memo is reproduced in Jesse Ventura, *63 Documents the Government Doesn't Want You to Read* (New York: Skyhorse, 2011), p. 99.
70. *Ibid.*
71. Noam Chomsky, *Understanding Power* (New York: Vintage, 2003), p. 328.
72. Gerald Posner's *Case Closed: Lee Harvey Oswald and the Assassination of JFK* (New York: Random House, 1993).
73. Vincent Bugliosi, *Reclaiming History*, (New York: Norton, 2007).
74. On Castro's powers of fascination see Servando Gonzalez, *The Secret Fidel Castro* (Oakland, California: Spooks Books, 2001), pp. 31-43. See also Servando Gonzalez, "How Jesse Ventura Fell Under Castro's Powers of Fascination. — and Never Recovered," *NewsWithViews.com,* June 27, 2017, https://newswithviews.com/how-jesse-ventura-fell-under-castros-powers-of-fascination-and-never-recovered/.

It seems that another who initially fell under Castro's powers of fascination was John F. Kennedy. In his book *The Strategy for Peace*, Senator Kennedy described Castro as "part of the legacy of Bolivar." John F. Kennedy, *The Strategy for Peace* (New York: Popular Library, 1961), pp. 167-168.

75. Jon Margolis, "*JFK* Movie and Book Attempt to Rewrite History," *The Chicago Trubune*, May 19, 1991.
76. *Ibid.*
77. George Lardner Jr., "On the Set: Dallas in Wonderland. How Oliver Stone's Version of the Kennedy Assassination Exploits the Edge of Paranoia," *The Washington Post*, May 19, 1991.
78. In the globalist conspirators' lingo, a "serious" scholar is one who systematically supports with questionable data the theories created to scare the people and justify the creation of a New World Order.
79. *The San Francisco Examiner IMAGE*, February 16, 1992, p. 14.
80. *Ibid.*, p. 15.
81. Dan Rather, an unknown T.V. journalist in Dallas, was one of the few people allowed to watch the Zapruder film. Luckily, he saw Kennedy's head move in a direction that agreed with the Commission's single bullet theory. This jump-started his meteoric career, joining the CFR and becoming one of its best professional disinformers. Eventually, however, the Rockefellers decided they didn't need his services anymore and threw him under the bus.
82. The United States Senate Select Committee to Study Governmental Operations with Respect to Intelligence, a.k.a. Church Committee because it was chaired by Idaho Senator Frank Church in 1975.
83. Jefferson Morley, "The Political Rorschach Test," Opinion, *The Los Angeles Times*, December 8, 1991,
84. Philip Shenon, *A Cruel and Shocking Act* (New York: Henry Holt, 2013).
85. David Talbot, "The JFK Assassinaion: CIA and New York Times are Still Lying to Us," *Salon.com*, November 6, 2013, http://www.salon.com/2013/11/06/the_jfk_assassination_we_still_dont_know_what_happened/
86. David Talbot, *The Devil's Chessboard* (New York: Harper Perennial, 2015).
87. *Ibid.*, pp. 337-350.
88. In a letter to Castro, Che Guevara advises: "Hatred as an element of the struggle; a relentless hatred of the enemy, impelling us over and beyond the natural limitations that man is heir to and transforming him into an effective, violent, selective and cold killing machine. Our soldiers must be thus; a people without hatred cannot vanquish a brutal enemy.

We must carry the war into every corner the enemy happens to carry it: to his home, to his centers of entertainment; a total war." Ernesto (Che) Guevara, "Message to the Tricontinental Conference," April 16, 1967, https://www.marxists.org/archive/guevara/1967/04/16.htm. It is good to remember that Guevara's hatred turned into fear when he was captured in Bolivia, after he dropped his own fully functional rifle, with a near full magazine, and cowardly begged, "Don't shoot! Don't shoot! I am Che Guevara and I am worth more to you alive than dead!" See Dan White, "Che Guevara Worth More To You Alive Than Dead," *The Historical Truth Project,* November 26, 2014, https://historicaltruthproject.com/tag/che-guevara-worth-more-to-you-alive-than-dead
89. Most of the pople Talbot call "thugs" actually were farmers whose land was stolen and small bussiness owners whose properties had been confiscated by Castro.

Chapter 6

1. Peter Collier and David Horowitz, *The Rockefellers: An American Dynasty* (New York: Signet, 1976), p. 4.
2. *Ibid.*, p. 8.
3. *Ibid.*
4. Daniel Yergin, *The Prize: The Epic Quest for Oil, Money, and Power* (New York: Pocket Books, 1993), p. 43.
5. *Ibid.*, pp. 10, 43.
6. Collier and Horowitz, *op. cit.*, p. 23.
7. See, Myer Kutz, *Rockefeller Power* (New York: Pinnacle, 1974), p. 36.
8. Gary Allen, *The Rockefeller File* (Seal Beach, California: '76 Press, 1976), p. 23.
9. Ida Tarbell, "The Standard Oil Company," in Earl Latham (ed.), *John D. Rockefeller: Robber Baron or Industrial Statesman?* (Boston: D.C. Heath and Company, 1949.), p. 33.
10. See, Appendix II, "The Evaluation of Information."
11. Yergin, *op. cit.*, p. 75.
12. *Ibid*, p. 54.
13. Collier and Horowitz, *op. cit.*, p. 22.
14. Tarbell, *op. cit.*, p. 10.
15. Yergin, *op. cit.*, p. 102.
16. Tarbell, *op. cit.*, pp. 30-31.
17. Matthew Josephson, "The Robber Barons," in Earl Latham (ed.), *John D. Rockefeller: Robber Baron or Industrial Statesman?* (Boston:

D.C. Heath and Company, 1949.), p. 36.

18. *Ibid.*, p. 40.

19. *Ibid.*, p. 43.

20. Lewis Galantière, "John D.: An Academy Portrait," in Earl Latham (ed.), *John D. Rockefeller: Robber Baron or Industrial Statesman?* (Boston: D.C. Heath and Company, 1949.), p. 86.

21. Ferdinand Lundberg, *The Rockefeller Syndrome* (New York: Zebra Books, 1976), pp. 134-135.

22. *Ibid.*, p. 142.

23. William Manchester, *Rockefeller Family Portrait,* quoted in Gary Allen, *The Rockefeller File* (Seal Beach, California: '76 Press, 1976), p. 23.

24. Matthew Josephson, *op. cit.*, p. 43.

25. Collier & Horowitz, *op. cit.*, pp. 108-110.

26. *Ibid.* p. 113.

27. The system is very similar to the system Apple uses to pay its semi-slave workers in China.

28. See United Fruit Company in Colombia, http://ufcincolumbia.weebly.com/santa-marta-massacre-of-1928.html

29. Fitzhugh Green, *American Propaganda Abroad* (New York: Hyppocrene, 1988), p. 99.

30. *Ibid.*

31. Nelson's memorandum to Eisenhower in John Loftus and Mark Aarons, *The Secret War Against the Jews* (New York: St. Martin's Press, 1994), p. 279.

32. See "The Icon of Industrial Greed Meet the Rockefellers," *Bobab Press*, Vol. 4, N o. 13, http://www.mega.nu/ampp/rockfam.html

33. Anderson's report was published in the *San Francisco Chronicle* on December 26, 1979.

34. We must keep in mind that in the CFR conspirators' lingo, "Communist" actually means anybody who threats Rockefeller's intersts.

35. On David Rockefeller using his goon Kissinger and the CIA to overthrow Allende see Stephen Kinzer, *Overthrow: America's Century of Regime Change From Hawaii to Iraq* (New York: Times Books, 2006) pp. 176-194.

36. See Servando Gonzalez, "Fidel Castro: Asesino de Allende?" http://www.servandogonzalez.org.

37. Charles Higham, *Trading With the Enemy: An Exposé of the Nazi-American Money plot 1933-1949* (New York: Delacorte Press, 1983).

38. *Ibid.* For the whole story, see Chapter 3, "The Secrets of Standard Oil."

39. See, Loftus and Aarons, *Op. Cit.,* pp. 64-73.

4.0 For the full story see, Stephen Schlesinger, "Cryptanalysis for Peacetime: Codebreaking at the Birth and Structure of the United Nations," *Cryptologia* 19 (July 1995), pp. 217-235.

41. See, i. e., Michael Rivero, "The Clinton Body Count," *What Really Happened,* http://www.whatreallyhappened.com/RANCHO/POLITICS/BODIES.php#axzz4uGb8nZNJ; also "Chilling Similarities Between Seth Rich Murder and 'Clinton Body Count' Victims," *WorldNewDaily*, May 16, 2017, http://www.wnd.com/2017/05/chilling-similarities-between-seth-rich-murder-and-clinton-body-count-victims/

42. Operation Keelhaul at the end of WWII, Operation Phoenix in Vietnam, the killing of thousands of civilians during the invasion of Panama, and the unnecessary killing of thousands of defeated Iraqi soldiers in the so-called "highway of death" during the Gulf War, are some of the most notorious war crimes committed by this criminal Mafia, but not the only ones.

43. The term "useless eaters" was coined by Adolf Hitler early in his career as Chancellor to describe the mentally retarded he planned to kill.

Chapter 7

1. Peter Grose, *Continuing the Inquiry* (New York, Council on Foreign Relations, 1996), p. 1.

2. Evolutionary biologist and theorist Richard Dawkins coined the term *meme* (pronounced like "gene") in his 1976 book *The Selfish Gene*, (New York, New York: Oxford University Press, 1976). According to Dawkins, a meme is any unit of cultural information, such as a practice or idea, that is transmitted verbally or by repeated action from one mind to another similar to the transmission of viruses. Based on that, some people have called memes "mind viruses."

3. Controller: intelligence lingo for a case officer; the person in the field directly responsible for an operation, usually of a covert nature, including, but not limited to, the running of all types of agents. A case officer must be good in handling people, by creating a psychological dependence on him. His agents most feel that they can fully rely on him, as he is the only link with the organization they are risking so much for — including betraying their owncountries.

4. *Ibid.*, p. xx.

5. Grose, *op. cit.*, p. 1.

6. James Perloff, *The Shadows of Power: The Council on Foreign Relations and the American Decline* (Appleton, Wisconsin: Western

Islands, 1988), p. 32.

7. Lawrence E. Gelfand, *The Inquiry: American Preparations for Peace, 1917-1919* (New Haven: Yale University Press, 1963), pp., 340-342.

8. *Ibid.*, pp. 44, 317.

9. *Ibid.*, p. 41.

10. *Ibid.*, p. 316.

11. *Ibid.*, p. 5.

12. *Ibid.*, p. 121.

13. *Ibid.*, p. 87.

14. See, *Fact Book on Intelligence*, Office of Public Affairs, Central Intelligence Agency, April 1983, p. 16.

15. Grose, *op. cit.*, p. 1.

16. A partial list of the initial members appeared in Edward Mandell House and Charles Seymour, *What Really Happened in Paris* (New York: Charles Scribner's Sons, 1921), p. 7.

17. Rhodes quoted in Carroll Quigley, *Tragedy and Hope: A History of the World in Our Time* (New York: Macmillan, 1966), p. 62.

18. *Ibid.*, p. 950,

19. Cristopher Andrew, *For the Presidents Eyes Only: Secret Intelligence and the American Presidency from Washington to Bush* (New York: Haper Perennial, 1996), p. 60.

20. Perloff, *op. cit.*, p.32.

21. Grose, *op. cit.*, p. 4.

22. *Ibid.*, p. 5.

23. Godfrey Hodgson, *Woodrow Wilson's Right Hand: The Life of Colonel Edward Mandell House* (New Haven, Connecticut: Yale University Press, 2006), p. 150.

24. Contrary to common belief, the Federal Reserve Bank is a private corporation, that has nothing to do with the Federal Government of the United States. The true owners of the Fed are not the American people, but a select group of international bankers: Rothschild Bank of London, Warburg Bank of Hamburg, Rothschild Bank of Berlin, Lehman Brothers of New York, Lazard Brothers of Paris, Kuhn Loeb Bank of New York, Israel Moses Seif Bank of Italy, Goldman Sachs of New York, Warburg Bank of Amsterdam and Chase Manhattan Bank of New York.

25. Cover story: 1. A fictitious, but plausible story used to explain the visible evidences of a clandestine operation. 2. A relatively plausible justification used to explain an operation that goes wrong. 3. A plausible story played by an intelligence officer used to conceal his real mission. Also called a legend.

26. U.S. Foreign Policy: Basic Aims of U.S. Foreign Policy. No. 7. Study

by Council on Foreign Relations, United States. Congress. Senate. Committee on the Judiciary,1959, https://books.google.com/books/about/U_S_Foreign_Policy.html?id=SFezAQAACAAJ

27. *Ibid.*

28. President George H. W. Bush, "Address Before a Joint Session of the Congress on the State of the Union," January 29, 1991, http://www.presidency.ucsb.edu/ws/?pid=19253. Also "Bush's Talk of a 'New World Order:' Foreign Policy Tool or Mere Slogan?", *Washington Post*, May 26, 1991.

29. Grose, *op. cit.*

30. On page 58 of his book *The Rockefeller File* (Seal Beach, California: '76 Press, 1976), Gary Allen quotes from page 42 of the CFR 1952 Annual Report mentioning the fact that, because of their government jobs, some Council members are obliged to suspend or curtail their membership for some time. He also mentions that, during the investigation of the CFR by the Reece Congressional Committee in 1953, it was discovered that the CFR had secret members. Two of them whose cover was eventually blown were alleged pro-communist industrialist Cyrus Eaton and Senator William Fulbright.

    Currently, I suspect that two of the most important secret CFR members are Barack Obama and Gen. James Jones. My suspicion arises not only from the fact that at this final phase of the conspiracy nobody can reach the position of President of the United States or National Security Advisor without being a CFR trusted member, but also because their actions exactly follow the CFR's party line.

31. *Foreign Affairs*, Volume 25, Number 4, July *1947,* https://www.foreignaffairs.com/articles/russian-federation/2016-10-31/sources-soviet-conduct-excerpt

32. Joseph Brewda, "Kissinger's 1974 Plan for Food Control Genocide," *Executive Intelligence Review*, December 6, 1995, http://www.larouchepub.com/other/1995/2249_kissinger_food.html. You may download a copy of NSSM Memorandum 200 at: pdf.usaid.gov/pdf_docs/Pcaab500.pdf

33. *Rebuilding America's Defenses: Strategy, Forces and Resources For a New Century*, A Report of the Project for the New American Century, September 2000. You may download the document at: www.newamericancentury.org/RebuildingAmericasDefenses.pdf.

34. An agent of influence is an agent of some stature who uses his or her position to influence public opinion or decision making to produce results beneficial to the country or organization who controls the agent.

Agents of influence are often the most difficult agents to detect. As normally there is no material evidence connecting them to a foreign power, they can be among the most effective means of influencing opinion and actions as they hold considerable credibility among the target audience. See Richard H. Shultz and Roy Godson, *Dezinformatsia: Active Measures in Soviet Strategy* (New York: Pergamon-Brassey's, 1984), pp. 132-133.

35. Carter's recruitment process is told in some detail in Brzezinski's book *Power and Principle: Memoirs of the National Security Adviser 1977-1981* (New York: Farrar, Straus, Giroux, 1983), p. 5.

36. Information about Brzezinski recruiting Obama in Webster Griffin Tarpley, *Obama: The Postmodern Coup – Making of a Manchurian Candidate* (Joshua Tree, California: Progressive Press, 2008), p. 65. Tarpley mentions that in the 1920s and 1930s Columbia University was the American university most friendly to Benito Mussolini's Fascist — which perhaps is another clue to Obama's fascist proclivities. It is interesting to note that Fidel Castro's infatuation with Fascism began when he was a student at the Jesuit's Belen High School in Havana.

37. Tarpley, *op. cit.*, p. 65.

38. Even a CFR apologist had to admit that CFR members don't like democracy because they only are "the happiest when others agree with them." See Robert D. Schulzinger, *The Wise Men of Foreign Affairs: The History of the Council on Foreign Relations* (New York: Columbia University Press, 1984). p. 32.

39. Lyndon Johnson hated the Kennedy brothers because they treated him like dirt. He most likely knew about the coming assassination attempt on JFK. Nevertheless, Johnson was not a CFR member and, contrary to most CFR members, he didn't hate his country and wanted to fuse it into a New World Order. Johnson's photos of his final days in the Oval Office show a man tortured by grief.

40. "Beware the Obama 'Evil Eye'," *The Drudge Report*, drudgereport.com, June 30, 2009.

41. Information of FDR as a CFR puppet in Curtis D. Dall, *FDR, My Exploited Father-in-law* (Washington, D.C.: Action Associates, 1970), pp. 23-24, 92, 185.

42. John Prados, *Safe for democracy: The Secret Wars of the CIA* (Chicago: Ivan R. Dee, 2006), p. 43.

43. *Ibid.*

44. Smith, *OSS: The Secret History of America's First Intelligence Service* (Berkeley: University of California Press, 1972).

45. *Ibid.*, p. 6.
46. *Ibid.*, p. 10.
47. Actually, this was not a difficult mission for the OSS. Most OSS officers had links to corporations that traded with the Nazis or had cartel agreements with German companies. For a detailed study of how the OSS helped Nazis avoid punishment, see, Thomas M. Bower, *The Pledge Betrayed: America and Britain and the Degasification of Post-War Germany* (New York: Doubleday, 1982), especially Part 4.
48. *Ibid*, p. 15.
49. Higham, *op. cit.*, p. 216.
50. *Ibid.*, p. 11. For detailed information about the OSS penetrated by leftists and Communists, see Smith, *op. cit.*, pp. 9-15.
51. *Ibid*, p. 15.
52. Formerly called the Chase Manhattan Bank.

Chapter 8

1. Bible verse etched in marble in the Lobby's wall at CIA headquarters, most likely as a reminder to CIA officers of the true reason why they should never tell the truth about what they do to the American people. The verse was selected by professional liar Allen Dulles.
2. It is interesting to note that a few non-CFR- controlled Republicans in Congress opposed the legislation, which was promoted by liberal "pro-gressive" Democrats, mostly because it gave too much power to the President. With the passage of time, however, they were co-opted, and now "conservative" Republicans are the strong supporters of the imperial presidency, particularly when there is a Republican in the White House. See, William Greider, *Who Will Tell the People: The Betrayal of American Democracy* (New York: Simon & Schuster, 1992), p. 365-366.
3. John Ranelagh, *The Agency: The Rise and Decline of the CIA* (New York: Touchstone, 1986), p. 18.
4. Actually, however, Pearl Harbor was *not* a surprise attack because people at the highest levels of the U.S. Government, including President Roosevelt, not only knew about it but also allowed it to happen. This explains why the CIA has been unable to prevent similar attacks such as the 9/11 events. See, Robert Stinnett, *Day of Deceit: The Truth About FDR and Pearl Harbor*, also David Ray Griffin, *The New Pearl Harbor: Disturbing Questions About the Bush Administration and 9/11*.
5. The Containment Doctrine was first expressed by CFR agent George Kennan in the famous article he wrote for *Foreign Affairs* under the

synonym "X," and later polished by the CFR's "Wise Men." See Evan Thomas, *The Very Best Men: The Daring Early Years of the CIA* (New York: Simon and Schuster, 2006), pp. 9, 29.

6. The Marshall Plan was actually written by CFR secret agent Richard Bissell. See, Thomas, *op. cit.*, p. 10.

7. Though generally attributed to JFK, actually the first person who mentioned the Alliance was CFR secret agent Fidel Castro. On May 2, 1959, during a session of the Economic Assembly of the Latin American States, Castro suggested that, in order to avoid problems in Latin America, the U.S. should help the Latin American countries economically. See, Herbert Matthews, *Fidel Castro* (New York: Simon and Schuster, 1969), pp. 166-167. The next month, during a speech in New York's Central Park, he called for an American "Marshall Plan" for Latin America in order to avoid communism. See, *Hispanic American Report*, Vol. XII, (No. 4, 1959), p. 205. Now, where did Castro get the dea? Most likely from his friend and mentor David Rockefeller.

8. See, David I. Walsh, Letter to James V. Forrestal, 15 May 1945 in Ferdinand Eberstadt, *Unification of the War and Navy Departments and Postwar Organization for National Security*, U.S. Congress, 79th Congress, 1st session, Senate, Committee on Naval Affairs, Senate Committee Print (Washington: Government Printing Office, 1945) iii–iv. 136; Demetrios Caraley, *The Politics of Military Unification: A Study of Conflict and the Policy Process*, (New York: Columbia University Press, 1966); also, Jeffrey M. Dorwart, *Eberstadt and Forrestal: A National Security Partnership, 1909-1949*, (College Station, Texas: Texas A&M University Press, 1991).

9. See Charles A. Stevenson, "Underlying Assumptions of the National Security Act of 1947," in *Joint Force Quarterly*, Issue 48, 1st Quarter 2008, p. 130.

10. Paul Y. Hammond, "The National Security Council as a Device for Interdepartmental Coordination: An Interpretation and Appraisal," *American Political Science Review*, December 1960, p. 899.

11. National Security Act of 1947, P.L. 80-253, ◊ 101(a), 61 State.

12. Influenced by insights from Bernard Baruch, another CFR hand, Eberstadt considered the NSRB as the key mechanism to unify a larger corporate political-economic organization by coordinating military, industry, labor, and business in a national security program — actually it officialized the already existing military-industrial complex later mentioned by President Eisenhower in his farewell speech.

13. National Security Act of 1947, P.L. 80-253, 101(a), 61 State.

14. Speech by Allen Dulles at Yale University, February 3, 1958.
15. Intelligence agencies carry out clandestine or secret operations, mostly espionage, secretly gathering information about a friend or foe. Event though these operations are concealed, if discovered, the service carrying them generally acknowledges being responsible. In contrast, covert operations, seeking to influence or change how a country is governed, are activities intended to remain concealed and, if discovered, plausibly denied. As I explained on Chapter 2, in June 28, 1961, Kennedy signed National Security Action Memorandum 55 that virtually cancelled NSA 10/2.
16. William M. Leary, ed., *The Central Intelligence Agency: History and Documents* (University, Alabama: The University of Alabama Pres, 1984), p. 133.
17. Evan Thomas, *The Very Best Men: The Daring Early Years of the CIA* (New York: Simon and Schuster, 2006), pp. 9, 29.
18. John Loftus, *The Belarus Secret* (New York: Alfred A. Knopf, 1982), p. 69.
19. William Corson, *The Armies of Ignorance* (New York: Dial Press, 977), p. 305. Also Peter Grose, *Gentleman Spy: The Life of Allen Dulles* (New York: Houghton Mifflin, 1994), p. 293.
20. The Church Committee's 1977 congressional report on "Alleged Assassination Plots Involving Foreign Leaders," see Jesse Ventura, *63 Documents the Government Doesn't Want You to Read* (New York: Skyhorse, 2011), pp. 24-25.
21. William M. Leary, *Ibid.* p. 144.
22. Christy Macy and Susan Kaplan, *Documents: A shocking collection of Memoranda, letters, and telexes from the secret files of the American intelligence community* (New York: Penguin, 1980), pp. 153-159.
23. *Ibid.*, p. 162.
24. After retiring from CIA Wisner committed suicide. See, Evan Thomas, *The Very Best Men: The Daring Early Years of the CIA* (New York: Simon and Schuster, 2006), pp. 319-320.
25. *Ibid.*, p. 15.
26. *Ibid.*, p. 11.
27. See John Ranelagh, *The Agency: The Rise and Decline of the CIA* (New York: Touchstone, 1987), pp. 151-152.
28. Ronald Kessler, *Inside the CIA* (New York: Pocket Books, 1992), p. 85.
29. Jesse Ventura, *They Killed Our President* (New York: Skyhorse, 2013), p. xxii. Nevertheless, if some anti-Castro Cubans in the U.S.

participated in the JFK assassination, they did it acting as CIA agents, not as free-lance anti-Castro Cubans.

30. False flag recruiting: 1. The recruiting of an agent by an intelligence service passing as a different one. A technique by which an informant, defector in place or agent is recruited through the disguise of telling him he will be working for the "good guys" —another country or service different from the one who is actually making the recruitment.

Usually, after a talent spotter detects a prospect for recruitment, he learns as much as he can about the target's political sympathies. Then an agent or intelligence officer approaches him pretending he is working for the country or organization for whom the target is sympathetic, while in reality he is working for another.

Talent spotter: 1. An intelligence officer or operative whose function is to detect and assess individuals who might be of value for an intelligence service and potential recruits for intelligence work. 2. A deep-cover agent who recruits agents to work against their own country or organization.

The Israeli Mossad operatives are experts in false flag recruitment. Being able to produce agents who can pass for just about any nationality under the sun, the Mossad has carried out some remarkable operations with false flag recruitment.

31. These true patriots inside the CIA are the same ones wrongly accused of treason by Rowan Scarborough in his book *Sabotage: America's Enemies Within the CIA* (Washington, D.C.: Regnery, 2007).

32. Nelson's memorandum to Eisenhower in John Loftus and Mark Aarons, *The Secret War Against the Jews* (New York: St. Martin's Press, 1994), p. 279.

33. Tyler Durden, "High-Ranking CIA Agent Blows Whistle On The Deep State And Shadow Government." *ZeroHedge*, Sep 16, 2017, http://www.zerohedge.com/news/2017-09-15/high-ranking-cia-agent-blows-whistle-deep-state-and-shadow-government

34. Servando Gonzalez, *Psychological Warfare and the New World Order* (Oakland, California: Spooks Books, 2010), pp. 108-115.

35. I have used the name favored in Cuba to designate the war, because, contrary to what is written in most American history textbooks, when the early imperialist conspirators decided to create the *USS Maine* incident as a pretext to enter the war, the Cuban patriots had already been fighting the Spaniards for many years. Actually, the 1898 war was the third war the Cubans waged against colonialist Spain, and they were winning.

On U.S. military interventions all around the world see William Blum,

The CIA: A Forgotten History (London: Zed Books, 1986).

36. A good source for discovering the true cause of most of U.S. interventions around the world is William Engdahl's *A Century of War: Anglo-American Oil Politics and the New World Order* (London: Pluto Press, 2004) See also, Daniel Yergin, *The Prize: The Epic Quest for Oil, Money, and Power* (New York: Pocket Books, 1993).

37. Butler joined the Marine Corps when the Spanish American War broke out. During his 34 years of Marine Corps service, Butler was awarded two Congressional Medals of Honor, the first one for the capture of Veracruz, Mexico in 1914, and the second one for the capture of Ft. Riviere, Haiti in 1917. In addition, he was awarded numerous medals for heroism including the Marine Corps Brevet Medal (the highest Marine medal at its time for officers). Butler was one of only 19 people to be twice awarded the Congressional Medal of Honor.

38. General Smedley D. Butler, *War is a Racket* (Los Angeles: Feral House, 2003), p. 23.

39. Trevor Monroe, *The Politics of Constitutional Decolonization* (Kinston: University of the West Indies, 1947), p. 27.

40. Written in China 2,000 years ago, Sun Tzu's, *The Art of War* is considered a sort of Bible of intelligence, espionage and warfare. The book contains principles still relevant today.

41. Joseph Trento, *The Secret History of the CIA* (Roseville, California: Prima Publishing, 2001), p. 44.

42. Dulles quoted in David Wise and Thomas B. Ross, *The Espionage Establishment* (New York: Random House, 19670), p. 290.

43. Michael Parenti, *Dirty Truths* (City Lights: San Francisco, 1996) pp. 185-186.

44. Stanfield Turner, *Secret and Democracy: The CIA in Transition* (Boston: Houghton Mifflin, 1985), p.46.

45. See, *Final Report of the Select Committee to Study Governmental Operations with Respect to Intelligence Activities, United States Senate*, Book I, Chapter VIII, April 26, 1976.

46. Turner, *op. cit.*, p. 76.

47. *Ibid.*, pp. 84-85.

48. *Ibid.*, p. 186.

49. The fact was mentioned by Professor Roy Godson in a Panel on "The Future of Intelligence Research," at the Annual Convention of the International Studies Association, Anaheim, California, March 7, 1986.

50. In his autobiography of sorts, *Honorable Men: My Life at the CIA* (New York: Simon and Schuster, 1978) William Colby calls them

"honorable men." I don't think there was anything honorable in what they did. Nevertheless, Colby ended his career by doing something honorable: denouncing their crimes. But some time later he paid with his life for his transgression. A few years after he retired, Colby drowned in a rather suspicious boating accident while kayaking near his vacation home in Maryland. See Zalin Grant, "Who Murdered the CIA Chief?" *Pythia Press*, 2011, http://www.pythiapress.com/wartales/colby.htm

51. Evan Thomas, *The Very Best Men: The Daring Early Years of the CIA* (New York: Simon and Schuster, 2006), pp. 9, 29.

52. *NBC*, "Evening News," January 13, 1978.

53. In a series of well-researched books, professor Antony Sutton proved beyond any reasonable doubt that the CFR conspirators created the Soviet Union's military machine. See Sutton's massive *Western Technology and Soviet Economic Development* (Three volumes) (Stanford, California: Hoover Institution Press, 1968-1973); also his *Wall Street and the Bolshevik Revolution* (New Rochelle, New York: Arlington House, 1974); and *The Best Enemy Money Can Buy* (Billings, Montana: Liberty House Press, 1986).

54. Barton J. Bernstein, "American Foreign Policy and the Origins of the Cold War," in Barton J. Bernstein, ed., *Politics and Policies of the Truman Administration* (Chicago: Quadrangle, 1970), pp. 16-17.

55. H.W. Brands, *The Devil We Knew: Americans and the Cold War* (New York: Oxford University Press, 1993), p. vi.

56. Frank Kofsky, *Harry S. Truman and the War Scare of 1948* (New York: St. Martin's Press, 1993), p. 308.

57. Anderson's article appeared in the *San Francisco Chronicle*, December 26, 1979.

58. Both Castro and the CIA collaborated in destabilizing the Allende government — the CIA by painting him as a radical leftist and Castro by openly criticizing him for not being radical enough. Moreover, Allende did not commit suicide: his Cuban security chief, General Patricio de la Guardia, killed him, following Castro's direct orders. See my article "Fidel Castro: Asesino de Allende?," http://www.servandogonzalez.org.

59. John Loftus and Mark Aarons, *The Secret War Against the Jews* (New York: St. Martin's Press, 1994), pp. 64-73.

60. Charles Higham, *Trading With the Enemy: An Exposé of the Nazi-American Money plot 1933-1949* (New York: Delacorte Press, 1983)

61 *Ibid*. For the whole story, see Chapter 3, "The Secrets of Standard Oil."

62. In early 1970s I met a man who had been hired by the National Bank of Cuba to search for gold in sunken Spanish galleons. He didn't find much gold, but found two of the underwater fuel tanks and even a sunken German submarine close to the Cuban coast.

Chapter 9

1. See Earl T. Smith, *The Fourth Floor* (New York: Random House, 1962).
2. Wieland was a protegé of CFR member Sumner Welles, notorious for his homosexual scandals, who was Under Secretary of State from 1937 to 1943. In 1950 the Senate disclosed a Washington police estimate of 3,500 homosexuals in federal jobs — many of them in the State Department. See Truxton Decatur, "We Accuse Sumner Welles," *Confidential* magazine, March 1956, http://www.reformation.org/welles-confidential-magazine.html
3. The operation by which the CFR infiltrated and eventually took control of the U.S. Department of State is described in detail in Lawrence H. Shoup and William Minter, *Imperial Brain Trust: The Council on Foreign Relations & United States Foreign Policy* (New York: Monthly Review Press, 1977), pp. 148-156.
4. For an in-depth analysis of the Bogotazo riots and the assassination of Gaitán see Servando Gonzalez, *Psychological Warfare and the New World Order* (Oakland, California: Spooks Books, 2010), pp. 150-179.
5 John Loftus and Mark Aarons, *The Secret War Against the Jews: How Western Espionage Betrayed the Jewish People* (New York: St. Martin's Press, 1994) p. 8.
6. Though del Pino claimed to be a University student, he actually was a student of the Escuela de Artes y Oficios [School of Arts and Trades], which was not a part of the University of Havana.
7. Confidential Dispatch No. 336, April 26, 1948, U.S. Embassy, Havana. http://www.icdc.com/~paulwolf/gaitan/archives/mallory26april1948.htm.
8. See Ramón B. Conte, *Historia oculta de los crímenes de Fidel Castro* (Self-published, n.p., 1995), pp. 15-30.
9. Heavy, a.k.a. slag. CIA vernacular for assets of girth and muscle the Agency uses in situations where brute force is more important that wit. Heavies also serve as bodyguards for CIA top officers.
10. In his book *Inside the Company: CIA Diary* (New York: Bantam, 1989), p. 396, CIA defector Philip Agee identified Isabel Siero Pérez, del

Pino's aunt, as a CIA's Miami station agent.

11. Both in his book and in a phone interview I made with him, Conte mentions a Mr. William Beulieu. After much research, however, I was unable to find any information about such person. So, I concluded that he was actually talking about Willard D. Beaulac, later to be appointed U.S. Ambassador to Colombia.

12. Conte, *Ibid.*, pp. 17-18.

13. You may listen to Conte's interview (in Spanish) at my website: http://www.intelinet.org/sg_site/intelligence/sg_entrevista_conte.html

14 .Tim Weiner, *Legacy of Ashes: The History of the CIA* (New York: Doubleday, 2007), p. 102.

15. Information on Pawley in Mario Lazo, *Dagger in the Heart: American Policy Failures in Cuba* (New York: Twin Circle, 1968), pp. 144-145, 170-171. Also in Jim Hogan, *Spooks: The Haunting of America — The Private Use of Secret Agents* (New York: William Morrow, 1978), pp. 310-311.

16. CFR member George Marshall already had experience in the creation of the Communist menace: he was instrumental in the implementation of a plan developed by the CFR conspirators by which Chiang Kai-Shek was betrayed and China was given on a silver platter to Mao Tse-tung and his "agrarian reformers."

17. False flag operation: an operation designed to be untraceable to the sponsor due to misrepresentation or disguise. Usually, false clues are planted to implicate another group or country as the perpetrator of the operation.

18. Francisco Fandiño Silva, *La Penetración Soviética en América y el 9 de abril*, (Bogotá: Nuevos Tiempos, 1949).

19. *U.S. News & World Report*, April 23, 1948, pp. 13-14.

20. Adm. Hillenkoetter was the CIA Director at the time of the Bogotazo riots. CFR agent Allen Dulles managed to blame Hillenkoetter for the CIA's failure to predict the riots. Eventually, the CFR conspirators fired Hillenkoetter and appointed Dulles CIA Director.

21. Senate Internal Security Subcommittee, *Communist Threat to the United States Through the Caribbean*, Hearings, Part II, August 3, 1959, Appendix, "Communist Anti-American Riots — Mob Violence as an Instrument of Red Diplomacy" (staff report), p. 116.

22. Jack Davis, "The Bogotazo," *Studies in Intelligence* Vol. 13, (Fall 1969).

23. *Ibid.*

24. "Communist Involvement in the Colombian Riots of April 9, 1948," Office of Intelligence Research (OIR), Report 4696, U.S. Sate Department, October 14, 1948.

25. Russell Jack Smith *The Unknown CIA: My Three Decades with the Agency* (Washington, D.C.: Pergamon-Brasseys, 1989), p. 38. The story shows not only that Marshall, a trusted CFR agent, was lying, but also that honest CIA officers like Smith, who worked in the CIA' intelligence branch, were left in the dark about the Bogotazo operation.

26. Confidential Dispatch No. 336, April 26, 1948, U.S. Embassy, Havana. http://www.icdc.com/~paulwolf/gaitan/archives/ mallory26april1948.htm.

27. Jules Dubois, *Fidel Castro: Rebel — Liberator or Dictator?* (New York: Bobbs-Merrill, 1959), p. 18.

28. It seems that far from being a Communist, Betancourt was more close to the ideology of the Caribbean Legion, an organization of non-communist, nationalist left wingers counting among them President Figueres of Costa Rica and Cuba's Prío Socarrás. See Nathaniel Weyl, *Red Star Over Cuba* (New York: Hillman/MacFadden, 1960), p. 69.

29. Alberto Niño H., *Antecedentes y secretos del 9 de abril* (Bogotá: Editorial Pax, 1949), p. 77. Niño was Colombia's former Security Chief.

30. Activities of Wieland, Rubbotom and Castro in Bogotá, Colombia, in Hearings, *Communist Threat to the U.S. Through the Caribbean*, Senate Internal Subcommittee, 86th-87th Congress, Parts 1-12, pp. 725, 756, 806; also in Mario Lazo, *Dagger in the Heart* (New York: Twin Circle, 1968), pp. 144-145.

31. Weyl, *Ibid.*, pp. 74-75.

32. *Ibid.*, p. 75.

33. Richard E. Sharpless, *Gaitán of Colombia: A Political Biography* (Pittsburgh: University of Pittsburgh Press, 1978), p. 173.

34. Dubois, *op. cit.*, p. 19.

35. Castro's interview was published in English in the *Illustrated Weekly of India*, and later translated into Spanish in the newspaper *El Tiempo* of Bogotá. See, Angel Aparicio Laurencio, *Antecedentes desconocidos del nueve de abril* (Madrid: Ediciones Universal, 1973), p. 21.

36. A few months later Castro married Mirtha Díaz Balart.

37. Niño, *op. cit*, p. 77.

38. President Eisenhower mentioned the existence of a U.S. military-industrial-complex in his Farewell address to the nation. What Eisenhower conveniently didn't mention, however, was that at the time

the military-industrial-complex had already changed into the military-industrial-banking complex, with the bankers fully in control of it, and also that he owed his meteoric military career to those bankers, particularly the Rockefellers.

39. Kennan's memorandum mentioned in Gonzalo Sánchez, (ed.), *Grandes potencias: El 9 de abril y la violencia* (Bogotá: Planeta, 2000) p. 50.

40. See, *The Final Act of Bogotá*, Foreign relations of the United States (FRUS), 1948, Volume IX. http://www.icdc.com/~paulwolf/gaitan/finalactofbogota.htm. The Bogotazo operation was essentially based on the Hegelian principle of thesis, antithesis, synthesis.

41. Psychological warfare operations, also called PsyOps, are operations to convey selected information and indicators to foreign audiences to influence their emotions, motives, objective reasoning, and ultimately the behavior of foreign governments, organizations, groups, and individuals. The purpose of psychological operations is to induce or reinforce foreign attitudes and behavior favorable to the originator's objectives.

The Joint Chiefs of Staff has defined psychological operations (PsyOps) as those that: "include psychological warfare, and, in addition, encompass those political, military, economic, and ideological actions planned, and conducted to create in neutral or friendly foreign groups the emotions, attitudes, or behavior to support achievement of national objectives." Another Dept. of Defense publication develops "the concept of 'strategic psychological operations' as aimed at influencing, and shaping decision-makers' power to govern, or control their followers."

Though, by definition, PsyOps are directed against foreign audiences, the American people has been among the groups being targeted by the conspirators, and effectively controlled through PsyOps. The CFR, however, could not accomplish their goals without complicity of the mainstream news media, which they absolutely control. The RAND Corporation, The Hudson Institute and the Stanford Research Institute are three of the institutions the CFR conspirators have used to develop their PsyOps against the American people.

42. The Bogotazo also helped the CFR conspirators to reach a secondary, and perhaps an initially unintended goal: getting rid of CIA Director Adm. Hillenkoetter, a man of honor and integrity they didn't fully control, and eventually replacing him with their trusted secret agent Allen W. Dulles.

43. Jefrey T. Richelson, *A Century of Spies: Intelligence in the Twentieth*

Century (New York: Oxford University Press, 1959), p. 217.

44. See, OSS Sabotage Instructions, May 7, 1943, and Simple Sabotage Instructions, C. 1945. http://www.icdc.com/~paulwolf/oss/ossso.htm#sabotage.

45. For more information about the OSS' Morale Operations Branch, see, http://www.icdc.com/~paulwolf/oss/ossmo.htm.

46. Black: Said of any operation whose true source is hidden or falsely attributed to another source. In the case of propaganda, "black" also means that the content is mostly fake or forged.

47. Black propaganda could be either true or false. For morale operations purposes, the truth or falsity is irrelevant. It is the effect on the target's mind that mattered.

48. One of the best sources of the War Scare is Frank Kofsky's, *Harry S. Truman and the War Scare of 1948* (New York: St. Martin's Press, 1993).

49. https://history.state.gov/historicaldocuments/frus1950v01/d212

50. Peter H. Smith, *Talons of the Eagle: Dynamics of U.S.-Latin American Relations* (New York: Oxford University Press, 1996), p. 126.

51. Weyl, *op. cit.*, p. 84.

52. Weyl, *Ibid.*, p. 76. This conversation between del Pino and Gaitán's assassin allegedly took place just and hour and a half before the assassination took place.

53. U.P. report quoted in Weyl, *op. cit.*, p. 77.

54. Rafael Azula Barrera, *De la revolución al orden nuevo* (Bogotá: Editorial Kelly, 1956), p. 379

55. Bracker mentioned in Weyl, *op. cit.*, p.84.

56. *Ibid.*, 233-234.

57. *Ibid.*, p. 237.

58. Arturo Alape, *El Bogotazo: Memorias del olvido* (La Habana: Casa de las Américas, 1983) pp. 603-604.

59, *Ibid.*, pp. 600-601.

60. Smith, *op. cit.*, p. 12.

61. Servando Gonzalez, *The Secret Fidel Castro: Deconstructing the Symbol* (Oakland, California: Spooks Books, 2001), pp. 309-315.

62. What happened to Castro's close friend Rafael del Pino after the Bogotazo? In 1957 del Pino joined Castro in Mexico when Castro was training his men for invading Cuba. But del Pino, an American citizen, got word that Castro was planning to kill him and escaped to the U.S. In July 1959, just six months after Castro took power in Cuba, Castro managed to capture del Pino and locked him in a Cuban jail. Soon after,

Servando Gonzalez

del Pino allegedly committed suicide by hanging himself with one of his socks. Del Pino was a witness of Castro's recruitment by the CIA in 1948, and Castro knew that dead men don't tell tales.

63. German philosopher Georg Wilhelm Friedrich Hegel (1770-1831) made change the cornerstone of his philosophical system, which he called Dialectics. According to Hegel, an idea or principle — which he called the thesis— is challenged by its opposite —the antithesis. Eventually, from this conflict emerges a new idea or principle that is a synthesis of both.

In practice, however, the first step (thesis) has been to artificially create a threat to the people's lives and well-being. The second step (antithesis) is to generate fear, hysteria and panic about it. The third step (antithesis), consists in offering a solution to the non-existing problem by taking measures which would not have been possible without having previously psychologically conditioning the people to accept them as the lesser of two evils by the fear and panic created in step two.

A recent example of Hegel's principle in action is the American sheeple happily accepting the losing of their freedoms and fascist aberrations such as the Office of Homeland Security, the Transportation Security Administration and the militarization of police, after the fear, hysteria and panic generated by the 9/11 false flag events. Another example is the phony environmental crisis used to terrorize gullible Americans into willingly accepting a drastic lowering of their standards of living.

64. In the Prologue to Melvin Beck's *Secret Contenders: The Myth of Cold War Counterintelligence* (New York: Sheridan Square, 1984), Thomas Powers explains how in his book, "Beck concludes that propaganda operations have little impact on uncontrolled foreign audiences; the real target of operations in the field was opinion at home. This is a subtle point, but a significant one; I have never seen it argued so clearly elsewhere." p. xiv.

65. A notable exception is Rhodri Jeffrey's-Jones' *The CIA and American Democracy*: Second Edition- (New Haven: Yale University Press, 1998), pp. 42-62.

66. So, the creation of the CIA's covert operations branch — the true purpose for the CIA's existence — was the result of a big lie: the threat of international communism. Any similarity to the creation of the Department of Homeland Security to oppose the threat of terrorism is not the result of a coincidence.

67. Epilogue to Church Report, https://history-matters.com/archive/
church/reports/ir/html/ChurchIR_0150a.htm

Chapter 10

1. Contrary to Castro, the son of a wealthy landlord, Cuban President
Fulgencio Batista was a black man of very humble origins.
2. Keep in mind that in 1957 the average price for a medium size house
in Cuba was about $2,000.00.
3. Department of Economic and Social Affairs, *Economic Survey of Latin
America 1957* (New York: United Nations, 1959), p. 177.
4. Louis A. Pérez, Jr., *On Becoming Cuban* (Chapel Hill: University of
North Carolina Press, 1999), p. 307.
5. *Ibid*, p. 53. Pérez's book studies in detail the growing similarities
between the American and the Cuban economy, culture and society.
6. K. S. Karol, *Guerrillas in Power* (New York: Hill and Wang,
1970), p. 324.
7. The whole story is told in detail in Mario Lazo, *Dagger in the Heart:
American Policy Failures in Cuba* (New York: Twin Circle, 1968), pp.
169-178.
8. It seems that millionaire William Pawley also played a role in the
Kennedy assassination. After he was targeted for questioning in 1977 by
the House Select Committee on Assassination (HSCA), Pawley, in bed in
his mansion in Miami Beach with a nervous ailment, allegedly put a gun
to his chest and committed "suicide." See Gaeton Fonzi, *The Last
Investigation* (New York: Thunder's Mouth Press, 1993), p. 82. For a
long list of people related to the Kennedy assassination who committed
suicide under strange circumstances see Peter Dale Scott, "William
Pawley, the Kennedy Assassination, and Watergate," *Global Research*,
November 29, 2012, http://www.globalresearch.ca/william-pawley-the-
kennedy assassination-and-watergate-tilt-and-the-phase-three-story-of-
clare-boothe-luce/5313486
9. Fonzi, *Ibid*., p. 175.
10. The whole story is told in detail by Ambassador Smith himself. See,
Earl E. T. Smith, *The Fourth Floor: An Account of the Castro Communist
Revolution* (Washington, D.C.: Selous Foundation Press, 1987) pp. 169-
174.
11. Smith, *Ibid*., p. 196.
12. Alexandra Obrenovich, *Who is Responsible?* (New York: Carlton

Press, 1962).

13. Evidence of Bruce McColm to the author at the Freedom House in New York.

14. See Humberto Fontova, "Former CIA station-chief in Cuba bashes Fontova's book (because it exposes how the CIA backed Castro and Che Guevara!)," babalublog.com, May 24, 2014, http://babalublog.com/2014/05/24/former-cia-station-chief-in-cuba-bashes-fontovas-book-the-longest-romance/

15. Tad Szulc, *Fidel: A Critical Portrait* (New York: William Morrow, 1986), p. 427. Actually, Szulc's portrait of Castro is very uncritical.

16. Jesús Arboleya, *The Cuban Counterrevolution* (Athens, Ohio: Ohio University Center for International Studies) p. 61.

17. Jaime Suchlicki, *Cuba: From Columbus to Castro* (New York: Scribner's, 1974), pp. 143.

18. *Bohemia Libre*, December 1961.

19. Daniel James, *Cuba: The First Soviet Satellite in the Americas* (New York: Avon, 1961), p. 34.

20. Daniel James, *op. cit.*, 55.

21 R. Hart Phillips, *The Cuban Dilemma* (New York: Ivan Obolensky, 1962), p. 18.

22. Mario Llerena, *The Unsuspected Revolution,* (Ithaca, N. Y.: Cornell Univ. Press, 1978), Chapter 5, note 7.

23. Lee Lockwood, *Castro's Cuba, Cuba's Fidel.* (New York: Macmillan, 1967), pp. 50, 52, 55.

24. *Ibid.*, p. 57.

25. Carlos Franqui, *Family Portrait with Fidel* (New York: Random House, 1984), p. 13; also in Lockwood, *op. cit.*, pp. 7, 22.

26. The full text of Castro's confession of Marxist faith was published in *Hoy*, the Cuban communists' organ, on December 2, 1961, and in the evening edition of *Revolución*, Castro's government official newspaper, December 2, 1961.

27. Loree Wilkerson, *Fidel Castro's Political Programs from Reformism to Marxist Leninism* (Gainesville, Florida: University of Florida Press, 1965).p. 81. Wilkerson's is by far the best analysis of Castro's "I am a Marxist" speech.

28. An illegal is an intelligence officer placed in a foreign country with false identity to operate independently from any of his country's embassies or consulates. Illegals are not covered by diplomatic immunity, therefore they normally operate under deep covers and use false documentation. A sleeper is an intelligence officer who has been implanted

into a country under a false identity and has been living a normal life as a native for a rather long amount of time, waiting to be roused into action. The main job of a sleeper is to wait, as unnoticed as possible, until he receives the wake up order, regardless of the length of time required.

29. *Editorial Research Reports* July 9, 1967.

30. Hugh Thomas, *Cuba: The Pursuit of Freedom* (New York: Harper & Row, 1971) p. 1489.

31. New York *Herald Tribune*, December 7, 1961.

32. Mario Lazo, *Dagger in the Heart* (New York: Twin Circle, 1968), p. 248. We don't know for sure if St. George was a CIA officer acting under a journalist's cover or a *bona fide* journalist recruited by the CIA, but many people, including his own wife, had strong suspicions about his true job. It is known that Che Guevara believed St. George was an FBI agent. In a series of articles about Guevara's guerrilla activities in Bolivia St. George is described as having done "a spell in the U.S. military intelligence service." See *Sunday Telegraph*, July 7, 1968.

33. Earl E. T. Smith, *The Fourth Floor* (New York: Random House, 1962), pp. 34-35.

34. Carl Bernstein, "The CIA and the Media," *Rolling Stone*, October 20, 1997. Bernstein claimed that a senior CIA officer told him that between 1950 and 1966 the *NYT* provided cover for about ten CIA operatives. See also Frank J. Donner, *The Age of Surveillance* (New York: Alfred A Knopf, 1980), p. 270. According to Donner, from around 1950 to 1975, some correspondents for the *New York Times*, CBS News, *Time* magazine, and many other press organizations, served as conduits for planted CIA stories, leaked information to the CIA, and in some cases even provided operational assistance. In addition, major news organizations such as the *NYT* wittingly allowed CIA operatives to pose as clerks or part-time correspondents and provided cover for others. Also, propaganda and disinformation disseminated abroad by the CIA was "blown back" to the U.S. and reprinted as bona fide news by American newspapers.

35. M-26-7, *Movimiento 26 de Julio*, (26th of July Movement), was Castro's revolutionary organization.

36. Mario Llerena, *The Unsuspected Revolution* (Ithaca, New York: Cornell University Press, 1978), pp. 104-105.

37. Even young Senator John F. Kennedy fell for the ruse. In his 1960 book *The Strategy for Peace*, he described Castro as part of the legacy of [Latin American patriot] Bolívar.

38. Daniel Schorr, *Clearing the Air* (New York: Houghton Mifflin, 1977).

39. Smith, *The Fourth Floor,* p. 231.

40. Smith, *Ibid., p.* 33.

41. Wise and Ross, *Ibid.*, p. 266.

42. Smith, *Ibid.*, pp. 135, 47.

43. Llerena, *Ibid.*, pp. 144-145.

44. Lawrence Shoup and William Minter, *Imperial Brain Trust* (New York: Monthly Review Press, 1977), p. 42; and in Dan Smoot, *The Invisible Government* (Dallas: The Dan Smoot Report, 1962), p. 18. It is interesting to notice that Castro's visit to the CFR is one of the best-kept secrets of his visit to the U.S. It was not mentioned in any other book about Castro.

45. Philip Bonsal, *Cuba, Castro, and the United States* (Pittsburgh: University of Pittsburgh Press), 1971, p. 64.

46. Like Hitler, Castro had what is known as a photographic or eidetic memory. Castro's photographic memory suddenly appeared when he was a student at the Colegio de Belén high school in Havana. It was at Belén where he suddenly changed from a mediocre student to an excellent one, consistently obtaining high grades in all subjects. Though there is no clear information about the cause for this sudden change, it seems that Castro's eidetic memory suddenly appeared after he hit his head against a wall at Belén and was unconscious for several days. Similarly, Hitler's eidetic memory seems to have appeared after he was unconscious for several days as the result of a gas attack when he was a soldier in WWI.

47. Lawrence Shoup and William Minter, *Imperial Brain Trust*, p. 42, and in Dan Smoot, *The Invisible Government*, p. 18.

48. Pascal Fletcher "U.S. Policy Experts Encouraged by Talks in Cuba," *Reuters* (Havana), February 18, 2001. Also, Rockefeller-led U.S. delegation cozies up to Castro. http://www.cubanet.org/CNews/y01/feb01/23e11.htm

49. Octavio Guerra, "The Cuban Conspiracy (Two): Castro & Rockefeller," *HavanaSchool*, October 1, 2010, https://havanaschooleng.blogspot.com/2010/10/cuban-conspiracy-two-castro-rockefeller.html?showComment=1485533239611#c5581495971165 12350

50. In his *Memoirs*, David wrote, "For more than a century ideological extremists at either end of the political spectrum have seized upon well-publicized incidents such as my encounter with Castro to attack the Rockefeller family for the inordinate influence they claim we wield over American political and economic institutions. Some even believe we are part of a

secret cabal working against the best interests of the United States, characterizing my family and me as 'internationalists' and of conspiring with others around the world to build a more integrated political and economic
structure —one world, if you will. If that's the charge, I stand guilty, and I
am proud of it." David Rockefeller, *Memoirs* (New York: Barnes and Noble,
2002), p. 405.
51. My theory that Castro's Cuba is actually a successful testing ground
for the Rockefellers' New World Order is explained in some detail in my
book *Psychological Warfare and the New World Order* (Spooks Books:
Oakland, California, 2010), pp. 274-286.

Chapter 11

1. Edmond Paris, *The Secret History of the Jesuits* (Chino, California:
Chick Publications, 1975), p. 65.
2. H. Boehmer, *Les Jesuits*. (Paris: Armand Collin, 1910), pp. 238-241.
3. Fidel Castro, *History Will Absolve Me* (New York: Center for Cuban
Studies, n. d.), p. 62.
4. Hugh Thomas, *Cuba: The Pursuit of Freedom* (New York: Harper &
Row, 1971), p. 819.
5. Carlos Franqui, *Vida, aventuras y desastres de un hombre llamado Castro*
(Barcelona: Planeta, 1988), pp. 69-70; see also Georgie Annie Geyer,
Guerrilla Prince (Boston: Little, Brown and Company, 1991), p. 49.
6. Among the many nicknames Fidel had since an early age was *"el loco
Fidel"* (crazy Fidel). The descriptive nickname followed him to the
Colegio de Belén, and later to the University of Havana.
7. Thomas, *op. cit.*, p. 812.
8. Tad Szulc, *Fidel: A Critical Portrait* (New York: William Morrow,
1986), p. 191.
9. Tad Szulc, "Exporting the Cuban Revolution," in John Plank, ed.,
Cuba and the United States (Washington, D.C.: Brookings Institution,
1967), p. 79.
10. Mario Lazo, *Dagger in the Heart* (New York: Twin Circle, 1968), p.
195.
11. Geoffrey Warner, "Latin America," in Geoffrey Barraclough, ed.,
Survey of International Affairs 1959-1960 (London: Oxford University
Press, 1964), pp. 478-479.
12. Quoted in Andrés Suárez, *Cuba: Castroism and Communism, 1959-
1966* (Cambridge, Mass.: M.I.T. Press, 1967), p. 94.
13. FBI report of agent William Stevens, File # 105-655, 24 October

1962, in Gus Russo, *Live by the Sword* (Baltimore: Bancroft Press, 1998), p. 223.

14. "Communist Activities in Latin America," *Report of the Subcommittee on Inter-American Affairs*, U. S. House of Representatives Committee on Foreign Affairs (July 1967), p. 7.

15. Paul D. Bethel, *The Losers* (New Rochelle, N.Y.: Arlington House, 1969), pp. 424-425.

16. Confidential information surfaced from secret sources in Cuba seem to confirm their claims. Apparently, the notorious Ilich Sánchez Ramírez (aka "Carlos" and "the Jackal") was one of Castro's hit men, and had an active role in the assassination of Somoza. When Carlos had his operations center in Paris in the 1960s, he received Cuban logistic and economic support. His Cuban handler was Armando Pérez Orta, an officer of the Cuban intelligence services operating under the pseudonym "Archimedes."

17. Leo Janos, the *Atlantic*, June 1973.

18. The Washington *Star*, June 25, 1976.

19. Michael R. Beschloss, *Taking Charge: The Johnson White House Tapes, 1963-1964* (New York, Simon and Schuster, 1997).

20. Daniel Schorr, "The Assassins," the *New York Review of Books*, October 13, 1977.

21. The *Washington Post*, July 27, 1975; see also G. Robert Blakey and Richard N. Billings, *The Plot to Kill the President*. (New York: Times Books, 1981), p. 140.

22. The *Washington Post*, November 25, 1983; also in G. Blakey and Billings, *op. cit.*, pp. 137, 176.

23. See, i.e., Norberto Fuentes, *Dulces guerreros cubanos* (Barcelona: Seix Barral, 1999), p. 275.

24. Anthony Summers, *Conspiracy* (New York: McGraw-Hills, 1980), p. 441.

25. *Human Events*, 24 July, 1979, pp. 13-15.

26. *Alleged Assassination Plots Involving Foreign Leaders*, U.S. Senate, November 20, 1975, 94th Congress, 1st Session, pp. 86-90.

27. JFK fired Dulles after the Bay of Pigs disaster, but Dulles, through his people inside the CFR and the CIA, kept conspiring against Kennedy.

28. Edward Jay Epstein, "Sixty Versions of the Kennedy Assassination," in Harold Haynes (ed.), *Smiling Through the Apocalypse* (New York: McCall, 1969), p. 486.

29. Igor Efimov, *Who Killed President Kennedy?* (Moscow: Terra

Publishing House, 1991).

30. Simone quoted in Michael Parenti, *Dirty Truths* (San Francisco: City Lights, 1996), p. 158.

31. U.S. Senate Select Committee to Study Governmental Operations with Respect to Intelligence Activities, *Final Report, Book Five, The Investigation of the Assassination of President John F. Kennedy: Performance of the Intelligence Agencies*, 94th Congress, 2nd sess., 1976, pp. 4, 60.

32. I think their fears were totally unfounded. Had the U.S. proved beyond any reasonable doubt that Castro had been involved in the Kennedy assassination, the Soviets either would have remained silent, or would have joined the Americans in their condemnation. The alleged fears were actually a false excuse to avoid conducting a thorough investigation of the Castro connection which may have brought up very damaging information about some people in the CFR, the CIA, the State Department and some other branches of the American government.

33. As it is difficult to understand the American liberals' love for Fidel Castro, it is also difficult to understand their love for John F. Kennedy. It was Kennedy who invented the non-existent missile gap that boosted the fortunes of the military-industrial-complex. He was personally involved in political assassination. He created the Green Berets and introduced the dirty game of counter-insurgency. Camelot, Kennedy's bright and shining moment, was a post-mortem concoction of his friend Theodore H. White and his wife Jacqueline Kennedy. Actually, the bright and shining moment never existed. It was a fiction. Far from being a liberal, in some aspects John F. Kennedy was a very conservative and even reactionary individual. See, i.e., Ira Stoll, *JFK Conservative* (New York: Houghton Mifflin Harcourt, 2013).

34. See, i.e., Peter Kornbluh and James Blight, "Our Secret Dialogue With Castro: A Hidden History," *The New York Times Review of Books*, October 6, 1994. For a detailed account of how this alleged accommodation actually never took place see Carlos Ripoll, "Kennedy y Castro: el abrazo imposible," www.eddosrios.org/obras/politica/kennedy.htm.

35. *Cigar Aficionado*, September-October, 1999.

36. See Claudia Furiati, *ZR Rifle: The Plot to Kill Kennedy and Castro* (Melbourne: Ocean Press, 1994). Furiati, a pro-Castro Brazilian journalist, got the information for her book directly from Cuba's chief of counterintelligence, General Fabián Escalante. Ocean Press, the publisher of Furiati's book, was created and is financed by the Cuban

intelligence services to disseminate pro-Castro propaganda in English.

37. Ted Sorensen, *Kennedy* (New York: Bantam, 1965), p. 814.

38. Ronald Kessler, *Inside the CIA* (New York: Pocket Books, 1992), p. 53.

39. *Ibid.*, p. 83.

40. One of Castro's main motivations in life was revenge. One of the very first things people discovered in early 1959 was, as Ruby Hart Phillips, the *New York Times* correspondent in Cuba put it, "the ruthlessness and vindictiveness of the new government." She also wrote that "What surprised me most was the vindictiveness of Castro and his fanatical followers. I had never considered this a characteristic of the Cuban people." See Ruby Hart Phillips, *The Cuban Dilemma* (New York: Ivan Obolensky, 1962), pp. 15, 23.

Ms. Phillips was right. Cubans are not a vindictive people. Proof of this is the generosity of Cubans toward the defeated Spaniards after the war. But Fidel Castro was not a typical Cuban.

41. Effeminate homosexuals (*maricones*) have always occupied a special place in Fidel Castro's shit list, and calling somebody a *maricón* (faggot) was his ultimate verbal abuse. At least on two occasions, first to Panamá's General Omar Torrijos, and several years later to Spain's Prime Minister Felipe González, he sent his special envoy, writer Gabriel García Márquez, to deliver a personal message to the target of his anger. The message was a very short one, and García Márquez delivered it *verbatim*: "*Dice Fidel que usted es un maricón.*" ("Fidel says that you are a faggot."). See Norberto Fuentes, *Dulces guerreros cubanos* (Barcelona: Seix Barral, 1999) pp. 200-202. For the repression of homosexuals in Castro's Cuba and their imprisonment in concentration camps see my book *The Secret Fidel Castro: Deconstructing the Symbol* (Oakland, California: InteliBooks, 2001), pp. 222-225.

42. This was not new. In September 26, 1960, in an address to the UN General Assembly, Castro already had called Kennedy "an illiterate and ignorant millionaire." http://www.un.org/ga/search/view_doc.asp?symbol=A/PV.872, p. 130.

43. During the Cuban missile crisis President Kennedy created the Executive Committee of the National Security Council, later abbreviated as "ExComm."

44. Theodore C. Sorensen, *Kennedy* (New York: Konecky & Konecky, 1965), p. 802.

45. "When Castro Heard the News," The *New Republic*, Vol. 149, No. 23 (December 7, 1963), pp. 7-9.

46. Castro's *l'Express* interview with Daniel in Thomas G. Buchanan,

Who Killed Kennedy? (New York: MacFadden, 1965), pp. 15-16.
47. Frank Mankiewicz and Kirby Jones, *With Fidel* (New York: Ballantine, 1975), pp. 140-148.
48. Robert Sam Anson, *"They've Killed the President!"* (New York: Bantam, 1975), pp. 264-265.
49. Mark Falcoff, "How to Think about Cuban-American Relations," in Irving Louis Horowitz, ed., *Cuban Communism, Fifth Edition* (New Brunswick, N.J.: Transaction Books, 1984), p. 547.
50. Mario Lazo, *op. cit.,* p. 182.
51. Blakey and Billings, *op. cit.,* pp. 145-146.
52. Amanda Cochran, "JFK book makes startling revelation: Fidel Castro questioned by Warren Commission," *CBS News* October 25, 2013, https://www.cbsnews.com/news/jfk-book-makes-startling-revelation-fidel-castro-questioned-by-warren-commission/
53. Mankiewicz and Jones, *op. cit.,* pp. 140-148.
54. Speech to the U.N. General Assembly, September 26, 1960, reproduced in Martin Kenner and James Petras, eds., *Fidel Castro Speaks* (New York: Grove Press, 1969), p. 30.
55. Daniel Schorr, "Oswald as Avenger," *The Washington Post*, November 25, 1983, https://www.washingtonpost.com/archive/politics/1983/11/25/oswald-as-avenger/cc9ab63e-8aeb-4ca9-8b41-15be6dc85830/?utm_term=.affb4bf5d426
56. Early in November 1960, six months before the invasion took place, Castro and Major Félix Duque had carefully inspected the Bay of Pigs area. See Peter Wyden, *The Bay of Pigs* (New York: Simon and Schuster, 1979), p. 104.
57. A typical case of this is Gen. Edward Lansdale openly telling during a meeting with JFK and his boss Allen Dulles that the invasion was to fail. According to a witness, after Lansdale listened to Allen's unrealistic plans for the invasion to land at the Bay of Pigs swamps, he could not remain silent and said: "We're going to get clobbered." Dullles cut Lansdale off and told him harshly to shut his mouth: "You are not a principal in this!" After the meeting broke off, Dulles took Lansdale aside and ordered him to be "discreet" about his negative assessments, "as a favor for past favors." See Cecil B. Currey, *Edward Lansdale: The Unquiet American* (Boston: Houghton Mifflin, 1988), pp. 211-2112.
   In 1963 Dulles had written to Gen. Curtis LeMay, who didn't know Lansdale, "suggesting" him to promote Lansdale to Major General.
58. Patrick Oppman, "Fidel Castro Survived 600 Assassination Attempts, Officials Say," *CNN*, November 26, 2016. http://www.cnn.com/2016/08/

12/americas/cuba-fidel-castro-at-90-after-assassination-plots/

59. Fabián Escalante, *Executive Action: 634 Ways to Kill Fidel Castro* (Melbourne: Ocean Press, 2006).

60. Due to the fact that all CIA's alleged attempts on Castro's life may have failed not because of his extremely good luck, but because of other reasons, I have not mentioned them. I, for one, take those Castro-CIA assassination stories with a grain of salt. In the world of intelligence and espionage things are seldom as they seem.

61. Desmond Fitzgerald was the CIA's chief of the Cuban Task Force who since 1962 supervised some of the alleged failed attempts on Castro's life. As a way of payment for his good job, in 1965 Fitzgerald was promoted to CIA's Deputy Director of Plans (covert operations).

62. See Taylor Branch and John Rothchild, "The Incident," *Squire*, March 1977, p. 57. http://archive.esquire.com/issue/19770301

63. Tracy Wilkinson, "Eden Pastora, a Sandinista Hero Who Broke With His," *UPI*, May 16, 1986. https://www.upi.com/Archives/1986/05/16/Eden-Pastora-a-Sandinista-hero-who-broke-with-his/8371516600000/

64. For Castro's powers of fascination see, Servando Gonzalez, *The Secret Fidel Castro: Deconstructing the Symbol* (Oakland, California: InteliBooks, 2001), pp. 33-45.

65. Harry R. Haldeman, *The Ends of Power* (New York: Times Books, 1978), p. 39.

66. *Ibid.*

67. Dave Davies, "The Final Documents on JFK's Assassination Are Being Declassified," *NPR*,'s *Fresh Air* interview with Philip Shenon, August 10, 2017, http://www.npr.org/2017/08/10/542531879/the-final-documents-on-jfk-s-assassination-are-being-declassified

68. Paul G. Kengor, "Remembering an Unknown Hero: Morris Childs, America's Greatest Cold War Spy, " *The Center for Vision and Values*, Grove City College, December 15, 2008, http://www.visionandvalues.org/2008/12/remembering-an-unknown-hero-morris-childs-americas-greatest-cold-war-spy/

69. John Newman, *Oswald and the CIA* (New York: Carroll & Graf, 1985), pp. 427-430.

70. Seth Cantor, *The Ruby Cover-Up* (New York: Zebra, 1978), pp. 249-252.

71. *Ibid.*, pp. 261-262.

72. George Crile III, "The Mafia, the CIA, and Castro," the *Washington Post*, May 16, 1976, C4.

73. Mark Riebling, *Wedge* (New York: Knopf, 1994), p. 171.

74. *Ibid.*, pp. 171-172.

75 .*The New York Times*, March 17, 1977, A23.

76. House Assassinations Committee Report, 173, and House Assassinations Committee, *Hearings*, Vol. 5, 345-48, 373-77.

77. *Alleged Assassination Plots Involving Foreign Leaders*, U.S. Senate, November 20, 1975, 94th Congress, 1st Session, pp. 60-61; also blind memo, 12/2/63, CIA FOIA #1384-491-B.

78. *Ibid.*, pp. 60-61.

79. Henry Hurt, *Reasonable Doubt* (New York: Holt, Rinehart and Winston, 1985), pp. 421-422.

80. James Johnston, "Did Cuba Murder JFK?" *The Washington Post*, November 19, 1989, p. D-5.

81. Riebling, *Op. Cit.*, p. 203

82. Daniel Schorr, "Oswald as Avenger," *The Washington Post*, November 25, 1983, https://www.washingtonpost.com/archive/politics/1983/11/25/oswald-as-avenger/cc9ab63e-8aeb-4ca9-8b41-15be6dc85830/?utm_term=.affb4bf5d426

83. *Ibid.*

84. Grayston Lynch, a former CIA agent in Florida, told Gus Russo, "The AM/LASH plot was known to Castro. We believed Cubela was a double agent." See Russo, *Live by the Sword* (Baltimore: Bancroft Press, 1998), p. 242.

85. A memorandum of the meeting of the Special Committee concluding that attacks on U.S. officials were unlikely was furnished to the Select Committee of the United States Senate to Study Government Operations, which published parts of it in its final report in 1976.

86. *The New York Times*, October 8, 1963.

87. Tony de la Guardia commanded a group of professional assassins. He jokingly called them "the *killers*," using the word "killers" in English. Tony belonged to an upper middle-class Cuban family and had been educated in the U.S. See Norberto Fuentes, *Dulces Guerreros Cubanos* (Barcelona: Seix Barral, 1999), p. 90.

88. *Foreign Broadcast Information Service*, "Report on Cuban Propaganda - No 12: Havana's Response to the Death of President Kennedy and Comment on the New Administration," December 31, 1963; also Neil A. Lewis, "Documents Indicate Cuban Forces Were Put on Alert After Kennedy Assassination," *The New York Times*, August 20, 1997; and George Lander, Jr., "Castro 'Frightened' After JFK Killing," *The Washington Post*, August 20, 1997, p. A9.

Chapter 12

1. John Newman, *Oswald and the CIA* (New York: Carroll & Graf), 1995.
2. Philip H. Melanson, *Spy Saga: Lee Harvey Oswald and U.S. Intelligence* (New York: Praeger, 1990).
3. This is the case of Edward Jay Epstein's book *Legend: The Secret World of Lee Harvey Oswald,* a book I consider a very unreliable source, particularly in relation to Angleton.
4. Ron Rosenbaum, "The Shadow of the Mole," *Harper's*, October, 1983; Seymour Hersh, "Angleton: The Cult of Counterintelligence," *The New York Times Magazine*, June 25, 1978; Edward Jay Epstein, *Deception: The Invisible War Between the KGB and the CIA*; David C. Martin, *Wilderness of Mirrors*; Tom Mangold, *Cold Warrior: James Jesus Angleton: The CIA's Master Spy Hunter*; William Hood, *Mole*; David Wise, *Molehunt: The Secret Search for Traitors That Shattered the CIA*; and, most recently, Jefferson Morley, *The Ghost,* just to mention a few.
5. Aaron Latham, *Orchids for Mother*; Robert Littell, *The Company*; and William F. Buckley *Spytime.*
6. *The Good Shepherd*, starring Robert DeNiro, and *The Company*, starring Michael Keaton, both of them loosely based on Littell's novel *The Company*. Unfortunately, Littell, otherwise an excellent writer of spy fiction, painted a very unrealistic picture of Angleton in this novel and took too many freedoms in dealing with well-known facts.
7. During the secret preparations for the invasion of Normandy, British Premier Winston Churchill said: "In wartime, truth is so precious that she should always be attended by a bodyguard of lies." During a radio broadcast in October 1939 he said: "I cannot forecast to you the action of Russia. It is a riddle, wrapped in a mystery, inside an enigma."
8. Martin, *op. cit.*, p. 204.
9. Dulles and Angleton kept their association after the OSS was dissolved and before Dulles was appointed CIA director. This explains Angleton's role in the Bogotazo.
10. The CIA's *Family Jewels* is the name commonly used to refer to a set of reports about illegal activities conducted by the CIA over the span of close to three decades, from the 1950s to the mid-1970s. The reports were compiled with the authorization of William Colby, CIA director in the mid-1970s, who helped in the compilation of the reports. In order to understand Colby's behavior one must keep in mind that, despite the fact that he had become a CFR member, he was never accepted in its inner

circles. Colby was a trusted man with impeccable OSS credentials, but he had humble origins and was not part of the Old Boys club. In April 27, 1996, Colby, already retired, died under suspicious circumstances.

11. Given the fact that Angleton got his marching orders from Allen Dulles, and that Dulles got his orders from David Rockefeller, it is safe to deduce that operation Chaos was a creation of the Rockefellers and their CFR lackeys. We must keep in mind that the Vietnam War was a boon for the warmongering military-industrial-banking-complex.

12. Oswald was one of a series of former U.S. military members who had defected to the Soviet Union between 1958 and 1960. Some of them had been "turned" by the Soviets; others, Oswald among them, appear to have accomplished their CIA mission. See John Newman, *Ibid.*, pp.169–73, 182–90.

13. Joan Mellen, "Who Was Lee Harvey Oswald." http://www.maryferrell.org/pages/Essay_-_Who_Was_Lee_Harvey_Oswald.html

14. The most complete information on Oswald working for the CIA is in John Newman, *Oswald and the CIA* (New York: Carroll and Graf, 1995). For information about how the CIA used Oswald as a patsy and fall guy, see, Joan Mellen, "Who Was Lee Harvey Oswald?" a lecture given during the symposium Making Sense of the Sixties at the Hecht Institute, October 5, 2008, http://www.maryferrell.org/wiki/index.php/Essay_-_Who_Was_Lee_Harvey_Oswald.

15. Newman, *op. cit.*, p. 43.

16. *Ibid.*

17. After Gary Powers' U-2 was shot down over the Soviet Union — most likely as the result of Pentagon-CIA sabotage — the price of shares of arms manufacturing companies rose sharply on the New York Stock Exchange, and government military-contract awards increased substantially. Just two months after the incident, the Eisenhower administration allocated the biggest military appropriations ever approved at that time, $48,300 million for fiscal 1960-61. See V. Cherniavsky, "U.S. Intelligence and the Monopolies," *International Affairs* (January 1965). In the same fashion, the U.S. defense budget for the fiscal year that began July 1, 1962, was $56.6 billion. Of these, $15.4 billion was designated for purchasing new weapons, $11.5 billion to operations and maintenance, and $6.7 billion to research and development. In the decade of mid-1953 to mid-1963, the U.S. spent more than $400 billion in defense. See, *U.S. News and World Report*, October 8, 1962, p. 50. Fear has always been good for business, and everybody knows that the business of America is

business.

18. L. Fletcher Prouty, "The Sabotaging of the American Presidency," https://ratical.org/ratville/JFK/SAP.html#begin

19. Church Committee Deposition, 9/17/75, p. 16.

20. Newman, *op. cit.* pp. 6, 38

21. Lisa Pease, "This Was One of Those Occasions," *Probe*, July-August, 2000 (Vol. 7, No. 5), http://www.ctka.net/pr700-ang.html.

22. A CIA internal memorandum declassified in 1976 proves that, while conducting investigations for the Warren Commission, Allen Dulles secretly met with a CIA officer (most likely Angleton) sent by Deputy Director Richard Helms, during which Dulles instructed that all allegations that Oswald was connected to the CIA must be refuted with straightforward language "which made clear that Lee Harvey Oswald was never an employee of the CIA." See Melanson, *op. cit.*, p. 131.

23. Dr. Locard's principle quoted in Zakaria Erzinclioglu, *Every Contact Leaves a Trace: Scientific Detection in the Twentieth Century* (London: Carlton, 2001), p. 10.

24. García Márquez story in Juan Carlos Gaitán Villegas, "El misterioso elegante del 9 de abril," *El Tiempo*, Bogotá, February 26, 2003.

25. Sir Norman Smith, Scotland Yard Report, pp. 9-10. www.intelinet.org/sg_site/Scotland_Yard_Report.htm. Angleton's physical description in Tom Mangold, *Cold Warrior: James Jesus Angleton: The CIA's Master Spy Hunter* (New York: Touchstone, 1991), p. 31.

Some time after the riots, the Colombian government asked the British Scotland Yard to conduct an impartial invertigation of the assassination of Gaitán and the Bogotazo riots. The Report is quite interesting because it revealed some very important information about the activities of Castro and del Pino purposedly kept hidden by the local investigators.

26. According to Tom Mangold, Angleton "was rarely photographed in public." Mangold, *op. cit.*, p. 31.

27. *Ibid.*

28. *Ibid.*, pp. 32, 359.

29. *Ibid.*, p. 44.

30. *Ibid.*, p. 361.

31. *Ibid.*

32. Nina Burleigh, "The Mysterious Murder of Mary Pinchot Meyer — Revisited," *The Daily Beast*, April 2, 2002, http://www.thedailybeast.com/the-mysterious-murder-of-mary-pinchot-meyerrevisited

33. Philip Shenon, "Why did the CIA's Angleton want to cut off ques-

tions about Oswald?" jfkfacts.org, http://jfkfacts.org/cias-angleton-want-cut-off-questions-oswald/
34. *Ibid.*
35. Arturo Abella, *Así fue el 9 de abril* (Bogotá: Ediciones Aqu' Bogotá, 1973), p. 19.
36. Guillermo Tovar, "Nueva visión del crimen de Jorge Eliécer Gaitán que partió en dos la historia del país," *Colombia.com*, April 10, 2006, http://www.colombia.com/entretenimiento/noticias/DetalleNoticia3951.asp.
37. *Ibid.*, p. 598.
38. Smith, Scotland Yard Report, p. 8.
39. Posner's book is probably one of the most asinine ever written about the JFK assassination — unless he was actually trying to get an invitation to join the CFR.
40. Judyth Vary Baker, "David Ferrie: Mafia Pilot, Participant in Anti-Castro Bioweapon Plot, Friend of Lee Harvey Oswald and Key to the JFK Assassination," http://www.thesecrettruth.com/davidferriebook.pdf
41 FBI Interview of David Ferrie, November 25, 1963 & November 27, 1963, Warren Commission Document 75, pp. 285–297, 199–200.
42. Dick Russell, *The Man Who Knew Too Much* (News York: Carroll and Graf, 1992).
43. William Tuner, *The Assassination of Robert Kennedy: The Conspiracy and Coverup* (New York: Thunder's Mouth, 1993).
44. *Ibid.*, p. 196-198.
45. See, John Marks, *The Search for the Manchurian Candidate: The CIA and Mind Control* (New York: McGraw-Hill, 1980).
46. Everything indicates that Sirhan Bishara Sirhan, Robert Kennedy's alleged assassin, was also both a patsy and a Manchurian candidate.
47. See "CIA Documents Tell of 1954 Project to Create Involuntary Assassins," *The New York Times*, February 9, 1978, p. A17.

As early as September 1942 the OSS had begun experimenting with mind control, searching for a drug that would force men under interrogation, such as captured Nazi submarine crews, to reveal secrets. On May 1943, OSS officers used THC acetate to obtain information from a subject. They referred to the THC acetate simply as "TD," a cryptonym for "Truth Drug." See "The Evolution of an Assassin: A Clinical Study of Lee Harvey Oswald," *Life*, February 21, 1964, p. 72.

But it was not until 1947, after the creation of the CIA, that the Navy's Project CHATTER initiated the United States first serious foray into truth serums. In 1949, the CIA began project BLUEBIRD using Nazi scientists to find a truth serum. Project BLUEBIRD evolved into Project ARTI-CHOKE and eventually into MK-ULTRA. Project MK-ULTRA was much larger in scope, focusing on mind control and the means to achieve it, was not limited to drugs and psychedelics. MK-ULTRA experiments included using hypnosis, lobotomy, electroshock, sensory deprivation, ESP, and drugs experiments and sexual abuse. These subjects are described in detail in Marks, *op. cit.*

Chapter 13

1. Most pro-Castro authors who have studied the Assassination of President Kennedy always include anti-Castro Cubans among the possible culprits. Nevertheles, even if some anti-Castro Cubans may have played a minor role in the opertion, given the fact that they were fully under the CIA's tight control, they should be considered as CIA-agents.

On the other hand, it is difficult to understand how anti-Castro Cubans in the U.S. who, according to some Cuban officials, failed in nearly 600 attempts to assassinate Castro, were so successful in their first attempt to assassinate Kennedy. See Patrick Oppmann, "Fidel Castro Survived 600 Assassination Attempts, Officials Say," *CNN*, November 26, 2016, http://www.cnn.com/2016/08/12/americas/cuba-fidel-castro-at-90-after-assassination-plots/index.html

2. Donald Gibson, *The Kennedy Assassination Cover-Up* (San Diego, California: Progressive Press, 1999-2014), p. 236.

3. Dan Smoot, *The Invisible Government* (Boston: Western Islands, 1965). The book was initially published in 1962 by the Dan Smoot Report. Also, David Wise and Thomas B. Ross, *The Invisible Government* (New York: Bantam, 1962).

4. The logical positivist philosophers believed that all differences between people arise either from using the same name to denote two different things or using different names to denote the same thing. Even though I don't think that all differences are just semantic, I think that in this case the logical positivists were right.

5. Emanuel Josephson, *Rockefeller "Internationalist" : The Man Who Misrules the World* (New York: Chedney Press, 1952).

6. *Ibid.*, p. 237.

7. *Ibid.*, p. 245.

8. Dan Smoot, *The Invisible Government* (Boston: Western Islands, 1962).

9. *Ibid.*, p. 3.

10. John Stormer, *None Dare Call it Treason* (Florissant, Missouri: Liberty Bell Press, 1964).

11. Gary Allen, *None Dare Call it Conspiracy* (Rossmoor, California: Concord Press, 1972).

12. Phoebe Courtney, *The CFR, Part II* (Littleton, Colorado: The Independent American,1975).

13. Woodrow Wilson, *The New Freedom* (New York: Doubleday, Page and Co., 1931), pp. 13-14.

14. Do not confuse Smoot's book with another book with the same title written by David Wise and Thomas B. Ross. These authors believed that the Invisible Goventment was actually the CIA. As you have seen in this book, the CIA is justg a tool of the Invisible Government.

15. See, i.e., Evan Gahr, "Looking at Philanthropy: The Gift of Giving: Paymasters of the PC Brigades," *The Wall Street Journal*, January 27, 1995; Bob Feldman, "Alternative Media Censorship: Sponsored by CIA's Ford Foundation?," *Disinfo.com*, September 18, 2002, http://old.disinfo.com/archive/pages/article/ id2709/pg1/index.html; Joyce Price, "Media Give Liberal Causes Millions More, Study Says," *The Washington Times*, Nov. 14. 1993; Marshall Robinson, "The Ford Foundation: Sowing the Seeds of a Revolution," *Environment*, v. 35 n. 3 (April 1993), 10-20; Goldie Blumenstyk, "New Head of Ford Fund's Education Program is Champion of Women and Minority Students," *The Chronicle of Higher Education*, v. 39 n. 16 (Dec 9, 1992), A27; Daniel Brandt, "Philanthropists at War," *NameBase NewsLine*, No. 15 (October-December, 1996).

The fact perhaps may explain why the American Left is one of the most reactionary leftist movements in the world. Nevertheless, they see themselves as "progressives." I call them "regressives."

16. Dinesh D'Souza, "The 'Anti-Fascist' Fascist," *The Daily Caller*, July 31, 2017, http://dailycaller.com/2017/07/31/the-anti-fascist-fascist/

17. Termination with extreme prejudice: CIA euphemism for assassination.

18. According to author Peter Dale Scott, Angleton created a "second CIA within the CIA." Peter Dale Scott, *Deep Politics and the Death of JFK* (Berkeley, California: University of California Press, 1993), p. 54. This statement, however, is not only naïve but also not true. Angleton was a tool of Allen Dulles, who was himself a tool of David Rockefeller, the one who created a CIA within the CIA when the National Security

Council illegally passed NSC 10/2 authorizing the Agency to conduct covert operations.

19. I always refer to whatever happened on September 11, 2001 as "the 9/11 *events*," because I am not convinced that a foreign terrorist "attack" ever took place that day. For a good introduction at what really happened that fateful day see the monumental chronology created by Paul Thomson, *The Terror Timeline* (New York: Harper, 2004). For a critical analysis of the 9/11 events see Webster Griffin Tarpley, *9/11 Synthetic Terror Made in USA* (Joshua Tree, California: Progressive Press, 2006); also David Ray Griffin, (ed.), *9/11 and American Empire* (Northampton, Massachusetts: Olive Branch, 2007).

20. The only exception was Allen Dulles, and we know what happened to President Kennedy for firing him.

21. For recent examples of how unethical CIA analysts have wittingly cooked the books to produce erroneous intelligence estimates to please their bosses, see Melvin A. Goodman, *Failure of Intelligence: The Decline and Fall of the CIA* (Lanham, Maryland: Rowman and Littlefield, 2008), pp. 93, 136, 183.

22. William Blum, *Killing Hope* (Monroe, ME: Common courage Press, 2003).

23. CFR honcho Allen Dulles callously called them "the disposal problem," as if they were trash to get rid of. See Peter Wyden, *The Bay of Pigs* (New York: Simon and Schuster, 1979), p. 100.

24. Burton Hersh, *The Old Boys: The American Elite and the Origins of the CIA* (St. Petersburg, Florida: Tree Farm, 2002), p. 418.

25. LBJ, Allen Dulles, and other CFR members repeatedly expressed this concern. Actually, as I explained in detail in my book *The Nuclear Hoax: Nikita Khrushchev and the Cuban Missile Crisis*, the reason why the Soviet Premier placed the dummy missiles on Cuban soil was to provoke the Americans to invade Cuba to do for him the dirty job of overthrowing Castro. After the U.S. had invaded Cuban and overthrown Castro, Khrushchev would have gone to the U.N. and strongly protested blaming American imperialists for it, but he had inherited Fidelism without the troublesome Fidel the same way some years later Castro inherited Guevarism without the troublesome Che Guevara.

26. Giancana's evaluation of Castro in Roselli's deposition to the Church Committee, quoted in Gus Russo, *Live by the Sword* (Baltimore: Bancroft Press, 1998), p. 523, n. 19.

27. Wet affairs (*mokrie dela*), KGB euphemism for assassination.

28. Edward McCarthy, *Working Press*, pp. 9-19, quoted in Gus Russo,

op. cit., p. 228. See also Lucia Newman, "In Rare Admission, Castro Says Cuba has Dispatched Spies Across U.S.," *CNN*, October 20, 1998.
29. A notable exception is Gus Russo's *Live by the Sword* (Baltimore: Bancroft Press, 1998). Russo's book brought out a wealth of new information about Castro's attempts to kill JFK that cannot be ignored.
30. According to a U.S. Justice Department source, the FBI and the CIA were investigating the possibility that Castro was plotting to use his agents in the U.S. to kill both President Ford and his Republican presidential contender Ronald Reagan in August, 1976. An FBI informer told the Bureau that San Francisco Bay Area radicals of the Emiliano Zapata terrorist group, in coordination with Andrés Gómez, a Castro agent, had plans to kill both men. See Daryl Lempke, "Cuban Spy Link to Ford, Reagan Death Plot Probed," *The Los Angeles Times*, March 19, 1976.
31 Steven Edwards, "Oppressors Running for U.N. Rights Council, *Ottawa Citizen National Post,* May 6, 2009, https://www.unwatch.org/issue-191-un-watch-releases-report-human-rights-council-candidates/
32. After his regime was condemned at the 2000 meeting of the U.N. Human Rights Commission in Geneva, Castro began uttering strong epithets, accusations and even veiled threats against the leaders of the countries that voted against him. See "Castro insulta y se aísla del continente," *El Nuevo Herald*, April 29, 2001.
33. For revealing details about John F. Kennedy's involvement in political assassination see Seymour Hersh, *The Dark Side of Camelot* (New York: Little, Brown and Company, 1997), particularly Chapter 13, Executive Action. Like Castro, John F. Kennedy was never worried about the ethical or moral issues involving political assassination, only about how to do it without getting caught.
34. Senate Select Committee to Study Governmental Operations with Respect to Intelligence Activities, *Alleged Assassination Plots Involving Foreign Leaders: An Interim Report*, 94th Congress, 1st sess., November 20, 1975, p. 138.
35. David Rockefeller, *Memoirs*, p. 222.
36. *Ibid*, p. 405.
37. Lawrence Shoup and Willliam Minter, *Imperial Brain Trust (*New York: Monthly Review Press, 1977), p. 42.
38. Andrew Glass. "Fidel Castro Visits the U.S., April 15, 1959," Politico.com, April 15, 2013, http://www.politico.com/story/2013/04/this-day-in-politics-april-15-1959-090037.
39. Peter Collier and David Horowitz, *Deconstructing the Left: From Vietnam to the Persian Gulf* (Studio City, California: Second Thoughts,

1991), p. 98.

40. Pascal Fletcher "U.S. Policy Experts Encouraged by Talks in Cuba," *Reuters* (Havana), February 18, 2001.

41. Arthur M. Schlesinger, Jr., *Robert Kennedy and His Times* (New York: Houghton Mifflin, 1978), p. 695.

42. *Ibid.*

43. For a description of how the CFR Mafia controls the media, see Denis W. Mazzoco, *Networks of Power: Corporate TV's Threat to Democracy* (Boston, Massachusetts: South End, 1994); Michael Parenti, *Inventing Reality: The Politics of Mass Media* (New York: St. Martin's Press, 1986). Also, James R. Bennett, *Control of the Media in the United States: An Annotated Bibliography* (New York: Garland, 1992).

44. See Antony Sutton, *Wall Street and the Rise of Hitler* (Seal Beach, California: '76 Press, 1976); also Charles Higham, *Trading With The Enemy: An Exposé of the Nazi-American Money Plot, 1933-1949* (New York: Delacorte Press, 1983).

45. See, i.e., Emanuel M. Josephson, *The Truth About Rockefeller: "Public Enemy No. 1"* (New York: Chedney Press, 1964), in which he expresses his theory that Nelson Rockefeller was a criminal psychopath. Another author who studied the Rockefellers' sociopathy is Ferdinand Lundberg in his book *The Rockefeller Syndrome* (New York: Kensington Publishing, 1975).

46. Operation Keelhaul at the end of WWII, Operation Phoenix in Vietnam, the killing of thousands of civilians during the invasion of Panama, and the unnecessary killing of thousands of defeated Iraqi soldiers on the so-called "highway of death" during the Gulf War, are some of the most notorious war crimes committed by this criminal Mafia, but not the only ones.

47. One exception to the rule is Fidel Castro, who was both a sociopath and a psychopath. Contrary to Nelson and David, Castro has killed many people with his own hands. See, Servando Gonzalez. *The Secret Fidel Castro: Deconstructing the Symbol* (Oakland, California: Spook Books, 2001), pp. 105-118.

48 Robert Hare, *Without Conscience* (New York: Simon & Schuser, 1994).

49. Kevin Barrett, "David Rockefeller dies—link to JFK assassination exposed!," *VeteransToday*.com, March 20, 2017, https://www.veteranstoday.com/2017/03/20/rockefeller/

Epilogue

1. In April 2000, David Rockefeller and a select group his CFR minions visited Castro's Communo-Fascist Cuba. After the visit, they told the press that Castro's Cuba was the social and economic model to follow. Unknowingly, they were showing their hand as to what they have in mind for America to become. See Pascal Fletcher "U.S. Policy Experts Encouraged by Talks in Cuba," *Reuters* (Havana), February 18, 2001. See also Paul Joseph Watson, "Austerity Fascism Is Coming And It Will Be Brutal," *PrisonPlanet.com*, June 8, 2010, http:// www.prisonplanet.com/austerity-fascism-is-coming-and-it-will-be-brutal.html

2. See Servando Gonzalez, *Barry Soetoro (a.k.a. Barack Hussein Obama): The Puppet and His Puppeteers* (Hayward, California: Spooks Books, 2016).

3. David Rockefeller gave this speech to the 1991 Bilderberg meeting and it was later leaked to the French press. It first appeared in the June 1991 issue of the French weekly *Minute* and later in the July-August 1991 issue of *Lectures Francaises*. Following the non-written rule, however, the American media ignored it. This explains why David thanked them for their complicity of silence.

4. Executive action: CIA euphemism for assassination following orders from the highest levels of the Invisible Government of the U.S.

5. Jim Garrison, closing speech at the trial of Clay Shaw (28th February, 1969), http://spartacus-educational.com/JFKgarrison.htm

6. You may read Brewster's article at https://www.foreignaffairs.com/ articles/united-states/1972-04-01/reflections-our-national-purpose

7. *Ibid.*

8. President John F. Kennedy Washington, D.C. January 20, 1961, https:/ /www.jfklibrary.org/Research/Research-Aids/Ready-Reference/JFK-Fast-Facts/Inaugural-Address.aspx

9. *Ibid.*

10. *Ibid.*

11. See Ted Sorensen, "JFK's inaugural address was world-changing" *The Guardian*, April 22, 2007, https://www.theguardian.com/ theguardian/2007/apr/22/greatspeeches1

12. John F. Kennedy, "Foreign Aid," *House Documents, 87th Congress,*

1st Session, Doc. No. 117, Washington, D.C.: Government Printing Office.

13. Remarks of Senator John F. Kennedy in the Senate, February 19, 1959, *John F. Kennedy Presidential Library and Museum,* https://www.jfklibrary.org/Research/Research-Aids/JFK-Speeches/United-States-Senate-Economic-Gap_19590219.aspx

14. President John F. Kennedy, Commencement Address at AmericanUniversity, Washington, D.C., June 10, 1963, http://www.presidency.ucsb.edu/ws/?pid=9266

15. Early in July 1955, at a closed plenum of the Central Committee of the Communist Party, Premier Khrushchev laid out the new goals of Soviet policy. He solidified this concept of a new approach in Soviet foreign policy in 1956 at the 20th Congress of the Communist Party of the Soviet Union, and again at the Party's 21th Congress, held in Moscow from January 25 to February 5, 1959. This new policy was later known as his "Doctrine of Peaceful Coexistence," accompanied by the slogan "To catch up and overtake the West" in economic well-being, and an improvement in the Soviet Union's internal affairs.

16. Lyman B. Kirkpatrick, Jr., *The Real CIA* (New York: McMillan, 1968), p. 261.

17. Kennedy's words about splintering the CIA quoted in Taylor Branch and George Crile, "The Kennedy Vendetta," *Harper's*, August 1975, p. 50. Nevertheless, some researchers have questioned the veracity of the quote. See, i.e., Matt Novak "The Real Story About That JFK Quote About Destroying the CIA," *Gizmodo*, March 3, 2017, https://paleofuture.gizmodo.com/the-story-behind-that-jfk-quote-about-destroying-the-ci-1793151211

18. There is strong evidence that the whole chemical attack on the Syrian people by its own government was a fabrication, part of a CIA PsyOp to justify U.S. military intervention in Syria on behalf of some transnational oil corporations who wanted to stop the construction of new oil pipelines in the country.

19. Javier De Diego and Jamie Gangel, "Bush 41 Calls Trump a 'blowhard,' White House Strikes Back," *CNNpolitics*, November 5, 2017, http://www.cnn.com/2017/11/04/politics/the-last-republicans-bush-book/index.html

20. Listen to Trump's full the speech at https://www.youtube.com/watch?v=qjVWpmk2a1Y

21. According to some analysts, the main reason why the "No" won the

plebiscite was because of the several mentions of special treatment for LGBT people. See Nicholas Casey, "Colombian Opposition to Peace Deal Feeds Off Gay Rights Backlash." *The New York Times*, October 8, 2016. The initial document allegedly was created in Cuba but, given the fact that the LGTB has become a 5th-column for the globalists' New World Order, one may safely assume that it was actually written at the Counil on Foreign Relations.

22. See Robert Jonathan, "President Obama Creating an Anti-Trump Shadow Government, Author Ed Klein Claims," Inquisitr.com, December 19, 2016, http://www.inquisitr.com/3812099/president-obama-creating-an-anti-trump-shadow-government-author-ed-klein-claims/.

23. Sydney Schamberg, "The War Secrets Senator John McCain Hides," in Russ Kick (ed.), *The Disinformation Guide to Media Distortion, Historical Whitewashes and Cultural Myths* (New York: The Disinformation Company, 2001), pp. 88-94.

24. In 1956 FBI Director J. Edgar Hoover (not a CFR member) received hundreds of letters from concerned citizens and members of Congress, accusing the Council on Foreign Relations of treason and promoting communism through its agents infiltrated in the U.S. government. Hoover ordered an investigation but, soon after, President Eisenhower (CFR) dictated an order prohibiting the FBI from investigating federal government employees. For the whole story see "Warning! How the FBI's Criminal-Espionage Investigation of the CFR Was Foiled," http://www.whale.to/c/fbiinvestigation.pdf

25. Robert Morrow. "Jeb Bush, Oliver North and the Murder of CIA Drug Smuggler Barry Seal in 1986," *Daily Kos.com,* May 13, 2013. http://www.dailykos.com/story/2013/04/03/1199001/-Jeb-Bush-Oliver-North-and-the-Murder-of-CIA-Drug-Smuggler-Barry-Seal-in-1986.

26. On George Marshall's treachery see Senator Joseph R. McCarthy, *America's Retreat from Victory: The Story of George Catlett Marshall* (Boston: Western Islands, 1965).

27. On Eisenhower's treachery see Robert Welch, *The Politician* (Belmont, Mass.: Privately Printed, 1963).

28. On Kissinger's treachery see Phyllis Schlafly and Chester Ward, *Kissinger on the Couch* (New Rochelle, N.Y.: Arlington House, 1975).

29. A November 29, 1963, memorandum from FBI Director J. Edgar Hoover to the Director of the Bureau of Intelligence and Research at the Department of State refers to the fact that information on the assassination of President Kennedy was "orally furnished to Mr. George Bush of

the Central Intelligence Agency." http://jfkmurdersolved.com/bush3.htm
30. According to Castro-admirer Jesse Ventura, "John F. Kennedy was murdered by a conspiracy involving disgruntled CIA agents, anti-Castro Cubans, and members of the Mafia." Jesse Ventura, *They Killed Our President* (New York: Skyhorse Publishing, 2013), p. xii. In his book *Brothers: The Hidden History of the Kennedy Years* (New York: Free Press, 2007). David Talbot, another Castro admirer, arrived at a similar conclusion. Nevertheless, as *bona fide* Castro admirers, both Talbot and Ventura failed to specify that, though some anti-Castro Cubans may have participated in the operation, they actually were naturalized American citizens and did it as CIA agents not as free-lance anti-Castro Cubans.

In is book *The Devil's Chessboard* (New York: Harper Perennial, 2015), Talbot raises the ante by expressing his admiration for Castro and Guevara because they have guns and also for shooting their opponents on the wall (p. 338). He fails to tell, though, that most of the people shot in the wall without a fair trial were farmers and small business owners who opposed Castro because he had stolen their properties.
31. Even though Angleton never appeared in the CFR membership roster, to all practical effects he was a secret member.
32. A typical example of money without power is Bill Gates. Though he had accumulated an enormous fortune, he was not interested in politics and had no real power. This explains why, after being threatened by the CFR conspirators with dismembering Microsoft, he saw the message on the wall, joined the CFR and, soon after, created the Bill and Melinda Gates Foundation. Its main goal, disguised under the banner of women's reproductive rights, is the depopulation of Africa and other Third World countries.
33. Though not an official CFR member, Hillary is a secret one. In a speech at the opening of the new CFR headquarters in Washington D.C. in July, 2009, she mentioned how she was delighted about having a CFR branch just across the street from the State Department, so "I won't need that far to go to be told how we should be doing and what we should think about the future." See "Hillary Clinton Admits CFR Control Over Government Policy," *Examiner.com*, July 21, 2008, www. examiner.com/article/hillary-clinton-admits-cfr-control-overgovernment- policy/
34. In 1974, CFR honcho Henry Kissinger's signed National Security Study Memorandum 200 delineating a policy of depopulation in Africa and the exploitation of the continent's natural resources. It was not a coincidence that, less than a year later, Castro launched his military action in Angola and other African countries.

35. After Kennedy fired him from his job as CIA Director, CFR agent Allen Dulles turned his Georgetown home into a sort of anti-Kennedy government in exile, planning for the overthrown of President Kennedy. See David Talbot, *The Devil's Chessboard* (New York: Harper Perennial, 2017), p. 7.

In the same fashion, after CFR asset Hillary Clinton lost the 2016 presidential election, CFR asset Barack Obama Obama has turned his enormous rented mansion in Washington D.C. into a sort of anti-Trump government in exile, "with a staff and lots of electronic communications gear, requiring the seizure of a quarter of a mile of a quiet residential street to be guarded by a Secret Service detail not much smaller than the platoon of heavily armed agents who kept him safe, sound and ready for action at 1600 Pennsylvania Avenue." See Wesley Prudent, "The Latest News From the President in Exile," *The Washington Times*, May 25, 2017, https://www.washingtontimes.com/news/2017/may/25/obama-attempts-government-in-exile/

So, it seems that, as the CFR conspirators used in the Kennedy assassination the same *modus operandi* they had used in the assassination of Gaitán, now they are planning to use against Trump the same *modus operandi* they used against Kennedy. They accused Kennedy of being a Communist and now are accusing Trump of being controlled by Moscow. Definitively, the CFR conspirators lack imagination.

36. Seemingly, "conservative" Republicans are very insecure people. Their strong fixation on the so-called "national security" has been very profitable for the military-industrial-banking complex. In their "conservative" eyes, any traitor who claims to be strong on national security issues gets their votes. Paradoxically, the more money we throw into the national security black hole the more insecure we are, because "national security" is nothing but a big hoax very similar to "global warming." Actually, national security is the "conservative" Right's equivalent of the "progressive" Left's global warming, and their Al Gore is John McCain.

37. See Servando Gonzalez, "Why I Hate Republicans (Including Tea Partiers), Even More Than I Hate Democrats," *Intelinet.org,* May 6, 2012, http://www.intelinet.org/sg_site/articles/sg_hate_republicans.html

38. Or perhaps he is so clever that we cannot even fathom his secret strategy.

39. You may find a good source of CFR treachery in my book *I Dare Call It Treason: The Council on Foreign Relations and the Betrayal of America.*

Appendix I

1. The *Salem Daily Capital Journal*, November 4th, 1915. Facsimile reproduced in http://truthstreammedia.com/2014/12/13/a-century-ago-rockefellers-funded-eugenics-initiative-to-sterilize-15-million-americans/. Rockefeller Jr. was referring to a play called "The Unborn," financed with Rockefeller money.

2. Cera R. Lawrence, "The Eugenics Record Officer at Cold Spring Harbor Laboratory (1910-1939)," *The Embrio Project Encyclopedia,* April 21, 2011, https://embryo.asu.edu/pages/eugenics-record-office-cold-spring-harbor-laboratory-1910-1939

3. After the discrediting of eugenics, the Cold Spring Harbor Laboratory became, with Rockefeller funding, the center of the Human Genomics Program.

4. Paul Lombardo, "Eugenic Sterilization Laws." *Eugenics Archive*, n.p., n.d., http://www.eugenicsarchive.org/html/eugenics/essay8text.html. Current programs for "women's reproductive care," a euphemism for wholesale abortion, are the modern version of the sterilization laws.

5. Edwin Black, "The Horrifying American Roots of Nazi Eugenics." *History News Network*. n.p., Sept. 2003. Web. 07 May 2014. http://hnn.us/article/1796

6. Bryan Nelson, "Was Genghis Khan history's greenest conqueror?," *MotherNatureNetwork*, Jan 24 2011, http://www.mnn.com/earth-matters/climate-weather/stories/was-genghis-khan-historys-greenest-conqueror.

7. *U.S. Senate, Committee of the Judiciary, Subcommittee to Investigate the Administration of Internal Security Act*, "Castro's Network in the United States," Hearing, 88th Congress, First Session, Part 6, February 8, 1963.

8. Jon Lee Anderson, *Che Guevara: A Revolutionary Life* (New York: Grove Press, 1997), p. 545.

9. *Verde Olivo*, December 22, 1968. An interesting detail is that, though Guevara wrote the editorial in 1962, it was not published until 1968, when the Cuban-Soviet differences over armed struggle had finally come out in the open.

10. *Granma Weekly Review*, December 22, 1963.

11. Andrés Suárez, *Cuba: Castroism and Communism, 1959-66* (Boston: MIT Press, 1967), p. 94.

12. *Le Monde*, November 24, 1997; also in "Castro Fond of Missiles," *AP* report, August 16, 1997.

13. *Le Monde, Ibid.*

14. For a controversial analysis of the missiles in Cuba see Servando Gonzalez, "Thirteen Lies (and Perhaps a Single Truth)," *LewRockwell.com*, http://www.lewrockwell.com/orig/gonzalez1.html.

15. *Le Monde, Ibid.*

16. *Fortune*, November 1961, pp.112-115.

17. Leonard C. Lewin, *Report From Iron Mountain: On the possibility and Desirability of Peace* (New York: The Free Press, 1996).

18. Alan B. Jones, *How the World Really Works* (Paradise, California: ABJ Press, 1996), pp. 132-13.

19. According to an author, Nelson "was fixated on the possibility of Soviet nuclear attack." See Jeffrey Frank, "The Big Spender: Nelson Rockefellers' Grand Ambitions," *The New Yorker*, October 13, 2014, https://www.newyorker.com/magazine/2014/10/13/big-spender-2

20. Nehru quoted in *Newsday*, December 12, 1973.

21. Michael Kramer and Sam Roberts, *"I Never Wanted To Be Vice-President of Anything!" An Investigative Biography of Nelson Rockefeller* (New York: Basic Books, 1976), p. 219.

22. Phil Tracy, "The Albany Bunker," *The Village Voice*, February 15, 1973.

23. Fidel Castro "Cuba no firma desnuclearización mientras E.U. sea una amenaza atómica," *Revolución*, August 27, 1965, pp. 1-2.

24. Juan Vivés, *Los amos de Cuba* (Buenos Aires: Emec Editores, 1982), pp. 181-182.

25. Not related to Rafael del Pino Siero, who accompanied Castro in his Bogotazo adventure.

26. Ernesto Betancourt, *"Is Castro Planning a Preemptive Strike Against the U.S.?"* (Washington, D.C., 1996), p. 4.

27. Jeanne Kirkpatrick, "Is a Stubborn Castro Testing U.S. Defenses?," the *Miami Herald*, March 31, 1991, p. 3C.

28. Joseph B. Treaster, "Defecting General Says Cuba Has Plan to Raid Base in the U.S. if It Is Attacked," the *New York Times*, October 11, 1987.

29. Following a Cuban usage in Spanish, I have capitalized the word *Island* when it stands for Cuba.

30. "Running Against Fidel," *Newsweek*, March 9, 1992.

31. Alina Fernández, *Castro's Daughter* (New York: St. Martin's Press, 1998), p. 194. As the Soviet army approached Berlin, Hitler ordered the floodgates to be opened and drowned thousands of German citizens who

had taken refuge in the city's subway. Havana has no subway, so perhaps Castro was hurriedly building a makeshift one just in case.

32. "Tunnel Vision," *Newsweek*, February 24, 1992, p. 4.

33. See, William J. Broad, "Details Emerge of Cold War Nuclear Threat by Cuba," the *New York Times*, September 22, 2009, p. D4.

34. *Ibid.*

35. Christopher Andrew and Vasili Mitrokhin, *The World Was Going Our Way: The KGB and the Battle for the Third World* (New York: Basic Books, 2005), p. 126.

36. William Kristol, "And Now Iran: We Can't Rule Out the Use of Military Force," *The Weekly Standard*, January 23m 2006, Vol. 11, Issue 18. According to Kristol, Iran is a rogue state whose threat to the U.S. cannot be ignored. Nevertheless, one can easily say that CFR agents have changed the United States into a rogue state whose threat to the world cannot be ignored.

37. Graham T. Allison, *Nuclear Terrorism: The Ultimate Preventable Catastrophe* (New York: Owl Books, 2004), pp. 161-162.

38. Probably one of the most despicable CFR's warmongers is Senator John McCain.

39. I foresee that it is going to be difficult for the CFR warmongers to paint Kim Jong-un, a character seemingly taken out of a Three Stooges film, as an evil monster similar to the Emmanuel Goldstein Orwell depicted in his novel *1984*.

40. See, Paula Demers, "Eliminate the Useless Eaters," http://www.jesus-is-savior.com/Evils%20in%20Government/AIDS%20and%20Population%20Elimination/kill_the_useless_eaters.htm

41. Adrian Salbuchi, "Argentina: Targeted by World Government – Danger over 'Patagonia'!," October 21, 2010, http://www.asalbuchi.com.ar/2010/10/argentina-targeted-by-world-government-danger-over-patagonia/. Also, Adrian Salbuchi, "La Patagonia argentina y chilena en peligro," *RT*, January 10, 2012. http://actualidad.rt.com/mas/blogs/salbuchi/blog_34659.html

42. Servando Gonzalez "Billionaires for Eugenics," *The Intel Hub*, May 8, 2011, theintelhub.com/2011/05/08/billionaires-for-eugenics/.

43. Pereyra Mele Córdoba, "La patagonia para los Rockefeller Boys?," February 13, 2006, http://mamanga.blogspot.com/2006/02/la-patagonia-para-los-rockefeller-boys.html.

44. The Castros and their close associates were frantically buying real estate mostly in Chile.

Appendix II

1. Ellsberg quoted in Michael Parenti, *History as Mystery* (San Francisco: City Lights, 1964), p. 153.
2. Gus Russo, *Live by the Sword* (Baltimore: Bancroft Press, 1998), pp. 72-73.
3. Rebecca Leung, "For the Record: Bush Documents," CBS News, September 15, 2004,https://www.cbsnews.com/news/for-the-record-bush-documents-15-09-2004/
4. Quoted in Michael Warner, "Wanted: A Definition of 'Intelligence.' Understanding Our Craft," CIA's Center for the Study of Intelligence, https://www.cia.gov/library/center-for-the-study-of-intelligence/csi-publications/csi-studies/studies/ vol46no3/article02.html. Nevertheless, the author of the article reminds that intelligence is an elusive concept, and there are many different definitions of the term. In the same fashion, the concept of information, the raw material out of which intelligence is produced, is even more elusive, to the point that there is no agreement among scientists about its true nature. The fact explains why Claude Shannon, the creator of Information Theory, decided to call it "Communication Theory" instead. See, Claude Shannon, "A Mathematical Theory of Communication," *Bell System Technical Journal* No. 27 (July and October, 1948).
5. Quoted in Allen Dulles, *The Craft of Intelligence* (New York: Signet, 1965) , p. 11.
6. Sun Tzu, *The Art of War* - translated by Samuel B. Griffin (London: Oxford University Press, 1963), p. 144.
7. Intelligence Cycle: The process by which information is acquired, converted into intelligence, and made available to policymakers. There are usually five steps which constitute the intelligence cycle: 1. Planning and direction, 2. Collection, 3. Processing, 4. Analysis and evaluation, and 5. dissemination — analysis and evaluation being the most important step of the intelligence cycle.
8. According to Communication Theory, the amount of information is directly proportional to the unexpectedness of the message. This law also applies to the field of intelligence and espionage.

Bibliography

Abraham, Larry and Franklin Sanders, *The Greening*. Atlanta, Georgia: Soundview, 1993.

Aguilar, Alonso. *Latin American and the Alliance for Progress*. New York: Monthly Review Press, 1963.

Alape, Sergio, *El Bogotazo: memorias del olvido*. La Habana: Casa de las Américas, 1983.

Alexander, Robert J. *Communism in Latin America*. New Brunswick, N.J.: Rutgers University Press, 1957.

Allen, Gary, *None Dare Call it Conspiracy*. Rossmoor, California: Concord Press, 1972.

———. *The Rockefeller File*. Seal Beach, California: '76 Press, 1976.

———. *Say "No" to the New World Order*. Clacakamas, Oregon: Emissary, 1991.

Allen, Robert Loring. *Soviet Influence in Latin America: The Role of Economic Relations*. Washington, D.C.: Public Affairs Press, 1959.

Alsop, Stewart and Thomas Braden. *Sub Rosa: The OSS and American Espionage*. New York: Harcourt, Brace and World, 1964.

Alvarez Díaz, José R. *Un estudio sobre Cuba*. Coral Gables, Fla: University of Miami Press, 1963.

Bamford, James. *Body of Secrets*. New York: Random House, 2001.

Barnet, Richard J. *Intervention and Revolution*. New York: World, 1968.

Bennett, James R. *Control of the Media in the United States: An Annotated Bibliography*. New York: Garland, 1992.

Bernstein, Irving. *Promises Kept: John F. Kennedy's New Frontier*. New York: Oxford University Press, 1991.

Bethel, Paul D. *The Losers*. New Rochelle, N.Y.: Arlington House,1969.

Bishop, Jim. *The Day Kennedy Was Shot*. Toronto: Harper Collins,1968.

Blakey, G. Robert, and Richard N. Billings. *The Plot to Kill the President*. New York: Times Books, 1981.

Bluestone, Barry and Bennet Harrison. *The Deindustrialization of America*. New York: Basic Books, 1982.

Blumberg, Paul. *Inequality in an Age of Decline*. New York: Oxford University Press, 1980.

Bonsal, Philip W. *Cuba, Castro and the United States*. Pittsburgh. Penn.: University of Pittsburgh Press, 1971.

Boward, Walter. *Operation Mind Control*. Ft. Bragg: Flatland, 1994.

Braun, Herbert. *The Assassination of Gaitán: Public Life and Urban Violence in Colombia*. Madison, Wisconsin: The University of Wisconsin Press, 1985.

Breuer, William B. *Vendetta: Castro and the Kennedy Brothers*. New York: John Wiley, 1997.

Brooke, Tal. *One World*. Berkeley, California: End Run, 2000.

Brown, Walt. *Treachery in Dallas*. New York: Carroll & Graf, 1995.

Brzezinski, Zbigniew. *Between Two Ages: America's Role in the Technetronic Era*. New York: Viking, 1976.

Buchanan, Thomas G. *Who Killed Kennedy?* New York: G. P. Putnam's Sons, 1964.

Bundy, William P. *The Council on Foreign Relations and Foreign Affairs*. New York: CFR, 1994.

Burks, David D. *Cuba Under Castro*. Headline Series # 165, Foreign Policy Association, New York, June 29, 1964.

Burner, David, and Thomas R. West, *The Torch is Passed: The Kennedy Brothers and American Liberalism*. New York: Atheneum, 1984.

Burns, James MacGregor. *John Kennedy: A Political Profile*. New York: Hartcourt, 1960.

Butler, Gen. Smedley D. *War is a Racket*. Los Angeles: Feral House, 2003.

Canfield, Michael and Alan Weberman. *Coup d'état in America*. New York: Third Press, 1975.

Casuso, Teresa. *Cuba and Castro*. New York: Random House, 1961.

Chossudovsky, Michel. *The Globalization of Poverty and the New World Order*. Shanty Bay,Ontario, Canada: Global Ourlook, 2003.

Colby, Gerard and Charlotte Dennett. *Thy Will Be Done*. New York:

HarperCollins, 1995.

Colby, William, *Honorable Men: My Life in the CIA*. New York: Simon & Schuster, 1978.

Coleman, John. *The Committee of 300*. Carson City, Nevada: WIR, 1997.

Collier, Peter and David Horowitz. *The Rockefellers: An American Dynasty*. New York: Signet, 1976.

——. *The Kennedys: An American Drama*. New York: Summit, 1984.

Constantine, Alex. *Virtual Government: CIA Mind Control Operations in America*. Venice, California: Feral House, 1997.

Conte, Ramón B. *Historia oculta de los crímenes de Fidel Castro*. Miami: n. p., 1995.

Corson, William R. *The Armies of Ignorance: The Rise of the American Intelligence Empire*. New York: The Dial Press, 1977.

Courtney, Kent and Phoebe Courtney. *America's Unelected Rulers*. New Orleans, Louisiana: Conservative Society of America, 1962.

Courtney, Phoebe. *The CFR, Part II*. Littleton, Colorado: The Independent American, 1975.

Crasweller, Robert D. *Cuba and the U.S.; The Tangled Relationship*. New York: Foreign Policy Association, 1971.

Cuddy, Dennis L. *The Globalists: The Power Elite Exposed*. Oklahoma City, Oklahoma: Hearthstone Publishing, 2001.

——. *The Road to Socialism and the New World Order*. Highland City, Florida: Florida Pro-Familiy Forum, 2000.

Curry, Jesse. *JFK Assassination File*. Dallas, Texas: American Poster and Printing Company, 1969.

Dall, Curtis D. *My Exploited Father-in-law*. Washington, D.C.: Action Associates, 1970.

Darling, Arthur B., *The Central Intelligence Agency: An Instrument of Government to 1950*. The Pennsylvania State University press: University Park, Penn., 1990.

Delgado, José. *Physical Control of the Mind*. New York: Harper and Row, 1969.

Devlin, Kevin. *The Soviet-Cuban Confrontation: Economic Reality and Political Judo*. Research Department of Radio Free Europe, 1 April, 1968.

Diamond, Sigmund. *Compromised Campus: The Collaboration of Universities with the Intelligence Community, 1945-1955*. New York: Oxford University Press, 1992.

DiEugenio, James. *Destiny Betrayed: JFK, Cuba and the Garrison Case*. New York: Sheridan Square, 1992.

Domhoff, G. William. *The Higher Circles*. New York: Vintage, 1971.

Duffy, James R. *Conspiracy: Who Killed JFK?* New York: S.P.I./ Shapolski, 1992.

Edmonds, Robin. *Soviet Foreign Policy 1962-1973: The Paradox of Superpower*. London: Oxford University Press, 1975.

Eland, Ivan. *The Empire Has no Clothes: U.S. Foreign Policy Exposed*. Oakland, CA : The Independent Institute, 2004.

Engdahl, William, *A Century of War*. London: Pluto Press, 1992.

Epperson, A. Ralph. *The Unseen Hand: An Introduction to the Conspiratorial View of History*. Tucson Arizona: Publius Press, 1985.

Evans, Stanton Medford. *The Assassination of Joe McCarthy*, Boston: Western Islands, 1970.

——. *The Usurpers*. Boston: Western Islands, 1968

——. *The Liberal Establishment*. New York: The Devin-Adair Co., 1965.

Facts on File. *Cuba, The U.S. and Russia, 1960-63*. New York: Facts on File, 1964.

Falk, Pamela. *Cuban Foreign Policy: Caribbean Tempest*. Lexington, Mass.: Lexington Books, 1986.

Farren, Mick. *CIA: Secrets of the Company*. New York: Barnes & Noble, 2003.

Fitzsimmons, Louise. *The Kennedy Doctrine*. New York: Random House, 1972.

Fosdick, Raymond B. *John D. Rockefeller, Jr. A Portrait*. New York: Pinnacle, 1974.

Flynn, Ted. *Hope of the Wicked: The Master Plan to Rule the World*. Sterling, Virginia: MaxKol, 2000.

Garret, Garet. *The Revolution Was*. Caldwell, Idaho: Caxton, 1944.

Garrison, Jim. *On the Trail of the Assassins*. New York: Warner Books, 1988.

Gelfand, Lawrence E., *The Inquiry: American Preparations for Peace, 1917-1919*. New Haven: Yale University Press, 1963.

Gerassi, John. *The Great Fear in Latin America*. New York: Collier, 1965.

Geyer, Georgie Anne. *Guerrilla Prince*. Boston: Little, Brown and Co., 1991.

Gibson, Donald. *Battling Wall Street: The Kennedy Presidency*. New York: Sheridan Square, 1994.

——. *The Kennedy Assassination Cover-Up*. San Diego, California: Progressive Press, 2014.

Goldwater, Barry. *With No Apologies*. New York: William Morrow, 1979.

Gonzalez, Servando. *The Secret Fidel Castro: Deconstructing the Symbol*. Oakland, California: Spooks Books, 2001.

———. *The Nuclear Hoax: Nikita Khrushchev and the Cuban Missile Crisis*. Oakland, California: Spooks Books, 2002.

———. *Psychological Warfare and the New World Order: The Secret War Against the American People*. Oakland, California: Spooks Books, 2010.

———. *La CIA, Fidel Castro, el Bogotazo y el Nuevo Orden Mundial*. Hayward, California: Spooks Books, 2012

———. *I Dare Call It Treason*. Hayward, California: Spooks Books, 2013.

———. *Barry Soetoro: The Puppet and His Puppeteers*. Oakland, California: Spooks Books, 2016

———. *American Inventors: An Inside View of the U.S. Secret Government in Action*. Hayward, California. El Gato Tuerto, 2016.

Goodman, Melvin A,. *Failure of Intelligence: The Decline and Fall of the CIA*. Lanham, Maryland: Rowan and Littlefield, 2008.

Greider, William. *Who Will Tell the People: The Betrayal of American Democracy*. New York: Simon & Schuster, 1992.

Griffin, David Ray. *The New Pearl Harbor: Disturbing Questons about the Bush Administration and 9/11*. Northhampton, MA: Olive Branch, 2004.

Griffin, David Ray and Peter Dale Scott. *9/11 and American Empire*. Northampton, MA: Olive Branch, 2007.

Griffin, Des. *Fourth Reich of the Rich*. Clackamas, Oregon: Emissary, 1976.

Griffin, G. Edward. *The Capitalist Conspiracy*. Westlake Village, CA: American Media, 1971.

———. *World Without Cancer*. Westlake Village, CA: American Media, 1974.

———. *The Creature from Jekyll Island: A Second Look at the Federal Reserve*. Westlake Village, California: American Opinion, 1994.

Groden, Robert J. and Harrison Edward Livingstone. *High Treason: The Assassination of President John F. Kennedy - What Really Happened*. New York: Conservatory Press, 1989,

Grupp, Jeffrey. *Corporatism: The Secret Government of the New World Order*. Joshua Tree, California: Progressive Press, 2009.

Hersh, Burton, *The Old Boys: The American Elite and the Origins of the CIA*. St. Petersburg Florida: Tree Farm Books, 1992.

Hoffman, William. *David: Report on a Rockefeller*. New York: Lyle Stuart, 1971.

Isaacson, Walter, and Evan Thomas, *The Wise Men: Six Friends and the World They Made*. New York: Touchstone, 1986.

Jeffrey-Jones, Rhodri, *The CIA and American Democracy*. New Haven: Yale University Press, 1989.

Jones, Alan B., *How the World Really Works*. Paradise, California: ABJ Press, 1996.

Josephson, Emanuel, *Rockefeller "Internationalist": The Man Who Misrules the World*. New York: Chedney Press, 1952.

——. *The Truth About Rockefeller: Public Enemy No. 1*, New York: Chedney Press, 1964.

Johnson, Loch K., *America's Secret Power: The CIA in a Democratic Society*. New York: Oxford University Press, 1989.

Kessler, Ronald, *Inside the CIA*. New York: Pocket Books, 1992.

Knightly, Philip, *The Second Oldest Profession: The Spy as Patriot, Bureaucrat, Fantasist and Whore*. London: Pan Books, 1986.

Kutz, Myer. *Rockefeller Power*. New York: Pinnacle, 1974.

Lane, Mark. *Plausible Denial: Was the CIA Involved in the JFK Assassination?* New York: Thunder's Mouth, 1991.

Lawrence, Lincoln and Kenn Thomas Kempton. *Mind Control, Oswald & JFK: Were We Controlled?* Kepton, IL: Advcentures Unlimited, 1987.

Lazo, Mario. *Dagger in the Heart*. New York: Twin Circle, 1968.

Leary, William M., ed., *The Central Intelligence Agency: History and Documents*. Montgomery, Alabama: The University of Alabama Press, 1984.

Lewin, Leonard C., *Report From Iron Mountain: On the Possibility and Desirability of Peace*. New York: The Free Press, 1996.

Livingstone, Harrison Edward. *Killing the Truth: Deceit and Deception in the JFK Case*. New York: Carroll and Graf, 1960.

Llerena, Mario, *The Unsuspected Revolution*. Ithaca, N. Y.: Cornell University Press, 1978.

Loch K. Johnson, *America's Secret Power: The CIA in a Democratic Society*. New York: Oxford University Press, 1989.

Loftus, John and Mark Aarons, *The Secret War Against the Jews*. New York: St. Martin's Press, 1994.

Lundberg, Ferdinand, *The Rockefeller Syndrome*. New York: Zebra Books, 1976.

Macy, Christy and Susan Kaplan, *Documents: A Shocking Collection of Memoranda, letters, and Telexes From the Secret Files of the American Intelligence Community* (New York: Penguin, 1980).

Mangold, Tom, *Cold Warrior: James Jesus Angleton: The CIA's Master Spy Hunter*. New York: Simon & Schuster, 1991.

Manrara, Luis V. *Cuba Disproves the Myth that Poverty is the Cause of Communism*. Miami: The Truth About Cuba Committee, 1963.

Marchetti, Victor, and John D. Marks. *The CIA and the Cult of Intelligence*. New York: Dell, 1974.

Marrs, Jim. *Rule by Secrecy*. New York: HarperCollins, 2000.

———. *Crossfire: The Plot That Killed Kennedy*. New York: Carroll & Graf, 1989.

Marks, John. *The Search for the Manchurian Candidate: The CIA and Mind Control*. New York: McGraw-Hill, 1980.

Martin, David C. *Wilderness of Mirrors*. New York: Ballantine, 1980.

May, Stacy and Galo Plaza. *The United Fruit Company in Latin America*. New York: National Planning Association, 1958.

McGehee, Ralph W. *Deadly Deceits: My 25 Years in the CIA*. New York, Sheridan Square Publications, 1983.

Melanson, Philip H. *Spy Saga: Lee Harvey Oswald and U.S. Intelligence*. New York: Praeger, 1990.

Monteith, Stanley. *Brotherhood of Darkness*. Oklahoma City, OK: Hearthstone Publishing, 2000.

Moscovit, Andrei. *Did Castro Kill Kennedy?* Washington, D.C: The Cuban American National Foundation, 1998, n.d.

Nelson-Pallmeyer, Jack, *Brave New World Order*. New York: Orbis, 1992.

Newman, John M. *JFK and Vietnam: Deception, Intrigue, and the Struggle for Power.* New York: Warner Books, 1992.

Oswald, J. Gregory, and Anthony J. Strover, eds. *The Soviet Union and Latin America*. New York: Praeger, 1970.

Parenti, Michael, *Dirty Truths*. City Lights: San Francisco, 1996.

———. *Inventing Reality: The Politics of Mass Media*. New York: ST. Martin's Press, 1986.

Parmar, Inderjeet. *Think Tanks and Foreign Policy: A Comparative Study of the Role and Influence of the Council on Foreign Relations and the Royal Institute of International Affairs, 1939-1945*. New York: Palgrave McMillan, 2004.

Perloff, James. *The Shadows of Power: The Council on Foreign Relations and the American Decline*. Appleton, Wisconsin: Western Islands, 1988.

Persico, Joseph E. *The Imperial Rockefeller: A Biography of Nelson A, Rockefeller*. New York: Simon and Schuster, 1982.

Prados, John. *Safe for democracy: The Secret Wars of the CIA*. Chicago: Ivan R. Dee, 2006.

Project for the New American Century, "Rebuilding America's Defenses: Strategy, Forces and Resources For a New Century," September, 2000.

Prouty, L. Fletcher. *The Secret Team*. Englewood Cliffs, NJ: Prentice Hall,1973.

———. *JFK, the CIA, Vietnam and the Plot to Assassinate John F. Kennedy*. New York: Birch Lane/Carol, 1992.

Quigley, Carroll, *Tragedy and Hope: A History of the World in Our Time*. New York: Macmillan, 1966.

Ranelagh, John. *The Agency: The Rise and Decline of the CIA*. New York: Touchstone, 1987.

Ratliff, William E. *The Selling of Fidel Castro*. New Brunswick: Transaction Books, 1987.

Robertson, Pat. *The New World Order*. Dallas: Word Publishing, 1991.

Rockefeller, David. *Memoirs*. New York: Random House, 2002.

Rockefeller, Nelson A. *The Future of Federalism*. Cambridge: Harvard University Press, 1962.

Rothkopf, David. *Running the World: The Inside Story of the National Security Council and the Architects of American Power*. New York: Public Affairs, 2004.

Scarborough, Rowan. *Sabotage: America's Enemies Within the CIA*. Washington, D.C.: Regnery, 2007.

Scheflin, Alan W. and Edward M. Opton, Jr. *The Mind Manipulators*. New York: Paddington Press, 1978.

Schlaffly, Phyllis and Chester Ward. *Kissinger on the Couch*. New Rochelle, N.Y.: Arlington House, 1975.

Schlesinger, Jr., Arthur M. *A Thousand Days*. London: André Deutsch, 1965.

———. *The Imperial Presidency*. Boston: Houghton Mifflin Company, 1973.

Scott, Peter Dale. *Deep Politics and the Death of JFK*. Los Angeles, CA: Tom Davis, 1971

Shepardson, W. H. *Early History of the CFR*. Stamford, CT: Overbeek Press, 1960.

Shoup, Lawrence H. and William Minter. *Imperial Brain Trust: The Council on Foreign Relations & United States Foreign Policy*. New York: Monthly Review Press, 1977.

Schulzinger, Robert D. *The Wise Men of Foreign Affairs: The History of*

the Council on Foreign Relations. New York: Columbia University
   Press, 1984.
Smith, Earl T. The Fourth Floor. New York: Random House, 1962.
Smith, Peter H.. Talons of the Eagle: Dynamics of U.S.-Latin American
   Relations. New York: Oxford University Press, 1996.
Smith, R. Harris. OSS: The Secret History of America's First Intelligence
   Service. Berkeley: University of California Press, 1972.
Smith, Russell Jack. The Unknown CIA: My Three Decades with the
   Agency. Washington, D.C.: Pergamon-Brasseys, 1989.
Smoot, Dan. The Invisible Government. Boston: Western Islands, 1962.
Srodes, James. Allen Dulles. New York: Regnery, 1999.
Still, William. New World Order. Lafayette, Louisiana: Huntington
   House, 1990.
Stormer, John. None Dare Call it Treason. Florissant, Missouri: Liberty
   Bell Press, 1964.
Suárez, Andrés. Cuba: Castroism and Communism, 1959-1966 (Cam-
   bridge, Mass.: M.I.T. Press, 1967)
Sutton, Antony C. Wall Street and FDR (New Rochelle, New York:
   Arlington House. 1975.
——. Wall Street and the Rise of Hitler. Seal Beach, California: '76
   Press, 1976.
——. Wall Street and the Bolshevik Revolution. New Rochelle, New
   York: Arlington House. 1981.
——. The Best Enemy Money Can Buy. Billings, Montana: Liberty
   House, 1986.
Tarpley, Webster Griffin. 9/11: Synthetic Terror Made in USA. Joshua
   Tree, California: Progressive Press, 2006.
——. Obama: The Postmodern Coup – Making of a Manchurian Candi-
   date. Joshua Tree, California: Progressive Press, 2008.
Thomas, Evan. The Very Best Men: The Daring Early Years of the CIA.
   New York: Simon and Schuster, 1995.
Tzu, Sun. The Art of War - translated by Samuel B. Griffin. London:
   Oxford University Press, 1963.
United States Department of State. Events in the United States-Cuban
   Relations: a Chronology, 1957-1963. Washington, D.C.: U.S.
   Government Printing Office, 1963.
Wala, M. The Council on Foreign Relations and American Policy During
   the Early Cold War. Oxford: Berghahan, 1994.
Walton, Richard J. Cold War and Counter-Revolution: The Foreign
   Policy of John F. Kennedy. New York: The Viking Press, 1972.

Weiner, Tim. *Legacy of Ashes: The History of the CIA*. New York: Doubleday, 2007)

Weisberg, Harold. *Whitewash: The Report on the Warren Report*. Hyattstown, MD: Dell, 1966.

Welch, Robert. *The Politician*. Privately printed edition, 1963.

Westerfield, H. Bradford, ed. *Inside CIA's Private World*. New Haven: Yale University Press, 1995.

Wilcox, Robert. *Target Patton: The Plot to Assassinate General George S. Patton*. Washington, D.C.: Regnery, 2008.

William Hood. *Mole*. New York: Ballantine, 1982.

Wise, David and Thomas B. Ross. *The Espionage Establishment*. New York: Random House, 1967.

Wise, David. *The Politics of Lying*. New York: Random House, 1973.

——. *Mole*. New York: Random House, 1992.

——. *Molehunt: The Search for Traitors That Shattered the CIA*. New York: Random House, 1992.

Wise, David, and Thomas B. Ross. *The Invisible Government*. New York: Bantam, 1962.

Wofford, Harris. *Of Kennedys and Kings*. New York: Farrar Straus Giroux, 1980.

Wormser, René A. *Foundations: Their Power and Influence*. Tennessee: Covenant House Books, c1993.

Wyden, Peter. *The Bay of Pigs*. New York: Simon and Schuster, 1979.

Index

www.ingramcontent.com/pod-product-compliance
Lightning Source LLC
Chambersburg PA
CBHW072045020426
42334CB00017B/1397